Lean Thinking in Industry 4.0 and Services for Society

Katarzyna Antosz
Rzeszow University of Technology, Poland

Jose Carlos Sa
School of Engineering, ISEP, Polytechnic of Porto, Portugal

Małgorzata Jasiulewicz-Kaczmarek
Poznan University of Technology, Poland

Jose Machado
University of Minho, Portugal

IGI Global
PUBLISHER of TIMELY KNOWLEDGE

A volume in the Advances in Logistics, Operations, and Management Science (ALOMS) Book Series

Published in the United States of America by
IGI Global
Business Science Reference (an imprint of IGI Global)
701 E. Chocolate Avenue
Hershey PA, USA 17033
Tel: 717-533-8845
Fax: 717-533-8661
E-mail: cust@igi-global.com
Web site: http://www.igi-global.com

Library of Congress Cataloging-in-Publication Data

Names: Antosz, Katarzyna, 1977- editor. | Sá, José Carlos, 1972- editor. | Jasiulewicz-Kaczmare, Małgorzata, 1962- editor. | Machado, José, 1972- editor.
Title: Lean thinking in industry 4.0 and services for society / Katarzyna Antosz, José Carlos Sá, Małgorzata Jasiulewicz-Kaczmarek, and José Machado, editor.
Description: Hershey, PA : Information Science Reference, [2023] | Includes bibliographical references and index. | Summary: "The aim of the book is to present an insight into Lean Thinking as a philosophy that allows you to identify problems / wastes in various areas, analyze them and identify activities that allow you to improve processes in many areas. As Lean Thinking is a philosophy that applies to many areas, the book will have an impact on research in the areas of resource management, production systems management, quality management, knowledge management, maintenance management, logistic management, and decision support systems"-- Provided by publisher.
Identifiers: LCCN 2022040856 (print) | LCCN 2022040857 (ebook) | ISBN 9781668456064 (hardcover) | ISBN 9781668456071 (paperback) | ISBN 9781668456088 (ebook)
Subjects: LCSH: Project management. | Industry 4.0. | Information technology--Management.
Classification: LCC HD69.P75 L396 2023 (print) | LCC HD69.P75 (ebook) | DDC 658.4/04--dc23/eng/20220913
LC record available at https://lccn.loc.gov/2022040856
LC ebook record available at https://lccn.loc.gov/2022040857

This book is published in the IGI Global book series Advances in Logistics, Operations, and Management Science (ALOMS) (ISSN: 2327-350X; eISSN: 2327-3518)

British Cataloguing in Publication Data
A Cataloguing in Publication record for this book is available from the British Library.

Advances in Logistics, Operations, and Management Science (ALOMS) Book Series

ISSN:2327-350X
EISSN:2327-3518

Editor-in-Chief: John Wang Montclair State University, USA

MISSION

Operations research and management science continue to influence business processes, administration, and management information systems, particularly in covering the application methods for decision-making processes. New case studies and applications on management science, operations management, social sciences, and other behavioral sciences have been incorporated into business and organizations real-world objectives.

The **Advances in Logistics, Operations, and Management Science** (ALOMS) Book Series provides a collection of reference publications on the current trends, applications, theories, and practices in the management science field. Providing relevant and current research, this series and its individual publications would be useful for academics, researchers, scholars, and practitioners interested in improving decision making models and business functions.

COVERAGE

- Decision analysis and decision support
- Organizational Behavior
- Production Management
- Services management
- Operations Management
- Finance
- Networks
- Computing and information technologies
- Marketing engineering
- Information Management

IGI Global is currently accepting manuscripts for publication within this series. To submit a proposal for a volume in this series, please contact our Acquisition Editors at Acquisitions@igi-global.com or visit: http://www.igi-global.com/publish/.

The Advances in Logistics, Operations, and Management Science (ALOMS) Book Series (ISSN 2327-350X) is published by IGI Global, 701 E. Chocolate Avenue, Hershey, PA 17033-1240, USA, www.igi-global.com. This series is composed of titles available for purchase individually; each title is edited to be contextually exclusive from any other title within the series. For pricing and ordering information please visit http://www.igi-global.com/book-series/advances-logistics-operations-management-science/37170. Postmaster: Send all address changes to above address.

Titles in this Series

For a list of additional titles in this series, please visit:
www.igi-global.com/book-series/advances-logistics-operations-management-science/37170

Futuristic Technology Perspectives on Entrepreneurship and Sustainable Innovation
Sanjay Misra (Ostfold University, Norway) Amit Jain (Amity University, India) Manju Kaushik (Amity University, India) and Chitreshh Banerjee (Amity University, India)
Business Science Reference • © 2023 • 300pp • H/C (ISBN: 9781668458716) • US $250.00

Cases on International Business Logistics in the Middle East
Islam Abdelbary (University of Plymouth, UK) Sandra Haddad (Arab Academy for Science, Technology and Maritime Transport, Egypt) and Ghada Elkady (Arab Academy for Science, Technology and Maritime Transport, Egypt)
Business Science Reference • © 2023 • 325pp • H/C (ISBN: 9781668446867) • US $240.00

Handbook of Research on Promoting Logistics and Supply Chain Resilience Through Digital Transformation
Ilyas Masudin (University of Muhammadiyah Malang, Indonesia) Mohammad Nabil Almunawar (Universiti Brunei Darussalam, Brunei) Dian Palupi Restuputri (University of Muhammadiyah Malang, Indonesia) and Ploy Sud-On (Mahidol University, Thailand)
Business Science Reference • © 2023 • 400pp • H/C (ISBN: 9781668458822) • US $315.00

Leadership and Workplace Culture in the Digital Era
Ebtihaj Al-A'ali (University of Bahrain, Bahrain) and Meryem Masmoudi (University of Bahrain, Bahrain)
Business Science Reference • © 2023 • 287pp • H/C (ISBN: 9781668458648) • US $240.00

Examining the Vital Financial Role of SMEs in Achieving the Sustainable Development Goals
Dalila Taleb (University of Abou Bakr Belkaïd, Algeria) Mohammed El Amine Abdelli (University of Brest, France) Afef Khalil (University of Tunis, Carthage, Tunisia) and Asma Sghaier (University of Sousse, Tunisia)
Business Science Reference • © 2023 • 325pp • H/C (ISBN: 9781668448342) • US $250.00

IGI Global
PUBLISHER of TIMELY KNOWLEDGE

701 East Chocolate Avenue, Hershey, PA 17033, USA
Tel: 717-533-8845 x100 • Fax: 717-533-8661
E-Mail: cust@igi-global.com • www.igi-global.com

Table of Contents

Detailed Table of Contents

This chapter aims to explore how lean manufacturing (LM) can leverage Industry 4.0 resources to achieve better industrial performance while achieving cleaner processes. In today's environment, to remain competitive, companies need to incorporate new resources to respond to environmental concerns - especially in the fight against climate change - without compromising efficiency. The goal is not only to clarify and extend the literature on the relationship between LM and Industry 4.0, but also to do so by simultaneously studying the impact on throughput and CO2 emissions reduction. Moving away from the usual separate assessment, the authors propose a comprehensive analysis that allows us to evaluate how LM can establish the right conditions on the shop floor for the development of 4.0 technology-intensive environments, and how these technologies can subsequently be leveraged to enhance the contribution of lean practices to industrial performance and sustainability.

Lean manufacturing and management systems have become a new paradigm for excellence in value generation and delivery for the most competitive companies in the world. With the effect of digital transformation, organizations prefer to apply these approaches in order to create value by providing quality products and services to the

improvement opportunities throughout the productive chain. This article aims to present the solutions developed to reduce wastes in the internal logistics department. Subsequently, the application and evaluations of the impact of lean tools, it was possible to calculate the impact in the internal logistics which results in a decrease of 16% in the production costs.

The main purpose of the article was the reduction of the machine changeover time in practical terms, on the example of a forming machine in the production process of a trunk shelf, based on the use of the SMED method. The article presented the stages of development and the foundations of the lean management concept. The description of the SMED methodology was made. A forming machine was selected in the manufacturing process of a trunk shelf. The identification and measurement of changeover times in the real model were performed. Two alternative models were proposed. The first of them was made based on the division of activities into external and internal, and the delegation of external activities to be performed by the production staff. The second alternative model included investments. The proposed and implemented improvement actions brought benefits in a reduction of the changeover time of the tested machine.

This paper presents the advantages of modelling an application destined for automotive using automotive standard architecture (AUTOSAR). This standard is structured in layers and is trying to make the software application independent from the microcontroller unit (MCU) specifications. By structuring an application in this way, it reduces the time and the cost of developing new ones for a different microcontroller or for creating new applications with a similar purpose for the same microcontroller. Also, the diagnosis for the errors is improved a lot, because it provides mechanisms to detect them, and, having a very structured form, it is easy to find them in comparison with the older procedures used for the soft-ware development that are different from one producer to another. This standard architecture helps to get better results in software development and embedded systems for the automotive area. Here is presented a primitive implementation for an electric automatic gearbox that can be developed more when new features are required.

In the recent trend, many manufacturing industries are looking to develop and optimise their operational excellence to match the raising complexity of integrating lean concept and Industrial 4.0 (I4.0). Through literatures of previous researchers, the authors can state that the lean principle and concept are the backbone for the industrial operational excellence which has been the primary objective across all sectors. Industry 4.0 has numerous technologies advanced to back up the process optimisation and supplement need for greener environment in industries. In this chapter, the study primarily focusses on exploring and identifying the best suited Industry 4.0 technologies, which can enhance lean and green paradigms in industry through which a clear pathway can be created for smooth transfer of technology within a system. Also, the authors have discussed the enhancement of lean tools by application of Industry 4.0 technologies and have developed a relationship matrix between Industrial 4.0 technologies and lean practices.

Lean thinking is a phenomenon that originated in the production sector; nevertheless, it has been warmly welcomed by the service industry. Healthcare practitioners are also keen to benefit from that notion being aware of the potential contributions that lean operations would bring in their field. Healthcare operations have much in common with the production sector, yet it has its own characteristics which ought to be handled separately. This chapter is dedicated to providing a guideline for healthcare practitioners to apply statistical quality control tools within a correspondence to four main components of lean thinking: problem detection, process redesign, process reliability and sustainability, and continuous improvement. By this means, practitioners will be able to start their own journey in the world of lean healthcare systems through substantial statistical tools as well as systems thinking.

Preface

The Lean Thinking is defined as the way to specify value, line up value creating actions in the best sequence, conduct these activities without interruption whenever someone requests them, and perform them more and more effectively. The five principles of Lean Thinking—define "value" from the customer's perspective, identify the "value stream," create a continuous flow, "pull" production, and seek perfection—were introduced to address the various challenges that occur within and between business units from the differences in business culture and management thought processes. Evidence of Lean Thinking implementation is found in various areas, such as services, healthcare and different industries, e.g., the automotive industry, aerospace industry, power plants, textile industry, food industry, oil and gas industry among others. Such evidence points to a number of universality and the use of the Lean Thinking tools in different contexts increasing its importance as an approach to continuous improvement.

OBJECTIVE

The objective of the book is to give an insight into Lean Thinking as a philosophy that allows readers identifying problems/wastes in various areas, analyze them and identify activities that allow you to improve processes in many areas. As Lean Thinking is a philosophy that applies to many areas, the book will have an impact on research in the areas of Sustainable Development (environment sustainability and energy efficiency) resource management, production systems management, quality management, knowledge management, maintenance management, logistic management, healthcare, and decision support systems.

The benefits of Lean Thinking Implementation are divided in two fields. Firstly, by elimination of wastes and unnecessary resources utilization, decreasing delivery, lead and cycle times, decrease inventories, and increase the productivity. Secondly, by improving the workers satisfaction, good communication, and decision-making process. This approach has been used in many types of organizations, starting by being used in manufacturing companies - Lean Manufacturing, including Lean Maintenance - and later, among many others, such as in sustainable environment and energy efficient companies, as well as in healthcare organizations.

With new trends in resource management and respective energy efficiency achievement, Lean Thinking is a real added value for organizations working in this domain, mainly the ones related with energy efficiency management. Also, in the healthcare area, lean health care is a management philosophy to develop a hospital culture characterized by increased patient, and other stakeholder, satisfaction through continuous improvements, in which all employees (managers, doctors, nurses, laboratory people, technicians, office people etc.) actively participate in identifying and reducing non-added value activities (waste).

Finally, Lean concepts such as work standardization, organization and transparency are highlighted as support for implementation of solutions linked to Industry 4.0. At the same time, through the analysis of implementation cases in the industry, Lean processes' improvement capacity is highlighted from its integration with I4.0. Lean methods are seen as facilitators of I4.0, and where I4.0 is analyzed as a factor that strengthens Lean.

TARGET AUDIENCE

Target users of the book are scientists working in Academia and engineers employed in companies who want to have an insight and more deep understanding of Lean Thinking and respective applications in the context of Industry 4.0, covering industry applications and services for the society, bringing added value for all the involved stakeholders.

THE CHALLENGES

Topics and challenges covering *Lean Thinking in Industry 4.0 and Services for Society* are related to:

- Lean manufacturing
- Lean Thinking in healthcare
- Lean Maintenance
- Lean Six Sigma
- Lean Industry 4.0/Lean thinking in the digital era
- Lean thinking for knowledge work
- Lean thinking in support processes

- Lean thinking in services
- Methods and tolls of Lean Thinking
- Industrial systems for lean implementation
- Lean improvement monitoring
- Lean Safety
- Lean Green
- Lean Sustainability

ORGANIZATION OF THE BOOK

The book is organized into 11 chapters. A brief description of each of the chapters is described below:

Chapter 1 explores how Lean Manufacturing (LM) can leverage Industry 4.0 resources to achieve better industrial performance while achieving cleaner processes. The main goal of the paper is not only to clarify and extend the literature on the relationship between LM and Industry 4.0 but also to do so by simultaneously studying the impact on throughput and CO2 emissions reduction. Moving away from the usual separate assessment, it is proposed a comprehensive analysis that allows evaluating how LM can establish the right conditions on the shop floor for the development of 4.0 technology-intensive environments and how these technologies can subsequently be leveraged to enhance the contribution of Lean practices to industrial performance and sustainability.

Chapter 2 reports how the lean management approach requires the direct support of both sustainability and industry 4.0 concepts in order to develop the respective principles and tools. On the other hand, UNDP's Sustainable Development Goals have a very important place when it is aimed to support sustainable industrialization, strengthen innovation, and ensure operational excellence. It is presented the way how to find answers to "How Industry 4.0 and Sustainable Development Goals can enhance Lean practices?" by performing content analysis in various databases in the existing literature.

Chapter 3 presents a study that aims to understand how the concept of Industry 4.0 has impacted the Portuguese business fabric, focusing on the purchasing area. The transformation in the processes led to discover new forms of digital technologies in the products processes to generate competitiveness in the market. New business models are a driving force for evolution and progress in the digital era. These models are based on the pillars of Industry 4.0, bringing sustainability to the industry, reducing waste, and forecasting more accurately the market.

Chapter 4 investigates the impact of applying Lean Thinking techniques to eliminate operations that do not bring business value in an organization. For this purpose, the authors decided to use the methodology of increasing the efficiency of business processes to identify the current process and indicate its optimization potential. The applied process optimization methods, focusing on the elimination of waste, are one of the main principles of Lean Thinking.

Chapter 5 throws light of new or different factors the disputable view which has presume that, at any point in future, the global automobile industry can reach a maturity level and would naturally resettle in the key developing countries where the auto market is expected to grow fast-paced and wages are significantly bottommost. The authors analysed that the gateway facing by a developing country is trying to create domestic automobile industry which have arisen due to recent developments: a wave faced due to technological and structural innovation; pressure caused by pandemic.

Chapter 6 presents a result of the work carried out in a company responsible for designing and projecting automated material handling and storage systems. The main goal is to present the developed solutions to reduce wastes in the internal logistics department.

Chapter 7 addresses a proposal for the reduction of the machine changeover time in practical terms, on the example of a forming machine in the production process of a trunk shelf, based on the use of the SMED method. The stages of development and the foundations of the Lean Management concept and description of the SMED methodology are presented. A forming machine was selected, in the manufacturing process of a trunk shelf, and respective identification and measurement of changeover times, in the real model, were performed.

Chapter 8 proposes the advantages of modelling an application destined for automotive using Automotive Standard Architecture (AUTOSAR). This standard is structured in layers making the software application independent from the microcontroller unit (MCU) specifications. By structuring an application in this way, it reduces the time and the cost of developing new ones for a different microcontroller or for creating new applications with a similar purpose for the same microcontroller. The main goal consists of presenting a primitive implementation for an electric automatic gearbox that can be developed, in a more detailed way, when new features are required.

Chapter 9 presents a general overview, focussing on exploring and identifying the best suit Industry 4.0 technologies which can enhance lean and green paradigms in industry through which a clear pathway can be created for smooth transfer of technology within a system. Also, discusses about enhancement of lean tools by application of Industry 4.0 technologies and have developed a relationship matrix between Industrial 4.0 technologies and lean practices.

Chapter 10 presents and analyses how healthcare practitioners are also keen to benefit from Lean being well aware of the potential contributions that lean operations would bring in their field. This work is devoted to provide a guideline for healthcare practitioners to apply statistical quality control tools within a correspondence to four main components of lean thinking: problem detection, process redesign, process reliability & sustainability and continuous improvement. By this means, practitioners will be able to start their own journey in the world of lean healthcare systems through substantial statistical tools as well as systems thinking.

Chapter 11 highlights the benefits of using Lean Maintenance, showing and discussing obtained results from studying industrial companies and concluding about used tools and level of this concept implementation in their activity. For obtaining the base results for this work, surveys were used for research carried out in enterprises. Some questionnaires were sent to companies, in Poland, for being possible to acquire some data from their experience and results by using Lean Maintenance.

Katarzyna Antosz
Rzeszow University of Technology, Poland

José Carlos Sá
School of Engineering, ISEP, Polytechnic of Porto, Portugal

Małgorzata Jasiulewicz-Kaczmarek
Poznan University of Technology, Poland

José Machado
University of Minho, Portugal

Chapter 1
Integrating Industry 4.0 Technologies Into Lean Thinking for the Development of Efficient, Low-Carbon Processes

Antonio Sartal
University of Vigo, Spain

Fernando León-Mateos
https://orcid.org/0000-0003-3230-3105
University of Vigo, Spain

Roberto Bellas
https://orcid.org/0000-0003-4118-8313
University of Vigo, Spain

ABSTRACT

This chapter aims to explore how lean manufacturing (LM) can leverage Industry 4.0 resources to achieve better industrial performance while achieving cleaner processes. In today's environment, to remain competitive, companies need to incorporate new resources to respond to environmental concerns - especially in the fight against climate change - without compromising efficiency. The goal is not only to clarify and extend the literature on the relationship between LM and Industry 4.0, but also to do so by simultaneously studying the impact on throughput and CO2 emissions reduction. Moving away from the usual separate assessment, the authors propose a comprehensive analysis that allows us to evaluate how LM can establish the right conditions on the shop floor for the development of 4.0 technology-intensive environments, and how these technologies can subsequently be leveraged to enhance the contribution of lean practices to industrial performance and sustainability.
DOI: 10.4018/978-1-6684-5606-4.ch001

INTRODUCTION

The production model of the late 20th century, focused on continuous improvement to reduce costs and time while fabricating higher quality goods, remains a crucial element in the minds of industrial managers. However, the pressure of today's society regarding the environmental, social and economic aspects of manufacturing stimulates the adoption of innovative solutions in industry. Most of these solutions make use of technology to achieve sustainable manufacturing (Stock and Seliger 2016).

Notably, industrial production systems have been transformed recently, acquiring higher levels of digitalization. Digitization facilitates evolution toward more intelligent, connected and decentralized production. This technological change represents an opportunity for companies both to continue to maintain their levels of competitiveness and productivity and to face the new ecological challenges. These technologies—grouped under the umbrella of what has come to be known as Industry 4.0 (I4.0)—favor consistent digitization and information exchanges by linking production units that allow the creation of an interoperable environment. In this new context, deploying new manufacturing processes and technologies that contribute to an increase in both operational and sustainable performance is possible. This interconnection of systems across different processes and agents in manufacturing environments will enable the emergence of connected intelligent factories, facilitating the adaptation of operational excellence practices to new demand requirements (Oztemel and Gursev, 2020).

The increasing digitalization of industrial environments, coupled with operational excellence practices, the maximum exponent of which is lean manufacturing (LM), has begun to demonstrate its ability to optimize processes and reduce waste throughout the industry value chain (Sartal et al., 2018; Sartal et al., 2020a). In this sense, a growing stream of the literature has proposed using I4.0 technologies to facilitate solutions to LM principles to adapt them to new requirements (e.g., Fettermann et al., 2018; Sordan et al., 2021). The combination of both paradigms can contribute to improving both flexibility and process flows in production plants (Rossini et al., 2021). Moreover, it would allow better coordination of the supply chain, favoring the improvement of process times and the reduction of waste (Tortorella et al., 2020), which would translate into improved productivity and better adaptation to new demand requirements (Rossini et al., 2021).

In this context, this chapter aims to analyze the synergies between LM practices and I4.0 technologies and the ways that combining both paradigms can help manufacturing companies in their transitions to SM and decarbonization.

BACKGROUND

Climate Change and Sustainability

Sustainability, defined as "the use of resources to meet the needs of the present without compromising the needs of future generations" (Brundtland and Khalid, 1987), is a pressing need for today's society (Ahi and Searcy, 2013). As stated in the UN's Sustainable Development Goals (SDGs), the development of humanity must add social and environmental dimensions to the traditional economic ones (United Nations, 2015).

The perception of sustainability as a necessity did not appear, however, until the end of the 20th century. Since the beginning of the first Industrial Revolution in the second half of the 18th century, the production model has been based on a linear economic system in which raw materials and resources were considered unlimited, following a get, use and dispose approach. Nevertheless, an increasing number of authors emphasize the need to move from that linear economy towards a circular-type economy (Rizos et al., 2017; Sharma et al., 2021), based on the reuse of biological resources for the longest possible time in closed-loop schemes (Mendoza et al., 2017). The circular economy makes it possible to harmonize the ambitions of economic growth and sustainability (Lieder and Rashid, 2016).

Alternatively, industrialization has also influenced one of the greatest challenges today: anthropogenic climate change (León-Mateos et al., 2021; Rolnick et al., 2022). Since its inception, greenhouse gas (GHG) emissions, caused by human activity, have experienced exponential growth. These gases are primarily responsible for the global warming that causes anthropogenic climate change. According to the Sixth Assessment Report of the Intergovernmental Panel on Climate Change (IPCC, 2021), from 1850-2019, the likely range of total human-caused global surface temperature increase is between 0.8 °C and 1.3 °C, with a most likely estimate of 1.07 °C. The report concludes that unless GHG emissions are reduced immediately, rapidly and on a large scale, limiting global warming to 1.5 °C or even 2 °C will be an unattainable goal. IPCC experts estimate that a warming of 1.5 °C will lead to an increase in heat waves, longer hot seasons and shorter cold seasons; with a global warming of 2°C, extreme heat events would more frequently reach critical tolerance thresholds for sectors such as agriculture or health (IPCC, 2021).

In this context, manufacturing companies, largely responsible for both the overexploitation of natural resources and the emission of greenhouse gases, estimated to be responsible for the production of 40% of such gases (IEA, 2021), have an obligation to add environmental sustainability to their traditional objectives of profitability and efficiency (Garza-Reyes, 2015). However, it is difficult to marry short-term business requirements related to efficiency and profitability with long-term societal demands and new environmentally compatible environmental requirements (Wright and Nyberg, 2015; Ozcelik et al., 2021). To achieve these new green goals, industries must modify their processes, adopt a sustainable manufacturing (SM) framework, and implement strategies to mitigate and adapt to new environmental sustainability needs.

On the one hand, in terms of mitigation, issues such as the decarbonization of production (low-carbon transition), the reduction of GHG emissions or reuse and recycling can contribute to curbing both global warming and the overexploitation of natural resources. Such strategies should aim to increase the efficiency of production plants by optimizing their processes to reduce their carbon footprint. On the other hand, in terms of adaptation, it is essential for companies to anticipate potential adverse weather phenomena resulting from climate change or shortages of raw materials and energy sources that could compromise the operational continuity of supply chains. In a globalized and complex economy, establishing resilient supply chains that can face these new conditions of uncertainty with guarantees is a priority objective (Lim-Camacho et al., 2017; Ehrenstein et al., 2019).

The Concept of Sustainable Manufacturing and Decarbonization: Definitions and Approaches Over Time

Nowadays, escalating shortages and costs of material resources and energy, together with the limitations of waste treatment, force companies to improve the efficacy and sustainability of their operations (Despeisse et al., 2012). Moreover, companies are under pressure from consumers' growing concerns about the social and environmental aspects of the goods and services they use (Barber 2007).

In order to respond to environmental problems, the pursuit of enhanced energy efficiency and decarbonization must be achieved through resolute strategies and decisions that allow for improvements and relevant changes in production and/or energy systems. Decarbonization is mainly achieved through the application of technological advances in the production, logistics or end-use phase. The adoption of cutting-edge technologies is essential in order to achieve an equivalent or even higher level of productivity and service (Borowski 2021; Kueppers et al. 2021; Manfren, Sibilla, and Tronchin 2021).

Despite the importance given to sustainability in society and more specifically in the scientific community and the industrial world, a wide variety of definitions and interpretations of concepts relate to sustainability and SM. Many authors consider that there is not enough uniformity regarding the interpretation of the concepts associated with SM, which results in a lack of a unified terminology and vocabulary (Haapala et al. 2013; Millar and Russell 2011; Moldavska and Welo 2017).

This lack of uniformity and comprehensiveness regarding SM is seen in Ihlen and Roper's (2014) study on large corporations. One of the most striking findings is that corporations do not use a precise description of sustainability, so inevitably the strategies they use to achieve it are not very clear and often fuzzy. Despite this lack of clarity, corporations often choose to treat sustainability and sustainable development as an achieved and unproblematic goal, thus failing to address the fundamental issues involved in their operations' sustainability. Furthermore, many corporations do not see sustainability as a "journey", but instead claim they have already integrated sustainability principles and have been doing so for years. In fact, some authors have stated, "Sustainability should not be conceived as a single concept, nor even as a coherent set of concepts". Rather, could be considered "a complex behaviour pattern to which any manufacturing organization should tend to evolve" or "a process of collective thinking" that aims to integrate ecological, economic and social awareness in the longer term perspective (Moldavska and Welo 2017; Robinson 2004).

One of the most widely adopted definitions of sustainability is the definition stated at the 1987 UN Brundtland Commission report, where "sustainability" is referred to as, "Development which meets the needs of current generations without compromising the ability of future generations to meet their own needs". Such formulation has been widely adopted, for example, in a number of UN undertakings initiatives (e.g., the 2015 SDGs). Moldavska and Welo's (2017) aforementioned content-analysis-based literature review found that the most widely accepted definition of SM in the nearly 200 papers analyzed was that given the US Department of Commerce: "The creation of products through processes that minimize both negative environmental impacts and consumption of energy and natural resources, being also safe for employees, communities, consumers and economically viable".

The concepts related with SM have therefore evolved over the last 50 years. In the 1970s, the focus was on the economic-industrial aspects, optimizing design and production to reduce resource consumption. In this sense, the Triple Bottom Line (TBL) established by Elkington (Elkington 1998) broadens the dimensions of sustainability: social, environmental and economic. The TBL approach involves broadening the organization's responsibilities, which in many cases are limited to making a profit by respecting the law and complying with regulations. However, the TBL approach adds environmental and social responsibilities. Subsequently, from the 1980s onwards, SM incorporated environmental aspects, evolving from the 3Rs to the 6Rs, the product life cycle and the sustainable supply chain. Already in this century, several social aspects have gradually been incorporated. These developments are described in more detail below.

Of special relevance is the 3R approach: reduce, recycle and reuse (Sarkis 1995; Sarkis and Rasheed 1995). The main method to preserve the environment is to reduce consumption. At the same time, we can give a second life to a used object and prevent it from being thrown into the waste bin. In the latter case, if they are disposed in an appropriate container, they can be recycled, consuming less raw materials when manufacturing a new product. The 3R concept evolved considering three new activities (i.e., redesign, recover and remanufacture), thus arriving at the 6R strategy. To succeed in end-of-life recycling and remanufacturing, design and logistics must focus on facilitating product recovery and reuse of materials and components (Toffel 2003). This is where the concept of backward flow or reverse logistics comes in: As the levels of 6R implementation increase, product design and new "reverse" logistics need to be adapted to modify the entire product life cycle (PLC; Ilgin and Gupta 2010) .

Among the first studies on SM that gained some prominence are those related to environmentally conscious manufacturing (Owen 1999; Weissman and Sekutowski 1991). Major themes of this view include source reduction activities, fabrication and assembling oriented design; that is, "cradle-to-cradle" design (McDonough and Braungart 2002) or "ecological footprint" (Wackernagel and Rees 1996). In this context, the three dimensions of environmentally conscious manufacturing are identified: product, technologies and operations. Concerning the manufacturing process, the wide diffusion in recent decades of the LM philosophy (Womack, Jones, and Roos 1990) has contributed to the sustainability of manufacturing operations. LM adopts the just-in-time (JIT) principle of reducing waste and using fewer resources (i.e., materials, labor, space and investment in machines and tools), increasing the efficiency and thus the sustainability of manufacturing operations and associated services.

At the end of the 1990s, the environmental approach was expanded to include all phases of the life of products to address SM, thus creating the concept of life cycle assessment (LCA) methodology (Kaebernick, Kara, and Sun 2003), which allows the evaluation of the environmental impact, carried out throughout the entire PLC, from procurement of primary resources through to manufacturing, utilization, and End-of-Life disposal (i.e., "cradle to grave"; Guide, Srivastava, and Kraus 1997). LCA has been standardized through the extended use of environment standards, such as ISO14041. It allows the environmental performance of various manufacturing options to be assessed, comparing them to help identifying their advantages and drawbacks. A logical evolution of the concept is its expansion to incorporate social and economic aspects leading to the life cycle sustainability assessment (Kloepffer 2008).

On the other hand, it is also worth mentioning maintenance, which is no stranger to the aforementioned sustainable evolution. Maintenance has a great influence on most of the production, logistical, health and safety processes. After evolving from reactive to preventive, it has adopted, like all other processes, the lean philosophy and has finally become a green-sustainable process (Jasiulewicz-Kaczmarek and Gola 2019). The impact of maintenance on the economic dimension of sustainability is crucial, contributing to productivity, cost, quality, delivery reliability. It is also in the environmental dimension, preventing environmental accidents, reducing emissions, waste and energy consumption (Firdaus, Samat, and Mohamad 2019; Franciosi et al. 2020). On the social dimension, although less important, its impact must also be taken into account, especially in terms of safety and hygiene (Ramiya and Suresh 2021).

In the last decade, several authors have addressed various aspects of supply chain management (SCM) in a sustainable way, and it is common to see the term "sustainable" attached to the terminology (SSCM). In this way, the entire PLC is integrated from product design, supply chain management and even customer orientation to reduce environmental impact more efficiently (Jayal et al. 2010; Seuring and Müller 2008; Tan et al. 2010; Vachon and Klassen 2008). Large corporations with global supply chains and who sell products to image-sensitive consumers (e.g., fashion companies) are developing partnership programs with suppliers on a long-term basis comprising capacity training teams and traceability systems to improve their SSCM performance (Mejías et al. 2019). Encompassing almost all of the above concepts is Haapala and Zhang's (2015) definition of SM: "SM can be defined as the manufacture of products in a way that minimizes environmental impacts and takes into account social responsibility towards employees, the community and the consumers throughout the PLC, achieving economic benefit".

Regarding decarbonization, the term refers here to individual firms limiting anthropogenic warming through low-carbon operations management, minimizing the consumption of energy and resources from product design and industrialization to SCM (Böttcher and Müller, 2015, Sartal et al., 2020a). The goal is to reduce CO_2 emissions and CO_2 equivalent emissions, which are emissions of GHGs that would cause the same level of global warming as 1 ton of CO_2 would. Companies can decarbonize their processes using linear diagnostic tools, such as LCA or cradle-to-cradle analyses. They can also carry out eco-design initiatives (weight reduction, toxic substance removal, substitution of materials for other ecofriendly ones, etc.) and implement cleaner technologies (renewable-energy technologies, material-saving technologies and highly efficient devices, amongst others) or even end-of-pipe technologies (e.g., scrubbers and catalytic convertors on smokestacks).

Decarbonization therefore seems coherent with a management philosophy aimed at eliminating waste (King and Lenox, 2001; Galeazzo et al., 2014). These theoretical arguments do not seem to have much influence on business practice. The reduction in CO_2 emissions is not included among the key indicators of most firms or, at best, left in the background behind variables such as the cost of materials and processes (Andersen and Skjoett-Larsen, 2009). The fact is that few companies see CO_2

concern as a source of savings on resources or of improved productivity (Böttcher and Müller, 2015). Therefore, it is well worth examining the way CO_2 reduction interacts with main organizational routines such as inventory management, waste reduction, or empowerment, among others, identified in any LM program.

Evolution of Lean Thinking: From Origins to Lean-Green Manufacturing Challenges

The obsessive concern over producing higher quality, lower cost and in the shortest possible time remains a crucial element in ensuring the future of industrial plants. However, all management initiatives attempt to take the manufacturing sector beyond conventional wisdom to stimulate its adaptation to the new selection mechanisms that the environment is generating. Thus, although industrial management philosophies and tools (e.g., JIT, total quality management, Toyota Production System) have been synthesized into a dominant management paradigm around lean philosophy (Womack and Jones, 2003), the evolution of markets, with abrupt changes in preferences, increased customization and, above all, growing concern for the environment, is forcing companies to reconfigure their management strategies and incorporate issues such as process decarbonization into their corporate decisions (Sartal et al., 2020a). People have modified the chemistry of the atmosphere over two centuries of industrial development with devastating consequences, and despite the multitude of initiatives to combat climate change, CO_2 emissions continue to increase. Therefore, a new approach to reconciling process efficiency and sustainability is urgently needed, a possible roadmap to reconcile current competitiveness requirements with the decarbonization of manufacturing processes.

Thus, societies and governments in developed countries are concerned about two new focal points that condition the viability of their industrial companies: On the one hand, greater political and economic uncertainty implies internalizing within organizational routines a greater heterogeneity and variability of preferences that make expected demand more volatile; on the other hand, competitive pressures from low-cost countries and basic environmental consensuses in developed countries lead to a growing emphasis on the greening not only of energy sources, but also of industrial operations as a whole (Martinez-Senra et al., 2012).

Regarding the first issue, LM shows a growing weakness mainly in two areas. On the one hand, in highly volatile environments where customer demands lead to sudden changes in preferences and shorter product life cycles, principles and tools designed for "high volume-low variety" production environments have difficulty adapting quickly to demands for greater variability and, therefore, lower volume as well. Authors such as Narashimhan et al., (2006), and Browning and Heath (2009) indeed have called for a paradigm shift towards greater system agility, highlighting in particular that the systematic application of production leveling (Hines et al., 2004) or JIT (Bortolotti, Danese and Romano, 2013) reduces a firm's flexibility to adapt its production in the short term in the face of changes in demand.

Instead, the greater variety and volatility of demand has multiplied the need to make decisions in real time and on numerous positions that must be synchronized (Sartal et al., 2019). The need to deploy information technologies (IT) has increased accordingly, often generating spaces of latent tension between the large investments made and the organizational coherence with which they are deployed. In this regard, it is worth remembering that although the introduction of IT in the enterprise seems a priori perfectly aligned with the objectives of organizational efficiency, the mistrust of the past about the way it would affect the role of the human factor has left its mark. However, IT has not only evolved in terms of performance and ease of use, but the digitization of society through the technologies associated with I4.0 has facilitated its progressive incorporation into industrial environments.

Second, in relation to the greening of industrial operations and despite the efforts of many companies to incorporate environmental considerations into their organization, a considerable "gap" exists between theoretical developments and their application in practice. In this sense, few companies perceive sustainable operations as sources of resource savings, waste reduction or productivity improvement. Although part of the literature identifies LM as the management system par excellence capable of balancing the trade-off between effectiveness and sustainability (Galeazzo et al., 2014), other authors qualify the synergies between both types of initiatives to focus their analyses on dysfunctions. For example, Sartal et al., (2020a) suggest that as the complexity or frequency of shipments increases, JIT practices need to be readjusted to reduce CO_2 emission.

This background inspires the following headings, which reflect a further step in the development of efficient and sustainable production systems. Assuming that increasing carbon productivity and coping with demand volatility without losing efficiency are some of the main challenges of the current environment, the challenge is to determine how organizational routines should evolve to reconcile efficiency and sustainability in a reasonable way over time. The answer requires exploring the role that Technology 4.0 can play. A growing number of researchers and professionals support the vision that Industry 4.0 may provide answers to this dual challenge, competitive and environmental, in support of lean principles (e.g., Lopez-Manuel et al., 2020; Sartal et al., 2021). However, how to go about this process and which technologies of the 4.0 paradigm may be best suited to result in a sustainable and environmentally responsible competitive advantage are less clear.

OPPORTUNITIES FOR MANUFACTURING SUSTAINABILITY AND DECARBONIZATION THROUGH LEAN 4.0 INITIATIVES

The trend towards the MS is evident in developed countries as well as in emerging and developing countries, due to the current evolution towards an environmentally conscious global society. Today's customers, and most stakeholders, are increasingly concerned about the environmental impact of what they consume and are demanding that companies move beyond the deployment of purely efficiency-based management philosophies towards new environmentally efficient production models that guarantee the operations' sustainability.

To adapt LM to this changing scenario, several proposals have been made in the literature. Some authors suggest a transformation of lean principles towards new hybrid models such as lean-agile (Ding et al., 2021), lean green (Pampanelli et al., 2014), or lean, agile, resilient and green (Carvalho and Cruz-Machado, 2011). Others point to the need to evolve lean towards new systems such as agile manufacturing (Ghobakhloo and Azar, 2018) or world-class manufacturing (Chiarini and Vagnoni, 2015). Finally, a third stream proposes employing Industry 4.0 technologies to facilitate solutions to lean manufacturing principles to adapt them to new needs (Sartal et al., 2020b; Sordan et al., 2021).

Focusing on the latter, growing stream, authors such as Fettermann et al., (2018) suggest that I4.0 can contribute to operations management on issues such as process flexibility, process time reduction, manufacturing cost reduction or value chain coordination. Other works point out that I4.0, in combination with LM, can improve productivity and reduce waste, which favors cost reduction (Tortorella et al., 2020). It's should be noted that most academics and industrialists believe that I4.0 can have a positive impact on sustainability.

Since the 2016 World Economic Forum put I4.0 on its agenda as a global theme, it has been associated with transformations in all aspects of our socioeconomic life. One of the key questions is how the conditions can be created for the fourth industrial revolution and associated emerging technologies to deliver sustainability with benefits for people and society. In this perspective, the circular economy presents itself as the rational choice to the conventional linear approach and it is enhanced by the digitization and interconnection of all areas of production offered by I4.0 (Stock and Seliger 2016). This is evident in several sectors, a notable case being that of energy companies. According to Borowski (2021), smart grids, digital twins, IoT and other digital advances reduce costs by more than 20%, and the lifetime of a power plant can increase by up to 30% and enable the prosumers' engagement in the energy supply.

I4.0 is thus increasingly perceived as a core facilitator to the effectiveness of the industrial operations, making circular economy models viable and addressing societal challenges in accordance with the triple bottom line (Müller et al., 2018). As Kiel et al., (2017) state, "Overall, the digitization and interconnection of industrial processes intended by Industry 4.0 is facilitated by data analytics, machine learning (ML) and artificial intelligence (AI), resulting in potentials in all three dimensions of sustainability."

The use of advanced robotics and collaborative robots (cobots), for example, could also favor a more agile production flow with less waste and fewer defects (Tortorella et al., 2020), as well as reducing energy consumption, which is also a key aspect of increasing sustainability in manufacturing processes (Pizoń et al., 2022; Stączek et al., 2022). These new devices manage to overcome the rigidity of traditional robots in terms of production by being designed for direct interaction with operators (Galin et al., 2020), thus facilitating the automation with a human touch pursued by Jidoka by greatly reducing non-quality issues. Likewise, value stream mapping, a fundamental tool for identifying waste in the value chain, teamwork and establishing pull flow in LM (Abisourour et al., 2020), can be enhanced through the set of ICT technologies (industrial Internet of things [IIoT], Big Data and cloud computing) that enable greater interconnectivity as well as real-time data collection and analysis (Rosin et al., 2020).

As for JIT, the flow-practices supported by the IIoT and cloud computing, can bring flow-optimized autonomous decisions. For their part, the use of RFID sensors can contribute to real-time location of all stock, allowing smaller stock inventories to be maintained, thus helping to generate pull flow (Ramadan et al., 2017). Additive manufacturing contributes to achieving lean objectives in different ways: (i) It enables small batch manufacturing, facilitating product customization, setup time reduction and single-piece flow; (ii) through print-on-demand, it contributes to eliminating inventories, promoting pull flow; and (iii) it facilitates the reduction of material waste (Chen and Lin, 2017).

Rosin et al., (2020) note that IIoT facilitates both continuous flow and Kanban strategies by its ability to locate products instantly by sending real-time status updates. Meanwhile, Kolberg and Zühlke (2015) indicate that containers equipped with smart sensors can assess their occupancy level, automatically sending a digital Kanban to order refunds. For its part, production leveling (Heijunka) can improve its efficiency with the use of AI, ML, and genetic algorithms. These types of algorithms have proven their effectiveness in the optimization of logistics routes, allowing, in addition, the reduction of fuel consumption and, consequently, CO_2 emissions (Groba et al., 2018).

The incorporation of advanced technologies has also affected equipment and machine maintenance operations. The intelligence, connectivity and sensor integration of the new "smart machines" enable a variety of functions and capabilities: autonomy thanks to self-diagnostic with AI, remote monitoring, maintenance optimization

Table 1. Correspondence between lean initiatives and I4.0 technologies

	Industry 4.0 Technologies										
Lean Practices	CPS	IoT	Advanced Robotic	Cloud computing	VR and AR	Big Data	AM	Simulation	VHDI	AI - ML	AGVs
JIT	x	x		x	x	x	x		x	x	x
Pull system	x	x	x	x				x	x		
Standard work	x	x				x					
Takt time	x	x		x		x		x	x	x	
SMED	x	x					x				
Cell design		x	x			x				x	
Heijunka	x	x	x					x	x	x	
Continuous flow		x					x	x	x	x	
Kanban	x	x		x	x	x			x	x	x
Jidoka	x	x		x		x					
VSM	x	x		x	x	x		x	x		
Andon	x	x		x							
Line stops	x	x				x					
Poca yoke	x	x		x	x	x					x
TQM	x	x		x			x	x		x	
TPM	x	x		x	x	x	x			x	x
Six sigma	x	x		x		x		x		x	

Note: JIT: *Just In Time;* ***VSM:*** *Value Stream Map;* ***TQM:*** *Total Quality Management;* ***AGVs:*** *Automated Guided Vehicles;* ***TPM:*** *Total Productive Maintenance;* ***CPS:*** *Ciber Phisycal Systems;* ***IoT:*** *Internet of Things;* ***VR:*** *Virtual Reality;* ***AR:*** *Augmented Reality;* ***AM:*** *Additive Manufacturing;* ***VHDI:*** *Vertical and Horizontal Digital Integration;* ***AI:*** *Artificial Intelligence;* ***ML:*** *Machine Learning;* ***SMED:*** *Single-Minute Exchange of Dies.*

through algorithms and data analytics (Jasiulewicz-Kaczmarek and Gola 2019). As a result, we can also refer of Maintenance 4.0.

By way of summary, a detailed correspondence between lean initiatives and I4.0 technologies can be seen in Table 1.

In this regard, it is found that numerous authors mention LM as a preliminary requirement that favors the successful implementation of solutions for digital transformation in industrial organizations (e.g., Sartal et al., 2017, Bittencourt et al., 2019). Dombrowski et al., (2017), supporting Bill Gates's hypothesis that automating inefficient processes will increase their inefficiency, state that it is imperative to define processes efficiently, before companies begin automating these production processes. Other authors also highlight the importance of classic lean concepts, such as transparency, organization and standardization, as key elements when carrying out a successful I4.0 implementation (Tortorella and Fettermann, 2018).

This set of synergies described between lean and I4.0 led Metternich et al., (2017) to coin the term "Lean 4.0" to define the relationships between LM routines and

I4.0 technologies. These authors introduce for the first time this term in the German language paper *Lean 4.0—Between Contradiction and Vision*, which combined lean with Industry 4.0 (I4.0). In their research both authors reflect on the compatibility between lean philosophy and technologies under the umbrella of I4.0, concluding that lean appears to be a prerequisite for an efficient digitization. In fact, they agreed that lean enabled the successful introduction of I4.0 and concluded that both views complement each other. In addition, they present a detailed overview on how the most relevant lean tools can be complemented with I4.0 technologies.

In a similar way, Valamede and Akkari (2020) identify 25 points of synergy between lean and I4.0 that give rise to a digitized evolution of both pillars (JIT 4.0, Kaizen 4.0) and lean tools (Poka-Yoke 4.0, Kanban 4.0; Value Stream Mapping 4.0). For their part, Mayr et al., (2018) find that LM favors the success of I4.0 implementation because both paradigms are complementary. Like traditional LM, this new version 4.0 pursues process optimization and waste elimination, so version 4.0 remains a philosophy that fits perfectly with the goals of SM. To explore the sustainability and decarbonization opportunities lean and I4.0 offer, the most important aspects have been identified, based on related studies (Ghobakhloo 2018, 2020; Kamble et al., 2018; Norton et al., 2014).

Among the opportunities for environmental aspects, there is a growing consensus for I4.0 contributes to reducing waste generation by making better use of materials and consumables, recycling them and using energy wisely. Experts believe I4.0 offers numerous opportunities to reduce carbon emissions by increasing production efficiency and flexibility, reducing waste, and minimizing the rate of carbon emissions per product (e.g., Ghobakhloo 2020; Kamble et al., 2018). From a technological point of view, the development of new digitalized devices mitigates overall impact by using energy and resources more efficiently the development of new digitized equipment reduces the overall impact through efficient use of energy and resources; for example, the incorporation of various types of sensors not only in manufacturing processes, but also throughout the product life cycle, enables smarter processes and greater transparency of operations. Thanks to the information these sensors provide, precise measures can be taken to reduce negative effects on the environment. In this sense, the possibility of developing advanced models by applying system dynamics techniques, among others, is very useful (Sartal and Vázquez 2017). In addition, the use of cutting-edge technologies such as additive manufacturing helps to make the best use of raw materials and waste (Oettmeier & Hofmann, 2017). In the case of small batches or one-off designs, it even helps to reduce costs and improve productivity.

Another related environmental aspect is the transformation of energy and resources. Digitalized energy systems and the extended adoption of technologies such as identity of things (IDoT), wireless networks, offer great openings for the SM. IDoT, for example, facilitate the integration of grids and renewable energy sources, as does the exchange of surplus renewable energy between producers and consumers (Batista et al., 2017). Environmental responsibility can also be pointed out. The development of digitalization of manufacturing facilitates proactive environmentally friendly techniques and practices, such as LCA, SSCM and benchmarking of environmental performance (Niaki et al., 2019)

In terms of the economic dimension, Ghobakhloo's (2020) review of I4.0 highlights that economic sustainability functions and production efficiency are likely to be the main effect of I4.0, paving the way for the development of other socio-environmental sustainability functions. Through digitalization, I4.0 should contribute to a supply chain that is more sustainable and a circular economy. It would also enable less developed countries to accelerate the process of economic modernization. As already mentioned, it is widely recognized that I4.0 and lean-agile techniques enable production efficiency, cost reduction, flexibility and product customization (Ghobakhloo 2018).

As for the impact of decarbonization on manufacturing efficiency and labor productivity, a dynamic panel data study (Sartal et al., 2020a) yielded mixed results: material efficiency and labor productivity are positively moderated by decarbonization, but not inventory turnover or sales per worker. Thus, climate change targets affecting industrial firms may be difficult to meet if managers aim to achieve decarbonization at no cost by applying current organizational best practices.

Also noteworthy is the emergence of innovative business models focused on the exploitation of smart data to offer new and sustainable products and services, such as joint ventures for byproduct trading within different industries. The pervasiveness of the Internet and the exponential development of the IoT facilitate the collaborative economy. The emergence of collaborative business models leads to a socially sustainable economy (Morrar et al., 2017). The increased connection of producers with each other and with consumers facilitates the collaborative exchange of goods and services. The aforementioned exchange of surplus renewable energy is an illustrative example of these collaborative models.

Regarding the social dimension, no consensus currently exists on the real impact of I4.0 on labor needs (Müller et al., 2018). The most widely shared view is that the labor market will undergo serious disruptions. Low-skilled jobs with simple, routine tasks will be largely automated with 4.0 technologies such as intelligent robots, autonomous vehicles, inventory tracking, ML, and cloud computing. Instead, job opportunities will be created in a variety of fields related to computer science, data analytics, and the different areas of digitization. People will continue to perform tasks involving more creativity, although the tasks will likely be modified somewhat and complemented by new jobs involving cognitive and analytical skills, linked to information technologies and data analysis (Kiel et al., 2017; Sartal and Vázquez 2017). The aforementioned automation also contributes to better risk and safety management, reducing hazards for workers. From a training point of view, visual and simulation technologies such as AVR enable efficient, cost-effective, safer, faster and more productive forms of training. Operators of critical processes or equipment and maintenance personnel can safely practice delicate or hazardous operations or repairs and improve their readiness for potential troubleshooting. In this regard, and by way of synthesis, Table 2 outlines some of the main opportunities for sustainability and decarbonization of SM offered by LM and I4.0.

Table 2. Sustainability and decarbonization opportunities with LM and I4.0.

Sustainability and decarbonization opportunities	Description	Main advantages and disadvantages
Reduction of carbon emissions	I4.0 offers numerous opportunities to reduce carbon emissions by increasing production efficiency and flexibility.	Waste reduction Minimize carbon emissions rate per product
Energy and resource transformation	Production systems are more efficient in terms of energy and resource consumption (consumables, materials, equipment/machine time).	Efficient energy management Reduction of energy consumption Reduced resource consumption
Environmental responsibility	Digitization of manufacturing leads to environmentally friendly techniques and practices: additive manufacturing, environmentally friendly components, LCA, and SSCM.	Waste reduction Efficient consumption of resources Environmentally friendly materials
Economic development	Digitization should contribute to: - Sustainable supply chain management - Accelerating the economic modernization of less developed countries - A circular economy	SSCM Circular economy Bridging the economic gap of the least developed countries
Production efficiency and flexibility	IIoT enables the collection and analysis of data from industrial processes, helping to avoid unnecessary manufacturing steps, waste, and superfluous inventories. System integration allows closed-loop production processes and better adjustment to customer demand: quantity and product characteristics. Autonomous robots can contribute to the development of small, profitable workshops close to the end customer with consequent environmental and work-life balance benefits.	Cost reduction Product customization
New social and collaborative business models	The high degree of connectivity thanks to the widespread diffusion of the Internet and the exponential development of the IoT facilitates the collaborative economy.	To solve part of the current social and socioeconomic problems, with an emphasis on sustainability Smart grid technologies allow to commercialize surplus renewable energy Benefits not only for industry, but also for health care, education, and other sectors
Human Resources	Industrial robots, cobots, automated vehicles and inventory tracking affect low-skilled jobs but improve safety for other workers. Improved HR decision making through AI, ML, and data analytics New forms of industrial training through AVR virtualization	Labor market disruptions, reduction of low-skilled jobs New employment opportunities: AI-ML, data analytics, robotics, and mechatronics Efficiency of human resources Improved risk and safety management

Therefore, although the main trigger for the necessary evolution towards an SM appears to be the buyers' and other stakeholders' awareness, technology developments are the key drivers that will allow the shift towards a new SM model. However, the entire digital transition processes, and the implementation of associated technologies to I4.0 in general, present major challenges, including the uncertainty generated by the insufficient standardization of technologies, the high investments required, insufficient technological training, and the inertia of managers who must make the decisions (Müller et al., 2018).

Given the above, I4.0 implies great opportunities for decarbonization and global sustainability in all dimensions of the triple bottom line. However, to achieve this successfully, companies must keep in mind that the digital transformation process entails certain risks, especially for SMEs, so investments in technology must be carefully prioritized to reduce the chances of project failure and generate sustainable competitive advantages.

CONCLUSION

Manufacturing companies play a key role in achieving the sustainability objectives demanded by today's society. As they are largely responsible for both the overexploitation of natural resources and the emission of greenhouse gases, these companies need to incorporate environmental sustainability into their traditional objectives of profitability and efficiency (Garza-Reyes, 2015, Sartal et al., 2020). To meet these new ecological challenges without losing efficiency, industries must modify their processes, adopting sustainable manufacturing (SM) frameworks that allow them to adapt to the new environmental sustainability needs.

In this context, lean manufacturing (LM) can play a key role in companies' achievement of efficiency and sustainability. After all, LM, the dominant paradigm in manufacturing environments, pursues operational excellence through process optimization based on continuous improvement and waste reduction and therefore has many points of overlap with the objectives of SM. In fact, a wide stream of research in the literature identifies LM as the management system par excellence, capable of balancing the trade-off between efficiency and sustainability (Galeazzo et al., 2014, Sartal et al., 2020). However, in current environments marked by volatility in customer demand, leading to sudden changes in preferences and shorter product life cycles, principles and tools designed for "high volume-low variety" (HVLV) production environments seem to have some difficulty in adapting quickly to the new "low volume-high variability" (LVHV) conditions. Thus, as the complexity or frequency of shipments increases, LM may compromise certain objectives of the FS, making it necessary to readjust practices to reduce CO_2 emissions. In this sense, the technologies associated with Industry 4.0 (4.0 technologies), in support of lean principles, could contribute to minimizing some of these performance losses and help make efficiency and sustainability compatible (Carou et al., 2022).

Technologies 4.0 offer a wide range of opportunities for companies to improve both the efficiency and flexibility of their processes. This optimization of tasks can favor a better use of materials and consumables, facilitating their recycling, which translates into a reduction of waste, a minimization of carbon emissions and a smarter use of energy, factors that make it easier for companies to meet their SM objectives. One must also bear in mind that the interconnection possibilities offered by 4.0 technologies favor both vertical integration, at the company level, and horizontal integration, at the value chain level, smoothing the shift from a linear to a circular economy while helping to create more sustainable supply chains.

Table 3. Main contributions

	LM	I4.0 Technologies	Effects on sustainable manufacturing
JIT	Pull System	CPS, HVDI, AR, AM	- Production efficiency and flexibility - Inventory reduction - Carbon emissions reduction
	Heijunka	IA, ML and genetic algorithms, AGVs	- Logistics routes optimisation - CO^2 emissions reduction
	Continuous flow	CPS, CC, BDA, IA, ML, HVDI, AR, AM	- Inventory reduction - Waste minimisation/elimination - Carbon emissions reduction - Energy consumption reduction
	Kanban	BDA, AGVs, Simulation	- Automated logistic - Material reduction - Intermediate material stocks reduction - Waste minimisation/elimination
Jidoka	VSM	IT (IIoT, BD and CC)	- Wate reduction - Energy consumption reduction - Carbon emissions reduction
	Poca yoke	AGVs, CC, AR	- Error prevention - Waste minimisation/elimination - Reduction of energy consumption
	TQM	AM; AR	- Non-quality problems reduction - Waste reduction - Energy consumption reduction
	TPM	CPS, CC, BDA, AGVs, AM, AR	- Maintenance planning: early failure detection - Material reduction - Energy consumption reduction
RfP	Training	I4.0 Technologies	- More skilled employees - Material reduction - Energy consumption reduction
	Employees Engagement	CPS, AR, Simulation	- Critical process monitoring - Material reduction - Waste reduction - Energy consumption reduction

***AGVs:** automatic guided vehicles; **AM:** additive manufacturing; **AR:** advanced robotic; **BD:** big data; **BDA:** big data analytics; **CC:** cloud computing; **CPS:** cyber physical systems; **IA:** artificial intelligence; **HVDI:** horizontal and vertical digital integration; **IIoT:** Industrial Internet of Things; **IT:** information technologies; **ML:** machine learning*

In this regard, this chapter delves into the different resources and functionalities offered by 4.0 technologies, in support of lean principles, for the achievement of efficiency and sustainability goal. As described throughout the chapter, 4.0 technologies can become key instruments through which lean practices reinforce their effects on efficiency and, simultaneously and by their very nature, help address environmental challenges. Accordingly, consideration is given to the effects not only on productive systems but also on society and the environment in a broader context. Thus, it first assesses how lean principles enable the right conditions for the development of 4.0 environments and then discusses ways they can be leveraged to improve their contributions to firm performance and sustainability. Lastly, the possibilities provided by several key 4.0 technologies for decarbonization and sustainability are summarized. In line with this, Table 3 details the main contributions of the chapter. The table is structured in three columns. The first column lists the main LM practices. The second shows the 4.0 technologies that, combined with the practices in column one, can support lean 4.0. Finally, the last column lists the potential contributions of lean 4.0 that can facilitate the transition to SM.

Based on these contributions, we can conclude that the implementation of Lean 4.0 in manufacturing companies has the potential to favor the decarbonization of production while enabling greater energy efficiency, lower resource consumption and better waste management, all of which are objectives of SM. Therefore, this new paradigm should be considered by managers when exploring opportunities to smooth the transition to more environmentally sustainable production.

The insights gained should encourage practitioners to consider integrating both lean and 4.0, focusing on those synergies that maximize success. It should be noted that not all lean pillars show the same orientation toward environmental improvement. For example, JIT practices can lead to serious incompatibilities between environmental requirements and the ongoing quest for efficiency. This occurs, for example, when the synchronization of the supply chain intensifies CO_2 emissions or when the reduction of batch sizes requires more frequent product changes with more frequent maintenance of production equipment and the creation of waste (Garza-Reyes, 2015).

Because they consider some of the conflicts that arise between the efficiency requirements of an industry and the environmental interests of institutions, the reflections in this chapter may also be of interest to public policy makers. As mentioned above, 4.0 technologies can enable the generation of unique and competitively valuable organizational capabilities that become competitive advantages. However, it is also true that the capabilities these resources generate in support of lean principles need not necessarily be in line with market requirements and, therefore, may not represent sustainable competitive advantages for the enterprise. Thus, whenever it is in the interest of society, public policy makers can intervene by introducing specific policies that enable entrepreneurs to use such technologies or by directly supporting projects that can contribute to improving an organization's performance. This is not suggesting that public policies should be directed solely at promoting lean–4.0 research, but considering that public resources are scarce, focusing on initiatives that maximize the use of public money and contribute to improving the competitiveness of regions and countries is important.

Limitations and Future Research

Notably, this chapter is a first step, of an eminently exploratory nature, which should be endorsed by future research, preferably of a quantitative nature. Given that it is not sufficient to analyze only the starting point and the final objective of this type of project, we stress the need to carry out longitudinal case studies that allow observation of the evolution of the routine transformation process, considering the possibility of the emergence of new routines that combine organizational and technological aspects to balance sustainability and efficiency.

Another major limitation is that our analysis focuses on the manufacturing sector, and a rational extension of it is to replicate the evidence in other sectors, particularly within non-repetitive environments. This is mainly because researchers have questioned the suitability of lean principles (Portioli-Staudacher and Tantardini, 2012) and 4.0. initiatives (Strandhagen et al., 2017) for these types of processes. It may also be of enormous interest to transfer this analysis to the service sector due to the enormous importance that these types of activities are acquiring in developed countries.

In this same context, evaluating what the right pace of implementation should be for lean–4.0 initiatives would be interesting. Future research should investigate questions such as whether the implementation of LM and 4.0 technologies should be simultaneous or sequential—and if sequential, which should be implemented first—or how simultaneous or sequential implementation affects performance. The answers to these questions could facilitate decision-making for managers in the transition to SM.

As the chapter states, there is little doubt today about the ability of 4.0 technologies to maximize the speed with which information is exchanged, facilitate data processing and analysis or complement lean principles. However, fewer certainties exist about how those benefits are produced and with what pace and sequence specifically. To understand the complex factors involved in the joint deployment of lean-4.0 practices, analyzing only the starting point or the end goal is indeed not enough. One needs to look at the evolution of the transformation process, clarifying the nature of the causal relationships and identifying which elements precede others and with what timing.

Finally, unraveling the role that formal and informal institutions can play in the process of transforming lean 4.0 routines into competitive advantages would be interesting. From a macroeconomic perspective, it might also be interesting not only to assess the key institutional characteristics that influence the relationships between organizational routines, sustainability and value creation but also to understand why and how these characteristics affect the creation of new competitive advantages based on lean–4.0 practices.

REFERENCES

Abisourour, J., Hachkar, M., Mounir, B., & Farchi, A. (2020). Methodology for integrated management system improvement: Combining costs deployment and value stream mapping. *International Journal of Production Research*, *58*(12), 3667–3685.

Barber, J. (2007). Mapping the Movement to Achieve Sustainable Production and Consumption in North America. *Journal of Cleaner Production*, *15*(6), 499–512. doi:10.1016/j.jclepro.2006.05.010

Batista, N. C., Melício, R., & Mendes, V. M. F. (2017). Services enabler architecture for smart grid and smart living services providers under industry 4.0. *Energy and Building*, *141*, 16–27.

Bittencourt, V. L., Carvalho Alves, A., & Pinto Leão, C. (2019). Lean thinking contributions for industry 4.0: A systematic literature review. *IFAC-PapersOnLine*, *52*(13), 904–909.

Borowski, P. F. (2021). Digitization, Digital Twins, Blockchain, and Industry 4.0 as Elements of Management Process in Enterprises in the Energy Sector. *Energies 2021*, *14*(7), 1885. doi: 10.3390/EN14071885

Bortolotti, T., Danese, P., & Romano, P. (2013). Assessing the impact of just-in-time on operational performance at varying degrees of repetitiveness. *International Journal of Production Research*, *51*(4), 1117–1130.

Böttcher, C. F., & Müller, M. (2015). Drivers, practices and outcomes of low-carbon operations: Approaches of German automotive suppliers to cutting carbon emissions. *Business Strategy and the Environment*, *24*(6), 477–498.

Browning, T. R., & Heath, R. D. (2009). Reconceptualizing the effects of lean on production costs with evidence from the F-22 program. *Journal of Operations Management*, *27*(1), 23–44.

Brundtland, G. H., & Khalid, M. (1987). Our common future. Oxford University Press.

Carou, D., Sartal, A., & Davim, J. P. (Eds.). (2022). Machine Learning and Artificial Intelligence with Industrial Applications. Springer.

Carvalho, H., & Cruz-Machado, V. (2011). Integrating lean, agile, resilience and green paradigms in supply chain management (LARG_SCM). *Supply Chain Management*.

Chen, T., & Lin, Y. C. (2017). Feasibility evaluation and optimization of a smart manufacturing system based on 3D printing: A review. *International Journal of Intelligent Systems*, *32*(4), 394–413.

Chiarini, A., & Vagnoni, E. (2015). World-class manufacturing by Fiat. Comparison with Toyota production system from a strategic management, management accounting, operations management and performance measurement dimension. *International Journal of Production Research*, *53*(2), 590–606.

Ding, B., Ferras Hernandez, X., & Agell Jane, N. (2021). Combining lean and agile manufacturing competitive advantages through Industry 4.0 technologies: An integrative approach. *Production Planning and Control*, 1–17.

Dombrowski, U., Richter, T., & Krenkel, P. (2017). Interdependencies of Industrie 4.0 & lean production systems: A use cases analysis. *Procedia Manufacturing*, *11*, 1061–1068.

Ehrenstein, M., Wang, C. H., & Guillén-Gosálbez, G. (2019). Strategic planning of supply chains considering extreme events: Novel heuristic and application to the petrochemical industry. *Computers & Chemical Engineering*, *125*, 306–323.

Elkington, J. (1998). Partnerships from Cannibals with Forks: The Triple Bottom Line of 21st-Century Business. *Environmental Quality Management*, *8*(1), 37–51.

Fettermann, D. C., Cavalcante, C. G. S., Almeida, T. D. D., & Tortorella, G. L. (2018). How does Industry 4.0 contribute to operations management? *Journal of Industrial and Production Engineering*, *35*(4), 255–268.

Firdaus, N., Samat, H. A., & Mohamad, N. (2019). Maintenance for Energy Efficiency: A Review. *IOP Conference Series. Materials Science and Engineering*, *530*(1), 012047.

Franciosi, C., Voisin, A., Miranda, S., Riemma, S., & Iung, B. (2020). Measuring Maintenance Impacts on Sustainability of Manufacturing Industries: From a Systematic Literature Review to a Framework Proposal. *Journal of Cleaner Production*, 260.

Galeazzo, A., Furlan, A., & Vinelli, A. (2014). Lean and green in action: Interdependencies and performance of pollution prevention projects. *Journal of Cleaner Production*, *85*, 191–200.

Galin, R., Meshcheryakov, R., Kamesheva, S., & Samoshina, A. (2020, May). Cobots and the benefits of their implementation in intelligent manufacturing. *IOP Conference Series. Materials Science and Engineering*, *862*(3), 032075.

Garza-Reyes, J. A. (2015). Lean and green–a systematic review of the state of the art literature. *Journal of Cleaner Production*, *102*, 18–29.

Ghobakhloo, M. (2018). The future of manufacturing industry: A strategic roadmap toward Industry 4.0. *Journal of Manufacturing Technology Management*.

Ghobakhloo, M. (2020). Industry 4.0, digitization, and opportunities for sustainability. *Journal of Cleaner Production*, *252*, 119869.

Groba, C., Sartal, A., & Vázquez, X. H. (2018). Integrating forecasting in metaheuristic methods to solve dynamic routing problems: Evidence from the logistic processes of tuna vessels. *Engineering Applications of Artificial Intelligence*, *76*, 55–66.

Guide, V. D. R. Jr, Srivastava, R., & Kraus, M. E. (1997). Product structure complexity and scheduling of operations in recoverable manufacturing. *International Journal of Production Research*, *35*(11), 3179–3200.

Hines, P., Holweg, M., & Rich, N. (2004). Learning to evolve: A review of contemporary lean thinking. *International Journal of Operations & Production Management*.

Ihlen, Ø., & Roper, J. (2014). Corporate reports on sustainability and sustainable development: 'We have arrived'. *Sustainable Development*, *22*(1), 42–51.

Ilgin, M. A., & Gupta, S. M. (2010). Environmentally conscious manufacturing and product recovery (ECMPRO): A review of the state of the art. *Journal of Environmental Management*, *91*(3), 563–591.

IEA. (2021). *Greenhouse Gas Emissions from Energy: Overview*. IEA. https://www.iea.org/reports/greenhouse-gas-emissions-from-en ergy-overview

Jasiulewicz-Kaczmarek, M., & Gola, A. (2019). Maintenance 4.0 Technologies for Sustainable Manufacturing - An Overview. *IFAC-PapersOnLine*, *52*(10), 91–96.

Masson-Delmotte, V., Zhai, P., Pirani, A., Connors, S. L., Péan, C., Berger, S., ... Zhou, B. (2021). *Climate change 2021: The physical science basis*. Contribution of working group I to the sixth assessment report of the intergovernmental panel on climate change.

Kaebernick, H., Kara, S., & Sun, M. (2003). Sustainable product development and manufacturing by considering environmental requirements. *Robotics and Computer-integrated Manufacturing*, *19*(6), 461–468.

Kamble, S. S., Gunasekaran, A., & Gawankar, S. A. (2018). Sustainable Industry 4.0 framework: A systematic literature review identifying the current trends and future perspectives. *Process Safety and Environmental Protection*, *117*, 408–425.

Kiel, D., Müller, J. M., Arnold, C., & Voigt, K. I. (2017). Sustainable industrial value creation: Benefits and challenges of Industry 4.0. *International Journal of Innovation Management*, *21*(08), 1740015.

Kloepffer, W. (2008). Life cycle sustainability assessment of products. *The International Journal of Life Cycle Assessment*, *13*(2), 89–95.

Kolberg, D., & Zühlke, D. (2015). Lean automation enabled by industry 4.0 technologies. *IFAC-PapersOnLine*, *48*(3), 1870–1875.

León-Mateos, F., Sartal, A., López-Manuel, L., & Quintas, M. A. (2021). Adapting our sea ports to the challenges of climate change: Development and validation of a Port Resilience Index. *Marine Policy*, *130*, 104573.

Lieder, M., & Rashid, A. (2016). Towards circular economy implementation: A comprehensive review in context of manufacturing industry. *Journal of Cleaner Production*, *115*, 36–51.

López-Manuel, L., León-Mateos, F., & Sartal, A. (2020). Closing Loops, Easing Strains: Industry 4.0's Potential for Overcoming Challenges of Circularity in Manufacturing Environments. In Circular Economy for the Management of Operations (pp. 23-47). CRC Press.

Mayr, A., Weigelt, M., Kühl, A., Grimm, S., Erll, A., Potzel, M., & Franke, J. (2018). Lean 4.0-A conceptual conjunction of lean management and Industry 4.0. *Procedia Cirp*, *72*, 622–628.

Mejías, A. M., Bellas, R., Pardo, J. E., & Paz, E. (2019). Traceability management systems and capacity building as new approaches for improving sustainability in the fashion multi-tier supply chain. *International Journal of Production Economics*, *217*, 143–158.

Mendoza, J. M. F., Sharmina, M., Gallego-Schmid, A., Heyes, G., & Azapagic, A. (2017). Integrating backcasting and eco-design for the circular economy: The BECE framework. *Journal of Industrial Ecology*, *21*(3), 526–544.

Metternich, J., Müller, M., Meudt, T., & Schaede, C. (2017). Lean 4.0 - entre la contradicción y la visión. *Revista de economía de fábrica, 112*(5), 346-348.

Moldavska, A., & Welo, T. (2017). The concept of sustainable manufacturing and its definitions: A content-analysis based literature review. *Journal of Cleaner Production*, *166*, 744–755.

Morrar, R., Arman, H., & Mousa, S. (2017). The fourth industrial revolution (Industry 4.0): A social innovation perspective. *Technology Innovation Management Review*, *7*(11), 12–20.

Müller, J. M., Kiel, D., & Voigt, K. (2018). What Drives the Implementation of Industry 4.0? The Role of Opportunities and Challenges in the Context of Sustainability. *Sustainability*, *10*(1), 247.

Narasimhan, R., Swink, M., & Kim, S. W. (2006). Disentangling leanness and agility: An empirical investigation. *Journal of Operations Management*, *24*(5), 440–457.

Niaki, M. K., Torabi, S. A., & Nonino, F. (2019). Why manufacturers adopt additive manufacturing technologies: The role of sustainability. *Journal of Cleaner Production*, *222*, 381–392.

Norton, T., Beier, J., Shields, L., Househam, A., Bombis, E., & Liew, D. (2014). *A guide to traceability: A practical approach to advance sustainability in global supply chains*. The United Nations Global Compact and BSR Report.

Oettmeier, K., & Hofmann, E. (2017). Additive manufacturing technology adoption: An empirical analysis of general and supply chain-related determinants. *Journal of Business Economics*, *87*(1), 97–124.

Owen, J. V. (1999). Environmentally Conscious Manufacturing. *Manufacturing Engineering*, *111*(4), 44–55.

Ozcelik, N., Rodríguez, M., Lutter, S., & Sartal, A. (2021). Indicating the wrong track? A critical appraisal of water productivity as an indicator to inform water efficiency policies. *Resources, Conservation and Recycling*, *168*, 105452.

Oztemel, E., & Gursev, S. (2020). Literature review of Industry 4.0 and related technologies. *Journal of Intelligent Manufacturing*, *31*(1), 127–182.

Pampanelli, A. B., Found, P., & Bernardes, A. M. (2014). A Lean & Green Model for a production cell. *Journal of Cleaner Production, 85*, 19–30.

Pizoń, J., Gola, A., & Świć, A. (2022). The Role and Meaning of the Digital Twin Technology in the Process of Implementing Intelligent Collaborative Robots. In *International Scientific-Technical Conference Manufacturing* (pp. 39-49). Springer.

Ramadan, M., Al-Maimani, H., & Noche, B. (2017). RFID-enabled smart real-time manufacturing cost tracking system. *International Journal of Advanced Manufacturing Technology, 89*(1), 969–985.

Ramiya, S., & Suresh, M. (2021). Factors Influencing Lean-Sustainable Maintenance Using TISM Approach. *International Journal of System Assurance Engineering and Management, 12*(6), 1117–1131.

Rosin, F., Forget, P., Lamouri, S., & Pellerin, R. (2020). Impacts of Industry 4.0 technologies on Lean principles. *International Journal of Production Research, 58*(6), 1644–1661.

Rossini, M., Costa, F., Tortorella, G. L., Valvo, A., & Portioli-Staudacher, A. (2021). Lean Production and Industry 4.0 integration: How Lean Automation is emerging in manufacturing industry. *International Journal of Production Research*, 1–21.

Sarkis, J., & Rasheed, A. (1995). Greening the manufacturing function. *BUSINESS HORIZONS-BLOOMINGTON, 38*, 17–17.

Sartal, A., & Vázquez, X. H. (2017). Implementing Information Technologies and Operational Excellence: Planning, emergence and randomness in the survival of adaptive manufacturing systems. *Journal of Manufacturing Systems, 45*, 1–16.

Sartal, A., Llach, J., Vázquez, X. H., & de Castro, R. (2017). How much does Lean Manufacturing need environmental and information technologies? *Journal of Manufacturing Systems, 45*, 260–272.

Sartal, A., Martinez-Senra, A. I., & Cruz-Machado, V. (2018). Are all lean principles equally eco-friendly? A panel data study. *Journal of Cleaner Production, 177*, 362–370.

Sartal, A., Carou, D., Dorado-Vicente, R., & Mandayo, L. (2019). Facing the challenges of the food industry: Might additive manufacturing be the answer? *Proceedings of the Institution of Mechanical Engineers. Part B, Journal of Engineering Manufacture, 233*(8), 1902–1906.

Sartal, A., Rodríguez, M., & Vázquez, X. H. (2020a). From efficiency-driven to low-carbon operations management: Implications for labor productivity. *Journal of Operations Management, 66*(3), 310–325.

Sartal, A., Carou, D., & Davim, J. P. (Eds.). (2020b). *Enabling technologies for the successful deployment of Industry 4.0*. CRC Press.

Senra, A. I. M., Sartal, A., & Vázquez, X. H. (2012). Tintorerías de posguerra e innovación organizativa en Inditex: una perspectiva contractual de la gestión lean de la cadena de suministro. *UCJC Business and Society Review*, (34).

Sharma, N. K., Govindan, K., Lai, K. K., Chen, W. K., & Kumar, V. (2021). The transition from linear economy to circular economy for sustainability among SMEs: A study on prospects, impediments, and prerequisites. *Business Strategy and the Environment, 30*(4), 1803–1822.

Sordan, J. E., Oprime, P. C., Pimenta, M. L., da Silva, S. L., & González, M. O. A. (2021). Contact points between Lean Six Sigma and Industry 4.0: A systematic review and conceptual framework. *International Journal of Quality & Reliability Management.*

Stączek, P., Pizoń, J., Danilczuk, W., & Gola, A. (2021). A digital twin approach for the improvement of an autonomous mobile robots (AMR's) operating environment—A case study. *Sensors (Basel), 21*(23), 7830.

Stock, T., & Seliger, G. (2016). Opportunities of sustainable manufacturing in Industry 4.0. *Procedia CIRP, 40*, 536-541.

Toffel, M. W. (2003). The growing strategic importance of end-of-life product management. *California Management Review, 45*(3), 102–129.

Tortorella, G. L., & Fettermann, D. (2018). Implementation of Industry 4.0 and lean production in Brazilian manufacturing companies. *International Journal of Production Research, 56*(8), 2975–2987.

Tortorella, G. L., Pradhan, N., Macias de Anda, E., Trevino Martinez, S., Sawhney, R., & Kumar, M. (2020). Designing lean value streams in the fourth industrial revolution era: Proposition of technology-integrated guidelines. *International Journal of Production Research, 58*(16), 5020–5033.

Vachon, S., & Klassen, R. D. (2008). Environmental management and manufacturing performance: The role of collaboration in the supply chain. *International Journal of Production Economics, 111*(2), 299–315.

Valamede, L. S., & Akkari, A. C. S. (2020). Lean 4.0: A new holistic approach for the integration of lean manufacturing tools and digital technologies. International Journal of Mathematical. *Engineering and Management Sciences*, *5*(5), 851.

Wackernagel, M., & Rees, W. (1998). *Our ecological footprint: reducing human impact on the earth* (Vol. 9). New society publishers.

Womack, J., & Jones, D. (2003). *Lean Thinking*. Simon and Schuster.

Zhang, H., & Haapala, K. R. (2015). Integrating sustainable manufacturing assessment into decision making for a production work cell. *Journal of Cleaner Production*, *105*, 52–63.

KEY TERMS AND DEFINITIONS

6R Sustainable Approach: Applies a broad scope of environmental impact reductions by considering the following activities: reduce, reuse, recycle, recover, redesign, and remanufacture.

Artificial Intelligence(AI): A digital form of consciousness that can match or exceed human-like performance in any number of metrics. An AGI would be equally good at solving math equations, conducting a humanlike conversation, or guiding a vehicle.

AVR: Is a set of technologies that allow the user to visualize part of the real world through a technological device with graphical information, combining tangible physical elements with virtual elements.

Decarbonization: The process of stopping or reducing carbon gases, especially carbon dioxide, being released into the atmosphere as the result of a process, for example the burning of fossil fuels.

Greenhouse Gas Emissions (GHG): Any gas that has the property of absorbing infrared radiation (net heat energy) emitted from Earth's surface and reradiating it back to Earth's surface, thus contributing to the greenhouse effect.

Identity of Things (IDoT): Provides IoT devices with unique identity, ensures that the information generated by the device is sent in a secure manner.

Industrial Internet of Things (IIoT): The use of connected smart devices in industrial applications for purposes such as automation, remote monitoring and predictive maintenance.

Machine Learning: Is a branch of IA, the ML imitate the way that humans learn, gradually improving accuracy. Enable the generation of mathematical models and refining them as they are trained on additional data.

Sustainability: The use of resources to meet the needs of the present without compromising the needs of future generations.

Sustainable Manufacturing (SM): The creation of manufactured products through economically-sound processes that minimize negative environmental impacts while conserving energy and natural resources. Also enhances employee, community and product safety.

Sustainable Supply Chain (SSCM): Is one that fully integrates ethical and environmentally responsible practices into a competitive and successful model. End-to-end supply chain transparency is critical; sustainability initiatives must extend from raw materials sourcing, to last-mile logistics, and even to product returns and recycling processes.

Triple Bottom Line (TBL): Established by Elkington broadens the dimensions of sustainability: social, environmental and economic.

Chapter 2
How Industry 4.0 and Sustainable Development Goals Can Enhance Lean Practices

Esin Yücel Karamustafa
https://orcid.org/0000-0003-1440-1203
Altinbas University, Turkey

Burcu Arsan
https://orcid.org/0000-0002-9757-9391
Yeditepe University, Turkey

ABSTRACT

Lean manufacturing and management systems have become a new paradigm for excellence in value generation and delivery for the most competitive companies in the world. With the effect of digital transformation, organizations prefer to apply these approaches in order to create value by providing quality products and services to the end customer, while reducing production and environmental waste. In this context, the lean management approach requires the direct support of both sustainability and Industry 4.0 concepts in order to develop the principles and tools. On the other hand, UNDP's sustainable development goals have a very important place when it is aimed to support sustainable industrialization, strengthen innovation, and ensure operational excellence. This research aims to find answers to "How can Industry 4.0 and sustainable development goals enhance lean practices?" by performing content analysis in various databases in the existing literature.

DOI: 10.4018/978-1-6684-5606-4.ch002

INTRODUCTION

Due to the globalizing market and the intense competition, businesses are faced with new challenges in terms of cost, quality, and time. According to the increase in the number of competitors and the increase in customers' opportunities day by day, tough competition conditions are created in the market. In order to stay alive in this competitive environment, businesses aimed to design their processes and methods efficiently and flexibly throughout the entire value chain. In this respect, lean manufacturing philosophy is important for businesses, which can significantly increase the performance of a company by focusing on value-added activities and achieving high-efficiency processes. With the increasing importance of creating value with scarce resources, organizations have sought new production models (Ruano et al., 2019).

Lean management philosophy aims to eliminate everything wasted by making continuous improvements and adjustments in the production process. Lean manufacturing is a Japanese method of business organization that originated in Toyota Motor Plant (Türkan, 2010). The benefits of Lean Manufacturing have drawn the attention of organizations in various sectors, and within the modern world, it has spread globally, predominantly in the automotive sector, and then has taken its place in companies in other sectors. Lean manufacturing is an approach that encompasses a wide variety of management practices, including just-in-time production / distribution, quality systems, work teams, cellular manufacturing, supplier management in an integrated system (Shah & Ward, 2003).

The focus of lean manufacturing is synergistically creating a high-quality system that produces finished products with little or no waste based on customer demand (Zühlke,2015) In a broader sense, lean production can be defined as making use of all the potentials by using all production factors in the most flexible way, with the least waste, in the shortest time, with low cost, and error-free production with the least use of resources (Cinoğlu, 2013). For this purpose, Lean Manufacturing techniques such as Just-in-Time Production, Kaizen (continuous improvement), Continuous Flow, Kanban (pull system), SMED (Single Minute Exchange of Dies), and Productive Maintenance have been developed.

Over the last years, the international industrial terrain has crucially altered due to the emergence of many disruptive technologies that have resulted from innovations and developments. Therefore, with growing improvements in manufacturing processes, the I4.0 idea has emerged, becoming a progressively relevant international issue in the last few years (Zhou et al., 2016) In addition to the lean management philosophy, the Industry 4.0 revolution that has emerged in recent years also increases the performance of organizations by making their processes efficient.

Industry 4.0 is seen as one of the most promising approaches to tackling the challenges in the manufacturing environment and it was introduced at the Hannover Messe in 2011 (Dombrowski et al, 2017). Industry 4.0 is an umbrella term that includes digital concepts such as the internet of things, cyber-physical systems, big data, data analysis, cloud computing, virtual reality, etc. These digital concepts are seen as encouraging complements to the successful and holistic implementation of lean methods and can support overcoming existing barriers to lean implementation. In addition, Industry 4.0 and lean manufacturing can be considered as parallel concepts in many respects (Adetunji, 2019).

The technology and services offered with the Industry 4.0 revolution allow you to instantly see the effectiveness of automation and production technologies, and to predict regular data exchange and future process steps. It also helps the formation of structures called 'smart factory' or 'dark (unmanned) factory' through virtual systems. At the same time, lean manufacturing provides efficient and economical use of Industry 4.0 technologies by creating standardized, transparent, uncomplicated, and repeatable processes. Also, lean manufacturing provides efficient and economical use of Industry 4.0 technologies by reducing product and process complexity.

Sustainability is fundamentally defined and perceived as ecology and the ability of ecological systems to maintain their functions, processes, and productivity in the future (Chapin et al., 1996). Sustainability has been also defined with words such as "biological system", "ecosystem", "protection, "social equality". Also, it is perceived as ecology and the ability of ecological systems to maintain their functions, processes, and productivity in the future. On the other hand, while defining sustainability, it is predominantly considered together with economic concepts (Esty and Winston, 2008). Ensuring sustainability in terms of economic development requires sensitivity in resource use due to the limited resources of the world. Resource efficiency, pollution prevention-recycling, use of clean technology can be considered as practices that will increase the sustainability reputation of companies and reduce costs (Chapin et al., 1996).

Nowadays, organizations can take the first steps to being sustainable by designing their production processes leaner. Another way, replacing old technologies with environmentally friendly ones, seems to be an easier approach than designing a new system. Thus, while organizations integrate new technologies into their production processes, they also support the realization of sustainable development goals. The sustainable development goals were first introduced at the United Nations' *Conference on Sustainable Development* held in Rio de Janeiro in 2012. Its aim is to set universal goals that address environmental, political, and economic issues.

The sustainable development goals replaced the millennium development goals launched in 2000. In this direction, global sustainable development goals have been determined by the United Nations. Through these determined goals, it is aimed to identify and solve the problems that have common aspects in a more participatory and effective way. In this framework, for sustainable development 17 fundamental goals and 169 sub-goals have been determined to achieve (tr.undp.org). The accomplishment of this agenda fundamentally relies on whether society will be capable of maximizing synergies and fix existing trade-offs between the SDGs.

Resources on earth are gradually decreasing or, are being destroyed by the hands of human beings. Today, human beings should be more conscious than ever about the efficient use of scarce resources (Martin, 2002). It is also very important for organizations to pursue sustainable strategies while choosing technology-based lean methods as a production model. UNDP, which sets standard targets for a better world, also supports responsible production by avoiding waste.

In this study, lean production philosophy, sustainable development goals, and Industry 4.0 revolution were examined and their effects on each other also investigated and evaluated. In addition, it has been evaluated which sustainable development goals support the lean management model more effectively.

THEORETICAL BACKGROUND

Development of Industry 4.0

Industry 4.0, which was established in Germany and influenced the whole world since 2011, is described as the last point reached by the industrial revolution. When the industrial revolutions are examined, it is seen that their history dates back to the 1750- 1800s. England took the first step in industrialization. The technological advancement created by England, which developed the textile industry, spread over time with the involvement of other countries in this process. It has created competition in industrialization and has forced many countries to attach importance to R&D processes. The concept of Industry 4.0 was mentioned for the first time at the Hannover Fair in 2011. On the subject of Industry 4.0, named for the first time by the German government, the "Industry 4.0 Manifesto" was published by the German National Academy of Science and Engineering (ACATech) (Fırat & Fırat, 2017).

The basis of the industrial revolution is the accumulation of capital with the development of the bourgeoisie and the increase in the accumulation of knowledge with the development of trade (Görçün, 2016). In addition, social structure, industrial tradition, understanding of society, education systems, ability to produce and use technology, experience, and many other factors play a crucial role in the production and development of technology (Yücel, 2006).

To summarize the factors that caused the industrial revolution, these are changes in demographic structure, innovations in agriculture, trade revolution, diversity in

Figure 1. The Industrial Revolution: From Industry 1.0 to Industry 4.0

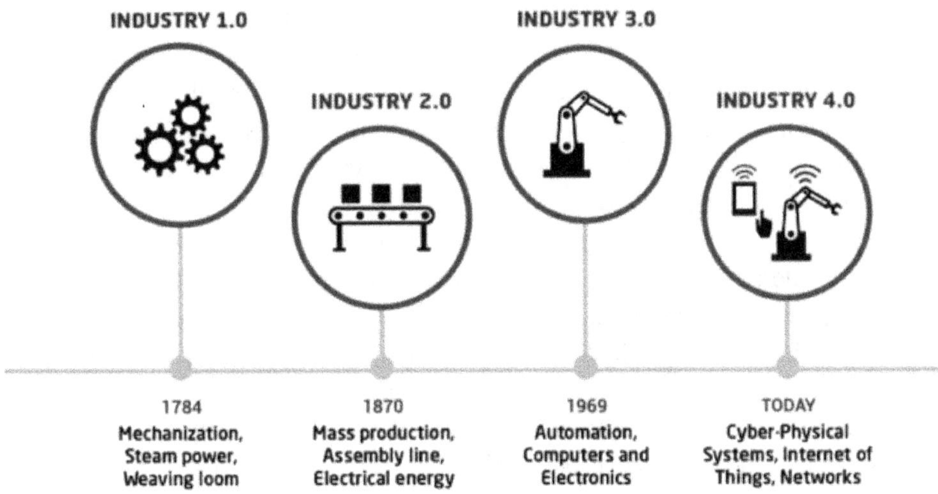

transportation channels, capital accumulation, knowledge for the development of industrial technology and developments in financial markets (Torun, 2003).One of the most important and fundamental developments that emerged with the industrial revolution is steam engines. With the invention of the steam engine, the age of steam has also been entered.

This period is when the primary production model shifts from human to machine power. The concept of production with machines spread rapidly, as fuel sources such as steam and coal made the use of machinery much easier and more convenient. Thus, the machines enabled faster and easier production and made all kinds of innovations and technologies possible within this period. Many concepts emerged with the effect of the industrial revolution. One of them is specialization. Adam Smith, in 1776, while describing the production processes, stated that the workers would contribute more due to the division of labor in the factories (Smith, 1776).

At the beginning of the 20th century, the world entered a second industrial revolution with the usage of steel and electricity in factories. The usage of electricity has allowed manufacturers increase productivity and make factory machinery more mobile. Thus, mass production concepts such as the assembly line emerged as a way to increase productivity. Historians also call Industry 2.0 the "Technological Revolution". Production systems and inventions based on theoretical knowledge emerged in this period. Another fundamental contribution in this process is that the parts of the machines produced were made to the same standard. As a result, the machines are composed of easily replaceable parts (Akbulut, 2011).

In 1911, Frederick Winslow Taylor put forward a new production method, which will be called Taylorism, in his book *Scientific Principles of Management*. The related method was accepted in industrial production in a short time and started to be applied in production processes. Taylor argued that a job should be divided into certain parts and produced by employees who specialize in separate processes. Taylor stated that his new production method will provide advancement in efficiency in the workflow (Görçün, 2016).

Following these advancements, industrialists had to look for new ways to compete and reconsidered their strategic decisions. Contrary to the production-oriented approach, the idea of producing in line with what consumers want has come to the fore. After this period, production cost reductions are the most important factor as consumers prefer to buy high-quality products at lower prices.

Industry 4.0 is essentially a project based on speed, flexibility, and efficiency. It has a much more intensive production approach with much lower costs. The Boston consultant team suggested that there are eight technological components that enable the transformation of the manufacturing industry to Industry 4.0 and listed them as follows: automation, IoT, simulation, additive manufacturing, cyber security, augmented reality, big data (Hermann, Pentek, and Otto, 2015). Industry 4.0 components can be defined as a system of digital products that are entirely surrounded and equipped with the internet (Doğruel, Anuşlu, & Fırat, 2019).

Based on all these, the impact of Industry 4.0 is not only limited to production. The development of artificial intelligence, 3D technology, cloud computing, augmented reality, and analysis of big data have great repercussions in many different sectors. By the means of data analysis methods, the demands of the target audience are determined, and production can be carried out accordingly. Thus, a profitable production process is possible, in which the margin of error is minimized, and waste is avoided. With the increasing production speed, the quality also increases. Today, high-performance, and nature-friendly devices with software and hardware have become possible with Industry 4.0 technology (Alahyari, 2019).

Industry 4.0 has clear implications when it comes to revenues, investments, and technological advancements, but employment remains one of the most mysterious aspects of the new industrial revolution. Industry 4.0 may be the pinnacle of technological advancement in manufacturing, but it still looks like machines will take over the industry. Consequently, it is important to further analyze this approach to draw conclusions about the demographics of labor in the future. This will help us prepare for the not-too-distant future. Industry 4.0, which is also expressed with similar words such as digital transformation, digitizing industry, fourth industrial revolution; It spreads in waves that will affect all manufacturing and service sectors and companies of all sizes.

The developing and evolving technologies of the Industry 4.0 revolution inevitably create change and transformation in many areas all over the world. As a result of this transformation, some undesirable negative consequences and threats also emerge, despite many desired positive results. In this context, it is very important to consider it within the scope of sustainability in order to maximize the positive results of the Industry 4.0 revolution, as well as to minimize its negative consequences and threats (Doğruel, Anuşlu, & Fırat, 2019).

Sustainability is generally discussed under three headings: economic, social, and environmental dimension. These three dimensions cannot be separated from each other with certain lines and there are many intersecting subtopics. One of the most important actors in this intersection area is innovation. The current Industry 4.0 revolution is highly related to the concept of innovation (Gürsoy, 2021). This relationship will affect the business processes, markets, and current structure of the industrial age and lead to a transition to a new era of digitalization, smarter production systems networks and interconnected business processes (Morrar, Arman, & Mousa, 2017).

Sustainable Development Goals

The definition of sustainable development, which is still the most frequently encountered and most cited in the literature, is the first definition made by the World Commission on Environment and Development (WCED) (Akpulat, 2019). WCED's definition of sustainable development is "Sustainable development is the development that meets the needs of the present without compromising the ability of future generations to meet their own needs".

Problems in the ecological balance were not noticed until the 1960s, due to the ignorance of the links between the environment and development. Development models that only focused on increasing per capita income ignore the future and cause irreversible damage to the environment. Damages to the environment due to unplanned consumption of limited fossil resources, unconscious use of natural resources, the proliferation of wastes caused by excessive consumption, and unscheduled, wrong urbanization; have caused consequences such as climate changes, global warming, pollution of water resources, depletion of the ozone layer, extinction of living species and loss of characteristics of natural habitats. In order to get rid of these effects that harm ecology, the necessity of sustainability in the environment and development has emerged (Reddy and Thomson, 2015).

The World Commission on Environment and Development was established by the United Nations (UN) in 1983. The Brundtland Report, titled "Our Common Future" with the contribution of many country leaders, has been a turning point for finding solutions to environmental problems and spreading the concepts of sustainable development. The Brundtland Report emerges as an economic concept based on rational resource use, beyond just an environmentalist understanding. It states that the fundamental condition for an environmentally friendly economy is "sustainable development".

The concept of sustainable development in the Brundtland Report was discussed at the Rio Summit in 1992 as a sine qua non of development. Afterwards, at the United Nations Sustainable Development Summit held in September 2015, "the 2030 Agenda for Sustainable Development" agreed upon by world leaders, was adopted with the signature of 193 countries. Afterwards, the 2030 Agenda was prepared as a continuation of the Millennium Development Goals (MDGs) implemented in 2000 and as an agenda that carries these goals further.

The scope of the 2030 Agenda aimed to include all societies in efforts to reduce poverty and increase welfare all around the world, protect cultural and social values, and prevent environmental damage. With the global sustainable development approach, in addition to social and environmental issues such as gender equality, observing the needs of disadvantaged groups, reducing food waste, combating desertification and drought, and protecting biodiversity, economic issues such as economic growth, technological development, employment and industrialization have also been brought to the agenda of sustainable development.

Within the scope of economic and social development objectives, sustainability should be taken as a basis in all developed and developing countries, which are oriented toward a market economy and central planning. Integrating economic and ecological considerations into decision-making processes is the basic principle of sustainable development strategy (Bilgili, 2017).

Sustainable development process has three fundamental dimensions: economic, social, and environmental (Tıraş, 2012): *Economic Dimension of Sustainable Development*: The generally accepted definition of the economic dimension of sustainability is the preservation of capital and the prevention of its degradation (Goodland, 2002). The potential for depletion of resources has a crucial place in the economic dimension of sustainability. Therefore, sustainability has always been a prominent element of the renewable natural resourceseconomy. Applications such as recycling energy and materials into raw materials, using fewer materials in the production of goods and services, and recycling wastes after production processes by consumers or producers can be evaluated at this point (Vivien, 2008). However, an economically sustainable system should be able to produce goods and services continuously; the government should be able to maintain the manageability of external debt and avoid sectoral imbalances that harm agricultural and industrial production (Holmberg and Sandbrook, 1992). From an economic perspective, sustainability is inextricably linked with environmental and social sustainability. It also shows the limits of economic growth (Reddy and Thomson, 2015).

Environmental Dimension of Sustainable Development; The environmental dimension of sustainable development emphasizes the carrying power of ecosystems and biodiversity and deals with the preservation of natural capital stock and its transfer to future generations (Bilgili, 2017). To ensure environmental sustainability, it is necessary to protect biodiversity, minimize the use of non-renewable resources, make recyclable designs, and ensure that environmental sustainability is decisive in the production of new services and products (Morelli, 2011). Advocates of strict environmental sustainability argue that non-renewable resources should not be used at any stage of production (Goodland & Daly, 1996).

Social Dimension of Sustainable Development: Social sustainability can be defined as the extent to which social values, social identities, social relations, and social institutions can continue into the future. Social sustainability requires preserving the integrity of society and its ability to work towards common goals. It should meet individual needs such as health and well-being, nutrition, shelter, education, and cultural expression (Moldan et al., 2012). A socially sustainable system should ensure the adequate delivery of social services, including the distribution of equality, health, and education, gender equality, political responsibility, and participation (Harris, 2000).

Five basic principles can be mentioned for the formation of a socially sustainable society: equality, loyalty, diversity, quality of life and democracy and governance (McKenzie, 2004).Although these three dimensions are different, they are closely related and affect each other.

The Sustainable Development Goals and Index Report, prepared by the Bertelsmann Stiftung and the Sustainable Development Solutions Network since 2016, is the first worldwide study to evaluate the position of countries to achieve their sustainable development goals. This report describes the current positions of countries in the context of sustainability goals and provides important clues as to which problems should be prioritized in the sustainable development goals expected to be achieved by countries by 2030 (Sachs, et al 2018).

Consequently, The Sustainable Development Goals (SDGs), also known as the Global Goals, are a universal call to action to eradicate poverty, protect our planet, and ensure that all people live in peace and prosperity. In order to achieve these goals, 17 sustainable development goals have been determined on a global scale.

With the increase in the population in the transition from the industrial society to the information society, the needs of the people went far beyond the predictions. The rapid consumption of natural resources to meet the increasing needs has caused significant damage to the sustainability of the world ecosystem. On the other hand, the point of communication technologies and the endless flow of data have eliminated the concepts of time and space for people (Vivien, 2008).

Figure 2. Sustainable development goals

Lean Thinking

Lean Thinking is a system of thought that consists of 5 basic principles and 3 basic values, put forward by James P. Womack and Daniel Jones are the authors of *The Machine That Changes the World* from 1996 to guide managers (Lean Concepts Dictionary, 2009). Although the origins of this thinking system, which consists of 5 basic principles, are based on the Toyota Production System, and Lean Thinking has started to become a phenomenon that we can find examples not only in production but also in service, health, construction, IT, and many other issues.

The Lean management philosophy, which became even more popular with the study published by Womack et al. in 1990, adds more value to the end user by using less input while saving the organization in terms of cost, time, and waste. Lean management philosophy is basically a set of practices that cover all activities within an organization and aim to reduce waste while improving the value chain (Furlan et al., 2011).The highest priority in the lean manufacturing philosophy is customer satisfaction, thus providing the customer with exactly the value and quality they want.

As it is known, with the emergence of the mass production system, which was revolutionary in the whole world, at the beginning of the 20th century, developments such as mechanization in the production phase and the loss of the human element formed the basis of some new currents of thought. During the transition to the mass production system, the age of labor-craft dependent production was left behind in a short time and the mass production system was adopted. This process, which developed together with the foundations of the capitalist way of thinking, constitutes the main philosophy of today's western business world.

Lean manufacturing is an ideal production system that does not contain any unnecessary elements in its structure and in which negative factors such as error, cost, stock, labor, production area, waste, and customer dissatisfaction are minimized. It adopts the principle of allocating time and resources as much as processes that add value to it by shaping materials and information in line with customer needs (Liker, 2004).

In the first stage, there is "waste hunting". Any cost that does not represent a "value" for the consumer is considered a waste. It sees all activities that do not add value as waste. It starts by separating the value-added and non-value-added activities on the product, in line with customer needs, and eliminates all non-value-added activities. In lean management, it should be considered that all kinds of disruptions, delays, overproduction, warehouses full to the ceiling and returns are also considered waste. Then the "value stream map" is rearranged by deleting all waste. This map is put into practice with an implementation plan and calendar (Jasti & Kodali, 2014).

Lean Thinking is a holistic methodology that includes all other management, improvement, and production systems such as TQM, TPM, TPS, 6-sigma, and has not only limited it to manufacturing and production technologies but has successfully applied in many sectors. Lean Thinking is not just a simple improvement activity, a managerial procedure, and/or a system that simply tries to reduce costs. The aim of the Toyota brand is based on the basic principles of how to create an automobile brand that can bring to market, is as affordable as possible, that people can buy, and where mistakes are minimal (Liker, 2004).

The lean production and management model is a Japanese management philosophy that aims to eliminate waste on a continuous basis. One of the post-modern or contemporary management approaches has emerged with the effect of total quality management. Total quality management, which attracted the attention of the whole western world especially after the 1974 oil crisis, is seen as a sub-system of the "Japanese management philosophy". At the same time, according to Sobek, Durward, and Lang (2010), the concept of Lean Management is an operations management approach that considers any process that does not add value to the end customer as waste. Lean methods are designed to identify wasted resources and eliminate waste by redesigning their systems so that managers and employees can improve their operational processes (Bayar, 2020).

Womack et al. evaluated lean production and management as value-creating and non-value-creating activities. While value-creating activities are defined as services or products that customers are ready to pay for, activities that do not create value are defined as the opposite, services and products that cannot be demanded on a customer basis (Jasti & Kodali, 2014). Organizations that can adapt lean management and production methods to their corporate culture can avoid eight types of waste: inventory, handling, overwork, defects, capabilities, overproduction, movement, and waiting.

Figure 3. The 5 lean management principles

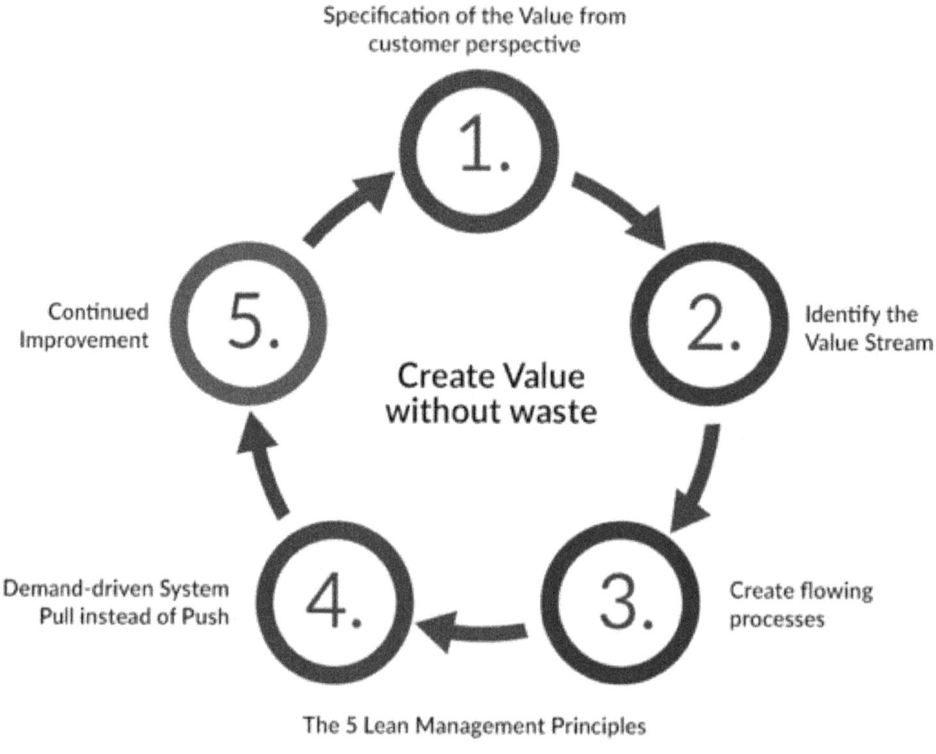

In order to achieve lean management goals, production processes; five lean management principles have been introduced, aiming to align with customer demand rate or takt time. These; identifying value, mapping the value stream, creating streams, attracting, and seeking excellence. The first step, also described as defining or determining value, is the first step organizations take towards becoming lean. In the related step, the value perception of the target customers and how the existing services and products meet this expectation are analyzed.

The second principle, the value stream, aims to map the stream. It covers the life cycle of the organization's product and service from the design to the final manufacturer. Continuous flow creation is the strategy-focused step of lean management and focuses on the uninterrupted process flow from production to shipping. A well-organized and coordinated work environment reduces production time and unnecessary inventory load and ensures that transportation processes work more effective. The fourth step, pull method, is directly related to creating flow. Since the continuity of the purchasing and production process, which is a part of the traditional production systems, even if there is no order, is considered a waste of resources in the perspective of lean management and production, the pull step is very important.

The last step, the pursuit of excellence, emphasizes that lean management and production processes are in constant development and the pursuit of error-free never ends.In this context, a successful and continuous value chain can only be mentioned when the principles outlined above are repeated and managed correctly (Womack & Jones, 1996). This management philosophy will become more and more widespread and be applied by all sectors. It is necessary to accept that it is very difficult to manage the new generations (especially the Z Generation) with the classical management approach.

SOLUTIONS AND RECOMMENDATIONS

Today, concerns about sustainability, insufficiency of natural resources, inequalities in wealth and income distribution, and social responsibility have become one of the main objects on the agenda of organizations. In this context, while organizations aimed to implement environmentally friendly management methods, they had to reconsider their production processes. This focus has led to the concept of environmentally responsible production, also called lean production.

The relationship between lean management and sustainability has been on the agenda of academics, decision-makers and, organizations for a while. In his research conducted in 2005, Rusinko stated that organizations under the influence of digitalization should consider quality management or lean management and production methods while adapting environmentally sustainable practices to their business processes. Thus, organizations will be able to develop their value chains by taking advantage of the principles such as economic and social development, continuous improvement, and personnel empowerment that exist between lean management and sustainability.

There are few studies in the literature that group the types of digitalization in terms of sustainability, rank and examine them based on environmental and social dimensions. Among these studies, Silvestre and Tîrcă (2019) state that any digital transformation varies depending on the degree to which it considers the environmental and social challenges of sustainability. While all developed economies are aware that only digitalization can stimulate new economic growth continuously, also developing countries are constantly pushing to upgrade their industrial structures through digitalization to increase their national competitiveness.

Although all efforts in society are aimed at improving living standards, it is seen that growth and development have a very significant effect on climate change and the consumption of fossil fuels such as oil. In other words, it can be stated that not all of the current advancements in production are sustainable. While the industrial sector continues to produce high quality products, it requires more sustainable manufacturing methods and equipment. From this point of view, the concept of Industry 4.0 is accepted as a strategy in constant motion and development to establish sustainable manufacturing systems. The technical, economic, social, and environmental impacts of Industry 4.0 adaptations on manufacturing are still discussed from a sustainability perspective. In studies investigating the environmental effects of smart and lean manufacturing systems; stated that smart and digitalized systems need very large mass data centers to feed their processes and network systems to receive support.

The effects of technological progress on the development of the relationship between economic growth and the environment are explained by endogenous growth theory, which considers that production processes are improved by increasing the capacity to replace polluting sources with other more environmentally friendly sources. These models are dedicated to the environment and are based on a society that can spend more resources to protect as the country's income increases. If revenues increase and emissions decrease accordingly, technology will play a key role and induced innovation will be the reason for the reduction in emissions.

The concept of sustainability continues to influence the business models of companies in three main dimensions as social, environmental, and economic, and within the scope of dozens of sub-titles under these three main dimensions (Fırat, Yurtsever, & Bilsel, 2015). These three main dimensions of the sustainability framework are not independent from each other, but they are in significant interaction and there are intersections in many sub-dimensions. In order to be sustainable at the organizational level, companies have developed lean thinking techniques. Because lean thinking and production methods prevent waste and use sustainable business models.

Many studies on the lean management model demonstrate that; lean principles parallel with the main objectives of sustainability, due to their potential to eliminate waste, process improvement and reduce the negative effects of construction projects (Cachadinha & Rueff, 2011). Similarly, Golzarpoor and González (2013) mentioned in their study that sustainable practices can be considered the natural return of lean management philosophy.

On the other hand, the United States Environmental Protection Agency (EPA) claims that lean models or processes promote sustainability by creating an organizational and cultural environment highly conducive to minimizing waste and preventing pollution in organizations (Golzarpoor & González, 2013). In addition, Mohammed S. Hashem M. Mahany stated that the concept of sustainability, digitalization, and lean management models are inseparable as they aim to reduce energy consumption, protect the environment, and reduce the amount of final waste (MSHM, 2015). Also, Saud Al Sulaiman, CEO of Four Principles, which provides consultancy to organizations on lean management processes, stated that when organizations and leaders adapt lean management principles to their organizations, they can achieve Sustainable Development Goals in their sectors more efficiently.

CONCLUSION

In the intense competition environment created by the direct effect of industrialization and digital transformation, companies implement lean management and production systems instead of classical production systems in order to ensure the continuity of their assets and to survive among their competitors. With the effect of rapid industrialization in the past, sufficient attention was not given to customer and employee satisfaction while defining targets in traditional mass production (Kennedy & Brewer, 2006).

For the last ten years, "digitalization" and "sustainability" have been at the center of business and academic research and constitute the most intense agenda in the policies and strategic plans of national and international organizations. This study fundamentally aims to determine how Industry 4.0 components and tools will influence lean management practices with the support of sustainable development goals and environmental performances. There are few studies in the literature on how the value created by Industry 4.0 with the effect of digitalization makes a difference in sustainable development. In terms of the economic, environmental, and social scopes of sustainability, Industry 4.0's powerful and versatile network structures have a great opportunity to realize sustainable industrial value creation together with the internet and smart technologies.

These opportunities will be effective in both macro and micro dimensions. From a macro perspective, the developed business models such as lean management and value creation networks will directly affect employment, people, and society and contribute to welfare in these areas. At the same time, the technology that emerged by force of lean thinking will also pay attention to waste management. From a narrowed perspective, when the equipment, people, organization, process, and product are taken into account, a "humane work" environment could be provided to people, and this will create an improvement of occupational health and safety in employment, and ergonomic work environments and conditions.

The feature of Industry 4.0 is that it can realize real-time communication, connection and definitions between people, machines, and products, and develop a digitalized smart manufacturing model customized according to customer demands with an extremely high flexibility. Pull, one of the most important components of the lean production model, comes into play at this point.

Lean manufacturing enables efficient and economical use of Industry 4.0 technologies by reducing product and process complexity. Therefore, lean processes are considered as a basis for efficient and economical implementation of Industry 4.0. The flexibility that has developed with Industry 4.0 helps to cope with the increasing complexity. Overall, there is a fundamental compatibility of lean manufacturing and Industry 4.0. This perspective can be attributed to similarities regarding objectives such as complexity reduction and lean principles. Accordingly, both paradigms are managed in a decentralized manner.

The emerging new technologies of the fourth industrial revolution (4IR) will inevitably change and transform the whole world in many ways. There are many outcomes from which great benefits are expected to occur in this transformation. Nowadays, R&D, innovation, and digitalization are mentioned together. It is important to consider the effects of new technologies and innovation studies based on sustainability, thus contributing to positive developments in terms of economic, environmental, and especially social sustainability. Based on the principle that people are at the beginning and at the heart of everything, social sustainability and therefore the welfare and development of people and society are the main targets.

Due to the digitization of purchasing processes, markets are evolving faster into buyers' markets. Thus, the customer impact will continue to increase with the development of Industry 4.0, and then the customer focus of lean thinking will become even more important during digitalization. However, new technologies lead to short lead times as well as new customer requirements and 100% quality product traceability throughout the production and delivery process that cannot be achieved with manual lean methods. Consequently, developing customer demands should be analyzed and lean methods should be complemented with digital technologies in order to meet these demands.

The elimination of waste, which is one of the basic points of the lean production philosophy, and the process excellence created through continuous improvement are essential for the effective implementation of Industry 4.0.In addition, activities such as flow, withdrawal, and just-in-time production/distribution can be successfully optimized and accelerated by integrating with Industry 4.0 technologies with methods such as value stream analysis or poka-yoke. However, data streams generated by scanning barcodes in each transport can be generated by data mining algorithms, and unusual transport routes and overstocks can be automatically identified.

For this purpose, all technological tools, information and communication technologies (ICT), network structures-internet, and innovation issues that are the supporters and triggers of the Industry 4.0 Revolution should all be considered in connection with economic competition and social welfare.

The developments promised by Industry 4.0 basically show many similarities with Lean Thinking. The only difference between the idea of Industry 4.0 to enable communication between machines and the Internet of Things and to take production management under control is a technology that is thought to be implemented in the closed future. According to the findings obtained from the research, while lean manufacturing, which is a foundation for Industry 4.0, complements Industry 4.0, Industry 4.0 increases the efficiency of lean manufacturing systems.In addition, it has been determined that enterprises should first improve their processes by applying lean production methods and thus increase their efficiency, and then apply Industry 4.0 technologies to their transparent, standardized, and waste-free systems. In this way, integrating Industry 4.0 technologies into lean production methods will increase operating efficiency. Otherwise, using Industry 4.0 technologies in their systems without applying lean production methods may not increase the efficiency of the business.

REFERENCES

Akbulut, U. (2011). *Sanayi Devrimleri Dünya Gidişini Değiştirdi*. www.uralakbulut.com.tr

Akpulat, F. (2019). *Sürdürülebilirlik kavramına farklı yaklaşımlar: Üniversite öğrencileri üzerine bir araştırma*. İstanbul Üniversitesi Sosyal Bilimler Enstitüsü.

Alahyari, H., Gorschek, T., & Svensson, R. B. (2019). An exploratory study of waste in software development organizations using agile or lean approaches: A multiple case study at 14 organizations. *Information and Software Technology*, *105*, 78–94. doi:10.1016/j.infsof.2018.08.006

Bayar, M. (2020). *Yalın Yönetim Anlayışının, Çalışanların Görev Performansına Etkilerine Yönelik Bir Araştırma, İşletme Araştırmaları Dergisi*, *12*(2), 1984–2001.

Bilgili, M. Y. (2017). Ekonomik, Ekolojik Ve Sosyal Boyutlarıyla Sürdürülebilir Kalkınma. *Uluslararası Sosyal Araştırmalar Dergisi*, *10*, 559–569.

Cachadinha, N., & Rueff, N. (2011). Lean construction and sustainability–complementary paradigms? A case study. 19th Annual Conference of the International Group for Lean Construction. Lima, Peru.

Chapin, F. S. III, Torn, M. S., & Tateno, M. (1996). Principles of Ecosystem Sustainability. *American Naturalist, 148*(6), 1016–1037. doi:10.1086/285969

Doğruel Anuşlu, M., & Fırat, S. Ü. (2019). Clustering analysis application on Industry 4.0-driven global indexes. *Procedia Computer Science, 158*, 145–152. doi:10.1016/j.procs.2019.09.037

Dombrowski, U., Richter, T., & Krenkel, P. (2017). Interdependencies of industries 4.0 lean production systems: A use cases Analysis. *Procedia Manufacturing, 11*, 1061–1068. doi:10.1016/j.promfg.2017.07.217

Esty, D. C., & Winston, A. S. (2008). *Yeşilden Altına*. MediaCat.

Golzarpoor, H., & González, V. (2013). *A green-lean simulation model for assessing environmental and production waste in construction.*

Goodland, R. (2002). Sustainability: Human, Social, Economic and Environmental, Ted Munn (Ed.), Encyclopedia of Global Environmental Change, içinde (1-3). John Wiley & Sons Ltd.

Goodland, R., & Daly, H. (1996). Environmental Sustainability: Universal And Non-Negotiable. *Ecological Applications, 6*(4), 1002–1017. doi:10.2307/2269583

Görçün, Ö. F. (2016). Dördüncü Sanayi DevrimiEndüstri 4.0. Beta Basım Yayım Dağıtım. Baskı, İstanbul.

Gürsoy, Ö. (2021). *Yalın üretim sisteminde dijitalleşme ve endüstri 4.0 uygulamaları ile süreç iyileştirme analizi: bir imalat işletmesinde uygulama (yayınlanmamış doktora tezi)*. Aydın Adnan Menderes Üniversitesi Sosyal Bilimler Enstitüsü.

Harris, J. M. (2000). *Basic Principles of Sustainable Development, Global Development and Environment Institute.* (Working Paper 00-04).

Hermann, M., Pentek, T., & Otto, B. (2015). *Design principles for Industrie 4.0 scenarios: A literature review.* (Working Paper No. 01).

Holmberg, J., & Sandbrook, R. (1992). Sustainable Development: What Is to Be Done? Making Development Sustainable: Redefining Institutions, Policy, and Economics. In J. Holmberg (ed.) International Institute for Environment and Development, p. 19-38. Island Press.

Jasti, N. V. K., & Kodali, R. (2014). A literaturereview of empirical research methodology in lean manufacturing. *International Journal of Operations & Production Management, 34*(8), 1080–1122. doi:10.1108/IJOPM-04-2012-0169

Kennedy, F. A., & Brewer, P. C. (2006). The lean enterprise and traditional accounting—Is the honeymoon over? *Journal of Corporate Accounting & Finance*, *17*(6), 63–74. doi:10.1002/jcaf.20234

Kolberg, D., & Zühlke, D. (2015). Lean automation enabled by Industry 4.0 technologies. *IFAC-PapersOnLine*, *48*(3), 1870–1875. doi:10.1016/j.ifacol.2015.06.359

Liker, J. (2004). *Toyota Way: 14 Management Principles from The World Greatest Manufacturer*. McGraw-Hill.

Martin, R. L. (2002). The Virtue Matrix, Harvard Business Review, 80(3), 68-75

Maware, C., & Adetuntji, O. (2019). Lean Manufacturing Implementation in Zimbabwean Industries: Impact on Operational Performance. *International Journal of Engineering Business Management*, *11*, 1–12. doi:10.1177/1847979019859790

McKenzıe, S. (2004). *Social Sustainability: Towards Some Definitions, Hawke Research Institute*. (Working Paper Series No 27).

Mehany, M. S. H. M. (2015). Lean construction principles past and present – a business model consistency. *51st Annual International Conference Proceedings*. ASC.

Moldan, B., Janousková, S., & Hak, T. (2012). How To Understand And Measure Environmental Sustainability. *Indicators And Targets, Ecological Indicators, 17*, 4–13. doi:10.1016/j.ecolind.2011.04.033

Morellı, J. (2011). Environmental Sustainability: A Definition for Environmental Professionals. *Journal of Environmental Sustainability*, *1*(1), 1–9. doi:10.14448/jes.01.0002

Morrar, R., Arman, H., & Mousa, S. (2017). The fourth industrial revolution (Industry 4.0):A social innovation perspective. *Technology Innovation Management Review*, *7*(11), 12–20. doi:10.22215/timreview/1117

Özçelik, T. Ö., and Cinoğlu, F. (2013). Yalın felsefe ve bir otomotiv yansanayi uygulaması. *İstanbul Ticaret Üniversitesi Fen BilimleriDergisi, 12*(23), 79-101.

Reddy, T., & Thomson, R. (2015). Environmental, Social and Economic Sustainability: Implications for Actuarial Science. ASTIN, AFIR/ERM and IACA Colloquia, 23-27.

Ruano, J., Hoyuelos, I., Mateo, M., & Angel, A. (2019). Lean School: A Learning Factory for Training Lean Manufacturing in A Physical Simulation Environment. *Management and Production Engineering Review*, *10*(1), 4–13.

Sachs, J., Schmidt-Traub, G., & Kroll, C., La Fortune, G. & Fuller, G. (2018). SDG Index and Dashboards Report 2018. Bertelsmann Stiftung and Sustainable Development Solutions Network

Shah, R., & Ward, P. T. (2003). Lean manufacturing: Context, practice bundles, and performance. *Journal of Operations Management, 21*(2), 129–149. doi:10.1016/S0272-6963(02)00108-0

Silvestre, B. S. andTircă, D. M. (2019). Innovations for sustainable development: Moving toward a sustainable future. *Journal of Cleaner Production.*

Smith, A. (1776). *Ulusların Zenginliği. Cilt 1*, Alan yayıncılık, 4. Baskı, İstanbul, 2004. *Sürdürülebilir Kalkınma Amaçları*, https://www.tr.undp.org/content/turkey/tr/home/sustainable-d evelopmentgoals.html

Tıraş, H. (2012). Sürdürülebilir kalkınma ve çevre: Teorik bir inceleme. *Kahramanmaraş Sütçü İmam Üniversitesi İktisadi ve İdari Bilimler Fakültesi Dergisi, 2*(2), 57–73.

Torun, İ. (2003). Endüstri Toplumu"nun Oluşmasında Etkili Olan İktisadi ve Sina-i Faktörler. *C.Ü. İktisadi ve İdari Bilimler Dergisi,* Cilt 4. *Sayı, 1*, 2003.

Türkan, Ö. U. (2010). Üretimde yalın dönüşümün temel performans kriterleri. *BalıkesirÜniversitesi Fen Bilimleri Enstitüsü Dergisi, 12*(2), 28–41.

Vivien, F. D. (2008). Sustainable Development.*An Overview ofEconomic Proposals, SAPIENS, 1*(2), 1–8. PMID:17337322

Yücel, İ. H. (2006). *Türkiye'de bilim teknoloji politikaları ve iktisadi gelişmenin yönü.* TC Başbakanlık Devlet Planlama Teşkilatı.

Zhou, K., Liu, T., & Zhou, L. (2016). Industry 4.0: Towards Future Industrial Opportunities and Challenges. In *International Conference on Fuzzy Systems and Knowledge Discovery,* (pp. 2147–2152). IEEE.

Chapter 3
Industry 4.0:
The Improvement of the Supply Chain Channel Based on Digital Transformation in Portugal

Marlene Rodrigues
Polytechnic Institute of Cávado and Ave, Portugal & CiTUR, Portugal

José Baptista Costa
Polytechnic Institute of Cávado and Ave, Portugal

Bruno Barbosa Sousa
https://orcid.org/0000-0002-8588-2422
Polytechnic Institute of Cávado and Ave, Portugal

Vítor Braga
https://orcid.org/0000-0002-3644-3992
ESTG, Polytecnhic Institute of Porto, Portugal

ABSTRACT

The supply chain has developed extensively in Portugal over the last ten years. There are three very important areas that integrate organizations; namely, the purchasing area, the production area, and the distribution area, which is commonly called the logistics area. Humans are moving towards a totally digital era, and so this study aims to understand how the concept of Industry 4.0 has impacted the Portuguese business fabric, focusing on the purchasing area. The transformation in the processes has led to the discovery of new forms of digital technologies in the products' processes to generate competitiveness in the market. New business models are a driving force for evolution and progress in the digital era. These models are based on the pillars of Industry 4.0, bringing sustainability to the industry, reducing waste, and forecasting more accurately the market.

DOI: 10.4018/978-1-6684-5606-4.ch003

INTRODUCTION

The first Industrial Revolution began somewhere between 1760 and 1840 in England, with the progressive replacement of machinery and tools by the exploitation of coal as an alternative energy to wood and other biofuels, and by the increasing use of steam power. The changes in production processes had significant economic and social consequences. The craftsman who had, hitherto, controlled the entire production process, from the exploitation of the raw material to the marketing of the final product, went to work for a boss who controlled the process, the raw material, the final product, and the profits. In the decades that followed and roughly until the end of the Second World War, developments were significant in industries such as chemical, electrical, and steel. The first steel boats were launched by powerful steam engines, revolutionizing the transportation of goods. There were also the first production lines that allowed mass production and low costs. Invention and innovation went hand in hand in this was the second Industrial Revolution. In the 1950s and 1970s, we began to conceive what would be considered the third Industrial Revolution, the digital revolution, with the proliferation and use of semiconductors, computers, automation and robotization in production lines, with information stored and processed in digital form, communications, mobile phones and the internet (Schwab, 2017; Rodrigues et al., 2019). Internet has become so widely used that it is not possible to talk about industry without talking about cyberspace - concepts that are relatively recent, but already well studied – this refers to the emergence of industry 4.0. An increasing number of firms are moving closer to the Industry 4.0 paradigm by connecting factories to the Internet in order to improve their efficiency and effectiveness. In this industrial context connected to the Internet, cyber security problems represent one of the most relevant challenges to be addressed (Lezzi et al., 2018). Among the new threats are unauthorized remote access, data manipulation, loss of intellectual property, loss of revenue and in extreme cases espionage. To compound these threats is the fact that all threats need to be detected in a timely manner, which is a real challenge.

Therefore, cyber security refers to the vulnerabilities that computer systems present, and in Industry 4.0 there is a strong correlation between several systems, this fact reveals the (im) possibility of data protection, either internal to the various processes that the company holds either external.

PURPOSE OF THE STUDY

With this study, we aim to explore the state of the art of the industry 4.0 implementation, in Portugal, and which concepts of Industry 4.0 are already being implemented. Briefly, our work aims to explore, analyze and understand the impact that these different concepts have on the Portuguese business fabric, with particular relevance for the purchasing and procurement processes. Considering that, in Portugal, the largest share of businesses are SMEs, the challenges associated with the implementation of digitalization is a theme that deserves all the attention. Therefore, exploring the importance of the digitalization of the industry in a SMEs populated county is critical and remains as the contribution of this study. In order to meet such objective, four specific objectives were designed: first, to assess the digital maturity in face of the application of Industry 4.0 concepts, through the implementation or the degree of importance that the concepts have for the company. Second, to understand which are the biggest challenges in the modernization of the purchasing and procurement processes. Third, to understand which IT in Industry 4.0 are considered the most relevant for the digitalization era; fifth to assess and analyze the relationship between Industry 4.0 and purchasing and procurement.

LITERATURE REVIEW

In order to frame our findings, a number of concepts need to be explored. This section briefly presents and explores the concepts associated to the industry 4.0 paradigm and related that to the supply chain management process.

Industry 4.0

According to Schwab (2017), in Germany the term Industry 4.0 appeared at the Hannover Fair in 2011, an expression that served to describe how this revolution is characterizing because it is based on transformation and digitization. Schwab (2017) argues that the fourth industrial revolution will bring about an inescapable change through technology, innovation and disruption. Schawb (2017) argues that all innovations and technologies have one fundamental feature in common: they leverage the power to disseminate digitization and information technology. All of the innovations described in this chapter are possible and enhanced through digital capability.

In addition to changing patterns of growth, the labor market and the future of work that naturally influence all organizations, there is evidence that the technologies that underpin the fourth industrial revolution are having a significant impact on the way companies are managed, organized and equipped. The first imperative of the commercial impact of the fourth industrial revolution is the urgent need to look at the organization with the premise of constant learning and change. Is there a history of rapid prototyping and investment decision making? Does culture accept innovation and failure? Everything we see indicates that the race will only accelerate, the changes will be fundamental, and the journey will require a hard and honest look at the ability of organizations to react with speed and agility.

Multiple sources of disruption trigger different forms of business impact. On the supply side, many industries look to the introduction of new technologies that create entirely new ways of meeting existing needs and significantly change existing value chains. The widespread adoption of 3D printing will make distributed manufacturing and the maintenance of spare parts easier and cheaper. Real-time information and knowledge will provide unique customer information and asset performance that will amplify other technology trends. Disruption also results from agile and innovative competitors who, by accessing global digital platforms for research, development, marketing, sales and distribution, can outperform established companies faster than ever before by improving quality, speed or prices. This is the reason why many business leaders consider their biggest threat to be competitors who are not yet considered as such. It would be a mistake, however, to think that competitive disruption will come only through startups. Scanning also allows large installed operators to overcome the barriers of their industry, leveraging their customer base, infrastructure or technology. Dimension can still be a competitive advantage if harnessed intelligently. Major changes on the demand side are also shifting business: increased transparency, consumer commitment and new consumer behavior patterns, increasingly built with access to mobile networks and data, force businesses to how they design, market and deliver new or existing products as well as services.

Industry 4.0: Implications for Logistics Management

According to Hofmann and Rüsch (2017), the objective is to answer the question: can be affected by Industry 4.0? We can include two dimensions:

The size of the physical supply chain: autonomous and self-controlled logistic subsystems such as transport (e.g., through autonomous lorries), turnover handling (e.g., by unloading robots or part removal) or order processing, through smart contracts in blockchain technology are interacting with each other. The dimension of the digital data value chain: the data of the machine and the sensor are physical processes throughout the supply chain. Through a layer of connectivity data collected are provided for any type of analysis (e.g., in the cloud), possibly resulting in potential value-added deals. From this two-dimensional application model, three customer value components are expected. First, the "value of availability", which means making products and services available to the customer through autonomous delivery. The creation of value through the availability of goods or services is the main added value of logistics activities and services. Second, the "value of digital integration" comes through permeable transparency and traceability throughout the supply chain. In addition, order processing systems are interconnected, making it easy to run business without interruption (e.g., self-service of objects, remote uses, or condition monitoring). Third, consumption normally exceeds the classic POS, but that does not mean that the supply chain ends at that point. There are a number of IT-based service options that go beyond simply distributing physical products or services ("value of digital service"). In addition to things with a digital load where physical products are "loaded" with additional digital services, the data itself creates value out of the original use case ("sensor as a service").

INDUSTRY 4.0 DIGITAL ENABLERS

Cyberphysical Systems (CPS)

Hofmann & Rüsch (2017) argue that industry 4.0 is characterized by an unprecedented internet connection or other and so-called CPS, which can be considered systems that integrate two strands; the physical world and the virtual world. Cyberphysical systems are computational integrations with physical processes. Embedded computers and networks monitor and control physical processes. In the industrial context it means that information related to the shop floor and virtual computing is highly synchronized.

Internet of Things (IoT)

Porter and Heppelmann, (2014) explain that the term "internet of things" has become popular in the first decade of the twenty-first century and can be considered the initiator of Industry 4.0. Smart products offer exponential opportunities through new features, increased reliability, greater and better use, and capabilities that transcend the traditional boundaries that are usually associated with the products we have hitherto known. In addition, IoT seems to envisage a society where all members have access to a full Internet in an environment filled with self-configuration, self-management, intelligent technology anytime, anywhere. It is hoped that IoT will create many economic opportunities. In the near future it will be considered one of the most promising technologies with enormous potential for expansion.

Internet Service (IoS)

We live in the so-called service society these days. There is strong evidence that, as in the case of the IoT concept, Internet service (IoS) is emerging, based on the idea that services are readily available through web technologies, enabling enterprises and private users combine, create and offer new types of services added. It can be assumed that the Internet-based marketplace service locations will play a key role in the industries of the future. While from a pure technological perspective, concepts such as service-oriented architecture (SOA), software as a service (SaaS) or business process outsourcing (BPO) are closely related to IoS.

Smart Factory

So far, CPS, IoT and IoS have been introduced as core components of Industry 4.0. It should be noted that these concepts are closely interrelated, since the CPS communicates through the IoT and IoS, thus allowing to spread the smart factory concept, which is based on the idea of a decentralized production system, in which human beings, the machines and the resources communicate with each other naturally. The close connection and communication between products, machinery, transport systems and man is expected to change the existing production logic. Intelligent factories can therefore be considered another important feature of Industry 4.0, products become increasingly autonomous and independent through production processes, easily identifiable and locatable at any time, pursuing the idea of an efficient cost, but highly flexible and individualized mass production. The smart factory concept will make the increasing complexity of manufacturing processes manageable for people working in organizations, thus ensuring that production can be both attractive and sustainable in order to generate an urban and profitable environment. Therefore, the potential that these new smart factory processes offer is immense. In addition to these key components, there is a growing array of other technologies in the wider 4.0 industry, such as watches, glasses or gloves, augmented reality applications, stand-alone vehicles, drones, blockchain, or even big data. Industry 4.0 implies profound changes in the way companies work and organize (Hofmann & Rüsch, 2017).

For instance, and according to Ratten et al., (2019), increasingly both business and government are focusing at low-income consumers and the role they play in the innovation process. This has meant greater emphasis has been given to understand the role of these consumers who are called ‘subsistence consumers’ because they live at the bottom of the pyramid and exist on low income and wages. Currently, there are many theories about the general repercussions of Industry 4.0, in this context, some critics have recently pointed out that automation and implementation of the smart factory concept can cause severe job destruction. Much is speculated as to the dangers of scanning and automation that the 4.0 industry will bring. Some studies advocate that this clever way of working will destroy a significant number of jobs. However, there are only a few stipulated examples of impacts on SCM. For this reason, with the primary objective of assessing opportunities, and possibly threats, as a result of the introduction of Industry 4.0 in each SCM function (Hofmann & Rüsch, 2017).

Additive Fabrication

The additive manufacturing commonly known as 3D Printing is being singled out as one of the most promising production technologies globally. 3D printing creates products by adding materials layer by layer over production processes with industrial machinery (Cotteleer et al., 2014). In this way it is possible to provide solutions in the manufacture of small lots of highly customized products, even in environments of mass production. One of the great advantages of this technology is its insensitivity to quantity and complexity, which improves production exponentially in terms of time, costs and especially in terms of design, as this is the great premise of the future. Another advantage is that it can be produced locally without the need to seek competitive countries in production costs, thus making productions closer to the target markets more profitable. This technology is promising by shortening the product development cycle to market launch and by reducing waste, which results in more efficient processes (Cotteleer et al., 2014; Ardito et al., 2018).

Augmented Reality

Bahrin et al., (2016) explain that systems based on augmented reality can carry out a variety of services, such as selecting parts in a warehouse or sending repair instructions through mobile devices.

SUPPLY CHAIN

The largest global organization of practitioners and academics in the area, which defines supply chain management, involves planning and managing all sourcing and procurement, conversion, and all logistics activities. It is important to note that supply chain management involves coordination and the search for collaboration between chain or channel partners, be they suppliers, intermediaries, logistics service providers or customers.

Since the 1990s, it has become evident for those companies with already high levels of logistics maturity that, in order to continue to achieve gains in terms of quality, time, cost and asset utilization, it is necessary to look at the supply chain as a whole rather than maintaining an internally focused view. Thus, a concertation with the business partners involved in the supply chain is required: namely with customers, suppliers, logistics providers, among others, and a capacity for integration of information and planning (Santos et al., 2022).

It is possible to define logistics as a process of managing flows of products, goods and services, with all of its associated information, reaching customers wherever the products and services they need, under the best conditions (Moura, 2006). Business logistics is a relatively new field of study of integrated management, traditional areas, finance marketing and production. The novelty derives from the concept, that logistics adds value to essential products and services, to consumer satisfaction and increased sales (Ballou, 2006; Guo et al., 2021).

According to Tjahjono et al., (2017), the introduction of Industry 4.0 has a huge impact on the entire supply chain. Collaboration between suppliers, manufacturers and customers is fundamental to increase the transparency of all stages of the logistics process, from when the order is received until the delivery of the product. In addition, due to the introduction of digitization and process automation, the supply chain management (SCM) structure needs to be redesigned. In order to understand the opportunities and threats possibly from the introduction of these new technologies, it is therefore necessary to analyze the impact of Industry 4.0 on the supply chain as a whole. Logistics deals with the creation of value, for the customers and suppliers of the company, and value for all those who have direct interests in it. The value of logistics manifested primarily in terms of time and place. Products and services are worthless unless they are held by customers when (time) and where (place) they intend to consume them. Good logistics management interprets each activity in the supply chain as a contributor to the value-adding process. When the value to be aggregated is not very expressive, the existence of this activity becomes questionable. However, value is added when consumers are willing to pay, for a product or service, more than the cost of making it available to them. Logistics has become an increasingly important process of value adding, for countless reasons (Ballou, 2006).

Logistics promotes competitiveness, not necessarily through isolated companies, or earlier through departments and areas of isolated companies, but rather in collaboration. When it is possible to share resources between them and competences in a supply chain or network of companies, it is only natural that the demand for competitive conditions and competitive advantages can be made jointly between cooperating companies. This is effectively how the logistics can open a window of opportunity to the creation of joint competitive advantages, promoting competitiveness. At bottom, the logic is that of collaborative competitiveness, although not forgetting the conditions of competitiveness. In the background, the logic is the determination of competitive advantages in a co-competitive way. According to Schwab (2017), in his book "The Fourth Industrial Revolution" there are four main changes expected in Industry in general: first, changes in customer expectations; second, smarter and more productive products; third, New forms of collaboration and partnerships; and fourth and final, The transformation of the operational model and conversion into a digital model.

Moura (2006) emphasizes that ICT facilitates the coordination of information flows throughout the logistics system, with an impact on its performance, in particular on continuous improvement. The use of ICT in logistics is very broad, covering the entire scope of its operations, from provisioning to physical distribution, through support to production operations. Glas and Kleemann (2016) thus characterize one of the functions that are part of this strategic chain: purchasing as the interface for the supply chain is of great importance in the digitization era. This will help to explore the phenomenon of industry 4.0 from this function, and the real objective is to analyze this impact and develop a conceptual basis so that it can sustain the growth of some of the concepts such as Procurement 4.0.

Integrated Supply Chain Management

Purchasing and supply chain management today reflect an increasing emphasis on the importance of suppliers. Supplier relations are changing with the aim of cooperating with selected suppliers. The activities that the modern shopping organization must implement are quite different from a few years ago. Supplier development, supplier design engagement, use of full-service providers, selection of total cost suppliers, long-term supplier relationships, strategic cost management, enterprise resource planning (ERP) and integrated Internet connections and shared databases as ways of creating new value within the supply chain. Buying behavior is changing dramatically to support the performance requirements of the new era. It is possible to come to three conclusions about 21st century shopping. First, the reshaping of the role of purchasing in the emerging global economy is underway in response to the challenges posed by global competition and the rapid change in technology and customer expectations. Second, the overall importance of the purchasing function is increasing, particularly for companies competing in sectors characterized by global competition and rapid change. Thirdly, purchases should continue to become more integrated as regards customer requirements, as well as operations, logistics, human resources, finance, accounting, marketing and information systems. This evolution will take time to fully occur, but integration is inevitable. The history and evolution of procurement management and supply chain, an appreciation of the growth, development and increased relevance of the profession in the last 150 years. Each historical period contributed something unique to the development of the procurement area, including the events that shaped the current emphasis on integrated supply chain management (Monzcka et al., 2009).

LEAN Supply Chain

Lean supply chains originate from the just-in-time philosophy, first adopted by American and European companies in the late 1980s. Just-in-Time (JIT) is a manufacturing philosophy based on the planned elimination of all and continuous improvement of productivity. It encompasses the successful execution of all operations activities required to produce an end product, from project engineering to delivery, and includes all steps of converting raw material into finished product. The primary elements of the Just-in-Time method must have only the necessary stock when needed; to improve the quality to zero defects; reduce wait times by reducing setup times, queue lengths, and batch sizes; incrementally review the operations themselves; and carry out these activities at a minimal cost. In the broad sense, it applies to all forms of production - job-shop, process and repetitive - and to many service industries as well. Companies that follow the JIT philosophy often experience remarkable improvements in their productivity (outputs / raw materials), stock levels and quality. To understand why the JIT caused such an impact we can consider the example of Toyota that brought a revolution to the way it was in the late 1980s, early 1990s. Toyota's factory needed fewer hours and lower stock levels to make its job. This ability to do more with less has led many people to refer to JIT as lean production. Likewise, the phrase just-in-time reflected the idea that the time and level of stock and production activities are closely related to demand. With average stock levels of only two hours, the Toyota plant was clearly only receiving parts and materials before they were needed.

The underlying emphases of JIT - to eliminate all forms of uncertainty and waste - are relevant to all organizations, regardless of the specific planning and control tools used. Second, although some techniques such as Kanban are not adequate. In certain production and service environments, it is quite possible that an organization can follow the JIT philosophy.

CHANGES AND CHALLENGES

Weking et al. (2020), concludes by pointing out that each economic and industrial revolution brings new challenges and determines new approaches within organizations. Companies wishing to travel the industry 4.0 should assess their capabilities and adapt their strategies to implement it in the appropriate scenarios. Overcoming these challenges will involve meeting certain requirements such as: addressing security and digital protection issues; standardization of communication interfaces; processes and organization of work; availability of trained labor force; insertion of SMEs; training and professional development; technological base; research and investment.

Therefore, while some companies are eager to introduce new technologies and improve the quality, efficiency and effectiveness of resources, reduce risks and remain competitive on the market, the lack of a clear understanding on the subject hampers the companies intending to embark on this new approach.

In short, one faces the following challenges:

- To use collaborative methods to foster innovation, which will allow disruptive innovations in a shorter period of time.
- To combine flexibility and efficiency in productive methods.
- To manage smaller series with shorter response times, which implies a greater logistical and coordination effort.
- To adapt more efficient and advanced logistics models.
- Adaptation to the transformation of channels: digitization, multi-channel and omni-channels.
- To leverage the information to anticipate the needs of the customers which implies the theme of BigData, with data collection and its treatment through advanced analytical methods.
- Adaptation to the hyper connectivity of the customer which means an ever greater digital interconnection between people and things, at any time or place.
- To manage the tracking (traceability) of products along the entire value chain.
- To manage the specialization through the coordination of value chains.
- To ensure sustainability in the long term, this notion of sustainability is economic, financial-energy (energy efficiency), optimization of resources, minimization of waste generation in order to have sustainable products.
- To offer customized products which implies a greater number of references, smaller volume of each series and reduced response times.
- To adapt the product portfolio to the digital world, which implies both the digitization of current products and the production of new digital and intelligent products, as in the technical textiles and intelligent fabrics that use nanotechnology and apply sensors to provide additional functionality.

RESEARCH METHODOLOGY

In terms of methodology, the search for information in this area is an endless process, since there is always something to discover. It is therefore important to delimit the scope of research by sticking to the substance and disseminating the results to ensure the progress of science, thus contributing to the creation of new knowledge. However, the research does not dispense with a method that should prove effective in the object of study. The method will be exploratory and bibliographical research, with a quantitative approach (enquires) to present a review of the main points already discussed in other exploratory studies already carried out in other countries on this issue. The question for all industries and companies without exception, is no longer: will there be a break in my company? But the question is: when will this breakdown occur, how long will the transition take and how will it affect my organization? A number of issues will be addressed, including: to understand the current importance of the supply chain in the Portuguese market; to understand if organizations are prepared to deal with the disruption that Industry 4.0 proposes; to analyze the implications and improvements that process automation will bring; to conjecture opportunities and threats that industry 4.0 will bring to the market. Considering the Portugal context, it is intended to understand how the supply chain, namely the purchasing sectors, are dealing with process digitization. It is also intended to understand what kind of changes are implied with the application of industry 4.0 in Portugal, and whether we will be re-industrialized. For instance, and according to Casais and Sousa (2019), industries and markets are competitive, and it is equally important to understand the role of corporate social responsibility in certain industries (e.g., tourism industry). In an interdisciplinary perspective, the present study intends to present contributions for the management and for the sustainable operation of the value chain in the current markets. Specifically, we intend to study the reality in Portugal. At the end, the main conclusions of the study will be presented (qualitative nature). In the final section, the limitations of the study will be presented and guidelines will be discussed for future research.

Questionnaire Preparation

The first aspect that was taken into account when constructing the questionnaire was the type of information that would be collected in order to build a measurement instrument that would allow relevant results to be obtained for the research (Weking et al., 2020). If the purpose of quantitative research is to quantify data and generalise the sample results to the target population (Malhotra, 2004), the questionnaire is a measurement instrument that translates the study objectives with measurable variables and helps to organise, standardise and control the data so that the information sought can be accurately collected. The quality of the results obtained depends largely on the reliability and validity of the measurement instrument.

The aim was to analyse the questions posed, their measurement and the choice or adaptation of measurement scales already in use. Based on the analysis of the information that needed to be collected, the type of questions to be included in the questionnaire was defined.

Identification of the Sample

Our sample includes a list of businesses that applied for the implementation of Industry 4.0 concepts through the Portugal 2020 Support Portal. Our sample has also been refined, as service-related sectors were not considered from the beginning for the study conceptualization. Emails were sent out to the general email address of companies and replies were received between November 1, 2019 and January 8, 2020. The sample is characterized by 54 valid questionnaires, out of a total of 140 sent, obtaining a response rate in the order of 39%. The data collected through the application of the questionnaire were statistically treated using the Statistical Package for the Social Sciences (SPSS) computer program.

DISCUSSION AND RESULTS

Our sample contains 85% of nationally owned businesses, with multinational companies representing a smaller share of our observations. SMEs represent 59% of the businesses included in our sample.

Most of the companies were created between the 1960's (19%) and 1990's (21%) and 25% of the sample included businesses started between 2006 and 2015.

As for the level of involvement of companies in the implementation of Industry 4.0 most are still indifferent to this reality, if we add the 3 responses associated with non-involvement we obtain an analysis universe of 64.81%. Only 13% of companies are very involved in digital transformation.

The companies surveyed expect to take an average of 4.98 years to implement the Industry 4.0 elements, and there is a strong positive correlation between the implementation of the elements in the company and in the purchasing department. Only 3.70% of the companies surveyed work fully with the digitalisation of the supply chain, this question shows us that the overwhelming majority of companies, around 80% (77.78%), are not even considering implementing the digital transformation in the purchasing department. Still 18.50% of businesses that are at the early stages of industry 4.0 implemention.

The suppliers of the companies surveyed are already entering the digitalisation era, around 53.70% are already implementing industry 4.0, and two of the possible reasons for an acceleration on the part of suppliers may be their size and location.

In Portugal, the degree of complexity of implementing Industry 4.0 is high or very high (79.80%).

The technologies that respondents consider as the most relevant for the creation of business value are the internet of things (IoT), artificial intelligence (AI), as well as cloud computing and big data. Cybersecurity is also an area that respondents highlighted as being relevant and of interest for the Industrial 4.0 era.

Regarding the expectations of respondents for the procurement area, 21% of the respondents think that digitalisation will bring an increase in competitiveness, 19.50% think that there will be a reduction in costs and it will facilitate the integration of information, eliminating duplication of work, in order to optimise resources and there will be greater responsiveness due to the growing integration and sharing of data and processes.

The greatest obstacles identified in the implementation are the management mentality (20%), with budget issues in second place (16%), and lastly the lack of knowledge or skills to adapt the new technologies to the organisation's daily tasks. Lastly, 12.70%, of respondents identify the lack of a digital strategy blocking the progress of business towards digitalisation.

The companies plan to invest in some digitalisation processes, and the one that is most emphasised, at this point, is electronic purchasing platforms, with 27.20% planning to invest in this resource. This is followed by big data analytics (17.40%) and planning to invest in cybersecurity, (14.10%). Only 6% of the companies have already evidenced investment in this area, 22.20% do not even have any planning for investment and 38.9% do not know how to mention the average timeframe or have no knowledge on the subject.

When analysing Industry 4.0 as being a topic for the procurement function, the respondents' view shows that they agree (18.50%) or partially agree (42.60%), leading one to conclude that digitalisation is important for the Industry 4.0 function.

Regarding the challenges in the procurement area, only 7.50% of the respondents partially or totally disagree with the question, as well as 5.60% was the percentage of disagreement, of the above question. One can conclude that the respondents agree that the implementation of I4.0 entails great challenges within the procurement area

None of the respondents completely disagreed with the challenge of the interconnection between customers and suppliers so that the supply channel flows with as little intervention as possible and 64.83% refer that order automation for the supply chain offers a challenge. With this study we conclude that this will be an important challenge, especially for companies with multi-suppliers and with a high level of purchases of raw materials, semi-finished or finished products.

CONCLUSION

Within the purchasing function, Industry 4.0 brings us a series of opportunities and threats. The implementation of certain technologies, such as virtual and augmented realities, 3D printing and simulation, are seen as opportunities. On the other hand, analysis of big data, cloud technology, cybersecurity, IoT, miniaturization of electronics, radio frequency identification (RFID), robotics, drones and nanotechnology, machine2machine (M2M) and business intelligence (BI), can be opportunities or threats for organizations. The fact that some technologies may result in opportunities and threats is because all different areas are interconnected, with no clear boundaries between them.

Some clear benefits can be identified from the implementation of the industry 4.0. The most relevant benefits are greater flexibility, quality standards, efficiency and productivity. This allows mass customization, permitting businesses to meet customer demands, creating value through the constant introduction of new products and services in the market. In addition, collaboration between machines and human beings could impact socially the life of the workers of the future, especially with regards to the optimization of decision-making.

Although the impacts of Industry 4.0 in Supply Chain have been discussed in this paper, due to their theoretical nature, some questions remain to be answered that, consequently, limit the generalization of this work, not only in its implementation, but also in its management. Therefore, we asked for empirical research in this area. It was useful to understand how Portuguese industry is preparing their organizations, in a holist way to the future market changes. It can be explored, in the future, in Portugal the concepts of Purchase 4.0 and Procurement 4.0. This document was our first attempt to help companies to better understand the implications of Industry 4.0 and its relevant technologies for the achievement of the Digital Supply Chain or Supply Chain 4.0. Our work contributes with empirical findings on the businesses evaluation on how they should digitally integrate their supply chain.

REFERENCES

Ardito, L., Petruzzelli, A. M., Panniello, U., & Garavelli, A. C. (2018). Towards Industry 4.0: Mapping digital technologies for supply chain management-marketing integration. *Business Process Management Journal.*

Bahrin, M. A. K., Othman, M. F., Azli, N. H. N., & Talib, M. F. (2016). Industry 4.0: A review on industrial automation and robotic. *Jurnal Teknologi, 78*, 6–13.

Ballou, R. (2006). *Gerenciamento da cadeia de suprimentos/logística empresarial.* Editora Bookman.

Casais, B., & Sousa, B. (2019). Portugal, the best destination: The case of a CSR communication that changed mentalities and increased business performance. *World Review of Entrepreneurship, Management and Sustainable Development, 15*(1/2), 29–41. doi:10.1504/WREMSD.2019.098474

Cotteleer, M., & Joyce, J. (2014). 3D opportunity: Additive manufacturing paths to performance, innovation, and growth. *Deloitte Review, 14*, 5–19.

Glas, A. H., & Kleemann, F. C. (2016). The impact of industry 4.0 on procurement and supply management: A conceptual and qualitative analysis. *International Journal of Business and Management Invention, 5*(6), 55–66.

Guo, D., Li, M., Lyu, Z., Kang, K., Wu, W., Zhong, R. Y., & Huang, G. Q. (2021). Synchroperation in industry 4.0 manufacturing. *International Journal of Production Economics, 238*, 108171. doi:10.1016/j.ijpe.2021.108171

Hofmann, E., & Rüsch, M. (2017). Industry 4.0 and the current status as well as future prospects on logistics. *Computers in Industry, 89*, 23–34. doi:10.1016/j.compind.2017.04.002

Lezzi, M., Lazoi, M., & Corallo, A. (2018). Cybersecurity for Industry 4.0 in the current literature: A reference framework. *Computers in Industry, 103*, 97–110. doi:10.1016/j.compind.2018.09.004

Malhotra, D. (2004). Trust and reciprocity decisions: The differing perspectives of trustors and trusted parties. *Organizational Behavior and Human Decision Processes, 94*(2), 61–73. doi:10.1016/j.obhdp.2004.03.001

Monzcka, R. (2009). Purchasing and Supply Chain Management, 4. Cengage Learning.

Moura, B. (2006). *Logística Conceitos e Tendências*. Edições Centro Atlântico.

Porter, M. E., & Heppelmann, J. E. (2014). How smart, connected products are transforming competition. *Harvard Business Review, 92*(11), 64–88.

Ratten, V., Jones, P., Braga, V., & Marques, C. S. (2019). Subsistence Entrepreneurship: The Role of Collaborative Innovation, Sustainability and Social Goals. In V. Ratten, P. Jones, V. Braga, & C. S. Marques (Eds.), *Subsistence Entrepreneurship* (pp. 1–6). Springer. doi:10.1007/978-3-030-11542-5_1

Rodrigues, M.; Sousa, B. & Batista da Costa, J. (2019). The improvement of the supply chain channel based on digital transformation: an exploratory study in the sustainable industry 4.0. *Book of Abstracts*, (pp. 66-77).

Santos, V. R., Vitorino, T. F., Dias, Á. L., Martinho, D., & Sousa, B. B. (2022). Developing a Commercial Ethics Framework for Analysing Marketing Campaigns. [IJSSMET]. *International Journal of Service Science, Management, Engineering, and Technology, 13*(1), 1–16. doi:10.4018/IJSSMET.290336

Schwab, K. (2017). *A Quarta Revolução Industrial.* Lisboa, Edição: Levoir, Marketing e Conteúdos Multimédia, S.A.

Tjahjono, B., Esplugues, C., Ares, E., & Pelaez, G. (2017). What does industry 4.0 mean to supply chain? *Procedia Manufacturing, 13*, 1175–1182. doi:10.1016/j.promfg.2017.09.191

Weking, J., Stöcker, M., Kowalkiewicz, M., Böhm, M., & Krcmar, H. (2020). Leveraging industry 4.0–A business model pattern framework. *International Journal of Production Economics, 225*, 107588. doi:10.1016/j.ijpe.2019.107588

KEY TERMS AND DEFINITIONS

Digital Supply Chain: Is a new media term which encompasses the process of the delivery of digital media, be it music or video, by electronic means, from the point of origin (content provider) to destination (consumer). In much the same manner a physical medium must go through a "supply chain" process in order to mature into a consumable product, digital media must pass through various stages in processing to get to a point in which the consumer can enjoy the music or video on a computer or television set.

Industry 4.0: Industry 4.0 or Fourth Industrial Revolution is an expression that encompasses some technologies for automation and data exchange and uses concepts of cyber-physical systems, Internet of Things and Cloud Computing. The focus of the Fourth Industrial Revolution is on improving process efficiency and productivity.

Technological Innovation: Is a term applicable to both process and product innovations. In general, it is any novelty implemented by the productive sector, through research or investments, which increases the efficiency of the production process or implies a new or improved product.

Chapter 4
The Synergy of Lean Thinking and Process Analysis as the Way to Reduce Waste in Intralogistics

Filip Nowak
https://orcid.org/0000-0003-1330-3230
Łukasiewicz Research Network - Poznań Institute of Technology, Poland

Jacek Krzywy
https://orcid.org/0000-0002-8453-3204
Łukasiewicz Research Network - Poznań Institute of Technology, Poland

Witold Statkiewicz
Łukasiewicz Research Network - Poznań Institute of Technology, Poland

ABSTRACT

The purpose of this article was to investigate the impact of applying lean thinking techniques to eliminate operations that do not bring business value in an organization. For this purpose, the authors decided to use the methodology of increasing the efficiency of business processes to identify the current process and indicate its optimization potential. The applied process optimization methods focusing on the elimination of waste are one of the main principles of lean thinking. With the usage of computer simulation, it was possible to verify the current performance of the process and to compare it with the effectiveness of the target solutions. The process analysis was carried out in a company dealing in wholesale distribution of fast-moving food products and concerned the process of picking order.

DOI: 10.4018/978-1-6684-5606-4.ch004

INTRODUCTION

In order to become more competitive, enterprises must constantly strive to increase the efficiency of their processes. Today's logistics companies face many challenges, and the current labor market situation such as limited human resources, frequent staff turnover, and a limited number of experienced employees makes meeting all challenges problematic.

One of the ways to improve the efficiency of logistics processes and at the same time to organize and standardize them, may be using methods related to Lean Thinking.

The authors of this publication focus on reviewing the available methods and test them in the logistics company which is responsible for the distribution of fast-moving food products with a focus on its order picking process. The result is to be a relatively quick and easy way to improve this process performance without incurring additional infrastructure investments or hiring additional people.

The work concerns the improvement of the order picking system using a simulation model, the implementation of various alternative scenarios and the interpretation of their results.

The paper is organized as follows: theoretical background provides knowledge about issues related to the picking process, Lean Thinking in order picking process and simulation in order picking. The next section described the research method used in this article. Section 3 describes the case study. This chapter also includes models of the product picking process in the current and target versions, as well as the results of a computer simulation. Lastly, the paper concludes with a summary, alternative solutions, contribution of the study and limitations and future research.

THEORETICAL BACKGROUND

Picking Process

Order picking means the process of retrieving the ordered quantities of one or more products from storage or buffer area in order to have them delivered for shipment. It is one of the most labour and time-intensive processes in internal logistics (E. Grosse et al., 2016; van Gils, Ramaekers, Caris et al., 2018). The recent changes in production and distribution have made the design and management of order picking more important and complex (Keshavarz et al., 2021; Winkelhaus & Grosse, 2020). In production, these changes include shifting to smaller batch sizes, point-of-use delivery, and order and product customization, among others. In distribution logistics, these changes relate to the requirements of customers who want fast and timely delivery within tight time windows, which in turn reduces the time spent on order picking.

Due to the wide range of external (e.g. customer demand pattern, overall product demand, etc.) and internal (e.g. mechanization level, organization, and operational policies) factors that affect the order picking system, the design of these systems is often complex.

The most frequently mentioned goals of planning and designing an order picking system are minimizing order fulfillment times, total costs or maximizing the use of space (Calzavara et al., 2018; E. Grosse et al., 2016; van Gils et al., 2017; van Gils, Ramaekers, Braekers et al., 2018).

To achieve these goals, many researchers suggest automating order picking to further reduce costs, faster delivery response times, better pick accuracy and space utilization (Damayanti et al., 2022; Elbert et al., 2018; Knigge, 2021; Loske & Klumpp, 2020; Wang et al., 2021; Żywicki & Buń, 2021). As such, recent research has increasingly focused on new automated technologies that can improve picking performance (Jaghbeer et al., 2020; van Gils, Ramaekers, Caris et al., 2018) present a literature review on the design of order picking system, taking into consideration material handling equipment. Winkelhaus and Grosse (Winkelhaus & Grosse, 2020) proposed the application of Internet of Things (IoT) and cyber-physical systems. Whereas Azadeh et al. proposed the application of picking robots, which can automate the entire picking process. Although there has been significant development of automated warehousing systems in recent years (Azadeh et al., 2019; Jaghbeer et al., 2020) most companies still rely on manual order picking processes by order pickers. The main advantage of manual packaging systems is their greater flexibility compared to the automated approach, which is particularly important in the case of changing product portfolios (Calzavara et al., 2018). Literature research shows that up to 80% of all order picking warehouses are operated manually (Calzavara et al., 2018; E. H. Grosse & Glock, 2015). Therefore, recently a lot of attention has been paid to the problems of manual order picking in logistics operations Grosse et al. discussed opportunities for integrating human factor into mathematical models of the order picking process (E. Grosse et al., 2014). On the other hand, in the literature one can also find methods of managing order picking based on the Euler graph and the dynamic programming procedure (Masae et al., 2021). Knigge (2021) in his consideration of the picking process analyzed the usefulness of VR HMD for planning and training in the context of manual order picking (Knigge, 2021). Pereira and other researchers proposed a localization system, to reduce one of the most time-consuming components of picking, the search time for products in the warehouse (Pereira et al., 2019). In addition to the above-mentioned proposals for improving the warehouse process, many authors also suggest a positive effect in the use of lean manufacturing methods and tools in the process of picking goods (Andjelkovic et al., 2017; Baby et al., 2018; Srisuk & Tippayawong, 2020).

Lean Thinking in Order Picking Process

Lean Manufacturing is a concept derived from the Toyota system. It is one of the best-known approaches to improving processes carried out in an enterprise. The main goal of Lean Manufacturing is to reduce costs by eliminating all possible sources of waste within the company (Jasiulewicz-Kaczmarek & Saniuk, 2018). Lean philosophy is based on three principles: identifying value, eliminating waste and generating value for the customer (Melton, 2005; Antosz et al., 2022a). Enterprises wishing to maintain and improve their competitive advantage should incorporate lean principles into their daily practices (Raghuram & Arjunan, 2021, Antosz et al., 2022b). To achieve this, all processes in the company must be organized respecting the principles of the lean strategy and eliminating activities that do not add value. Due to the fact that warehouse and warehouse operations are not only a source of costs but also a source of competitive advantage through a higher level of service, the implementation of lean tools can contribute to greater value and lower costs (Dehdari, 2014). Lean warehousing is focused on adequate and efficient implementation of activities and consists in minimizing activities that do not add value in all warehouse operations, including order picking (Buonamico et al., 2017; Raghuram & Arjunan, 2021). To eliminate waste in the order picking process, Pipatprapa proposed quick response code (QR) on mobile platforms of the smartphone (Pipatprapa, 2019). Srisuk & Tippayawong (2020) in their consideration showed that the implementation of the KAIZEN and Lean techniques in the raw material picking process allowed to shorten the picking time by 83%, and the total picking distance was reduced by 86%.

The main purpose of lean tools in the order picking system is the elimination of wasted time and costs, which is achieved, among others, by reducing travel time, and determining the correct sequence of human activities, which reduces costs and results in increased profitability. In Lean improvement, order picking processes must be analyzed using process mapping. One of the tools supporting the analysis of processes is simulation. The simulation can be used to develop a dynamic version of the process map and to model and visualize the need for changes in the current process.

Process Simulation Techniques

In business practice, the stage of business process modeling is often only the first stage on the way to process efficiency improvement. Process simulation is an essential element for successful process optimization. In the literature, we most often see the term that process simulation is a tool for managing change in an organization. Thanks to the simulation of processes, we can answer a number of questions related to: process implementation time, labor costs, the effectiveness of changes introduced in the organization, and the involvement of resources. In addition, the simulation of processes allows to predict how the introduced changes may affect the company. Process simulation is also a very important tool contributing to the elimination of misplaced changes in the organization (Barnett, 2003, Jasiulewicz-Kaczmarek & Bartkowiak, 2016). The most commonly used techniques for simulation modeling of business processes are (Jahangirian et al., 2010):

- DES - Discrete Event Simulation
- SD - System Dynamics
- ABS - Agent-Based Simulation
- Monte Carlo

Discrete event simulation is a method that allows you to simulate a process as an analysis of individual events taking place over time. It enables the analysis of dynamic behaviors and their interactions (Ferro et al., 2018; Karnon et al., 2012; Zhang, 2018). System dynamics is a method based on continuous simulation modeling. The Dynamics system deals with the modeling of the general behavior of the system, not with a detailed analysis of tasks (Hell & Petrić, 2021). Agent-based modeling is one of the newer techniques for simulation modeling of processes based on the interaction of autonomous "agents". These agents are described by simple rules and their interactions with other agents, which in turn has a direct impact on their behavior (Bonabeau, 2002; Macal & North, 2010). The Monte Carlo simulation method is a method used in business to assess the level of exposure to a specific risk. This type of simulation is most often used for the financial valuation of derivatives and the creation of various management scenarios (Johansen, 2010; Levy, 2008; Ruan, 2019).

When analyzing the cited characteristics of individual business process simulation techniques, it should be emphasized that the most appropriate process simulation method to be used in this article will be the process simulation method based on discrete event modeling. Due to the specificity of the modeled issue (goods picking process), this method will not only comprehensively develop the above-mentioned simulation model, but will also contribute to obtaining the most accurate results of the conducted research.

Simulation in Order Picking

Simulation is defined as the practice of creating models representing existing or future systems and experimenting to explain the system behavior, to improve performance or design new systems with desirable features (Qiao & Wang, 2021). The main feature of simulation is the ability to study several alternate solutions and evaluate them in terms of cost and efficiency (Ho & Lin, 2017). Greasley and Owen highlight that the simulation allows investigating complex systems, conducting 'what if' experiments without interfering with them (Greasley & Owen, 2018). Rodič adds that the simulation has been consolidated in the last decades in the most diverse sectors, contributing to the development and improvement of products, processes, and services (Rodič, 2017).

To meet these challenges, companies utilize various virtual tools and methods for product and production development. These techniques included discrete event simulation (DES), system dynamics (SD), agent-based simulation (ABS) (Santos et al., 2021). The discrete event simulation model plays an important role in continuous improvement (Baril et al., 2015; Shou et al., 2021). Various scenarios can be tested with a detailed discrete event simulation model. Nevertheless, developing a detailed discrete event simulation model is time-consuming as it requires data acquisition, process modeling and validation, model validation, and generation of improvement solutions (Bokrantz et al., 2017).

Caron et al., presented a DES approach for efficient manual-order-picking warehouse layout design (Caron et al., 2000). Petersen and Aase introduced a simulation model to examine the effect of several picking, routing, and storage policies on the total distance travelled within the warehouse to fulfil orders (Petersen & Aase, 2004). Simulation techniques are used to study picking processes in order to reduce operating costs (Chackelson et al., 2013). Altarazi and Bozer in their works they also took up the subject improving the picking process, among others (Altarazi & Ammouri, 2018; Bozer & Aldarondo, 2018).

Many authors indicate that DES can support the designers of lean systems in testing and verifying the proposed solutions in real conditions (the first publication to adopt DES in lean production research was in 1997 by I.D.Tommelein (Tommelein, 1997).

In research titled: "Using lean techniques and discrete-event simulation for performance improvement in an outpatient clinic", the authors used lean techniques with DES to reduce patient waiting times. The solutions proposed in the article make it possible to increase the capacity of the clinic by 303 patients (272%) or shorten the patient's waiting time during the visit by 28.5 minutes (Demirli et al., 2021). Abideen and Mohamad proposed an integrated approach of the value stream mapping (VSM) and DES in a Malaysian pharmaceutical production warehouse (Abideen & Mohamad, 2020).

DES can support lean project analysis by allowing the project team to test the performance of proposed solutions in a variety of scenarios and help decision makers make better decisions by examining various performance indicators such as wait times, lead times, and resource utilization.

Figure 1. Method of increasing the efficiency of business processes
Source: (Ragin-Skorecka & Nowak, 2017)

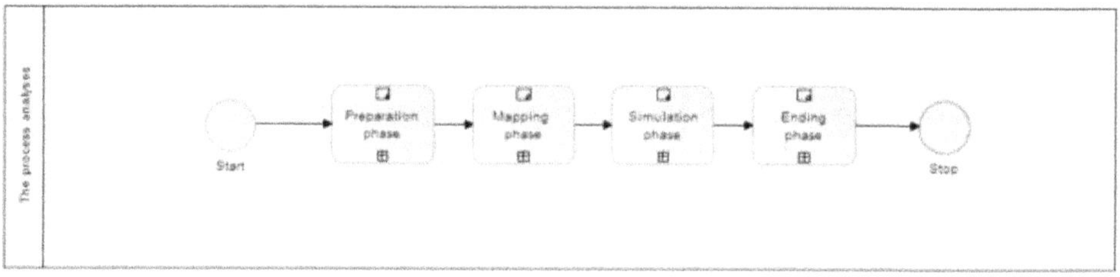

METHOD - INCREASING THE EFFICIENCY OF BUSINESS PROCESSES

In the research part, the method of process analysis based on a top-down approach was adopted. BPMN 2.0 was chosen as the mapping standard due to its widespread use. This standard is described in ISO/IEC 19510:2013 Information technology - Business Process Model and Notation. The advantages of this notation include:

- user-friendly way of describing the process,
- the ability to model virtually all business processes, regardless of the industry specificity,
- common knowledge of the standard symbols in business,
- the possibility of diagnosing unnecessary operations.

The described research was conducted in accordance with the method of increasing the efficiency of business processes (Fig. 1).

The preparatory phase includes collecting basic information and preparing assumptions on the basis of conducted research. A scenario is built according to the currently running process which will be tested. AS IS scenario includes, among others, information about the number of people working within the examined process, time of availability of the resources(working time), the quantity of process transactions, and the time when processes will be generated.

The process mapping phase is divided into two parts: AS IS mapping and TO BE mapping. The purpose of AS IS mapping is, on the one hand, to reflect the course of processes in accordance with the practice of their application and on the other hand to prepare conclusions showing the identified discrepancies in relation to the references contained in the arrangements with the process owner. The purpose of TO BE mapping is to illustrate the planned changes and then check their correctness and logic using a process analysis.

The simulation phase is divided into two parts: preparation and simulation of AS IS model and preparation and simulation of TO BE model. The purpose of simulating AS IS model is to verify whether prepared AS IS map reflects the actual state of current process. Completion of the work on AS IS model is the verification the of maps with the client, which enables the commencement of the second stage of work - the simulation of the target state based on the adopted scenarios of process changes.

The completion phase allows to merge all studies, analyzes and simulations into one report. Only after approval of this stage the results are presented to the client. Searching for potential changes that will increase the efficiency of the process takes place in the mapping and simulation phase. After preparing the current state map of the process (AS IS), it should be parameterized and calibrated on the basis of historical data. KPIs are defined and their values are measured in the current process. At this stage, there are sub-processes that might be improved. During creating a map of the desired state of a given process (TO BE), it is worth considering how many changes might be made. While stimulating TO BE process, changes should be introduced one by one and tested the effectiveness (referring to previously defined KPIs and their base values). When the obtained effect of simulating the introduction of a single change is positive, the total effectiveness of the proposed changes can be tested. It may turn out that for two or more changes the positive effect disappears (no synergy occurs). The best solution in the given conditions is obtained iteratively when the client considers that he has adequate process efficiency with the assumed use of resources (Ragin-Skorecka & Nowak, 2017).

CASE STUDY

Description of the Case

The process analysis was carried out in one of the largest companies dealing in the wholesale distribution of fast-moving food products, household chemicals, alcohol, drinks, and tobacco products. The current situation in the labor market - limited access to employees performing warehouse tasks, especially in special economic zones, implies an increased demand for warehouse employees. In response to these challenges, the company has taken steps to improve warehouse processes efficiency to eliminate the lack of human resources. The company wanted to investigate whether using one of the lean thinking techniques in the context of tasks that do not bring business value would improve the warehouse processes efficiency. On that account, the organization conducted an analysis of the order picking process. This chapter describes research conducted in a real-life scenario.

The aim of these works was to investigate the impact of applying Lean Thinking techniques to eliminate operations that do not bring business value in an organization, by measuring and comparing the operational efficiency of the person completing the goods before they are shipped from the warehouse.

Preparation Phase

According to the research methodology, in the first phase of the process analysis, assumptions were defined, and basic process data/parameters were obtained.

The simulation assumptions are as follows:

1. Process transactions: Number of products to be completed during one shift by one employee.
2. Transaction generators: 546 products.
    a) Business roles: 1 warehouse worker.
3. Process observation time:
    a) 1 employee shift.
    b) Working hours: 8:00 am - 4:00 pm.
4. Setup of simulation:
    a) Simulation time: Compressed.
    b) Simulation end: Transaction completed.

In the study, the duration of individual operations and their efficiency were measured on the basis of an employee indicated by management as a typical representative of a given business role. The simulation model (process activities and events) was supplied with data on the travel time and distance for each completed product. These data were obtained on the basis of actual data from the WMS (Warehouse Management System) of the analyzed entity.

The number of consolidated orders was a discrete variable because the ergonomic parameters of the tested products, the place of their storage, and the way of their transport were limited by the set of tested values {1,2,4,12}. They were verified by employees directly implementing the process as real parameters - possible for the application.

Figure 2. Order picking process – AS IS process
Source: own study

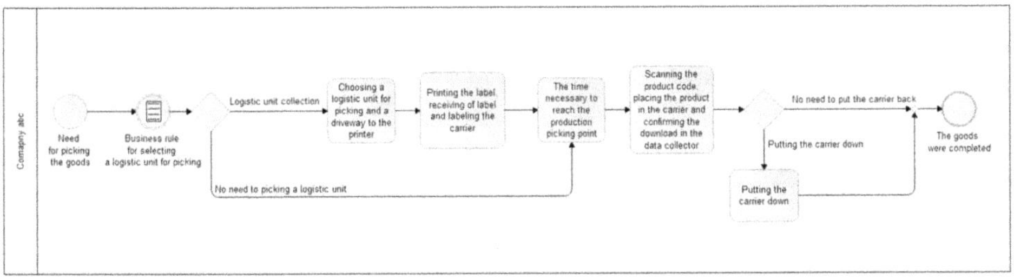

MAPPING PHASE

1. Current Situation - Process AS IS

The second phase of the process analysis concerning process mapping is related to the identification and mapping of the current order picking process (AS IS process). The BPMN 2.0 standard was used during the process mapping step. Currently, it is one of the most popular standards for mapping business processes. The currently identified and mapped process is presented in Figure no. 2.

The purpose of the order picking process is to take all products from the picking list and place them in the logistic unit. Currently, the warehouse worker is supported during this process by a data collector, which shows him the location of subsequent products. The order picking process begins with the business rule regarding the need to select a logistics unit for picking. After the business rule is executed, the warehouse worker has a choice of two flow paths. In the case of the first decision, the employee should pick up a new unit for picking, drive to the label printing station, collect the printed label and then stick it on the logistic unit. In the case of the second path of the process, the warehouse employee does not have to pick up a new logistic unit, because subsequent products can be completed for the current logistic unit. The next stage of the process is the employee's drive to the product location indicated by the data collector. When the employee is in the indicated place, he scans the product code, places it in the logistic unit and confirms the fact that the product has been placed on the data collector. Systemic product pick-up confirmations are extremely important from the point of view of maintaining the credibility of the current stock levels. After the system confirmation of product picking, another decision is made, this time regarding the need to put the logistic unit aside in place of the shipping of the products to the customer, or the no need to put the logistic unit back. The mapping phase also allowed to identify bottlenecks and provided data for making a comparison with the future state. In the current

Figure 3. Order picking process – TO BE 1 process
Source: own study

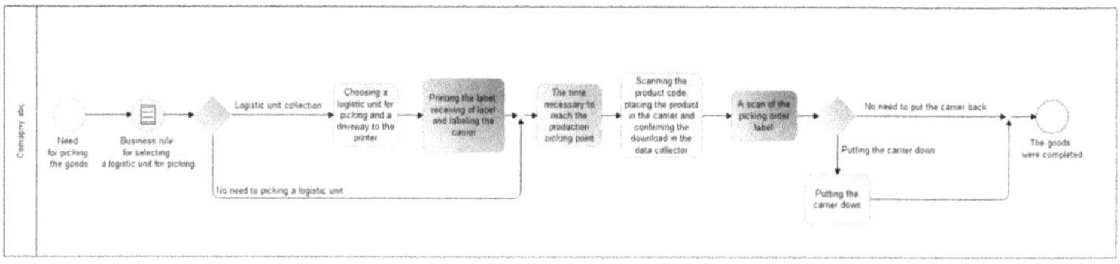

process, four steps with optimization potential have been identified. The above-mentioned steps of the process are marked in yellow in the picture (Figure 2. Order picking process – AS IS process). The first potential is to reduce the frequency of retrieval of new logistic units. Printing the label, receiving of label and labeling the carrier is the next stage of the process that will have an impact on the target solution. Researchers also identified the time necessary to reach the picking point as an element of process waste. The last element marked in yellow is the frequency of placing logistic units in place of shipping goods to the customer.

2. Proposed Solutions – Process TO BE 1

The next stage of process mapping was to develop proposals for target solutions influencing the effectiveness of the current process. In this case, it was decided to verify the effectiveness of three potential solutions to reduce waste in the order picking process (eliminating waste as one of the three basic lean thinking assumptions). In target solutions, the effectiveness of grouping many orders in one picking cycle was tested. In the case of the first solution - process TO BE 1 (figure 3), a dedicated bipartite picking platform was used, allowing one to complete two orders during a single picking cycle (picking path). This change will be possible to implement under the condition of a systemic combination of the possibility of simultaneous picking of two orders within one picking path.

In Figure 3, red marks those places in the process where elementary activities will extend the completion time of the order picking process. Belong to them:

- printing the label, receiving of label and labeling the carrier,
- a scan of the picking order label (It is an additional step in the process that must occur in order for the target solution to be complete).

Green, on the other hand, in the target process TO BE 1 marks those stages that will contribute to the acceleration of the process. These changes are due to the dedicated bipartite picking platform being used.

3. Proposed Solutions – Process TO BE 2

In the case of the TO BE 2 scenario (figure 4), the efficiency of simultaneous completion of 4 orders during a single completion cycle (picking path) was examined.

Figure 4. Order picking process – TO BE 2 process
Source: own study

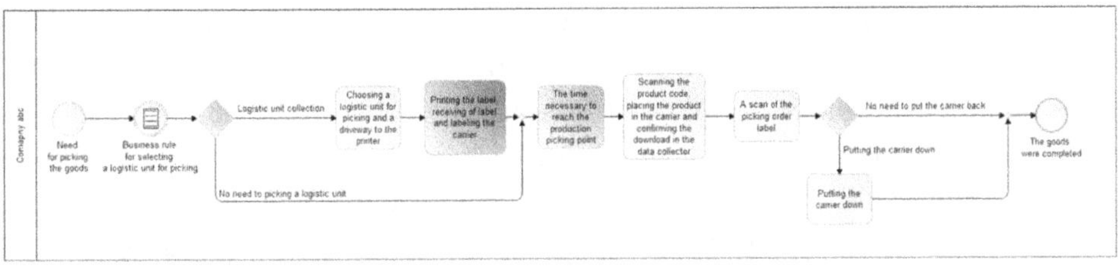

As in the case of the TO BE 1 scenario, red marks the activities that will extend compared to the previous version of the process. Due to the completion of four orders during a single picking cycle, the time associated with printing labels and marking the printed labels of logistic units will be longer. On the other hand, the proposed solution will contribute to reducing the frequency of picking new logistic units, the frequency of putting back the completed units, and shortening the picking path.

4. Proposed Solutions – Process TO BE 3

The last proposal of the target process - TO BE 3 scenario (figure 5), assumes the simultaneous completion of 12 orders during one completion cycle carried out by a warehouse employee.

In the solution assuming the completion of twelve orders during a single picking cycle, the time associated with printing labels and marking the printed labels on logistic units will be extended. Time savings will be possible by reducing the frequency of collecting new logistic units, the frequency of putting them back in place and shortening the picking path.

Figure 5. Order picking process – TO BE 3 process
Source: own study

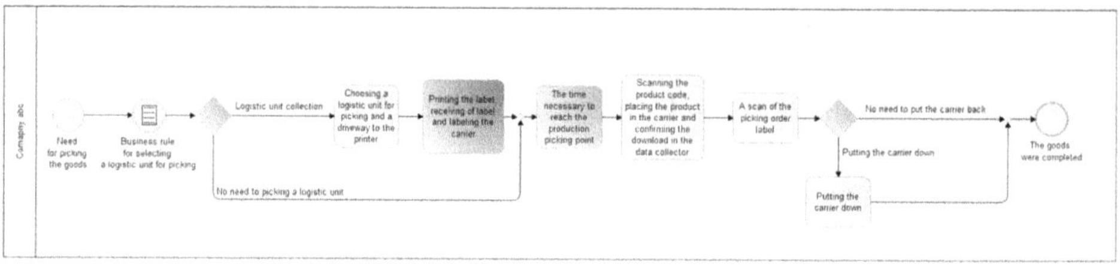

Simulation Phase

According to the adopted research methodology, after the development of process maps in the current state (process AS IS) and target state (processes TO-BE), the phase related to the process simulation was started. In this phase, simulation models of processes in iGrafx Process for Enterprise Modeling were developed. Thanks to the simulation of the processes, it was possible to determine the Key Performance Indicators (KPI) of the order picking process. Also, process simulation allowed to examine the current efficiency of the process and compare it with the potential efficiency after the implementation of the proposed solutions. In order to select the most favorable process change scenario, three KPIs were selected for the analysis: Average time of picking an assortment item, total working time (In terms of one working shift) and involvement of personal resources. The charts below show the results of selected KPIs.

Ending Phase

The obtained results of the comparative analysis of the product picking process showed that it is possible to improve the efficiency of this process using the Lean Thinking technique. All generated KPIs show the possibility of improving the efficiency of the examined process. For all KPIs, the greatest improvement can be achieved in the TO BE 3 scenario related to the simultaneous completion of 12 orders during one completion cycle carried out by a warehouse employee.

In terms of the average time of picking an assortment items, the necessary time in the AS IS process is 34 seconds, in TO BE 1 it is 32 seconds, in TO BE 2 it is 27 seconds, and in TO BE 3 it is 21 seconds. These results show that each subsequent process change contributes to the possibility of obtaining a higher efficiency of the implemented process.

Total working time, as in the case of the previous KPI, confirms the possibility of reducing waste in the order picking process. The total work time required to

Figure 6. Average time of picking an assortment item
Source: own study

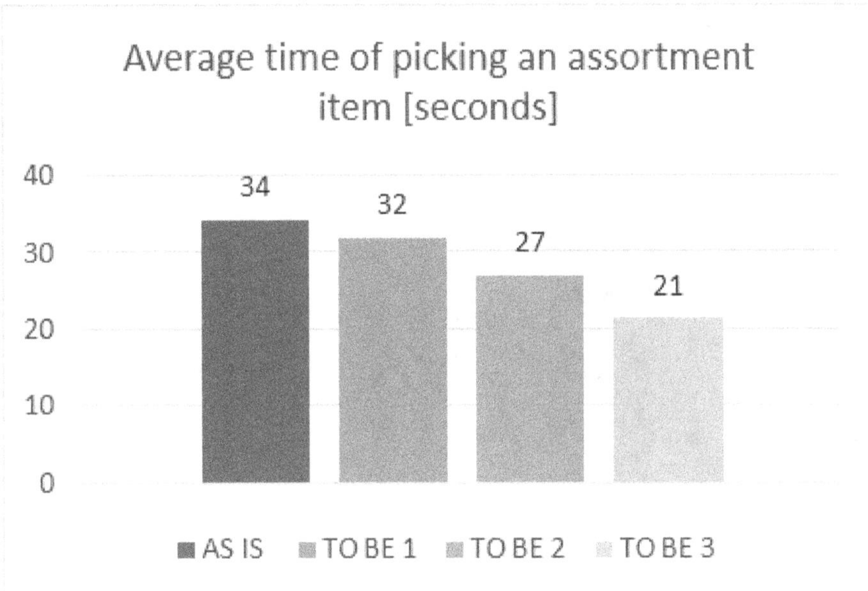

Figure 7. Total working time
Source: own study

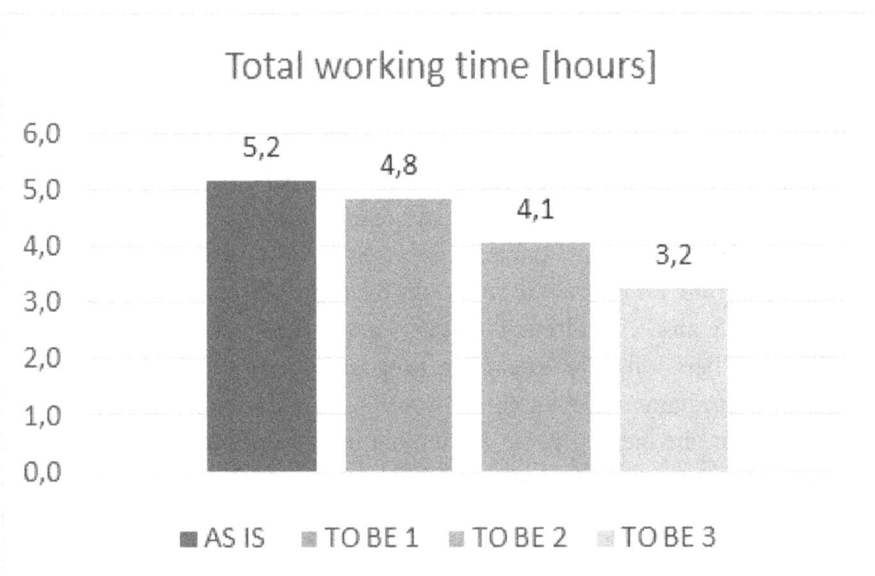

Figure 8. Involvement of personal resources
Source: own study

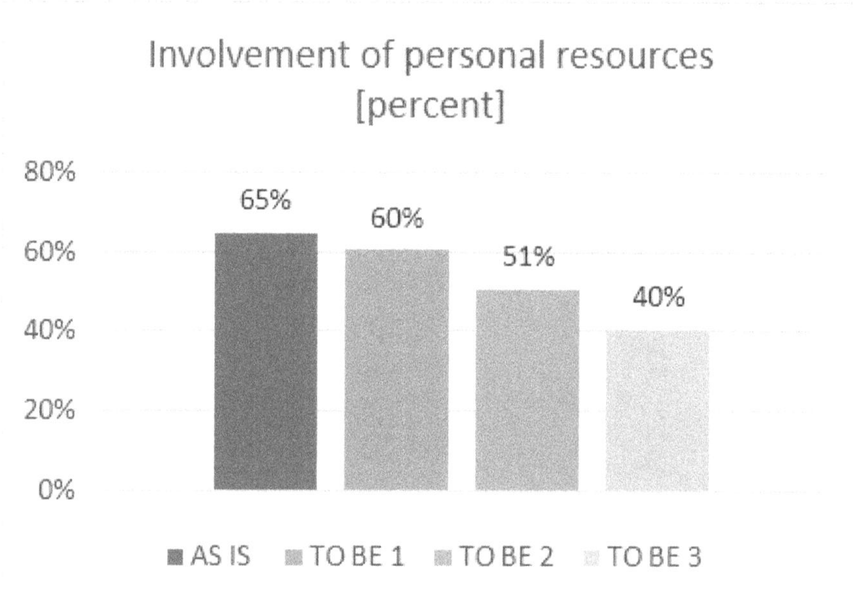

complete all picking orders on a given day is gradually decreasing. In the case of the AS IS process, the employee who picks orders needs 5.2 hours to handle the entire process, in the case of TO BE 1 - 4.8 hours, in the case of TO BE 2 - 4.1 hours and in the case of TO BE 3 only 3.2 hours. As can be seen from the results obtained, in the case of the TO BE 3 scenario (in relation to the currently implemented process), the organization can expect a daily time saving of 2 hours.

As in the case of the previous KPIs, the highest savings are expected for the TO BE 3 scenario. In the TO BE 3 target process, the picker needs only 40% of his commitment to complete the entire daily list of orders. In relation to the AS IS process, the organization can expect to save approximately 25% of the daily time of a warehouse employee. Of course, it is extremely important for the company's management to find suitable additional tasks for these employees, so that they can spend the saved hours on additional activities in the company.

In their considerations, the researchers proposed 3 scenarios of process change. Of course, the question arises whether it would be possible to combine subsequent picking orders in one picking cycle carried out by a warehouse employee. On the one hand, it is mathematically possible, of course, however, business practice shows that in organizations we are always dealing with some limitations. In this case, such a limitation was the type of assortment that could be combined with each other. We are talking about a similar weight and volume assortment transportable for picking.

The Simulation Model Validation

The model was validated by staff directly performing the goods-picking process. The current state model was supplied with real data (activities and process events were parameterized based on actual data from the company's Warehouse Management System). Afterward, one working shift performance was simulated to determine the key performance indicators, which were verified with the actual data recorded in the WMS, and confirmed by the employees who operated this process. The validated current state model was the basis for designing target processes.

CONCLUSION

The purpose of this article was to investigate the impact of applying Lean Thinking techniques to eliminate operations that do not bring business value in the picking process in the storage and distribution of fast-moving goods company. The study was carried out using the methodology of business process analysis, which involves the use of specialized computer software that allows the simulation of business processes - iGrafx® Process ™ for Six Sigma, as well as audit and cooperation with employees responsible for a given process at the management and operational level.

The conducted study proved the correctness of applying the Lean Thinking approach in the process of picking goods. The application of the methodology of business process analysis and their simulations additionally confirmed the effects empirically, which was described in the case study phase. It has been shown that under the currently used picking techniques, the most advantageous is to use picking based on the assumptions of the TO BE 3 scenario, i.e. grouping 12 orders within a single picking cycle (picking path). The proposed change in the organization of the picking process will be relatively easy to implement, as it assumes the use of the currently available warehouse infrastructure and no additional financial outlays are needed.

Continuation of the research should also include checking the processes related to the picking process, i.e. the process of goods receipt, the process of grouping orders that trigger the picking process, the process of preparing logistic units for completion and the process of goods release. It is presumed that selecting the most favorable scenario for these processes and then integrating them together will further increase their efficiency and productivity.

Another issue worth considering is carrying out research to these processes in other warehouses of the company or other similar organizations because they are usually based on a similar infrastructure and mode of operation. Simulation-tested and implemented processes with the use of Lean Thinking may constitute a set of good practices to be implemented in a number of companies conducting similar activities.

ALTERNATIVE SOLUTIONS

An alternative solution is full automation of the picking process, e.g., using a sorter. Undoubtedly, this solution is influenced by the possibility of a significant reduction in the use of human resources for the sake of process automation. However, this solution is expensive and time-consuming to implement. Another alternative solution is inventory location management. This proposal is difficult to implement because orders from the ecosystem of the company surveyed are characterized by high variability, which makes it difficult to forecast an adequate distribution of the supplies received in the central warehouse.

CONTRIBUTION OF THE STUDY

The company approved the effects of the work, considering them to be the right way to improve this process efficiency. The company's representatives also emphasized that thanks to the synergy of Process Analysis and the use of Lean Thinking techniques, it was possible to detect bottlenecks in intralogistics processes relatively quickly and indicate a simple and easy way to eliminate them. In addition, the results of the study indicated potential further areas for improvement with this method and led to further discussions on the continuation of the work.

LIMITATIONS AND FUTURE RESEARCH

The study developed a simulation model isolated from:

- variables related to other picking paths (more effective or less),
- warehouse ergonomics (types of racks and their arrangement in the warehouse),
- goods placement,
- the efficiency of warehouse trucks.

The analysis of the above variables would significantly hamper the examination of the effectiveness of consolidation of picking orders, which was the subject of the study. Because of that, the authors deliberately focused on the aspect related to the consolidation of picking orders, because it is easily applicable and does not require large investments related to the adaptation of the warehouse (equipment modernization). The results of the study indicate that the change of the examined parameter (the number of grouped picking orders) improves the efficiency of the examined process and may constitute a starting point for further multi-criteria analyzes.

It should be also remembered that the study was conducted on the example of one employee designated by the company, without analyzing other employees responsible for the same tasks. It is possible that their results will vary slightly because different people may perform certain tasks with different quality.

ACKNOWLEDGMENT

The research was carried out as part of the Applied Doctorate Program of the Ministry of Education and Science carried out in the years 2020-2024 (Agreement No. DWD/4/232020).

The case study described in the article was used to validate the research method, which detailed description will be published as a part doctoral dissertation entitled "The method of using a simulation experiment to transform information and make process decisions in small and medium-sized enterprises" by Filip Nowak, at the Faculty of Engineering Management, Poznan University of Technology.

REFERENCES

Abideen, A., & Mohamad, F. (2020). Improving the performance of a Malaysian pharmaceutical warehouse supply chain by integrating value stream mapping and discrete event simulation. *Journal of Modelling in Management*. doi:10.1108/JM2-07-2019-0159

Altarazi, S. A., & Ammouri, M. M. (2018). Concurrent manual-order-picking warehouse design: A simulation-based design of experiments approach. *International Journal of Production Research*, *56*(23), 7103–7121. doi:10.1080/00207543.2017.1421780

Andjelkovic, A., Radosavljevic, M., & Stošić Panić, D. (2017). Effects of Lean Tools in Achieving Lean Warehousing. *Economic Themes*, *54*(4), 517–534. doi:10.1515/ethemes-2016-0026

Antosz, K., Augustyn, A., & Kaczmarek, M. J. (2021). Application of VSM for Improving the Medical Processes-Case Study. In *IFIP International Conference on Advances in Production Management Systems* (pp. 413-421). Springer. 10.1007/978-3-030-85902-2_44

Antosz, K., Jasiulewicz-Kaczmarek, M., Paśko, Ł., Zhang, C., & Wang, S. (2021). Application of machine learning and rough set theory in lean maintenance decision support system development. *Eksploatacja i Niezawodnosc – Maintenance and Reliability, 23*(4), 695–708, . doi:10.17531/ein.2021.4.12

Azadeh, K., De Koster, R., & Roy, D. (2019). Robotized and Automated Warehouse Systems: Review and Recent Developments. *Transportation Science, 53*(4), 917–945. doi:10.1287/trsc.2018.0873

Baby, B. N. P., & Jebadurai, D. (2018). Implementation of Lean Principles to Improve the Operations of a Sales Warehouse in the Manufacturing Industry. *International Journal of Technology, 9*(1), 46. doi:10.14716/ijtech.v9i1.1161

Baril, C., Gascon, V., Miller, J., & Côté, N. (2015). Use of a discrete-event simulation model during a Lean process: A case study in healthcare. *European Journal of Operational Research, 249*. Advance online publication. doi:10.1016/j.ejor.2015.08.036

Barnett, M. W. (2003). *Modeling & simulation in business process management, 10*.

Bokrantz, J., Skoogh, A., Lämkull, D., Hanna, A., & Perera, T. (2017). Data Quality Problems in Discrete Event Simulation of Manufacturing Operations. W *SIMULATION* (T. 94). doi:10.1177/0037549717742954

Bonabeau, E. (2002). Agent-based modeling: Methods and techniques for simulating human systems. *Proceedings of the National Academy of Sciences of the United States of America, 99*(Supplement 3), 7280–7287. doi:10.1073/pnas.082080899 PMID:12011407

Bozer, Y., & Aldarondo, F. (2018). A simulation-based comparison of two goods-to-person order picking systems in an online retail setting. *International Journal of Production Research, 56*(11), 1–21. doi:10.1080/00207543.2018.1424364

Buonamico, N., Muller, L., & Camargo, M. (2017). A new fuzzy logic-based metric to measure lean warehousing performance. *Supply Chain Forum: An International Journal, 18*(2), 96–111. 10.1080/16258312.2017.1293466

Calzavara, M., Glock, C., Grosse, E., & Sgarbossa, F. (2018). An integrated storage assignment method for manual order picking warehouses considering cost, workload and posture. *International Journal of Production Research, 57*(8), 2392–2408. do i:10.1080/00207543.2018.1518609

Caron, F., Marchet, G., & Perego, A. (2000). Layout design in manual picking systems: A simulation approach. *Integrated Manufacturing Systems, 11*(2), 94–104. doi:10.1108/09576060010313946

Chackelson, C., Errasti, A., Cipres, D., & Lahoz, F. (2013). Evaluating order picking performance trade-offs by configuring main operating strategies in a retail distributor: A Design of Experiments approach. *International Journal of Production Research, 0*(20), 1–13. doi:10.1080/00207543.2013.796421

Damayanti, D. D., Novitasari, N., Setyawan, E. B., & Muttaqin, P. S. (2022). Intelligent Warehouse Picking Improvement Model for e-Logistics Warehouse Using Single Picker Routing Problem and Wave Picking. *Undefined.* https://www.semanticscholar.org/paper/Intelligent-Warehouse-Picking-Improvement-Model-for-Damayanti-Novitasari/3ff2de88c 48b081689f57638162a70613e50eb10

Dehdari, P. (2014). Measuring the Impact of Lean Techniques on Performance Indicators in Logistics Operations. *Measuring the Impact of Lean Techniques on Performance Indicators in Logistics Operations*, 1–191. doi:10.5445/ KSP/1000036424

Demirli, K., Kaf, A., Simsekler, M. C. E., Jayaraman, R., Khan, M., & Tuzcu, E. (2021). Using Lean Techniques and Discrete-Event Simulation for Performance Improvement in an Outpatient Clinic. *International Journal of Lean Six Sigma, ahead-of-print*. doi:10.1108/IJLSS-09-2020-0138

Elbert, R., Knigge, J.-K., & Sarnow, T. (2018). *Transferability of order picking performance and training effects achieved in a virtual reality using head mounted devices. 51*, 686–691. doi:10.1016/j.ifacol.2018.08.398

Ferro, R., Cordeiro, G. A., & Ordoñez, R. E. C. (2018). Dynamic Modeling of Discrete Event Simulation. *Proceedings of the 10th International Conference on Computer Modeling and Simulation - ICCMS 2018*, 248–252. 10.1145/3177457.3177477

Greasley, A., & Owen, C. D. (2018). Modelling People's Behaviour using Discrete-Event Simulation: A Review. *International Journal of Operations & Production Management, 38*(5), 1228–1244. doi:10.1108/IJOPM-10-2016-0604

Grosse, E., Glock, C., Jaber, M., & Neumann, W. (2014). Incorporating human factors in order picking planning models: Framework and research opportunities. *International Journal of Production Research*, *53*(3), 695–717. doi:10.1080/00207543.2014.919424

Grosse, E., Glock, C., & Neumann, W. (2016). Human factors in order picking: A content analysis of the literature. *International Journal of Production Research*, *55*(5), 1260–1276. Advance online publication. doi:10.1080/00207543.2016.1186296

Grosse, E. H., & Glock, C. H. (2015). The effect of worker learning on manual order picking processes. *International Journal of Production Economics*, *170*, 882–890. doi:10.1016/j.ijpe.2014.12.018

Hell, M., & Petrić, L. (2021). System Dynamics Approach to TALC Modeling. *Sustainability*, *13*(9), 4803. doi:10.3390u13094803

Ho, Y.-C., & Lin, J.-W. (2017). Improving order-picking performance by converting a sequential zone-picking line into a zone-picking network. *Computers & Industrial Engineering*, *113*, 241–255. doi:10.1016/j.cie.2017.09.014

Jaghbeer, Y., Hanson, R., & Johansson, M. (2020). Automated order picking systems and the links between design and performance: A systematic literature review. *International Journal of Production Research*, *58*(15), 1–17. doi:10.1080/00207543.2020.1788734

Jahangirian, M., Eldabi, T., Naseer, A., Stergioulas, L. K., & Young, T. (2010). Simulation in manufacturing and business: A review. *European Journal of Operational Research*, *203*(1), 1–13. doi:10.1016/j.ejor.2009.06.004

Jasiulewicz-Kaczmarek, M., & Bartkowiak, T. (2016). Improving the performance of a filling line based on simulation. In IOP Conference Series: Materials Science and Engineering (Vol. 145, No. 4, p. 042024). IOP Publishing. doi:10.1088/1757-899X/145/4/042024

Jasiulewicz-Kaczmarek, M., & Saniuk, A. (2018). How to make maintenance processes more efficient using lean tools. *Advances in Intelligent Systems and Computing* 605, 9 - 20 (AHFE 2017 International Conference on Social and Occupational Ergonomics)

Johansen, A. M. (2010). Monte Carlo Methods. W P. Peterson, E. Baker, & B. McGaw (Eds.), International Encyclopedia of Education (Third Edition) (s. 296–303). Elsevier. doi:10.1016/B978-0-08-044894-7.01543-8

Karnon, J., Stahl, J., Brennan, A., Caro, J. J., Mar, J., & Möller, J. (2012). Modeling using Discrete Event Simulation: A Report of the ISPOR-SMDM Modeling Good Research Practices Task Force-4. *Value in Health, 15*(6), 821–827. doi:10.1016/j.jval.2012.04.013 PMID:22999131

Keshavarz, A., Jaafari, D., Khalaj, M., & Dokouhaki, P. (2021). A Survey of the Literature on Order-Picking Systems by Combining Planning Problems. *Applied Sciences (Basel, Switzerland), 11*(22), 10641. doi:10.3390/app112210641

Knigge, J.-K. (2021). *Theoretical Background: The use of Virtual Reality Head-Mounted Devices for Planning and Training in the Context of Manual Order Picking. W J.-K. Knigge (Red.), Virtual Reality in Manual Order Picking: Using Head-Mounted Devices for Planning and Training*. Springer Fachmedien., doi:10.1007/978-3-658-34704-8

Levy, G. (2008). *Computational finance using C and C*. Academic Press.

Loske, D., & Klumpp, M. (2020). Smart and efficient: Learning curves in manual and human-robot order picking systems. *IFAC-PapersOnLine, 53*(2), 10255–10260. doi:10.1016/j.ifacol.2020.12.2757

Macal, C. M., & North, M. J. (2010). Tutorial on agent-based modelling and simulation. *Journal of Simulation, 4*(3), 151–162. doi:10.1057/jos.2010.3

Masae, M., Glock, C., & Vichitkunakorn, P. (2021). A Method for Efficiently Routing Order Pickers in the Leaf Warehouse. *International Journal of Production Economics, 234*, 108069. doi:10.1016/j.ijpe.2021.108069

Melton, T. (2005). The Benefits of Lean Manufacturing: What Lean Thinking has to Offer the Process Industries. *Chemical Engineering Research & Design, 83*(6), 662–673. doi:10.1205/cherd.04351

Pereira, M., Sousa, J. M. C., Pinto Ferreira, L., & Sá, J. (2019). Localization System for Optimization of Picking in a Manual Warehouse. *Procedia Manufacturing, 38*, 1220–1227. doi:10.1016/j.promfg.2020.01.213

Petersen, C., & Aase, G. (2004). A comparison of picking, storage, and routing policies in manual order picking. *International Journal of Production Economics, 92*(1), 11–19. doi:10.1016/j.ijpe.2003.09.006

Pipatprapa, A. (2019). QR Code on Mobile Platform for Improving Order Picking Process of Lean Factory Warehouse. *International Journal of Innovation, Management and Technology, 10*(1), 56–60. doi:10.18178/ijimt.2019.10.1.836

Qiao, D., & Wang, Y. (2021). A review of the application of discrete event simulation in manufacturing. *Journal of Physics: Conference Series, 1802*(2), 022066. doi:10.1088/1742-6596/1802/2/022066

Raghuram, P., & Arjunan, M. (2021). Design framework for a lean warehouse – a case study-based approach. *International Journal of Productivity and Performance Management, ahead-of-print*. doi:10.1108/IJPPM-12-2020-0668

Ragin-Skorecka, K., & Nowak, F. (2017). Process analysis as a tool for rationalization of the organization. *Studia i Prace WNEiZ, 48*, 77–88. doi:10.18276ip.2017.48/2-07

Rodič, B. (2017). Industry 4.0 and the New Simulation Modelling Paradigm. *Organizacija, 50*(3), 193–207. Advance online publication. doi:10.1515/orga-2017-0017

Ruan, K. (2019). *Cyber Risk Measurement in the Hyperconnected World. W K. Ruan (Red.), Digital Asset Valuation and Cyber Risk Measurement*. Academic Press., doi:10.1016/B978-0-12-812158-0.00004-1

Santos, C., Montevechi, J. A. B., Queiroz, J., Miranda, R., & Fabiano, L. (2021). Decision support in productive processes through DES and ABS in the Digital Twin era: A systematic literature review. *International Journal of Production Research*, •••, 1–20. doi:10.1080/00207543.2021.1898691

Shou, W., Wang, J., & Wu, P. (2021). The application of simulation in lean production research: A critical review and future directions. *Engineering, Construction and Architectural Management, ahead-of-print*. doi:10.1108/ECAM-10-2020-0853

Srisuk, K., & Tippayawong, K. Y. (2020). Improvement of raw material picking process in sewing machine factory using lean techniques. *Management and Production Engineering Review, 11*(1). Advance online publication. doi:10.24425/mper.2020.132946

Tommelein, I. D. (1997). *Discrete-Event Simulation of Lean Construction Processes*. 121–136. https://www.iglc.net/papers/details/25

van Gils, T., Ramaekers, K., Braekers, K., Depaire, B., & Caris, A. (2018). Increasing order picking efficiency by integrating storage, batching, zone picking, and routing policy decisions. *International Journal of Production Economics, 197*, 243–261. doi:10.1016/j.ijpe.2017.11.021

van Gils, T., Ramaekers, K., Caris, A., & Cools, M. (2017). The use of time series forecasting in zone order picking systems to predict order pickers' workload. *International Journal of Production Research, 55*(21), 6380–6393. doi:10.1080/00207543.2016.1216659

van Gils, T., Ramaekers, K., Caris, A., & de Koster, R. B. M. (2018). Designing efficient order picking systems by combining planning problems: State-of-the-art classification and review. *European Journal of Operational Research, 267*(1), 1–15. doi:10.1016/j.ejor.2017.09.002

Wang, Z., Sheu, J.-B., Teo, C., & Xue, G. (2021). Robot Scheduling for Mobile-Rack Warehouses: Human-Robot Coordinated Order Picking Systems. *Production and Operations Management*. Advance online publication. doi:10.1111/poms.13406

Winkelhaus, S., & Grosse, E. (2020). Logistics 4.0: A systematic review towards a new logistics system. *International Journal of Production Research, 58*(1), 18–43. doi:10.1080/00207543.2019.1612964

Zhang, X. (2018). Application of discrete event simulation in health care: A systematic review. *BMC Health Services Research, 18*(1), 687. doi:10.118612913-018-3456-4 PMID:30180848

Żywicki, K., & Buń, P. (2021). Process of Materials Picking Using Augmented Reality. *IEEE Access: Practical Innovations, Open Solutions, 9*, 102966–102974. doi:10.1109/ACCESS.2021.3096915

Chapter 5
From Resilience to Resurgence:
COVID-19 and the Automobile Industry

Vanshika Kakkar
UPES University, India

Anurag Singh
https://orcid.org/0000-0002-9568-3013
UPES University, India

ABSTRACT

This study throws light on new or different factors of the disputable view, which has presumed that, at any point in future, the global automobile industry can reach a maturity level and would naturally resettle in the key developing countries where the auto market is expected to grow fast-paced and wages are significantly bottommost. The authors analysed that the gateway facing by a developing country trying to create domestic automobile industry which has arisen due to recent developments: a wave faced due to technological and structural innovation, and pressure caused by pandemic. These results suggest that the automobile industry has been affected during the pandemic but expected to see effective growth in future. An abnormal situation in the pandemic every day signifies the decline in the auto market, and the deep impact it had on the auto sector market and its returns.

DOI: 10.4018/978-1-6684-5606-4.ch005

INTRODUCTION

Companies have been obliged to use current technologies to improve smart manufacturing as a result of growing market competition and fast changes in demand. Industry 4.0 refers to the current trend in industrial technology that promotes automation and data connection across systems. It is the fourth industrial revolution (also known as Industry 4.0), and it broadens the reach of advanced digital technologies to embrace cyber-physical systems (CPS), the internet of things (IoT), and cloud computing, among other things. Industry 4.0 need to adopt communication, technology, infrastructure, and information. Intelligent machines should be introduced in 'smart factories' with an automated process. Advanced production is required in an optimized way which should avoid time taking process and standstills. Machines need to be self-organized to lead to the decentralization of production. Individualization of production is needed to carry the requests of customers instantly.

The automotive industry is required digital technology which would not only reduce the burden of work but also have a structure of work (Marie-Claude et. al., 2000). Scholars have reported that unemployment will increase, and technology eliminates tens of millions of jobs in the manufacturing sectors. Increasing globalization, weak trade unions, disaggregation has led to a decline in wages, inadequate working conditions, displacement of workers is making the industry slow-paced in the present scenario all these requirements can be in pretty conditions by technological and infrastructure advancements (William T. Neese et. al., 2018).

The focus is required for two major reasons firstly, it employs non-agricultural industries, and second, the auto industry contributes to GDP (Gross Domestic Product) at a large scale of about 7.1% and 37 million people are employed directly or indirectly with the sector. The growth of labour productivity in India was 2.63% in 2019 as compared to China 9.8% per year. The changes in the automobile industry need to be brought by applying in the real world, not by discussions (Balon, V., Sharma, A. K., & Barua, M. K., 2016). The industry slummed 18.71% low from 22.45 lacs units to 18.25 lacs units and approx. 2.75 lacs jobs trimmed in the sector. The industry saw the steepest fall in 19 years. Due to such a crisis, the automotive industry requires pulling up their socks to get back on the tracks and requires to gain strategic advantage to have profits in future (Charan, P., Shankar, R., Baisya, R.K., 2009; Matsunaga, F., 2022). We all know the sweet truth that "None of us can change our yesterday but can shape a bright future of automobile industry in India." Looking at the problem identified we have established following objectives of the study*: a) To evaluate the challenges that auto industry are facing due to pandemic, b) To study the government policies and its endeavours for automobile industry, c)*

To assess the challenges raised by the foreign counterpart especially China, d) To give suggestions if required

LITERATURE REVIEW

This section provides a brief review of automobile industry literature during the Covid-19 pandemic. We find sufficient literature covering the automobile industry performance during the uncertain event. The industry's performance relies on various factors such as production, manufacturing, operational and marketing. The industry is facing a lot of constraint that affects the functions of an organization (Polonsky, et al., 2001). Market, financial, learning and reinvestment execution are some of the major production outcomes of the industry. (Morgan, 2012).

Countries like India, Indonesia, Malaysia, Philippines, Thailand, and Vietnam have been emerging in industrial and manufacturing areas in recent years. Manufacturers in these countries are facing lot of pressure to produce the products in an eco-friendly supportable approach, especially for those who are competing in the global areas and have to standby along with foreign eco-friendly standards and regulations. Consumers have become the matter of concern regarding the manufacturer's eco-friendly behaviour. (Science in environmental policy, 2013).

Sustainability occurs due to twofold constraint, i.e. external and internal. External constraints comprise of satisfying customer's demands, responding to competitor sustainability measures, supplier's appeal to alter the inputs conversely the internal constraints are cost and philosophy (Polonsky, 2001). The major concern lies in sustainable development mainly for automobile sector, which is known for carbon emissions and pollution (Gan, 2003). Mc Cann-Erickson, (2007) said that for strategic economic-development also means sharing between rich as well as poor and safeguarding the global issues while not putting at risk the necessities of future generation (Jones, Clarke-Hill, Comfort, & Hillier, 2008).

It is important to find out practical approaches inside the companies themselves, including its supply chains as done by Volkswagen (Koplin, 2007). The firms in auto sector has started adopting the green initiatives to reduce the constraints for brand image to maintain sustainability like management of the supply chain, advertisement, ecolabeling. (Smith, 2010). In the auto sector many firms started producing alternative fuel vehicles and few manufacturers are trying to adopt this segment to expand their business operations and adopt sustainability (Sierzchula, et al., 2012). China may become the world's largest CO2 emitter by id 21st century as from 1980 to 1997 total carbon emissions in China is increased from 1.5 to 3.6 billion tons which means 1.4 times approx. To improve its performance in the eco market, China is trying to adopt technological innovation to reduce the CO2 footprints

(Gan, 2003). According to Automotive Component Manufacturer Association, the passenger vehicles touched 3.23 million units in 2012-2013 and is expected to reach 11.7 million units by FY30 (Auto component industry in India, 2013). In India, the company India oil is focusing on CNG, LPG, ethanol blended petrol, biodiesel and Hydrogen Energy (Mishra & Sharma, 2010).

With the help of Japanese Government, Toyota is trying to capture market with the help of a program where consumers will purchase transport without owing a car as Toyota is trying to build a green image of themselves, for example, changing the engines in hybrid combustion electric (Polonsky, et al., 2001). Volkswagen, Ford, Nissan, Hyundai are trying to cope up in the similar direction in eco-friendly way. The demand for green vehicles is increasing and providing safeguard to the nature and managing with the regulations (Inter-brand, 2013). A California-based company known as electric Tesla Roadster was sold immediately in 2008. The firms are trying to design themselves in terms of product, strategy, overall visible activities, marketing and communication tactics including the gasoline products (Sing, Vrontis & Thrassou, 2011). Nissan Motors reported that Nissan leaf if first 100% electric along with no gas and tailpipe vehicle. It has a technology attached to it called inverter which works like pump & pumps and the electricity is stored in the battery which will power the vehicle. The consumers response towards it was overwhelming and a good number of bookings has already been made more than everyone's expectations (Xia & Tang, 2011).

It has been noticed that consumer awareness, lack of government intervention is the barrier which is the cause of lacking behind of Green Supply Chain Management (GSCM) in Indian automobile industry (Luthra et al., 2011). The findings confirmed that the effects are positive of eco-information which resulted in increase of green consumer behaviour (Sriwardena, Hunt, Teisl, & Noblet, 2012). The marketing strategy positively affecting the supply chain, marketing performance which is also affecting the financial performance of the firms (Jr. Green, Whitten, & Inman, 2012). Many motorcycle firms in Vietnam has started implementing innovation of the product to improve its organization's performance (Lin, et al., 2013). The Indian government is putting efforts to promote green market and eco-friendliness by promoting the banning of plastic material, helping the automotive industry to develop greener vehicles by supporting the electric vehicles (EVs) by stepping into greener cars (Shrikanth & Raju, 2012). The auto market is focusing on new consumers, new car consumers is more responsible towards to social pressure (Dijik & Yarime, 2010). Due to financial instability the car manufacturers moved to the small car manufacturing to reduce cost and increasing sales (KPMG, 2008). The automobile sector is facing pressure regarding environment, law, society, firm performance (Penna & Geel, 2012). Fuel efficiency and environment related products are considered most significant consumer buying issues (KPMG, 2010).

Few firms are investing largely in R & D like Honda, Toyota, GM, Ford, Daimler Chrysler, Suzuki, Hyundai, Tata, etc. Pradeepta K. Sarangi (2014) said that despite ups and downs automobile sector showed positive growth during FY14 in all the segments. Vandana Singh (2017) said that automobile industry has an effective multiplier effect and is capable to drive a good economic growth. A though aroused for a sound transportation system by which industry can be linked and can play a vital role in nation's fast economic and industrial growth. This study aims at making the approachable changes turning to physical changes. The forecast done in the study should clarify the projected trends on our current understanding. They are not inescapable and may help the industry players by discussing the possible future traits. The literature review indicates the methodological gap in accessing the impacts of the pandemic on automobile industry. We find that (Nayak, J., Mishra, M., Naik, B., Swapnarekha, H., Cengiz, K., & Shanmuganathan, V. (2021)) have conducted an event study to examine how the pandemic impacted the automobile industry.

Many automobile firms started working on green marketing to maintain ecological balance keeping in mind the consumer behaviour as the major concern while prioritizing the environment when purchasing any product. Green marketing contributes on huge basis to the firm's performance and also sustainability (Chan, et al., 2012).

METHODOLOGY

This research aims at determining how the technological opportunities leading to the rise in electric vehicles, connectivity and electrified power stations can influence the Indian consumer behaviors in the Indian automobile market. The Covid-19 pandemic affected the automobile sector and demand for electric automobiles, two-wheelers and three-wheelers suffered as a result of the disruption. However, as the sale of EVs are picking up, the market is expected to register positive growth during the forecasted period.

Due to automation, it is forecasted that about 6, 40,000 jobs will be lost. In nearest future, machine and man-led will not be there, instead, leadership, decisions and execution will be robots and humans who will suit them best to deliver the desired outcome. The automobile Industry needs to participate in ecosystems such as electrification and infrastructure. A global experience will be required for India to grab the opportunity and focusing in threats from the present for identifying new business model with advanced technological features.

Companies have been obliged to use current technologies to improve smart manufacturing as a result of growing market competition and fast changes in demand. The automobile industry requires digital technology which would not only reduce the burden of work but also have a structure of work.

The government of India has undertaken multiple initiatives to promote the manufacturing and adoption of electric vehicles in India:

- The Indian government has provided tax exemptions and subsidies to the EV manufacturers and consumers.
- The Ministry of Power issued a clarification starting that no license is required to operate the EV charging stations in India.
- The Ministry of Road and transport and Highways also announced that all battery-operated, ethanol-powered and methanol-powered transport vehicles would be exempted from the requirement of permits.

QUANTITATIVE ANALYSIS AND INTERPRETATION

In 2020 and 2021 the crisis rose globally, and the production level felt down sharply from about 15.4% because of lockdowns and the restrictions imposed by the government while resulted in sharp decline in the economy of the country as well. Passenger cars experienced a lot of downfalls from about 16.9% to 11.6% than commercial vehicles whereas the electric vehicles rose by 39% in FY20 to 3.2 units which made stock to reach a level up to 11.3 million units. The statistics was revealed from International Organization of motor vehicles manufacturers which showed decline in Latin America by 24.8% and North America by 24% whereas commercial vehicles sales drop down by 8.7% and passenger vehicle sales dropped by 15.9% which was 20% more than 2019. Exports in auto vehicle showed a slowdown due to restrictions imposed by pandemic and the exports came to a standstill in some of the states like Latin America, Eastern Europe, Middle East and the rest of the region saw a downfall of 40% to 50%. Despite the backdrop of overall auto market global rise in EV market was seen in Germany by 18%, Norway by 75%, Sweden by 32%, Netherlands by 25% and Denmark by 16%.

Rise of EVS Globally

EVs are in its early stage so the growth is potentially rising but not yet at top speed. Since 2015 the EVs has shown increased by 50% per year. If similar growth happens EVs would grow more up to 50% of all light-duty vehicles by 2026 and it is expected to be 60% to 75% EVs by 2030 followed by 2050. EV sales market share grew by 1% in 2010 and by 54% by 2020. It reached its tripling point and approached price parity with traditional vehicles whereas other countries need to employ few incentives to reach this tripling point and then they could reach a good amount of EV sales even more than Norway. By 2035 EVs are expected to reach 100% sales. European

Union said that they will likely to increase about 4 million battery manufacturing jobs by 2025 and American jobs plan is to increase 800,000 EV manufacturing jobs by 2025. India's plan to increase manufacturing jobs by 5.8 million jobs in another five years. EVs has consistently performed up to the market in the past but the main question arises that will the EV can continue to fight with the odds and make the 2025 to 2035 estimated figures a reality (see Table 1 and Figure 1).

Table 1. Global vehicle market size (2021-2028)

DETAILS	COVERAGE
Estimated Period	**2021 To 2028**
Estimated Period From 2020 To 2028 CARG	**24.3%**
2028 Forecasting	**USD 1,318.22 Billion**
Base Year Considered	**2020**

Source: Author's Compilation

Figure 1. Global expected sales of EV
Source: IEA (2021), Electric Vehicles, IEA, Paris https://www.iea.org/reports/electric-vehicles

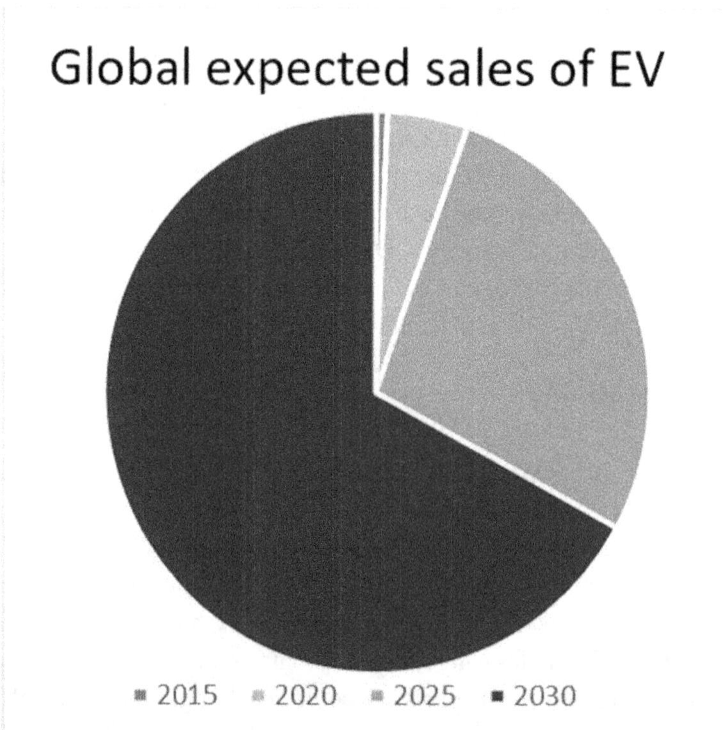

Interpretation: In the above graph global sales of electric vehicles in 201 was 0.60% (approx.), in 2020 it reached to 4.3% (approx.), in 2025 it is expected of about 25.0% and till 2030 it is estimated it will reach by 60.9%(approx.). Electric cars sales reached up to 3 million by 2020 and which is more than 40% that in 2019 but in 2020 the overall car sales went down by 16% due to pandemic. By 2030 followed till 2050 it is expected to reach of about 300 million car sales which means approx. 60% of EVs as compared to 4.6% in 2020

Automobile Sector and GDP

Economists generally agree that economy of a country will grow and develop by four factors: HR, capital, natural resources and technology which will also contribute to the GDP of the country. A skilled and well-trained manpower directly invest in the welfare of the economy whereas the unskilled labour may also contribute on an economy but may lead to high employment. Investment in roadways, equipment, machinery and factories will reduce cost efficiency and contribute to the GDP and will lead to higher productivity which will give maximum output. Natural resources like oil or mineral deposits, skilled labour force and capital will contribute to the GDP. Scientists may lead to more discoveries and managers may find the way to apply to the innovation production technique. Better education for workers will lead to economic output and better living environment. Economists may count a fourth or fifth factor for human welfare or entrepreneurial activity (see Table 2 and Figure 2).

Interpretation: The above graph interprets the list of the countries which contributes by Gross Domestic Product (GDP) in all the three sectors (industrial, agricultural and service). China contributes the highest in the GDP in industrial sector followed by Japan and European Union and it is expected that China and Europe will be the leading producers who will contribute in the GDP though industrial sector.

Table 2. GDP Of selected countries sector wise (In %) for the year 2018

Country	GDP(US$MM)	Agriculture	Industrial	Service
China	23,210,000	7.90	40.5	51.6
European Union	20,850,111	1.60	25.1	70.9
India	9,474,000	15.40	23.00	61.5
Japan	5,443,000	1.10	30.1	68.7
U. S	19,490,000	0.90	19.1	80.0
World	127,800,000	6.40	30	63.6

Data Source: World Development Indicators, World Bank, 2018

Figure 2. The above graph interprets the list of the countries which contributes by Gross Domestic Product (GDP) in all the three sectors (industrial, agricultural and service).
Source: Author's compilation

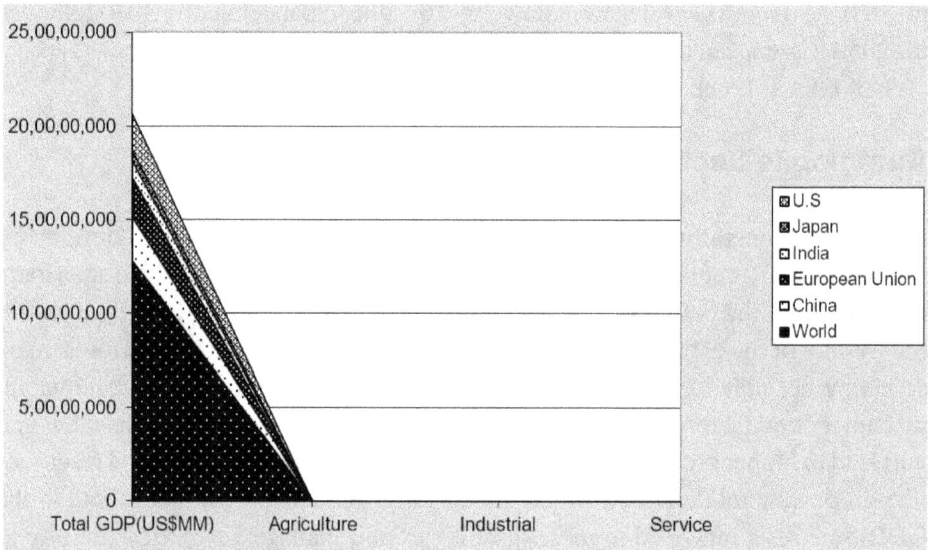

HISTORY OF AUTOMOBILE INDUSTRY IN INDIA

Specifically, the automobile sector would be divided into the following categories: automobiles and other four-wheeled vehicles (CARS), light commercial vehicles (LCV), medium and heavy commercial vehicles (HCV) and heavy commercial vehicles (HCV). It had been a relatively long time since the automobile industry in India had operated under the conditions of a 'protected market,' meaning that it had been shielded from both internal and external competition. It was not possible to enter the market or diversify (Indian Brand Equity Foundation, 2008). There were also restrictions on capacity expansion, overseas cooperation, and the importation of machinery and components. From the early 1980s to the present, the number of enterprises in various categories (sectors) of this industry was quite limited. Even in certain cases (for example, CARS), there were only one or two companies operating until the early 1980s (Aggarwal, R.N., 1988).

In the case of Heavy Commercial Vehicles (HCV), there was no change in the number of vehicles produced, with the chassis being manufactured by the same four companies. However, in the case of the ancillary sector, the production structure has undergone a significant transformation as a result of the government's policy of restricting the importation of specific components and encouraging the use of domestically produced alternatives.

Because of the presence of such a big oligopolistic structure, the majority of the enterprises were able to achieve high profit margins, rapid growth rates, and a significant market share. There was little incentive to upgrade technology at the time. As a result, there were no new products or new models released onto the market. The process of indigenisation and their efforts to adapt their products to the local conditions have, nevertheless, resulted in significant technological learning for some enterprises (particularly TELCO and BAJAJ) as part of their efforts to adapt their products to the local requirements.

Deregulation of the licencing framework, broad-banding, capacity re-endorsement, and liberalisation of controls and restrictions on clearances for foreign collaborations and the import of capital goods and components were among the significant changes in industrial policy introduced in India during the mid-1980s, according to the International Labour Organization. Furthermore, the governments' stance toward foreign direct investment has shifted significantly from a distrustful policy to a more supportive approach, which is a huge improvement. When Japan collaborated with Western auto manufacturers to upgrade and introduce various new models of automobiles starting in the mid-eighties, the result was a transformation of the structure that existed in the automobile industry (Shinde, G.P. and Dubey, M. 2011). This transformation was facilitated by deregulation and liberalisation during the mid-eighties.

The manufacture of automobiles in India increased significantly over this time period However, while the overall number of motor vehicles produced climbed from 126000 in 1980–1981 to 350 000 in 1989–1990, the car sector alone saw a growth from 47000 to 224 000 during the same time. The output of commercial vehicles (which includes HCVs and LCVs) grew as well, rising from 79000 units in 1980–1981 to 125 000 units in 1989–1990. However, within the commercial vehicle category, it is the light commercial vehicle (LCV) sector that has seen production surge by more than 100% during the same period. The HCV sector had a gain as well, though it was far less than both the LCV and the Car sectors combined.

The entry of new enterprises, the diversification of production, and the introduction of new products were all witnessed in this industry. The majority of the time, imported technology was used to facilitate entry and diversification. The entry of enterprises with overseas partnership compelled the existing firms to upgrade their technological capabilities to compete. The industry imagined a fiercely competitive environment in which the technology of the product being advertised was at the forefront. There were also various exits available.

Following deregulation, a study of the competitiveness of firms in the Indian motor vehicle industry (in terms of market shares—defined by the number of vehicles sold by firms in different categories) reveals a significant shift in the relative position of old and pioneering firms since deregulation. This is especially true in the case of CARS and light commercial vehicles (LCV) (Narayanan, K., 1998). The entry of enterprises using Japanese technology into these two categories has had a significant impact on the relative positions of all of the firms in the industry. While most of the old corporations were scrambling to keep their market shares from plummeting, the new ones, equipped with the most up-to-date technology, were attempting to seize control of the market. Within this, the Car sector appears to have seen a significant transformation in favour of the newly established firm, Maruti. The majority of new entrants in the light commercial vehicle (LCV) sector have successfully established themselves on the market, thanks to Japanese partnership. However, an Indian company, TELCO (the market leader in high-capacity vehicles), which joined this industry between 1984 and 1985, had captured 30 percent of the market by 1990. TELCO's new product is the culmination of its trajectory development and arm's-length acquisitions of technologies for components and components and components and parts. As a result, legislative changes implemented in the mid-1980s had a significant impact on the behaviour of enterprises in terms of technological advancement, modernization, and market structure.

DECLINE IN THE INDUSTRY BECAUSE OF PANDEMIC

Due to the increasing number of Covid-19 cases as a result of the pandemic and sporadic lockdowns, the automobile industry is experiencing setbacks and obstacles on its way to recovery, rather than depression (Rakshit, B, Basistha, D, 2020). Due to the pandemic, Maruti faced its first quarterly loss in 17 years. Hyundai Motor Limited also lost 2% year over year and 23% overall as a result of the pandemic's spread. Hero Motor Corp Ltd had a 3.9 percent decline in share price. Toyota suffered a 24.6 percent decline and numerous other setbacks. As stated previously, India's annual production will expand from 3 million to 4 million in seven years. To do this, we need to eradicate pandemics so that labour may work properly and effectively (Yonatan Strauch, Angela Carter and Thomas Homer-Dixon, 2020). It is yet uncertain whether or not there will be a rise in automotive sales during the Christmas season, since everything is contingent on the economy's recovery, consumer sentiment, and the evolution of the Covid-19.

If the automobile industry's output level is reduced in the future, the upcoming generation will be adversely impacted, as they will be living in a mobilised and fast-paced world, which indicates a technologically and industrialised environment. The automobile sector in India faces a difficult path ahead. According to CRISIL Research, India may face a double decrease as a result of this lockdown. According to the automobile research, passenger vehicles are predicted to fall by 24 to 26 percent, while two-wheeler vehicles are expected to decline by 21 to 23 percent. Commercial vehicle sales are predicted to fall by 26 to 28 percent. Domestic car sales are 45 percent lower than in March 2019, 90 percent lower across all vehicle classes in 2020, and 10-15 percent lower in 2021 for Passenger Vehicles (PVs), Commercial Vehicles (CVs), Two-wheeler (2W), and Three-wheeler (3Ws).

IMPACT OF PANDEMIC ON AUTOMOBILE INDUSTRY

The pandemic has put the humankind and globalization into danger. Due to this ongoing pandemic the government has put lockdown during 2020. Although after the lockdown the cases decreased but it affected the valuable chains of a country's most important industries which majorly impacted the automobile sector along with its key manufacturers either by following the orders passed by the government or with least staff due to number Covid-19 cases. Since past 12-18 months, already automobile sector is lacking behind due to architectural change like goods and services tax, load of a vehicle applied through wheels at both ends, changed to division of movability, cash-flow's critical point facing since lockdown began i.e; 24 March 2020. The sector was striving hard in terms of (Research and Development) R & D to mobilise resources as well as alternate fuels. Rajmohan (2020) conducted a study in which he explained how the stock market is particularly affecting automobile sector. The condition is moving fast-paced which affected in various fields like man force, supply chain, finance and cash-flow, tax and trade policies and strategies made by the automobile sectors. If the pandemic widens due to spreading of new variants, then a large employee may get sick which can directly cause loss in the sector.

POST-COVID-19 SITUATION OF AUTOMOBILE INDUSTRY

The pandemic has created a 'Do or Die' situation in which individuals are forced to labour for survival, and as Vivek Murthy[1], former US surgeon-general, has warned, the pandemic will not stop until 2022 or later. The CRISIL research indicates that, despite the epidemic, the Indian automobile sector is predicted to rise by 2022. Mr Sharma stated that by 2022, Electric Vehicles (EVs) will witness positive development, particularly in the two-wheeler segment. For instance, Operational Level Agreement (Ola) is looking forward for manufacturing electric vehicles.

By 2021, India would be the third largest market for passenger vehicles in the world. Can we, however, foresee that this will be possible in the future, given the pandemic? After analysing the Share and Trends Analysis Report, we can conclude that the Covid-19. Pandemic has prompted consumers to invest in alternate modes of transportation, with demand forecast to reach 6,920,991 units by 2027 and a Compound Annual Growth Rate (CARG) of 11.3 percent between 2020 and 2027. Certain companies are experimenting with alternative modes of vehicle sales, such as e-commerce websites, which will benefit OEMs in expanding their distribution networks and reducing infrastructure and labour costs. Tata Motors' small commercial vehicle sales have increased by 25% as the company has shifted its focus to e-commerce. As outlined in 'The Automobile Mission Plan,' the car industry's contribution will be enhanced by 12% between 2016 and 2026. The government is optimistic about the automobile industry and has set the following goals for 2030: to propel the auto industry toward becoming a tool for the 'MAKE IN INDIA' programme, to make the auto industry a significant contributor to the 'SKILL INDIA' programme, to increase the automobile industry's net exports, and to promote comprehensive and stable policy distribution.

INITIATIVES ENDEAVOURS FOR FUTURE

Infrastructure development and new fuel regulations will all contribute to India becoming a "Skill India." When India is compared to the rest of the globe, it will rank third by 2026 in engineering, manufacturing, and automobile exports. India's economy is expanding at a rate of more than 12% of GDP and has created 65 million jobs. If the automobile industry keeps to its stated objectives and goals, it has the ability to triple its revenue to $300 billion and continue to grow (Haugh, D., A. Mourougane and O. Chatal, 2010). The automotive industry is predicted to generate $300 billion in revenue and employ 65 million people by 2026. New Delhi: Department of Heavy Industries future (see Figure 3).

According to figure 1, between 2035 and 2040, electric vehicles will take up ranging from 60 to 100% of the market. Not only will the model 3 revolutionise the car industry and be a game changer, but it will also serve as a future game changer goods.

The government will not relinquish its goal of electrifying every automobile on the road. For the next decade, EVs will maintain a strong position in the premium and luxury mass categories. By the middle of 2020, when EVs will face significant competition from internal combustion engine (ICE) vehicles, robust competition is predicted. According to a senior analyst at Lux Research, while BEVs are currently more expensive and cumbersome to operate than gasoline-powered vehicles, the gap will soon decrease. Prices have declined in lockstep with the basic manufacturer's suggested retail price of a typical vehicle, which has decreased from $42,189 to $33,901. As a result, consumers profit from owning an electric vehicle. It's worth mentioning that the key focus should be on the battery supply chain, which must maintain flexibility and commitment; failing to do so may result in a lack of Battery Electric Vehicle (BEV) production plans. While larger OEMs should prioritise cost-effective BEV development, smaller Original, Equipment, manufacturer (OEMs) should prioritise flexibility in order to avoid sluggishness.

Electric vehicles are composed of less than 5% of total sales and the research firm has reaffirmed that despite pandemic, EVs are expected to grow more than half of all sales between 2035 to 2040 but pre- Covid-19 it is expected that EVs will face short-term setbacks.

Figure 3. Inflection points
Source: Murray, C. (2016, March). Retrieved from designnews.com

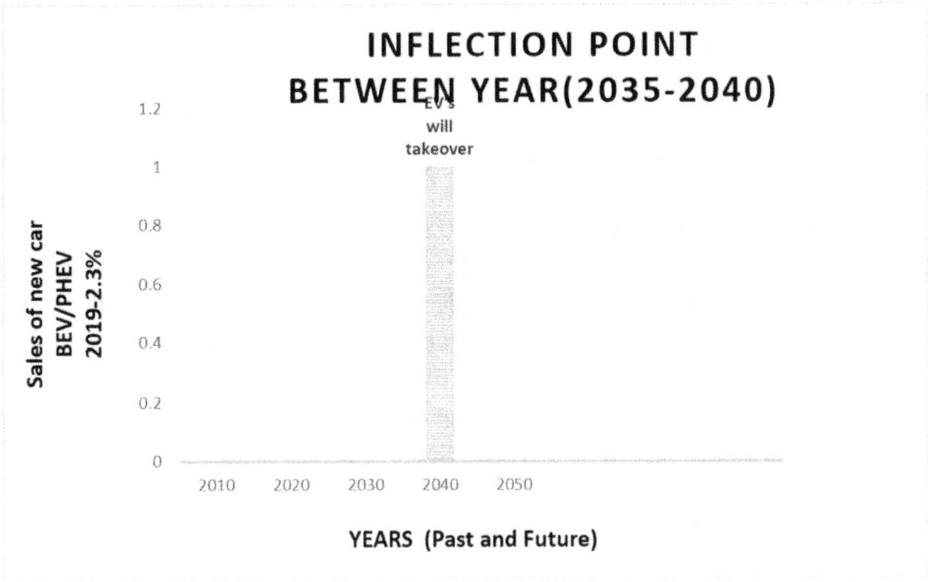

ROLE OF MASS PRODUCTION FOR TARGET SALES

The 2020 sales figures demonstrate that two-wheelers continue to dominate EV sales in India. We anticipate a future innovation that catapults it to mass market adoption. In this respect, it is anticipated that following lockdown, there would be a great increase and growth in demand for E2W in the low-speed market, due to its ease of use and low maintenance. Lockdown is a significant contributor to reduced pollution, and in order to continue this progress, there is a significant concentration of people toward EVs, which may result in increased demand in the low-speed category, resulting in great growth toward mass-market adoption in India (Chowdhury, S. G., and Chatterjee, S., 2020). Additionally, it is anticipated that post- Covid-19 will raise severe concerns about individuals opting for two-wheelers over crowded public transportation. Governments are likely to show concern in the future and mandate the use of EVs in industries such as e-commerce and couriers in order to make India a pollution-free country. They would reallocate monies already authorised under FAME 2 to support low-speed Electric two-wheeler (E2Ws) that meet the basic needs of the common man.

IMPOSED TAXES AND GDP

India's quarterly GDP growth got deflated by 23.9% in the month of April-June as compared to the previous year. In this quarter it is seen, growth wore out by 21.9%. If we look at the graph it has been seen like a *'V'* shape which indirectly means going on and then rising sharply. Economists saw there was $40 billion in new spending. Oxford Economics researchers say that by 2025, 'there will be long-term economic damage due to pandemic which will be double than the rising markets as compared to wealthy countries. A 2019 study showed a serious threat towards coastal cities like Mumbai, Chennai, and Kolkata by 2050. India's manufacturing value shows that there is a decline in GDP rate by 13.6% which is lowest than 1968. A report of Mc Kinsey examines that despite pandemic it is expected that households of Delhi will have a standard living and GDP per capita at purchasing power parity will be as that of Russia by 2025.

The vehicle market is narrowed because of the imposition of heavy taxes. Once the market expands, the automobile industry will also expand. According to JLR India, the Gross and Service Tax (GST) should deflate from 28% to 18% which will not only help in the recovery of the auto industry but also spur employment in the country. Volumes of automobiles will like to rise in future if GST imposition will be decreased which in turn lead to business stability and growth. It is noticed by JLR if the government will be imposed high GST on automobiles it will not only allow the market to grow but also restricts the hurdles in bringing more products in future. In the present scenario, luxury cars in India grab attention from the top GST slab of 28%, 20% cess on sedans and 22% on Sport Utility Vehicle (SUVs). Mr Suri exclaimed that demand for cars is high it will rise more if the taxation comes to a mark in future.

CRISIS THAT CAN BE FACED DUE TO DOWNWARD SLOPE

In April-June, India's quarterly GDP growth was deflated by 23.9 percent compared to the previous year. As can be seen, growth slowed to a 21.9 percent clip in this quarter (Manda, Vijaya Kittu and Beatrice, Betsy Babu, 2020). If we look at the graph, it resembles a 'V' form, which implies continuing and then abruptly rising. Economists estimated that new spending would total $40 billion. According to Oxford Economics experts, by 2025, 'long-term economic harm caused by pandemics will be double that caused by increasing markets in comparison to wealthy countries. According to a 2019 study, coastal cities such as Mumbai, Chennai, and Kolkata face a major threat by 2050. India's manufacturing value indicates a 13.6 percent fall in GDP, the slowest pace since 1968. According to a Mc Kinsey assessment, despite the pandemic, households in Delhi are predicted to enjoy a quality of living and GDP per capita at purchasing power parity equal to that of Russia by 2025.

Figure 4. Automobile Industry (Profit and peak point)
Source: Chen, J. (2020, May). Retrieved from Investopedia.

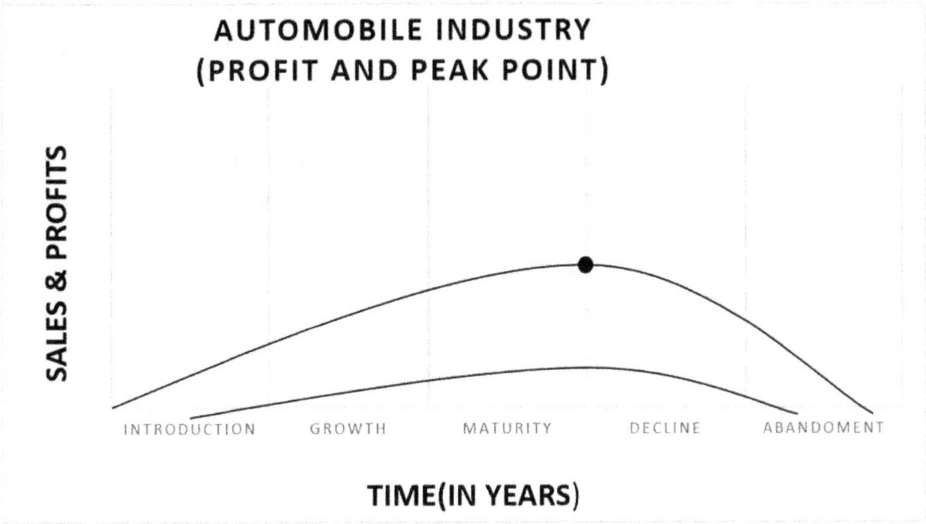

The car market has been more constrained as a result of the introduction of high taxes. When the market expands, so does the vehicle industry. According to JLR India, the GST should be reduced from 28 to 18 percent, which will aid in the revival of the auto industry while also stimulating employment in the country. Automobile sales will likely increase in the future if the GST is reduced, resulting in business stability and growth. JLR takes note of this. If the government imposes a high GST on autos, it not only allows the market to expand, but also reduces the barriers to introducing new products in the future. Luxury automobiles in India currently attract attention due to the top GST slab of 28 percent, a 20 percent cess on sedans, and a 22 percent cess on SUVs. Mr Suri asserted that demand for automobiles is high and will continue to climb if future taxation reaches a tipping point. High luxury car taxes are squeezing the market and limiting the local manufacture of more models: JLR India. High luxury automobile taxes are squeezing the market and prohibiting the local manufacture of more models: JLR India (see Figure 4).

The life cycle of a car is critical for both automobile planners and marketers, as seen in Figure 4. Between the maturity and decline stages of the car industry, a (.) peak point occurs; earnings drive the on-growth stage and emerge at the margin during the maturity stage.

COMPETITION CHALLENGES IN FUTURE

It is estimated by the *Society of the Automobile Industry* that the auto industry estimated a loss of INR 2,300 Cr. Per day during the global pandemic. The effect of this loss can be gained if Tesla enters the Indian industry. Tesla's quarterly report gave hints that it is planning to build its next Gigafactory in the US. However, Tesla watchers have been enthusiastically tweeting Elon Musk about the global EV revolution, when will India become a part of it? As promised by Elon Musk, Tesla Model 3 will enter the Indian market by 2021 but it is said that it will cover less than 1% Indian auto industry as compared to China which is 5% wholly set up under Tesla but could have a wide reach of over 10% till next decade. Roth Capital Irwin exclaimed that India will be as big as China in future or even more because there are no trade and geopolitics conflicts. Elon said that by 2024 that a key will be price models at the $25,000 level. As seen earlier regulations and demand were the issues, but now, the hands of India are open for Tesla which would bring 5000-7000 jobs in India (see Figure 5).

In Figure 5, an anticipated growth in the worldwide fleet of automobiles by 2050 is depicted. The statistic indicates that sales will double in comparison to the base year of 2000 and treble to 2 million by 2050. The increase in the overall fleet of cars is a result of the rapid growth of vehicle fleets in industrialised nations such as China, India, Latin America, and various African countries. The positive reality that there will be an increase of about 3.2 million cars by 2050 cannot be ignored.

"In the year 2032, it is estimated that the fleet will be doubled and it will be tripled by 2050. This significant fleet of vehicles showed a very fast development in countries

like China, India, Asia, Latin American and across African countries. Improvements can be expected in future if HEV, PHEV, RE-BEV contribute highly by reducing GHG emissions by 30-50%." [Paris, I. E. (2019). Scaling up the transition to electric mobility. Paris: Global EV Outlook].

Figure 5. Estimated increase of global fleet of vehicles
Source: Mamalis, A.G., Spentzas, K.N. & Mamali, A.A. The impact of automotive industry and its supply chain to climate change: Somme techno-economic aspects. Eur. Transp. Res. Rev. **5,** *1–10 (2013)*

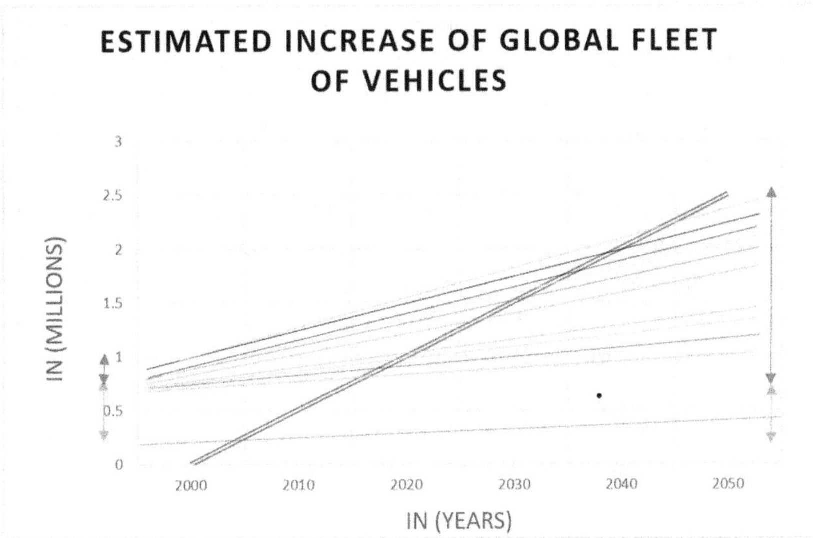

Highlights - OECD N.America OECD Europe ECD Pacific ECCA stern Europe China Other Asia India Middle East Latin America Africa

OECD- *NON-OECD-*

EFFECTS DUE TO CLIMATIC CHANGES

In the coming years, a rapid increase in CO2 emissions is expected to have serious change towards green energy. BEV should enter the Indian market in future to reduce the contribution of vehicles to climate change. Either though off- pick or by high demand hours operative adaptability of electricity channel is needed. Releasing fossil fuels in cars is a greater contributor to harming the environment (Bala, A., Munoz, P., Rieradevall, J., Ysern, P., 2008). About 14% transportation sector is responsible for CO2 emission. It is said by the *'global climate conference'* that there needs to be a target that Earth should have a maximum temperature of 2 degree Celsius till

2100. The impact of the automotive industry and its supply chain to climate change: Somme techno-economic aspects.

EXTENSIVE APPROACH IN FUTURE

A holistic strategy is required to cure India of future threats. India can win over China in the automotive industry by doing mass production. It is observed that China is a manufacturing hub of 80% air conditioners, 70% cell phones, 60% luxury brand, 60% shoes 74% solar cells globally. It is required that India should identify the international trade; 10,000 companies with Rs. 10+ crore business. The government need to take strategic decisions and should sign trade agreements by providing interest rates up to 5%. Pandemic provides an opportunity for India to build the automotive industry. Citizens should not misuse democracy but abide by the laws and regulations. We need to build strength in technology, legal, political, military and defence issues. Economic productivity is the key for Indians to work hard on demographic windfall into a higher standard of living for the par Indians. Investment rates of India are low which in turn has not led them to build manufacturing and production centres, railways, airports and ports. India invests only 30% of GDP as that of 50% of China, manufacturing is around 20% of India as compared to 30% of China. India needs to be strong in all three parts whether it is infrastructure, manufacturing or technology to be called a bread-and-butter country.

FUTURE OF AUTOMOBILE-IT SECTOR

The automobile industry has increased the use of renewable power both on-site and off-site. IT sector has a growth of 6% in 2019 and it is expected that the IT sector will roll out up to $350 billion by 2025. CISCO forecasts that Augmented Reality-Virtual Reality (AR-VR) traffic will rise by 12-fold in all fields of entertainment. Corporate surveys disclose that only 20% of engineering graduates will be employed in future due to their lack of skills and right attitude. Due to automation, it is forecasted that about 6,40,000 jobs will be lost. Cognitive skills, critical thinking, complex information thinking will be growing through 2030. In nearest future, machine and man-led will not be there, instead, leadership, decisions and execution will be robots and humans who will suit them best to deliver the desired outcome. Indian cybersecurity is likely to rise by $7.6 billion by 2022.

INDIA, THIRD LARGEST CAR SEGMENT HUB BY 2030

Pandemic has shown such time to India that they are unable to estimate the next quarter's sales and growth, but US keystone subsidiary of LaSalle Consulting estimators have forecasted that India will be 3rd automobile industry sector to be developed by 2030, after China and US. The automobile sector can be seen shrinking in countries like Korea, Europe and Japan due to aging factor of the inhabitants and increasing value of the ownerships whereas the per capita income will combust the two enormous growth.

By the next decade, the current markets will appear to be mature markets in America, Europe, Japan as the primary driver that is sales might rise up showing majorly increase of 69% of industry sales and 87% of the registrations of the vehicles. The motor sold till now will gear up its sales after 25 years than in the total history of the industry (Silva et al, 2022). In 2017 we saw China to be the leading producer and the largest manufacturer for cars even surpassed Japan. The countries which will get developed in future its propensity will increased over 600 per thousand. India and China are expected to see a potential increase in ownership rate of about 8% and 14%. The all trends have been estimated and forecasted by estimating its economic parameters and the sales across the world of top 30 motor vehicle market sold areas. The variable may consist of GDP, gross income, per capita income, growing population, elasticity of demand and elasticity of income.

According to KPMG Survey, India will see the auto sector will have 39% of electric vehicles. The auto industry will see a profitable rise and electric vehicles will grow in an extraordinary way by 2030 but the shortage of labourers and supply chain will still be a huge cause of concern will be requiring solutions. About 53% are confident about industry's future prospects while 38% are still concerned about the profit aspects and in about next 10 years it is expected to see increased number of charging points for EVs, tech- cars entrance, flying taxis, cars by subscription. But 50% of executives is concerned about price availability for semi-conductors, scarce elements, steel, supply chain and 55% of executives is concerned about shortage of labours. China will have CARG of about 10.60%, US CARG of about 1.30% and India's CARG of about 12.20%. The oil prices will have a secular and a high growth over years which may impact the sales over the 25-years period.

RESILIENCE IN SHAPING THE AUTO SECTOR FOR FUTURE

The automobile sector requires a push for the transformation that is required from various areas like regulatory, technological, economic, competitive and environmental. But the challenge industry is facing is pandemic which is an opportunity for the automobile sector to shape the new models, sub-systems, its parts and services. Technology has aroused which replaced the engine powered vehicles to battery and electric vehicles. Where the people think that Covid-19 is a huge loss to the economy but it also plays a major role in the transformation by accelerating commercial vehicle models and subscription-based vehicles. As the Covid-19 won't last forever where the supply chains and manpower is the key area where the attention needs to be paid up. The manufacturers should make the maximum use of digital technology to gain maximum output which will also wind up the gap between demand and supply force and it will also cover the gap between new products and offers. Based on our research, automobile can take a turn after the pandemic in the long-run if the manufacturers will invest and estimate the risks to develop market growth (see Table 3 and Figure 6).

Table 3. Turn in automobile sector post-Covid-19

	Input	Output
Community	Maximising the shares of auto market in urban areas	Maximisation of fashion cars and increasing magnitude of auto market
	Need for social distancing among the travellers to increase cleanliness	Renovation of auto market's body and interiors
Operable	Robotization for minimal human touch	New interface of auto sector
	Minimum dealings with auto sector care centres	AI for independence, multichannel approach, query handling
Commercial	To encourage for the purchase of new models	No interest loans to be charged on car service
	Vouchers and coupons for early purchasers	New-model will gain a significant output

Source: Authors compilation

The above graph 1.2 illustrates that private owned cars in US cities is about 77%, Philippines in about 45%, Germany is about 26%, Japan is about 12%, Finland is about 39%. The need for social distancing and safety will lead to increase in private owned cars. One-third of the population is working from home still they have demand of private owned cars. This will also potentially increase the demand for manufacturing of cars in auto sector. Emergency health care devices should be launched in cars to safeguard the trip for every passenger. This will also create opportunities to create revenue along with profits, service segment including new system for health purposes. This research talks about resurgence in auto market during post and ongoing pandemic. When government-imposed lockdown in China in March 2020, Tesla was the first one to observe increase in new car registrations.

In China 50,000 cars was still sold despite pandemic again in March which made them confident. The pandemic considered not only the commercial vehicles but also tech-savvy early adopters. The traffic jams and global demand to decrease carbon emissions has provided vouchers to use public transport despite private owned vehicles.

Figure 6. Percent increase of private ownership cars
Source: Authors compilation

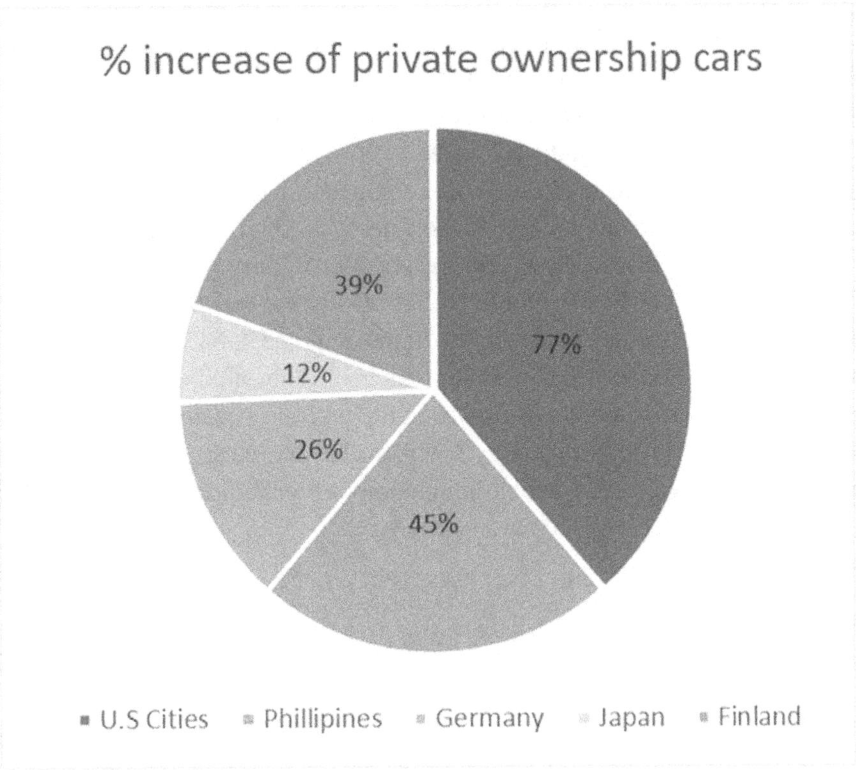

REIMAGINING THE AUTO SECTOR OF FUTURE

Disruptions may result in loss of auto sector but the auto markets who are reimagining their operations despite pandemic will perform the best during after post-pandemic. The major issues faced by the auto sector faced before pandemic were no EVs, machine-driven factories, dispel cars and the similar factors will be faced post-pandemic also. After seeing pandemic, the population is imagining the normal situation in auto sector which curtailed due to pandemic, decreased car sales, large layoffs. The changes in the auto sector is visible since few past months and if the changes will continue then the best is yet to come in the auto market.

At operating levels, the Covid-19 became an opportunity which can be seen through the increase of online traffic, willingness to purchase OEMs, propensity to focus on main activities to cooperate with its partners and challenges they are facing. If auto sector will work on the crisis, then only, they can reimagine the structure, working and performance of their organization. The auto sector can reimagine in a developed working phase if they focus on the digital modes of the channels they created which had already risen up by 13% which may result up to 28%, focusing on the profit and revenue which is recurring, evaluating asset arrangement, degrading the zero-based budget and building a resilient chain of supply by creating demand. The auto sector should take up the steps now otherwise it will change into never. Most people are checking the industries online in which it is surveyed.

The players of the auto industry weren't known about the uncertain time that is pandemic but despite this challenge some companies have moved ahead drastically (Pizoń, J., 2022). The automobile market needs to digitalize themselves so that the companies which are below average score can compete with B2B channels. About 96% of Business to Business (B2B) market has made changes by shifting themselves from go-to-market model to digitalized model, 64% people believe that that digitalization has become the need of an hour. The auto market needs to focus on its digital subscribers to have growth in the revenue system including lifestyle, podcasts, and multimedia channels. It will make the reach of about ten million subscribers base by 2025.Investing in autonomous technology, connection-based, shared mobility is challenge to automobile sector.

Figure 7. Estimated number of increases in ACES partnerships
Source: Authors compilation

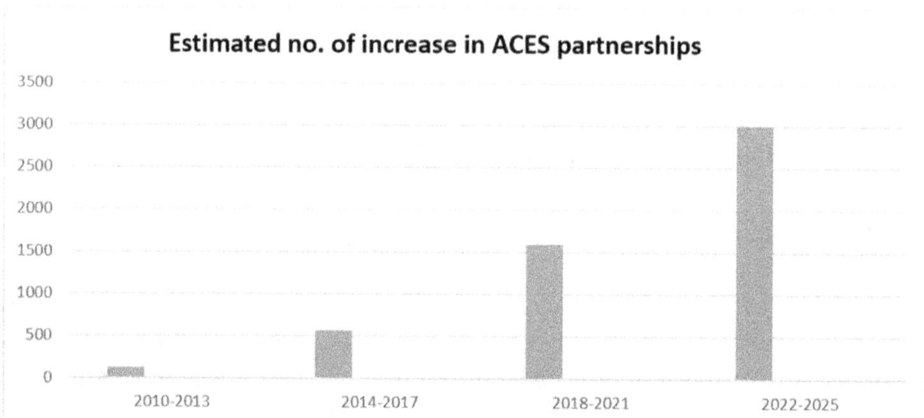

Figure 7 depicts the estimated increase in ACES (Autonomous, connectivity, electrification and shared mobility) partnerships in the self-driving driverless cars. Tech players have already seen the competitiveness in the auto sector and the pandemic is placing additional pressure on OEMs and they are required to mobilize it to build strong financial position. Auto sector is seeing the two phases, firstly, the success and reinvention, secondly, to maintain the status already captured. The auto players need to act now to survive and ensure success in the future.

MOBILISATION OF AUTOMOBILE INDUSTRY FOR FUTURE

Covid-19 is disturbing the global automotive sector and its value chain. Globally, Auto sector is facing uncertainty, decrease in sales, penance due to emission of CO2, changes in the demand of consumer. Auto sector is facing a storm since 2019 and to cover the gap they need to focus on ACES. Pandemic affected all the parts of the auto sector from suppliers on the way to dealers but mobilisation of auto sector can be done in six ways.

- **Organize Supply Chain –** Since auto sector along with OEMs rely on supply chain which has caused disruptions due to pandemic. Almost two-third of production was affected due to supply chain as it created industrial's shutdowns which impacted suppliers also. The Chinese made parts made heavy impact on the global production as after pandemic the imports were unable to be made. This need to managed by evaluating the risks and by creating complete picture by using big data systems, artificial intelligence (AI), ecosystem. This will help supply chain to adapt or adjust in the environment. They need to mobilize command Centre to figure out the risk and operate with safety measures. Protocols need to be taken to recover from risk and switch back to normal from disruptions.
- **Continuation Of Mass Production –** China is trying to cope up with the pandemic and are stabilizing day by day whereas US and European countries are facing huge loss due to uncertainty. OEMs are required to shift their procedure towards engineering, assembling and procurement to produce equipment so that the decrease in supply chain, losses of the job, downfall of percent of automobile production which will also create an impact to GDP. This all can be managed by keeping themselves in close contact with suppliers to ensure fast enhancement so that auto market can recover its production level and schedule up to the mark. Manpower's safety, social distancing and cleanliness are required to take up IoT concepts for increasing efficiency and

prepare for future protocols. Enable flexibility whenever needed to shift to emergency mode.

- **Cash-Flow –** Liquidity is the heart of the market but some OEMs have low cash with minimum operating cash flows and the cash reserves which are left are also depleting. Market capitalization needs focus to have high credit lines and without excess funding auto sector will be unable to accelerate themselves which will adversely affect ACES. This can be managed by staying in touch with banks and engage with a working capital to prioritize the pending dues. Develop a fixed-cost and with the help of AI management can develop cash-flows. Pay attention to financial health of suppliers, manufacturers, dealers and partners as they are also under distress.
- **High Vehicle Sales –** China is the leading producer of auto market but the sales dropdown in 2020 by 80% but they have still become a strong indicator for the direction of the global market. 9% of population aren't purchasing vehicles due to pandemic in US. A change in behaviour in consumer's response is depicted like less mobility, more online shopping and this might remain the same after pandemic too. The auto sector can manage it by focusing on online channels to reach its customers and start virtual events to compensate with the losses. They should try to implement the need of their consumers in such a way which will meet the health and hygiene needs of the customers. Reimagine the sales model and create digital channels to have good sales. Post-pandemic prices may go down and may create pressure on dealers but they should focus on costs and inventories to evaluate discount policies and balance market prices, brand image and profitability share.
- **Respond, Reset and Renew The Ongoing Crisis –** The auto sector needs to respond by implementing safety measures for its customers and ensure collaborations with organizations to set up a digital place for its own which will enable them to create transparency. They should reset by locating the hidden and caught up value in operating costs and consider a portfolio which will have good supply chain and be alert with the risks they might face in functional areas. They should renew by drawing strategic roadmaps, put investing efforts, scan for inorganic growth of the market by creating efficient operational strength and redesigning the operations digitally.

INDIAN AUTOMOBILE SEGMENT ANALYSIS

The mode of transport preferred by the citizens in countries like India, China, Indonesia, Vietnam, and Thailand is a 2-wheeler segment rather than a 4-wheeler segment. Urbanization and the expansion of economies have raised the demands of consumers from rural to urban areas. 2-wheeler starter motor leads the global demand. A prevailing share of the market of 82.48% in 2020 by passenger carrier is likely to be carried till 2026.

Figure 8. states that due to government limitations and rising petrol and diesel prices, it is projected that the three-wheeler sector would grow and traditional fuels such as petrol and diesel will transition to natural and electric by 2026.

Figure 9 depicts how the automobile business will function in the future like meat and potatoes (essential necessities). The global rental market for 2-wheelers and 4-wheelers is anticipated to reach about USD 180.93 billion by 2026, growing at a CARG of 10.2 percent."

Figure 8. Indian 3-wheeler market segment by FY26
Source: Authors compilation

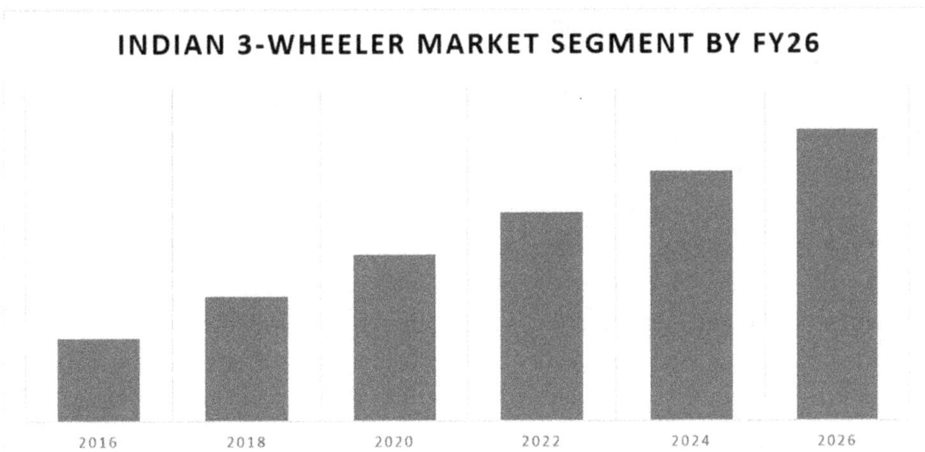

Figure 9. 2-wheeler and 4-wheeler rental segment from FY16 to FY26
Source: Authors compilation

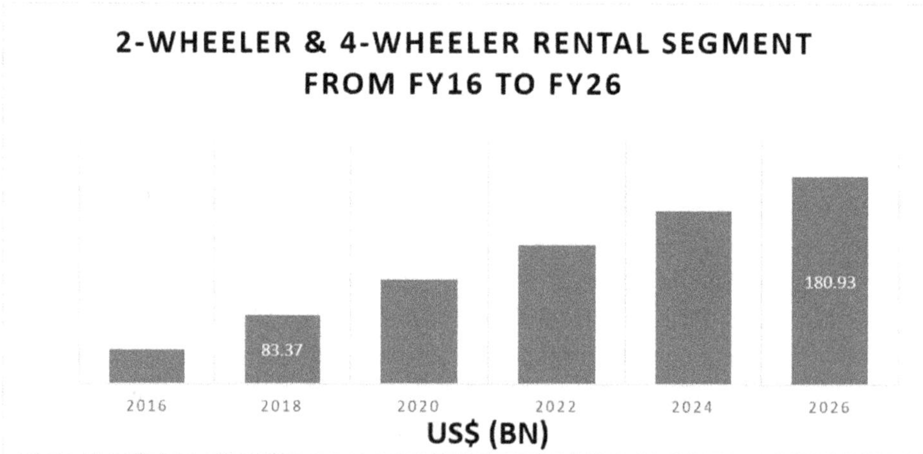

SUMMARY OF FINDINGS

The research question that drove us to conduct this study was the lack of sufficient literature examining the automobile sector during pandemic. Although the auto sector was examined in the past (for example see, Haugh, D., A. Mourougane and O. Chatal (2010)), we did not find such studies during the pandemic period. The market hypothesis indicates that pandemic reflect all available information and can react only to new information. We selected the widely used event study methodology with the industry 4.0 market to measure the automobile industry. We use the global pandemic effects around which the abnormalities in the market are to be examined. Our results suggest that the automobile industry has been affected during the pandemic but expected to see effective growth in future. An abnormal situation in pandemic every day signifies the decline in the auto market and the deep impact it had on the auto sector market and its returns. The global pandemic declaration did not significantly impact the abnormal returns of the automobile industry and during the global pandemic declaration, the automobile industry experienced significant abnormalities.

LIMITATION AND FUTURE RESEARCH

The proposed research may face limitations because within the targeted population it is uneasy to detect the exact number of people with the knowledge about the challenges and the technological opportunities for the automobile industry. The area of study is India, where the introduction of the electric cars has elicited sharp political and social reactions concerning the engagement of the foreign automotive companies in the Indian automobile market.

The inherit social attitudes and political influences are capable of influencing the response behavior of the people. Locating the reliable participants is another limitation t this research. The research requires the collection of data from 60 respondents, who are either in motion with their vehicles or scattered somewhere within the large population.

The paper carried out research in various fields like OEMs, mass production, vehicle segments, industry 4.O, electric vehicles, pandemic post and pre-effects, downfall, challenges, IT sector of automobile, profit and peak point and so on. However, we suggest that future research should be carried on top automobile companies, post Covid-19 effects, SCP model, Transport shares in all automobile industry, GDP, investment, rankings.

CONCLUSION

The changing preferences of consumers and technological challenges are shaping the new trends of mobility, which requires the automotive industries in India need to be the original in the coming future (Bhattacharyya, A., Ghosh, D. and Majumder, A., 2021). Consumers are seeking retro-fitment even for the level-2 car models by 2025. Due to changing preferences, 10 new cars may likely be a shared vehicle in future by 2030 which will cause a reduction in private-use vehicles. It is foreseen that Apple, Google and Tesla will be only the tip of the iceberg in future. A global experience will be required for India to grab the opportunity and focusing on threats from the present for identifying new business model with advanced technological features.

The auto industry needs to participate in ecosystems such as electrification and infrastructures. Tsunami faced by the industry since the 2019 to save feet, hands and eyes of automobile industry in future. India needs to shape the wired car to a separate network architecture to build the future of India. Robotics, cybersecurity, development of software allows the automobile industry to support start-ups and start with product development and innovation. Strategy, business development & human resource requirements to collaborate hands with the industry.

The boards and executives should build a future vision and measure progress by revisiting the set-up plan regularly. Is the driver required to drive the car? Will steering wheels be present? We need the automobile industry should not answer these questions but capture the international market by exporting all these questions into a reality check in future. Similar study can be conducted on more quantitative techniques. The government 'MAKE IN INDIA' initiative need to play an important role to achieve its targets. In place of "changing auto news story FY2020" OR "changing auto trends FY2020" we expect "This *Is the New Era of Automobile Industry.*"

ACKNOWLEDGMENT

This research received no specific grant from any funding agency in the public, commercial, or not-for-profit sectors.

REFERENCES

U.S. Department of Transportation & Bureau of Transportation Statistics. (2018). Transportation Statistics, Annual Report 2018. [Data set]. USFG.

Green, K. W., Whitten, D., & Inman, R.A. (2012). Aligning marketing strategies throughout the supply chain to enhance performance. *Industrial Marketing Management*, 1008–1018.

Smith, K.T. (2010). An examination of marketing techniques that influence millennia's perception of whether a product is environment-friendly. *Journal of Strategic Marketing*, *18*(6), 437–450.

Thakur, G., Singh, A., Rai, S., & Mishra, R. (2022). An Ounce of Prevention Is Worth a Pound of Cure: A Study on Emotional Regulation, Thwarted Social Needs, Disposable Income and Its Relationship with Psychological Well-Being. International. *Journal of Work Organisation and Emotion*, *13*(4), 1.

Shinde, G.P., & Dubey, M. (2011). Automobile Industry and Performance of Key Players. *Asian Journal of Technology and Management Research*, *1*(2).

Bala, A., Muñoz, P., Rieradevall, J., & Ysern, P. (2008). Experiences with greening suppliers. The Universidad Autònoma de Barcelona. *Journal of Cleaner Production*, *16*(15), 1610–1619. doi:10.1016/j.jclepro.2008.04.015

Balon, V., Sharma, A. K., & Barua, M. K.Author. (2016). Assessment of Barriers in Green Supply Chain Management Using ISM: A Case Study of the Automobile Industry in India. *Global Business Review*, *17*(1), 116–135. doi:10.1177/0972150915610701

Bhattacharyya, A., Ghosh, D., & Majumder, A. (2021). A Threadbare Analysis on the State of Affairs of Indian Automobile Sector in the Aftermath of Present Recessional Trend and Its Remedy, Pal, M.K. (Ed.) Productivity Growth in the Manufacturing Sector, 253-267. Emerald Publishing Limited. doi:10.1108/978-1-80071-094-820211019

Singh., A., Nagpal, E., & Mundi, H. S. (2020). Brand personification through celebrity ambassador: A study to investigate the impact on consumer attitude and loyalty. *International Journal of Business Excellence*, *1*(1), 1.

BuisnessLine. (2021). 39% of new vehicles sold in India will be electric vehicles by 2030: *The Hindu Business Line*.

Rakshit, B. & Basistha, D. (2020). Can India stay immune enough to combat Covid-19 pandemic? An economic query. *Journal of Public Affairs*, *20*, e2157. https://doi.org/10.1002/pa.2157

Chan, R. Y. K., He, H., Chan, H. K., & Wang, W. Y. C.Author. (2012). Environment orientation and corporate performance: The mediation mechanism of green supply chain management and the moderating effect of competitive intensity. *Industrial Marketing Management*, *41*(4), 621–630. doi:10.1016/j.indmarman.2012.04.009

Charan, P., Shankar, R., & Baisya, R. K.Author. (2009). Modelling the barriers of supply chain performance measurement system implementation in the Indian automobile supply chain. *International Journal of Logistics Systems and Management*, *5*(6), 614–630. doi:10.1504/IJLSM.2009.024794

Chowdhury, S. G., & Chatterjee, S.Author. (2020). Determinants of Indian Automobile Industry Growth. *Eurasian Journal of Business and Economics*, *13*(26), 65–91. doi:10.17015/ejbe.2020.026.04

Huang, C. (2020). Clinical features of patients infected with 2019 novel coronavirus in Wuhan, China. *Lancet*, *395*(10223), 497–506.

Shrikanth, R., & Raju D.S. N. (2012). Contemporary Green Marketing-Brief Reference to Indian Scenario. *International Journal of Social Science and Interdisciplinary Research*, *1*(1), 26–39.

COVID-19 will batter global auto sales and credit quality, March 23, 2020, S&P Global.

Da Silva, N. A., Abreu, J. L., Klingenberg, C., Antunes, J. A. V., & Lacerda, D. P. (2022). Industry 4.0 and micro and small enterprises: systematic literature review and analysis. *Production & Manufacturing Research, 10*(1), 696–726. doi:10.1080/21693277.2022.2124466

Siriwardena S., Hunt, G., Teisl, M.F., & Noblet, C.L. (2012). Effective environmental marketing of green cars: A nested logit approach. *Transportation Research Part D, Transport and Environment*, 37–242.

Financial Express. (n.d.). *India to be world's 3rd largest car market by 2030.* Financial Express. https://www.financialexpress.com/archive/india-to-be-worlds-3rd-largest-car-market-by-2030-study/158001/

Sarangi, P. K. (2014). Future Trend in Indian Automobile Industry: A Statistical Approach. *Journal of Management Sciences and Technology*, *2*(1), 28–32.

Singh, A., Das, U., & Kumar, S. (2022). Gender, technology and innovation: The role of women in Indian micro, small and medium enterprises. *World Review of Entrepreneurship, Management and Sustainable Development*, *18*(4), 429.

Belis-Bergouignan, M.C., Bordenave., G., & Lung, Y. (2000). Global Strategies in the Automobile Industry. *Regional Studies*, *34*(1), 41–53. doi:10.1080/00343400050005871

Gan, L. (2003). Globalization of the Automobile Industry in China: Dynamics and barriers in greening of the road transportation. *Energy Policy*, *31*(C), 537–551.

Singh, H. K., & Singh, A. (n.d.). Governance and Social Responsibility Practices in Indian Life Insurance Industry. *Pacific Institute of Management & Technology.*

Kushwaha, G.S.; Sharma, & Kumar, N. (2015). Green initiatives: A step towards sustainable development and firm's performance in the automobile industry. *Journal of Cleaner Production*.

Singh, S., Vrontis, D., & Thrassou, A. (2011). Green marketing and consumer behavior: The case of gasoline products. *Journal of Transnational Management*, *16*(2), 84–106.

Singh, V. (2017). Growth of Automobile Industry and its Economic Impact: An Indian Perspective. *International Journal of Commerce and Management Research*, *3*(8), 6–10.

Gurumurthy, A., Soni, G., Prakash, S., & Badhotiya, G. K. (2013). Review on Supply Chain Management Research—An Indian Perspective. *IIM Kozhikode Society & Management Review*, *2*(1), 1–19. doi:10.1177/2277975213496508

Haugh, D., Mourougane, A., & Chatal, O. (2010), *The Automobile Industry in and Beyond the Crisis, OECD Economics Department* (Working Papers, No. 745). doi:10.1787/5kmmp8wg6cmq-en

Hofstatter, T. & M. K. (2020, October). Reimagining the auto industry's future: It's now or never. p. 1. accenture. COVID 19: Mobilizing the automotive industry now accenture.

Strauch., Y., Carter, A., & Homer-Dixon, T. (2020). However, the pandemic unfolds, it's time for oil use to peak—and society to prepare for the fallout. *Bulletin of the Atomic Scientists*, *76*(5), 238–243. doi:10.1080/00963402.2020.1806577

IEA. (2021). Electric Vehicles. *IEA*. https://www.iea.org/reports/electric-vehicles

Singh, A., & Kumar, A. (2021). Impact of COVID-19 on monitoring human health behavior through digital medium system. *International Journal of Business Information Systems*, *1*(1), 1.

India Brand Equity Foundation. (2013). *Auto components industry in India.* IBEF. https://www.ibef.org/pages/33363

Aggarwal, R.N. (1988, October-December). Indian Automobile Industry: Problems and Prospects. *The Indian Economic Journal*, *36*(2).

Indian Brand Equity Foundation. (2008). *Automotive Market and Opportunities.* IBEF. https://www.ibef.org/download/Automotive_250608.pdf

Inter-brand. (2013). Creating and managing brand value. *Third annual best global green brands*. Grounded World.

International Organization of Motor Vehicle Manufacturers. (2022). *Media Reports, Press Releases, Union Budget 2021-22.* Department for Promotion of Industry and Internal Trade (DPIIT), Automotive Component Manufacturers Association of India (ACMA), Society of Indian Automobile Manufacturers (SIAM).

IvyPanda. (2021, July 22). *Research Methodology of the BMW Strategy*. IvyPanda. https://ivypanda.com/essays/research-methodology-of-the-bmw-strategy

Iyer, S. (2022). *Top 6 challenges in the Automobile Industry: The Post-COVID-19 Era.* Global Market Insights.

Jaguar. (2019). Future Jaguar Land Rover models could help stop the spread of superbugs. Jaguar Land Rover.

J.D. Power. (2020*). Post-coronavirus resurgence of car sales in China potentially bodes well for U.S. market*. J.D. Power.

KPMG International. (2008). *A rough road-financial crisis and automotive industry*. KPMG.

KPMG International. (2010). *Global Auto Executive Survey 2010 Industry Concerns and Expectations to 2014.* KPMG.

Krishnan, S., Gupta, S., Kaliyan, M., Kumar, V., & Garza-Reyes, J.A. (2021), Assessing the key enablers for Industry 4.0 adoption using MICMAC analysis: a case study, *International Journal of Productivity and Performance Management, 70*(5), 1049-1071. doi:10.1108/IJPPM-02-2020-0053

Luthra, S., Kumar, V., Kumar, S., & Haleem, A. (2011). Barriers to implementing green supply chain management in automobile industry using interpretative structured modeling techniques: An Indian perspective. *Journal of Industrial Engineering and Management*, *4*(2), 231–257.

Manda, Kittu, V., & Beatrice, B. B. (2020).The Indian Automobile Sector Slowdown (January 30, 2020). https://ssrn.com/abstract=3528891 or doi:10.2139/ssrn.3528891

Lin, R.J., Tan, K.H., & Geng, Y. (2013). Market demand, green product innovation, and firm performance: Evidence from Vietnam motorcycle industry. *Journal of Cleaner Production*, *40*(C), 101–107.

Matsunaga, F., Zytkowski, V., Valle, P., & Deschamps, F. (2022). Optimization of energy efficiency in smart manufacturing through the application of cyber–physical systems and industry 4.0 technologies. *Journal of Energy Resources Technology, 144*(10). doi:10.1115/1.4053868

Maurya, P., Singh, A., & Salim, M. (2022). The Application of Text Mining in Detecting Financial Fraud: A Literature Review. *Business Intelligence and Human Resource Management: Concept, Cases, and Practical Applications*, *243*(C).

Mishra, P. & Sharma, P.(2010). Green marketing in India, emerging opportunities and challenges. *Journal of engineering science and management education, 3*(C), pp.9-14.

Mishra, R., Rai, S., Thakur, G., Singh, A., & Shah, A. K. (2022). Impact of leadership styles on Emotional regulation strategies of followers in leader-follower relationship. *Journal of Positive School Psychology*, 130–141.

Penna, C.R., & Geels, F.W. (2012). Multidimensional struggles in the greening of the industry: A dialectic issue life cycle model and case study. *Technological Forecasting and Social Change*, *79*(C), 999–1020.

Narayanan, K. (1998). Technology acquisition, de-regulation and competitiveness: a study of Indian automobile industry. *Research Policy*, *27*(2), 215–228. doi:https://doi.org/10.1016/S0048-7333(98)00037-7

Nayak, J., Mishra, M., Naik, B., Swapnarekha, H., Cengiz, K., & Shanmuganathan, V. (2021). An impact study of covid-19 on six different industries: Automobile, energy and power, agriculture, education, travel and tourism and consumer electronics. *Expert Systems*. https://doi.org/10.1111/exsy.12677

Nayak, J., Mishra, M., Naik, B., Swapnarekha, H., Cengiz, K., & Shanmuganathan, V. (2021). An impact study of covid-19 on six different industries: Automobile, energy and power, agriculture, education, travel and tourism and consumer electronics. *Expert Systems*. https://doi.org/10.1111/exsy.12677

Nayak, J., Mishra, M., Naik, B., Swapnarekha, H., Cengiz, K., & Shanmuganathan, V. (2021). An impact study of covid-19 on six different industries: Automobile, energy and power, agriculture, education, travel and tourism and consumer electronics. *Wiley Online Library.*

Neese., W., Foxx., W., Eppler., D. B. & Wright, L.T. (2018). The influence of industry-specific personal characteristics on consumer reactions to domestic vs. foreign comparative advertising in the American automobile market. *Cogent Business & Management, 5*(1).

Paris, I. E. (2019). Scaling up the transition to electric mobility. Global EV Outlook

Pizoń, J., & Gola, A. (2023). The meaning and directions of development of personalized production in the era of industry 4.0 and industry 5.0. In Lecture Notes in Mechanical Engineering, 1–13. Springer International Publishing.

Polonsky, M.J., & Rosenberger, P.J. (2001).Revaluating Green Marketing: A strategic approach, *Business Horizon*, 21-30.

Rameshan, P. (2021). Crisis Leadership of Covid-19 Fightback: Exploratory Anecdotal Evidence on Selected World Leaders. *IIM Kozhikode Society & Management Review, 10*(2), 136–159. doi:10.1177/2277975220986274

Lai, C.-C. (2020). Severe acute respiratory syndrome coronavirus 2 (SARS-CoV-2) and corona virus disease-2019 (COVID-19): The epidemic and the challenges. *International Journal of Antimicrobial Agents*, *55*(105924). doi:10.1016/j.ijantimicag.2020.105924

Sharma, P., Khater, S. & Vashisht, V. (2020). Sales Forecast of Manufacturing Companies using Machine Learning navigating the Pandemic like covid-19, 2021 *2nd International Conference on Computation, Automation and Knowledge Management (ICCAKM),* 1-5, doi:10.1109/ICCAKM50778.2021.9357751

Singh, A. (2022). From Crisis to Resilience. In Handbook of Research on Challenges for Human Resource Management in the COVID-19 Era, p.89.

Singh, A., Singh, H., & Singh, A. (2022). People Analytics: Augmenting Horizon from Predictive Analytics to Prescriptive Analytics. In: Jeyanthi P.M., Choudhury T., Hack-Polay D., Singh T.P., & Abujar S. (eds) *Decision Intelligence Analytics and the Implementation of Strategic Business Management.* Springer. doi:10.1007/978-3-030-82763-2_13

Singh, D., Singh., A. & Karki, S. (2021). Knowledge Management and Web 3.0: Introduction to Future and Challenges. In S. Kautish, D. Singh, Z., Polkowski, A. Mayura., & M. Jeyanthi (Ed.)., *Knowledge Management and Web 3.0: Next Generation Business Models*, 1-14. Boston: De Gruyter. doi:10.1515/9783110722789-001

Singh, D., Singh, A., & Omar, A., (2022). Business Intelligence and Human Resource Management: Concept, Cases, and Practical Applications (S. B. Goyal, Ed.). CRC Press.

Xia, Y., & Tang, T.P. (2011). Sustainability in Supply chain management: Suggestions for the auto industry. *Management Decision*, *49*(4), 495–512.

Dijk, M., & Yarime, M. (2010). The emergence of hybrid-electric cars: Innovation path creation through co-evolution of supply and demand. *Technological Forecasting and Social Change*, *77*(8), 1371–1390.

Sierzchula, W., Bakker, S., Maat, K., & Wee, B.V. (2012). The technological diversity of emerging eco-innovations: A case study of the automobile industry. *Journal of Cleaner Production*, *37*(C), 211–220.

Von Paul, G., &, H.-W. K. (2016, January). *Automobile revolution-perspective towards 2030.*

World Bank. (2018). *World Development Indicators*. World Bank.

World Health Organization. (2020). *Laboratory testing for coronavirus disease 2019 (Covid-19) in suspected human cases: interim guidance, 2 March 2020. No. WHO/Covid-19 /laboratory/2020.4*. World Health Organization.

ENDNOTE

1 Former US surgeon-general, Nomura Research Institute

Chapter 6
Implementation of Lean Tools in Internal Logistic Improvement

José Carlos Sá
https://orcid.org/0000-0002-2228-5348
School of Engineering, Polytechnic of Porto, Portugal

Francisco J. G. Silva
https://orcid.org/0000-0001-8570-4362
School of Engineering, Polytechnic of Porto, Portugal

José Dinis-Carvalho
University of Minho, Portugal

Olga Silva
Polytechnic Institute of Viana do Castelo, Portugal

Bruna Costa
School of Engineering, Polytechnic of Porto, Portugal

Vanda Lima
ESTG, Polytechnic of Porto, Portugal

ABSTRACT

Lean thinking is a philosophy that allows organizations to move towards perfection through continuous improvement. With the applications of lean tools, it is possible to identify waste within an organization and present simple, effective, and cost-effective solutions to achieve higher productivity and profitability. The present article is a result of the work carried out in a company responsible for designing and projecting automated material handling and storage systems. Using lean tools such as value stream mapping (VSM), it was possible to identify several wastes and improvement opportunities throughout the productive chain. This article aims to present the solutions developed to reduce wastes in the internal logistics department. Subsequently, the application and evaluations of the impact of lean tools, it was possible to calculate the impact in the internal logistics which results in a decrease of 16% in the production costs.

DOI: 10.4018/978-1-6684-5606-4.ch006

INTRODUCTION

Currently, change is a constant in any market in which an organization belongs. Competitors become more aggressive, new opportunities, and new challenges arise such as as new technologies to support logistics, has contributing to force companies to adapt to changes to remain profitable and competitive (Dias et al., 2019). To this end, organizations must focus on identifying activities that add value, eliminate waste, increase the quality of their products and services, and thus increase customer satisfaction (Rosa et al., 2017).

Over the last years, continuous improvement, and the application of Lean tools have proved to be a key aspect on increasing the competitiveness of companies worldwide (Correia et al., 2018). The Lean philosophy aims to streamline companies to make them more dynamic, to be able to adapt to changes in the environment where they operate, eliminate waste, and promote a culture of continuous improvement within the entire organization (Pombal et al., 2019). Nevertheless, the application of Lean tools within an organization can lead to significant changes in its strategy (Silva & Gouveia, 2020), which can represent a change in the habits of employees, which often constitute a barrier to the implementation of these tools (Costa et al., 2018; Silva et al., 2022).

The work described in this article was developed in a company in the automation area, and its purpose was to propose the implementation of Lean tools to improve internal logistics processes, with regard to the flow of materials internally. The application of improvements proposed should cover stock management, visual management, 5S, and continuous improvement at Gemba, with the main objectives to be accomplished as follows: identifying the main wastes, reducing activities that do not add value, improving the supplies of materials at workstations and improvement in the organization and factory cleaning.

Background

Lean Thinking aims to identify and reduce waste in organizations by improving the efficiency of their processes to have a continuous flow of production without interruption (Pinto, et al., 2022). The application of lean philosophy and its tools can be extended to every industry, from quality, maintenance, supply chain and logistics to production itself. Several articles present successful case studies about the implementation of the most varied lean tools in different industries (Teixeira et al., 2021).

The work developed by Silva and Golveia (2020) which used a metalworking industry on the application of the 5S methodology, it was possible to see significant improvements, both in terms of production, as well as in quality and safety. It was possible to verify that with the increase in the levels of cleanliness and organization, their performance and productivity also increased. It was also possible to observe a decrease in the waste of materials and working time, which enabled the rentability of delivery dates and increased customer satisfaction. Silva et al. (2020), developed in an automation company, the application of Lean tools such as Total Productive Maintenance and Jidoka, combined with waste identification and other kaizen tools, allowed, not only to the reduction of cycle times by 25-40% but also the scrap reduction by 60% and the reduction by 70% of the necessary raw material which allowed the company to save 1786 €/ month. Rodrigues et al. (2019), researched if the application of Lean tools could also bring fast gains for organizations. In the study developed by the authors, it was verified that the tools such as Daily Kaizen, PDCA cycle, Visual Management, Gemba Walk, among others, were applied. The implementation of these tools in a company in the metalworking sector allowed, in just three months, to an increase of 8.5% in machine occupancy rate and a reduction of 27.9% regarding the costs per hour of defective products. Consequently, the ratio of costs associated with non-quality per hour decreased significantly by 27.9%. These results were achieved since the Lean tools can be rapidly and easily implemented and quickly understood by the workers.

The identification of waste and its subsequent elimination on a production line is essential when talking about Lean. Costa et al. (2018), in a company of the automotive sector, through Gemba observation, the identified points of improvement and with Lean Thinking, it was possible to save 2 159 000 €. This was equivalent to 10.9% of the total investment planned for this project. The main wastes eliminated were over-processing, transportation, and motion. In another company, the application of Standard Work, allowed to increase the stability and the autonomy of the employees, resulting in a reduction of defects between shifts of 90%. The implementation of preventive maintenance and Single Minute Exchange of Die (SMED), allowed, respectively, to reduce unplanned downtime from 12% to 5% and the reduction of setup times by 37% compared to the initial (Ribeiro et al., 2019).

The application of Lean tools extends beyond production, and another area where these tools are very beneficial is in the logistics and supply chain (Mourato et al., 2021). In a study carried out on a company whose goal was the implementation of Lean methodologies in the management of consumable materials, several benefits and improvements were registered. With the implementation of the 5S methodology and Visual Management, it was possible a reduction in the time required to locate the consumable material in the order of 70%. Improvements in stock control were also achieved through the reformulation of Kanban (approximately 30%) and a reduction in the time required to replenish material in the consumable's cabinet was ensured using the mizusumashi (with an expected improvement of 50%) (Pombal et al., 2019).

Pereira et al. (2019), developed a study that had as main objective the optimization of picking tasks and the improvement of warehouse operations, as well as inventory management . The solution involved the development and implementation of a tracking system to reduce one of the most time-consuming components of picking, the time wasted searching for products in the warehouse. This application led to a 93% reduction in unproductive time (waste), which led to an optimisation of picking activity, increasing warehouse preparation capacity by 63%. A similar solution was also implemented by Tellini et al. (2019).

When not individually combined, the application of lean has multiple advantages for organizations. Among the various examples existing in the scientific literature, below are some references as examples of these advantages. Ferreira et. al. (2019), mapped the value chain of an organisation through tools such as Value Stream Mapping (VSM), allowed the identification of waste and opportunities for improvement leading, for example, to the reduction of the changeover time in an assembly machine from 39 min to 17 min, thus presenting a 44% gain in manufacturing.Another example of the application of VSM in an organization allowed a reduction in setup times in two productive cells by approximately 50% by identifying opportunities for improvement in these areas and applying SMED to improve it (Monteiro et al., 2019). In a mold industry, with the application of Pareto's graphics, it was possible to identify which processes of the production line contributed the most to the continuity break in the production line. After this analysis and the application of improvements in these areas, the company managed to increase its global OEE value by 20% (Pereira et al., 2019).

The joint application of Lean tools allows for a reduction in budgeting time, improves communication and production management systems, optimizes storage spaces, increase organization, and reduce the time and complexity of logistics operations (Dias et al., 2019). Lean management includes a set of tools that allow companies to archive strong goals when implemented properly (Oliveira et al., 2017).

RESEARCH METHODOLOGY

This work is based on the action research methodology that was applied in a Portuguese company specialized in designing storage and material handling systems, carrying out the entire process from consulting, planning, defining the right solution for the client, equipment design, manufacture, assembly, software development, integration, and commissioning. This company presents solutions adapted to the needs of each client and their specific requirements in materials flow and, consequently, offers a wide range of products, all subject to high levels of customization.

The adopted methodology was based on the principles of action-research and is typically divided into five main steps (Martins et al., 2020; Marinho et al., 2021). The first step is to identify and diagnose the problem and define the main objectives. The next step is to prepare and develop actions through the mapping of the current state and later identification of existing wastes and problems. For this, the lean tool VSM was used. The next step is to study whether, through the application of other lean tools, it is possible to eliminate or minimize the identified problems and wastes. In the next phase, the defined measures are implemented, and their feasible gains are quantified. Afterward, an assessment of the work done must be carried out to determine whether the measures implemented have made it possible to achieve the goals initially defined and whether it is necessary to develop other solutions. Finally, a conclusion is put together about the work performed. The tools, the methodology followed, and the results obtained concerning the initial state are all described, and critical analysis and proposal for future work are presented in this final step (Azevedo et al. 2019).

CASE STUDY

Presentation of the Current Situation of the Company

In this research, for the consulted company the portfolio is subject to high levels of customization, which makes it hard to have a standard equipment assembly system and standardize its stages. In ordert to map the current state of the assembly process and further analyze the improvement opportunities, a Value Stream Mapping was used. Then, the equipment that was chosen to be analyzed was the Stacker crane Double Mast, as it integrates the orders taking place in the company. Concerning the assembly of a Double Mast, it is typically split into five phases: Columns, Platform, Base, Electrical Panel, and Final Assembly.

In carrying out the VSM, since the assembly of the Stacker crane consists of several phases, which occur individually, it was decided to map each one of them, resulting in a split of a macro VSM into five more detailed VSM as presented in Figure 1. A team with different levels of expertise and belonging to different departments was involved to make the most of the knowledge of the other team members.

The complete process of assembling for the Stacker crane project took 16 weeks. In Figure 1, a representation of the variation that existed between the non-value-added time (NVAT) values registered can be found, as well as its value-added time (VAT) in every stage of assembly.

Figure 1. VSM Stacker Crane

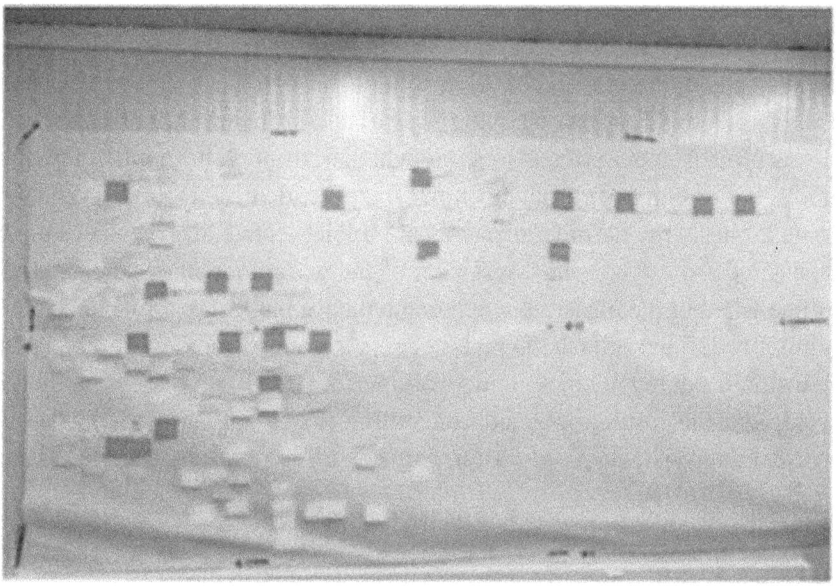

With the analysis of the Figure 2, except for the assembly of the columns, all the stages of Stacker crane assembly process registered NVAT values much higher than VAT. The most substantial difference was recorded in Final Assembly, since it was in this phase that the larger number of waits was recorded, followed by the assembly of the Platform, where the highest number of rework hours was registered.

Figure 2. Variation between NVAT and VAT in every stage of assembly

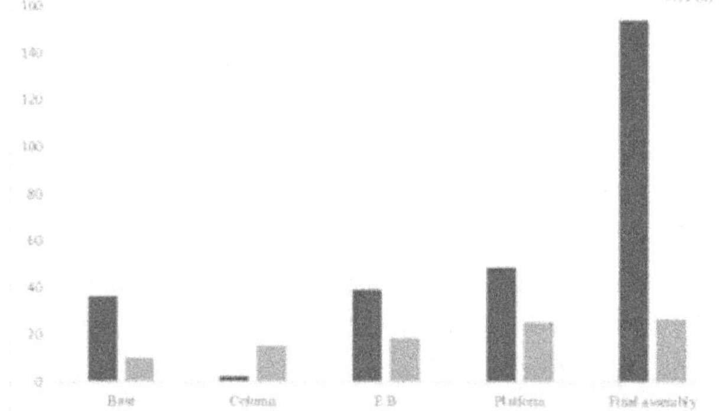

During the entire process, there was a total of 6 hours of waiting due to cargo handling at the factory, 80 hours due to delays or engineering changes, 1244 hours of delays from suppliers, and 818 hours of waiting due to lags between the launches of engineering and production planning. If the assembly process was not streamlined by the operators, the real impact of these waits on the lead time (LT) would be more substantial than that registered.

Regarding the rework register, it had its origin due to changes that were necessary to make when the project coming from the engineering department, and in total 97 necessary hours were necessary. The total of waits recorded, plus all rework resulted in 2245 hours of NVAT in the entire Stacker crane assembly process, with a cost of 40410 €. Thus, the total cost of assembly of the Stacker crane was 65070 €. The total process of assembling the Stacker crane registered a value-added percentage of 37.5%.

In addition to these values, waste, and problems along the value chain were also identify, such as extra processing, over-processing, and waiting. The waste and opportunities for improvement where the tools and improvements described in this paper were applied in the internal logistics of the organisation (Table 1).

Table 1. Problems identified in internal logistics

Lack of Planning
Difficulty in the Management of needs
Long waiting times and Workflow interruptions
Difficulty in Control of Materials Missing from workstations
Inexistence of Instructions of Work.

To meet the needs of Internal Logistics, approximately 3 hours are spent per day, with interruptions in material requests, that is, 3 hours a day of activities that do not add value to the product. These interruptions have a daily cost of € 54 per employee that is covered by them.

Improvement Proposal

Once the mapping and analysis of the current situation is complete, it is necessary to map the future situation, i.e. the desired situation in the future, with the elimination and reduction of waste through the implementation of Lean tools. In this way, a value stream design (VSD), which is the VSM of the future, of this assembly process was performed. The VSD of the future process was carried out at a macro level and aimed to eliminate all existing waits and all rework needs, with the Assembly Lead Time value defined as an objective to be achieved (Table 2).

The goal to be achieved is the reduction of 16 weeks needed to assemble the first Stacker Crane, to just 6 weeks. This reduction in LT to 6 weeks, represents a decrease of 41 364 € in assembly costs. This objective is possible to be achieved, not only through the improvements described here but also through other actions that were implemented during the analysis of the VSM and which have involved other sectors of the organization.

Table 2. Future lead time and costs to be archived

	Present LT (d)	Presente Cost (€)	Future LT (d)	Future Cost (€)
Base	44	7 380	5	1 980
Column	13	5 202	5	4 554
E.B.	49	11 232	12	5 184
Plataform	51	11 160	15	3 960
Final Assembly	29	30 096	15	8 028
Total	**16 (wks)**	**65 070**	**6 (wks)**	**23 706**

IMPLEMENTATION OF LEAN TOOLS

A set of improvements and Lean tools (table 3) were applied throughout the internal logistics department to combat waste and problems identified there. Besides, other Lean tools such as the 5S and the Gemba Walk were also applied throughout whole factory (Table 3).

As shown in Table 3, several improvements were implemented, however, the one that led to the most significant gains for the organization was the implementation of Kanban, with a cost reduction of 16%.

The creation of a Supply Kanban (Figure 3) for the assembly of the stacker crane aimed at reducing the variability of material waiting, allowing the creation of some stock that became essential to reduce waiting times and downtime, allowing some continuity and fluidity of work. This solution will also make it possible to contribute to workload at the internal logistics post and thus stabilize the working time since the Internal Logistics post is no longer in charge of 115 materials.

Table 3. Solutions implemented

Solutions	Description	Earnings
Logistic Kanban	Implementation of a kanban with 115 materials to support the assembly of Stacker Crane	10 620 € per year in logistics activities.
Visual Management in Internal Logistic	Implementation of an Internal Logistics Planning and Management Board	More organized workflow, delays and confusion in supplies are avoided and prioritizing supplies and needs is easier to manage.
Supply Kits	Aggregation of all materials in special cars, instead of being delivered in cartons, wood, or pallets.	Promotion of 5S, allows supplies in greater quantities and with more material and facilitates the identification of missing and overdue materials.
Standard Work	Work Instructions for Internal Logistic	Record the correct way to perform the functions of this workstation, standardize operations and train and assist other employees who may have to perform the duties of this job.
5S	Implementation of 5S in storage spaces	Safer, organized, clean and efficient work environments resulting in increased productivity.
Gemba Walk	Walk on the factory floor and aims to survey waste and opportunities for improvement.	Easier identification of improvement opportunities and waste leading to faster improvement actions.

Figure 3. Kanban Stacker Crane

CONCLUSION

This study focused on the application of Lean tools to contribute to improve the Internal Logistics process. In this sense, a description and analysis of the product Stacker crane was carried out, through the Value Stream Mapping tool. The VSM implementation involved a team made up of people who entered different departments. Several types of waste associated with the Stacker crane assembly process were identified, the times and percentages of activities that effectively added value to the product were quantified.

The entire process of assembling the Stacker crane had a cost of 65,070 € and a Lead Time of 16 weeks. With the drawing of the VSM, some opportunities for improvement were identified, having mapped the future process through a Value Stream Design, and then a plan was drawn out with the actions to be carried out perfectly defined to achieve the objectives planned in the VSD. The defined goals are to reduce the Lead Time for assembly of the Stacker crane to 6 weeks and to reduce the cost of assembly to 23,306 €.

To achieve these objectives, a set of improvement actions were defined, which were subsequently implemented in Internal Logistics. The actions defined for implementation were the 5S and a Gemba Walk.

Both application of 5S and the Gemba Walk represented non-measurable gains for the company, however, the application of improvements in Internal logistics constituted a reduction of 10 620 € per year, i.e., a decrease in 16% of the costs.

As future works, it is suggested to conclude the implementation of the Kanban supply to the stacker cranes, which is 80% of its conclusion, due to problems related to the administrative part concerning stock management and it is recommended to extend these measures to the rest of the equipment that is part of the company's portfolio.

REFERENCES

Azevedo, J., Sá, J.C., Ferreira, L.P., Santos, G., Cruz, F.M., Jimenez, G., & Silva, F.J.G. (2019). Improvement of Production Line in the Automotive Industry Through Lean Philosophy. *Procedia Manufacturing*, 41. doi:. doi:1023-1030

Correia, D., Silva, F. J. G., Gouveia, R. M., Pereira, M. T., & Ferreira, L. P. (2018). Improving manual assembly lines devoted to complex electronic devices by applying Lean tools. *Procedia Manufacturing*, *17*, 663–671. doi:10.1016/j.promfg.2018.10.115

Costa, C., Ferreira, L. P., Sá, J.C., & Silva, F.J.G. (2018). Implementation of 5S methodology in a metalworking company. *DAAAM International Scientific Book 2018*, 001-012.

Dias, P., Silva, F. J. G., Campilho, R. D. S. G., Ferreira, L. P., & Santos, T. (2019). Analysis and Improvement of an Assembly Line in the Automotive Industry. *Procedia Manufacturing*, *38*, 1444–1452. doi:10.1016/j.promfg.2020.01.143

Duas, J. A., Ferreira, L. P., Sá, J. C., Ribeiro, M. T., & Silva, F. J. G. (2019). Improving The Order Fulfilment Process At A Metalwork Company. *Procedia Manufacturing*, *41*, 1031–1038. doi:10.1016/j.promfg.2019.10.030

Ferreira, C., Sá, J. C., Ferreira, L. P., Lopes, M. P., Pereira, T., Ferreira, L. P., & Silva, F. J. G. (2019). iLeanDMAIC – A methodology for implementing the lean tools. *Procedia Manufacturing*, *41*, 1095–1102. doi:10.1016/j.promfg.2019.10.038

Marinho, P., Pimentel, D., Casais, R., Silva, F. J. G., Sá, J. C., & Ferreira, L. P. (2021). Selecting the best tools and framework to evaluate equipment malfunctions and improve the OEE in the cork industry. *International Journal of Industrial Engineering and Management*, *12*(4), 1–13. doi:10.24867/IJIEM-2021-4-295

Martins, R., Pereira, M. T., Ferreira, L. P., Sá, J. C., & Silva, F. J. G. (2020). Warehouse operations logistics improvement in a cork stopper factory. *Procedia Manufacturing*, *51*, 1723–1729. doi:10.1016/j.promfg.2020.10.240

Monteiro, C., Ferreira, L. P., Fernandes, N. O., Sá, J. C., Ribeiro, M. T., & Silva, F. J. G. (2019). Improving the Machining Process of the Metalworking Industry Using the Lean Tool SMED. *Procedia Manufacturing*, *41*, 555–562. doi:10.1016/j.promfg.2019.09.043

Mourato, J., Ferreira, L. P., Sá, J. C., & Silva, F. J. G. (2021). Improving internal logistics of a bus manufacturing using the lean techniques. *International Journal of Productivity and Performance Management*, *70*(7), 1930–1951. doi:10.1108/IJPPM-06-2020-0327

Oliveira, J., Sá, J. C., & Fernandes, A. (2017). Continuous Improvement through Lean Tools: An application in a mechanical company. *Procedia Manufacturing*, *13*, 1082–1089. doi:10.1016/j.promfg.2017.09.139

Pereira, A. M. H., Silva, M. R., Domingues, M. A. G., & Sá, J. C. (2019). Lean Six Sigma Approach to Improve the Production Process in the Mould Industry: A Case Study. *Quality Innovation Prosperity*, *23*(3), 103–121. doi:10.12776/qip.v23i3.1334

Pereira, M. T., Sousa, J. M. C., Ferreira, L. P., Sá, J. C., & Silva, F. J. G. (2019). Localization System for Optimization of Picking in a Manual Warehouse. *Procedia Manufacturing*, *38*, 1220–1227. doi:10.1016/j.promfg.2020.01.213

Pinto, C. M. A., Mendonça, J., Babo, L., Silva, F. J. G., & Fernandes, J. L. R. (2022). Analyzing the Implementation of Lean Methodologies and Practices in the Portuguese Industry: A Survey. *Sustainability*, *14*(3), 1929. doi:10.3390u14031929

Pombal, T., Ferreira, L. P., Sá, J. C., Pereira, M. T., & Silva, F. J. G. (2019). Implementation of Lean Methodologies in the Management of Consumable Materials in the Maintenance Workshops of an Industrial Company. *Procedia Manufacturing*, *38*, 975–982. doi:10.1016/j.promfg.2020.01.181

Ribeiro, P., Sá, J. C., Ferreira, L. P., Silva, F. J. G., Pereira, M. T., & Santos, G. (2019). The Impact of the Application of Lean Tools for Improvement of Process in a Plastic Company: A case study. *Procedia Manufacturing*, *38*, 765–775. doi:10.1016/j.promfg.2020.01.104

Rodrigues, J., Sá, J.C., Ferreira, L.P., Silva, F.J.G., & Santos, G. (2019). Lean Management "Quick-Wins": Results of Implementation. A Case Study. *Quality Innovation Prosperity*, *23*(3), 3-21. doi:10.12776/qip.v23i3.1291

Rosa, C., Silva, F. J. G., & Ferreira, L. P. (2017). Improving the Quality and Productivity of SteelWire-Rope Assembly Lines for the Automotive Industry. *Procedia Manufacturing*, *11*, 1035–1042. doi:10.1016/j.promfg.2017.07.214

Silva, F. J. G., & Gouveia, R. M. (2020). *Cleaner Production—Toward a Better Future; Springer Nature*. Switzertland. doi:10.1007/978-3-030-23165-1

Silva, F. J. G., Kirytopoulos, K., Ferreira, L. P., Sá, J. C., Santos, G., & Nogueira, M. C. C. (2022). The three pillars of sustainability and agile project management: How do they influence each other. *Corporate Social Responsibility and Environmental Management*, *29*(5), 1495–1512. doi:10.1002/csr.2287

Silva, S., Sá, J. C., Silva, F. J. G., Ferreira, L. P., & Santos, G. (2019). Lean Green—The Importance of Integrating Environment into Lean Philosophy—A Case Study. *Proceedings of the 6th European Lean Educator Conference*, 122, 211-219. Springer. 10.1007/978-3-030-41429-0_21

Teixeira, P., Sá, J. C., Silva, F. J. G., Ferreira, L., Santos, G., & Fontoura, P. (2021). Connecting lean and green with sustainability towards a conceptual model. *Journal of Cleaner Production*, *322*, 129047. doi:10.1016/j.jclepro.2021.129047

Tellini, T., Silva, F. J. G., Pereira, T., Morgado, L., Campilho, R. D. S. G., & Pereira, L. P. (2019). Improving In-Plant Logistics Flow by Physical and Digital Pathways. *Procedia Manufacturing*, *38*, 965–974. doi:10.1016/j.promfg.2020.01.180

Chapter 7
The Reduction of Machine Changeover Time by Using the SMED Method:
Case Study

Magdalena Dąbrowska
Collegium Witelona State University, Poland

Dawid Jagaczyński
Collegium Witelona State University, Poland

ABSTRACT

The main purpose of the article was the reduction of the machine changeover time in practical terms, on the example of a forming machine in the production process of a trunk shelf, based on the use of the SMED method. The article presented the stages of development and the foundations of the lean management concept. The description of the SMED methodology was made. A forming machine was selected in the manufacturing process of a trunk shelf. The identification and measurement of changeover times in the real model were performed. Two alternative models were proposed. The first of them was made based on the division of activities into external and internal, and the delegation of external activities to be performed by the production staff. The second alternative model included investments. The proposed and implemented improvement actions brought benefits in a reduction of the changeover time of the tested machine.

DOI: 10.4018/978-1-6684-5606-4.ch007

INTRODUCTION

The current economic crisis yielded by the worldwide crisis pulls on the corporation's pursuit of solutions extending effectiveness and performance of processes, among them production processes. In practice, multiple enterprises decide to implement the solutions based on the Lean Management philosophy. These answers allow the elimination of waste in various areas of the enterprise's functioning. Concerning the production companies and production processes, the losses relate to e.g. overproduction, downtime, machine losses, keeping the unnecessary inventory, or long-term research of the tools and machines.

The beginnings of the Lean Management conception can be dated to the times after the Second World War. This notion was initiated in the automotive industry in Japan. Its forerunner is the Toyota company, which began not only the new mode of action but also thinking (Dekier, 2012; Liker, 2004; Liker & Meier, 2006; Spear, 2004). The Lean Management conception was an answer to the present at that time issues in the market. The main concerns of the Japanese automotive market then were (Dave, 2020; Liker & Convis, 2012): the small size of the market, market demands requiring the offer of diversified products, economic problems in Japan caused by the war consequences, lack of financial resources, lack of raw materials, high inflation, and poverty. Due to the fragile condition of the enterprise, 1600 people left the company, while the workers who remained hired, were offered satisfying working conditions and salaries, as well as lifetime employment. During its thirteen years of operating, the company assembled only 2685 cars. Governing then president of the board - E. Toyoda, with the engineer - T. Ohno, were working on combining mass production with crafting methods. Because of the e.g., high employee competencies, workers' ingenuity, and openness for refreshed solutions, but also lack of resistance to the changes, conducting the experiments were possible. The great willingness for cooperation and flexibility of the managers led E. Toyoda to visit the Ford factory in the United States (more about the management system in Ford Company was discussed e.g., in: (Beynon, 1984), (Beynon & Nichols, 2006), (Buckman, 2009),(Levinson, 2002),(Monden, 2011),(Wilson, 1995)). Based on completed observations and experimentations, in the Toyota company, the Toyota Production System (TPS) was created. Its core consisted of (Haak, 2006),(Ohno, 1988), (Ohno & Bodek, 2019), (Pegels, 1984), (Wada, 2020), (Yang & Yang, 2013): complete waste elimination, striving to the reaching the most subordinate potential expenditures, guaranteeing the highest quality, and the process realization in the shortest possible amount of time. The evolution of Toyota Production System has been presented in the Table 1.

Table 1. The development of Toyota Production System

Year	Task	Characteristics
1948	Implementation of the suction system in the engines department	- raising an order to go back to the prior functional position in order to accumulate a stock of parts crucial for production; - seizing only the amount of goods, which is required once in the machining process and in the moment when it is mandated; -the elimination of the interoperation stocks through the insightful commodities control;
1949	Usage of the suction system in the treatment department	- the exclusion of the supplies appearance in the machining department; - the necessity to operate several machines by one worker; - employees conduct personal control, which increases the quality of manufactured products;
1950	Advancing of the pull system to the marketing activities, departments synchronization, and implementation of the triple lights system	- adaptation of the production policy exclusively for vehicles ordered by customers from dealers; - further reduction of the interoperation commodities; - shortening the time of notifying the supervision services about the occurring issues;
1953	Introduction of the kanban system (more about the kanban system see e.g., in:(Junior & Godinho Filho, 2010),(Lin et al., 2013),(Monden, 1994)	- exchange of the cards, which is a signal to renew production; - to simplify the production, purchasing, and transport process, the company implemented parts and components standardization;
1955	Heijunka (more about the heijunka system see e.g. in:(Hüttmeir et al., 2009),(Lippolt & Furmans, 2008)	- further reserves reduction through the controlling delivery of the parts to the production lines system; - balancing production (both in terms of quantity and assortment) with a simultaneous better use of machines and devices;
1957	Implementation of the triple light system in all production lines	
1961	Introduction by Toyota of the Kanban system to the factories of selected suppliers	
1962	Approach to the management in small sections	- extension of the existing kanban system to all branches and production corps; - introduction of the system preventing errors, which assignment is to eliminate shortages and prevent overproduction; - more effective usage of machines and devices, reduction of reserves, and reduction of producing lead times;
1963	Boosting the employee productivity	- employees operate an average of five machines;
1965	Expansion of the Kanban system on the external suppliers	
1971	Reduction of the retooling of the stamping presses	- the reduction of the changeover time of stamping press to three minutes was obtained; - the practices of transferring assembly workers between various operating positions were executed;
1973	Integration of suppliers	

Source: own study on the basis of (Ohno & Bodek, 2019), (Sutherland & Bennett, 2007), (Wada, 2020).

Until the end of the 70s in the 20th century, this method was used and implemented in Japan. Unfortunately, in the beginning, this conception was not enthusiastically received. American intellectuals found the success of Japanese enterprises in high automatization, low wages, and the support of the Japanese government toward local businesses. However, American scholars were wrong about this. The breakthrough came with the book "The Machine that Changed the World" written by D.T. Jones, D. Roos, and J.P. Womack. In this book, the authors confirmed that achieving better results by the Japanese factories, in comparison to American or European businesses, was a result of specific management practices. The writers for the first time introduced the terminology "Lean Management"(Womack et al., 1990).

In the subject literature there exist a multitude of definitions of "Lean Management". In the context of chosen definitions, Lean Management conceptions can be viewed as strategy, but in other descriptions as a philosophy or even a method(Bertagnolli, 2018), (Charron et al., 2014), (Helmold, 2020), (Jackson, 1996), (Lizak, 2016), (Womack & Jones, 1996). The foundations of the conception are (Table 2):

Table 2. Foundations of the "Lean Management" conception

Foundations	Explanation
Groupwork	The efficiency of the team is greater than the sum of the individual employees' performance (the so-called synergy effect). The team is given tasks and a range of responsibilities. The group is demanded to conduct independent decisions. As a result, the immediate control is changed for the team's self-control. The growth of the group discipline results in motivation growth and readiness to work.
Decentralization of the decisions	Decision-making is assigned to the lower branches of the organizational structures. The autonomy and team self-control grow. The decision decentralization may affect on lowering of the number of intermediate management level employees.
Focus on the client	Every worker is responsible for customer satisfaction and should endeavour to meet their requirements. The obligation for the product begins already at the level of materials suppliers, as well as raw materials, and components.
Constant improvement (kaizen)	All employees ought to take part in the gradual improvement of all areas of the company's activities. Enhancing the functioning of the establishment serves to compress production time, reduce costs, and improve quality. The significance of constant progress is "small steps today", not "big steps tomorrow".
Flattening of hierarchies	The horizontal organizational structure fosters better coordination of activities, more efficient information flow, and increase customer attraction.
Rejecting the mistake at the source	It is the detection of the error as close as possible to the location of its occurrence, as well as its elimination at the time of distinction. Determining the problem at its basis means lower production expenses. It is also the opportunity to analyse faster the deeper causes of deficiencies and the prevention of their repetition.
Avoidance of prolificacy	Processes that do not add significance are waste and they should be therefore eliminated.
Constant flow of the materials	Every material should be in circulation, whereas the number of manufactured goods ought to be managed by the customer.
Total quality management	The specification of the product is defined by the customer. It is essential to frequently improve the level of product quality through teamwork, self-control, and improving employee qualifications.

Source: own study on the basis of (Womack, 2007), (Womack et al., 1990), (Womack & Jones, 1996).

To the most important Lean Management tools mentioned in the subject literature belong (Mayr et al., 2018), (Wolniak, 2014): 5S, Kaizen, Just in Time, Just in Sequence, Heijunka, Kanban, SMED, TPM, VSM, Visual Management.

The fourth industrial revolution, also called the digital transformation of manufacturing, refers to the development and integration of technology-oriented companies in the processing industry. Solutions of the Industry 4.0 era allow innovative ways of producing products, providing services, managing assets, and running a business. They represent a potential for many industries, sectors, and fields. The implementation of the solutions of the fourth industrial revolution affects the entire value chain by streamlining production and engineering processes, enhancing the quality of products and services, optimizing relationships between customers and organizations, bringing tangible benefits, as well as transforming the current work environment (Ślusarczyk, 2019). The influence of Industry 4.0 on the organization of production processes is presented in Table 3.

Table 3. The impact of Industry 4.0 solutions on the functioning of the production processes.

Process "dimension"	Benefits
Usage of resources and process optimization	- real-time process monitoring; - quick, effective, and fully automated response to any circumstance during production; - transparent resource consumption cracking; - the possibility of accurately estimating the number of resources at each stage of production; - the possibility of accurately estimating the number of resources at each stage of production; - increasing the efficiency of processes
Assets usage	- optimal exploitation of the machine park; - constant and remote monitoring of the condition of machines; - reducing machine down time; - early detection of potential problems; - continuous maintenance of machines; - avoidance and early correction of defects; - lowering costs and increasing production efficiency
Work productivity	- increase in labor productivity; - shortening the waiting time between different stages in the production process; - acceleration of the research and development process (e.g., through 3D printing)
Improvement of quality	- real-time problem-solving; - advanced process control; - correction of errors to reduce the occurrence of unstable production processes or reworks

Source: own study on the basis of (Blunck & Werthmann, 2017).

Industry 4.0 enables integral production by providing data and tools to streamline operations and manage supply chain risk more efficiently (from product logistics and inventory management to machine maintenance). Intelligent solutions enable monitoring traffic and emergencies more efficiently, using the infrastructure, limiting power outages, reducing waste, and implementing intelligent pricing programs (Ślusarczyk, 2019). Industry 4.0 is a revolution in the approach to production control methodology. It consists, among other things, of the dynamic retooling of machines initiated by many factors, e.g., information transferred in the processed elements (Gajdzik & Grabowska, 2018).

The digital revolution became a stimulus for innovative system and process solutions with use of 4.0 technology (Valamede & Akkari, 2020). The basics of Industry 4.0 include (Kolberg & Zühlke, 2015), (Pereira et al., 2019), (Sanders et al., 2016):

- Big Data Analytics (see more (Chen et al., 2016), (Vaidya et al., 2018)),
- Automated Guided Vehicles (AGV) (see more (Bechtsis et al., 2017), (Mayr et al., 2018)),
- Virtual Simulation (VS) (see more (Bahrin et al., 2016)),
- Cybersecurity (see more (Craigen et al., 2014), (Ustundag & Cevikcan, 2018)),
- Cloud Computing (The Cloud) (see more (Furht, 2010), (Vaidya et al., 2018)),
- Additive Manufacturing (AM) (see more (Bahrin et al., 2016), (Bandyopadhyay & Bose, 2019)),
- Augmented Reality (AR) (see more (Mayr et al., 2018).

Currently, the Industry 4.0 revolution aims to achieve faster innovation in manufacturing process. They take into the account the growth of the value chain (Ben-Daya et al., 2019). Due to the focus on the automation flow process, Industry 4.0 enables flexibility and customization of products and services. It, however, consequently increases profitability (Abramowicz et al., 2015).

In the era of the Industry 4.0, there is a new approach to the Lean Management philosophy called also Lean 4.0.Lean 4.0 is a combination of the establishments and tools of the Lean Management concept (Lean Production, Lean Manufacturing) (Javaid et al., 2022), (Mayr et al., 2018). The evolution of the Lean 4.0 concept has so far proceeded in four stages (Ejsmont et al., 2020), (Gil-Vilda et al., 2021):

1. Defining the concept of Lean 4.0 - Lean 4.0 was used for the first time in 2017.
2. Identification of synergy points - in 2020, as many as 25 points of synergy were identified between Lean tools and Industry 4.0 solutions (Table 4).

Table 4. Synergy points between lean tools and Industry 4.0 solutions

LM TOOL	TECHNOLOGIES 4.0						
	Big Data Analytics	**AGVs**	**AM**	**The Cloud**	**Cybersecurity**	**VS**	**AR**
JIT	X	X	X	X			X
Kanban	X	X				X	
Poka-Yoke		X		X	X		X
VSM	X			X		X	
Kaizen	X			X		X	X
TPM	X	X	X	X		X	X

Source: (Valamede & Akkari, 2020).

3. Inclusion of artificial intelligence in decision-making processes.
4. Waste reduction to reach a new level of excellence.

Lean 4.0 is understood as a combination of the principles and tools of the Lean Manufacturing (or Lean Production) concept with Industry 4.0 technologies. The task of the Lean 4.0 concept is the synergy and complementarity of Industry 4.0 and Lean solutions in order to reduce waste and complexity (Gil-Vilda et al., 2021). Among the seven primary sources of waste, distinguished by T. Ohno in the production process indicated are (Ohno, 1988): waste of overproduction, waste of inventory, waste of transport, waste of waiting, waste of motion, waste of overprocessing and waste of defects. The failure rate of machines is undoubtedly a source of waste in the production process, understood as waiting. The leading causes of failure of the machine park include inadequate machine regulations, poorly performed retooling, or overloading the machine. In the literature on the subject, there are publications relating to the practical aspects of applying the SMED method in the conditions of Industry 4.0 (Ciano et al., 2021), (Jurík et al., 2020), (Peças et al., 2022).

The purpose of the article is the time reduction of the machine changeover in practical terms. The studies were conducted on the cause of a forming machine in the production process of a trunk shelf based on the SMED method.

SMED Methodology (Single Minute Exchange of Die)

The SMED methodology was developed by the Japanese engineer S. Shingo. It was implemented for the first time in Toyota manufactories (Kulkarni & Lahiri, 2014), (Pellegrini et al., 2012), (Simões & Tenera, 2010). The SMED methodology allows productivity and processes efficiency growth in the area of maintenance. This is an explicit consequence of shortening the machine changeover time(Shingo & Dillon, 2019). The use of SMED methodology enables constant and gradual advancement, and also the elimination of excessive activities. As a result, it enables efficient adjustment to the dynamic environment and altering market conditions. SMED allows the reduction of the machine changeover time. Thanks to that, the time intended for production increases, while at the same time the size of the production branch and the number of inventories lowers. As a result, it decreases production costs (Pacana & Czerwińska, 2020), (Pietraszek et al., 2020).

The starting point for implementing this method is the division of activities bonded with the changeover into the so-called internal and external activities. Internal activities are those, which are fulfilled on the turned-off machine. It is essential to emphasize, however, that the duration of the activity alone should be added to the start time, machine start-up time, and time to achieve full performance. External activities, on the other hand, are those, which are possible to do without the necessity of turning off the machine (they can be performed while the machine is running). These are most often preparatory activities striving for raising modifications. Internal activities not only cause the loss of work efficiency but also decrease the time intended for production. Changeover time is a time counted from the moment of producing the last good piece made for the "old order" to the time when the first piece for the "new order" is created (Rosa et al., 2017), (Ulutas, 2011), (Vieira et al., 2020).

The SMED methodology is based on the four steps (Birmingham & Jelinek, 2007), (Carrizo Moreira & Campos Silva Pais, 2011), (Stadnicka, 2015):

- step 0 - observation and the recording of the changeover process;
- step 1 - analysis of the collected materials and the division of the activities into internal and external retooling;
- step 2 –transformation of the internal activities into the external ones;
- step 3 - facilitating all aspects of changeover operations.

The first step is to specify all activities connected to the machine changeover. Later, every action should be described giving it the status of "internal activity" or "external activity" - following the adopted definition. Then, all of the measures are grouped. To the group of external actions, all external actions are sorted; likewise, the group of internal actions consists of all internal actions. Each of the activities is given its duration. As a result, the sum of the times of "external activities" and the sum of the times of "internal activities" is found. The "internal activities" need to have diverged in terms of the possibility of their implementation in the system of external activities. If there is a possibility, they are given the new status of "external action". The remaining activities do not have their status changed. In this way, a new division of activities is acquired, thereby decreasing the totality of the time of internal activities.

Characteristics of Changeover of a Forming Machine in the Production Process of Atrunk Shelf– Real Model

The research was conducted for one year and documented on an ongoing basis in paper and photo form. The audited company did not consent to make the concerned documentation public.

The forming machine (here: the hydraulic press) was analysed. The hydraulic press is a bottleneck in the production process of the trunk shelf (the average OEE coefficient calculated for the next 20 working days was 77.24%). The hydraulic press gives the materials the right shape. Thanks to the sheets, it cuts the product following the provided measurements. The activities of changing over the forming machine (hydraulic press), which are under the work instructions adopted in the examined enterprise, include 20 steps (Table 5).

Table 5. The activities of changing over the forming machine (hydraulic press) according to the instructions

Step	Activities of the changeover process
1.	Activities carried before the tool change: • preparing the trolley for replacement with an appropriate tool and placing it nearby before the end of the machine cycle; • preparation of the checklist for operators; • substitution of given materials for the assigned exchange product; • preparation of the key for replacement.
2.	Checking the checklist: • checking the previously prepared checklist.
3.	Panel operation: • the machine needs to be switched over from the automatic settings to the manual operation.
4.	Closing the press with inserts on distances: • insertion of the distances to the tool columns.
5.	Panel operations: • closing the press continued until the upper form touches the lower form.
6.	Preparation of the press for lifting: • On the control panel there is a requirement to unlock the tool.
7.	Disconnecting the wires and loosening the screws: • disconnection of the cooling and pneumatic lines; • disconnection of electric wires from temperature indication and tool code; • unscrewing the holding pins.
8.	Lifting the press: • reconnecting the power supply in the control panel; • opening the press and gently driving the molds with the press table.
9.	Lifting the curtains: • lifting up the rollers in the tool; • raising the right and left curtains all the way up and locking them.

continues on following page

Table 5. Continued

Step	Activities of the changeover process
10.	Tool removal • moving the trolley to be replaced under the press and pulling the tool in the press into the free space on the trolley; • driving the trolley and inserting the tool into the press from the second stand; • driving the cart outside the working area.
11.	Inserting the tool and lowering the press: • if the tool is not evenly inserted in the press, it should be straightened with a crowbar so that the holes fit the screws; • using the control pendant to lower the rollers in the tool; • deleting the barrier and lowering the press with the control pendant.
12.	Connecting the wires: • starting with the connection of cooling lines, then pneumatic lines, then electrical lines with temperature indication and tool code.
13.	Lowering the curtains: • lowering right and left curtain completely down.
14	Tool locking: • if the tool is closed, the tool must be locked by using the control panel.
15.	Tightening the screws: • tightening the screws on the front of the tool at the top; • then on the back, tighten the two screws on the top of the tool.
16.	Lifting the press and inserting the recipe: • lifting the press by the top part of the tool and inserting the recipe.
17.	Folding the trolley: • The trolley should be compounded to the required size by using the knob.
18.	Taking out the securities: • All protections on which the upper of the tool rests need to be removed.
19.	Applying the decor and fleece: • placing the decor (roll) on the feeder using a hoist, sliding it under the clamping bar, stop inserting when the sensor is initiated; • evening the decor, closing the clamp using a cassette; • then inserting the fleece on the spindle by carefully screwing the roller locks.
20.	Inserting the sommold: • inserting the sommold to the certain place in a box.

Source: internal materials of examined enterprise.

After getting to know the work instructions, the activities of forming machine (hydraulic press) changeovers were observed along with the time measurements of the activities conducted in the process of changing the tested machine (Table 6).

On the basis of conducted observations it can be inferred, that:

- there are discrepancies between the work instructions and the activities carried out by the operator;
- there are committed excessive activities linked to the searching for the tools and trolleys, as well as the transport of the tool for replacement, and their preparation takes the operator 1020 sec.

Table 6. Results of the observation of the activities in the process of changing over of the forming machine (hydraulic press) – real model

Operation of the changing over process	Time (s)
Panel operation - setting the working mode of the machine	5
Closing the press with inserts on distances	30
Operation on the press closing panel	30
Tool unlocking	120
Searching for a bolt wrench	300
Unscrewing the screws	180
Disconnecting the wires	120
Raising the press	30
Raising the rollers in the tool	10
Raising the curtains	30
Searching for a trolley and driving it to the press	300
Pulling out the tool onto the trolley	120
Driving the truck beyond the working area	120
Going for the tool and bringing it back	300
Inserting the tool from the trolley into the press	60
Manual correction of the tool in the press with a crowbar	180
Lowering the press	30
Connecting the wires	300
Lowering the curtains	30
Tool locking	120
Tightening the screws	180
Raising the press	30
Typing a prescription	10
Twisting the cart	30
Establishing a fleece	180
Applying the decor	180
Insertion of a sommold	60
Total	**3085**

Source: own study.

The Optimalization of the Machine Change Over Time– Alternative Models

Based on the carried observations and conclusions drawn from the real model analysis, the subsequent determinations were executed (alternative model I):

- setting the empty tools trolley next to the workplace;
- setting the empty tools trolley next to the workplace with a toll requiring the change;
- securing the position with the keys necessary to unscrew the screws;
- necessity to familiarize with the checklist by the operator.

Taking into consideration proposed improvements, the classification of activities related to the changeover of the forming machine (hydraulic press) into external and internal activities was created. The external activities, which do not require turning off the machine (they can be done before or during the changeover process) include (Table 7):

- creating the checklist and preparing the necessary tools;
- driving the empty trolley in front of the press before starting the changeover;
- driving the cart with the replaced tool out of the working area;
- placing a trolley with a tool under the press;
- assembling of the trolley used in the process.

The activities listed in Table 7 were conducted by the production staff, not by the operator, which allowed to shorten the time assigned for making them from 1020 seconds to 250 seconds, while at the same time widening the field of activities by preparing the checklist and taking care of all of the crucial tools before the changeover process. This operation lasted 100 sec.

The proposed improvements led to reducing the changeover time of the tested machine from 3083 sec. to 2035 sec., so by 1050 sec.

The further step was making the investments having the purpose improvement of the activities performed during the changeover (alternative model II). These investments absorbed € 120,000 and were related to:

- improving the press regulations;
- improvements to the speed of raising the curtains;
- purchase of the specialized trolley for transporting, inserting, and removing the tool from the machine;
- acceleration of the locking mechanism;

- improvements allowing for faster material changes;
- purchase of an electrical device that improves screw tightening;
- use of the multi-connectors.

Table 7. Division of the activities of the changeover process of the forming machine (hydraulic press)

Activities of the changeover process	Time (sec,)	External	Internal
Preparing the checklist and taking care of all the necessary tools	100	E	
Panel operation – setting the working mode of the machine	5		I
Closing the press with inserts on distances	30		I
Operation on the press closing panel	30		I
Tool unlocking	120		I
Unscrewing the screws	180		I
Disconnecting the wires	120		I
Raising the press	30		I
Raising the rollers in the tool	10		I
Raising the curtains	30		I
Leaving an empty trolley in front of the press	30	E	
Taking the tool out of the press and placing it on the trolley	120		I
Driving the truck beyond the working area	60	E	
Placing a trolley with a tool under the press	30	E	
Inserting the tool from the trolley into the press	60		I
Correcting the tool manually in the press with a crowbar	180		I
Lowering the press	30		I
Connecting the wires	300		I
Lowering the curtains	30		I
Tool locking	120		I
Tightening the screws	180		I
Raising the press	30		I
Typing a prescription	10		I
Twisting the cart	30	E	
Establishing a fleece	180		I
Applying the decor	180		I
Insertion of a sommold	60		I
Total		**250**	**2035**

Source: own study.

Among the investments were implemented solutions in Industry 4.0 related to the standardization and visualization of conversion activities.

Based on the made and implemented investments, another measurement of the changeover time of the forming machine (hydraulic press) was carried out. The results are pictured in Table 8.

Table 8. Results of the observations of the activities in the changeover of the forming machine (hydraulic press) – alternative model (before and after investments)

The activity of the changeover	Before	After
	Time (sec.)	**Time (sec.)**
Panel operation - setting the working mode of the machine	5	5
Closing the press with inserts on distances	30	10
Operation on the press closing panel	30	10
Tool unlocking	120	30
Unscrew the screws	180	30
Disconnecting the wires	120	10
Raising the press	30	5
Raising the rollers in the tool	10	10
Raise the curtains	30	10
Taking the tool out of the press and placing it on the trolley	120	5
Inserting the tool from the trolley into the press	60	5
Correcting the tool manually in the press with a crowbar	180	0
Lowering the press	30	5
Connecting the wires	300	20
Lowering the curtains	30	10
Tool locking	120	30
Tightening the screws	180	30
Raising the press	30	10
Typing a prescription	10	5
Establishing a fleece	180	30
Applying the decor	180	30
Insertion of a sommold	60	30
Total	**2035**	**340**

Source: Own study

The proposed improvements led to reducing the changeover time of the tested machine from 2035 sec. to 340 sec., so by 1695 sec.

CONCLUSION

The purpose of this article was to reduce the machine changeover time in practical terms, on the example of a forming machine in the production process of a trunk shelf, on the basis of the SMED method.

Founded on the conducted analyses, it can be concluded that:

1. there exist some dissimilarities between the work instructions in the field of the forming machine changeover and the activities performed by the operator,
2. there are performed some unwarranted activities related to looking for tools and trolleys, as well as the transport of the tools for the replacement, whereas their execution takes operator 1020 sec.,
3. the division of activities related to the changeover of the forming machine to the internal and external activities and the delegation of external activities to be done by the production staff, not by the operator, allowed to shorten the time of their performance from 1020 sec. to 250 sec., whereas widening the spectrum of activities by preparation checklist and taking care of all the required tools before the changeover process (the duration of the activity was additional 100 sec.),
4. suggested improvements in the area of the delegation of some activities to be conducted by the production staff allowed to reduce the changeover time of the examined machine from 3083 sec. (in the real model) to 2035 sec. (in the alternative model I), so by 1050 sec.,
5. making investments having the purpose of improving activities performed during the changeover (alternative model II) allowed reducing the changeover time of the examined machine from 3085 sec. (in the real model) to 340 sec. (in the alternative model II) by 2745 sec.,
6. making investments having the purpose of improving activities performed during the changeover (alternative model II) allowed reducing the changeover time of the examined machine from 2035 sec. (in the alternative model I) to 340 sec. (in the alternative model II) by 1695 sec.

REFERENCES

Bahrin, M.A.K., Othman, M.F., Azli, N.H.N., & Talib, M.F. (2016). Industry 4.0: a review on industrial automation and robotic. *Jurnal Teknologi*, *78*(6–13), 137–143.

Bandyopadhyay, A., & Bose, S. (Eds.). (2019). *Additive manufacturing*. CRC Press. doi:10.1201/9780429466236

Bechtsis, D., Tsolakis, N., Vlachos, D., & Iakovou, E. (2017). Sustainable supply chain management in the digitalisation era: The impact of Automated Guided Vehicles. *Journal of Cleaner Production*, *142*, 3970–3984. doi:10.1016/j.jclepro.2016.10.057

Ben-Daya, M., Hassini, E., & Bahroun, Z. (2019). Internet of things and supply chain management: A literature review. *International Journal of Production Research*, *57*(15–16), 4719–4742. doi:10.1080/00207543.2017.1402140

Bertagnolli, F. (2018). *Lean management*. Springer. doi:10.1007/978-3-658-13124-1

Beynon, H. (1984). *Working for Ford* (2nd ed.). Penguin.

Beynon, H., & Nichols, T. (2006). *The Fordism of Ford and Modern Management*. Edward Elgar Publishing.

Birmingham, F., & Jelinek, J. (2007). *Quick Changeover Simplified: The Manager's Guide to Improving Profits with SMED*. CRC Press.

Blunck, E., & Werthmann, H. (2017, October). Industry 4.0–an opportunity to realize sustainable manufacturing and its potential for a circular economy. *DIEM: Dubrovnik International Economic Meeting*, *3*(1), 644-666.

Buckman, J. (2009). Ford finds its way. *Quality Progress*, *42*(6), 14–15.

Carrizo Moreira, A., & Campos Silva Pais, G. (2011). Single minute exchange of die: A case study implementation. *Journal of Technology Management & Innovation*, *6*(1), 129–146. doi:10.4067/S0718-27242011000100011

Charron, R., Harrington, H. J., Voeh, F., & Wiggin, H. (2014). The lean management systems handbook. CRC Press.

Chen, Y., Chen, H., Gorkhali, A., Lu, Y., Ma, Y., & Li, L. (2016). Big data analytics and big data science: A survey. *Journal of Management Analytics*, *3*(1), 1–42. doi:10.1080/23270012.2016.1141332

Ciano, M. P., Dallasega, P., Orzes, G., & Rossi, T. (2021). One-to-one relationships between Industry 4.0 technologies and Lean Production techniques: A multiple case study. *International Journal of Production Research*, *59*(5), 1386–1410. doi:10.1080/00207543.2020.1821119

Craigen, D., Diakun-Thibault, N., & Purse, R. (2014). Defining cybersecurity. *Technology Innovation Management Review*, *4*(10), 13–21. doi:10.22215/timreview/835

Dave, P. Y. (2020). The History of Lean Manufacturing by the view of Toyota-Ford. *International Journal of Scientific and Engineering Research*, *11*(8), 1598–1602.

Dekier, Ł. (2012). The origins and evolution of Lean Management system. *Journal of International Students*, *5*(1), 46–51. doi:10.14254/2071-8330.2012/5-1/6

Ejsmont, K., Gladysz, B., Corti, D., Castaño, F., Mohammed, W. M., & Martinez Lastra, J. L. (2020). Towards 'Lean Industry 4.0 '–Current trends and future perspectives. *Cogent Business & Management*, *7*(1), 1781995. doi:10.1080/23311975.2020.1781995

Furht, B. (2010). Cloud computing fundamentals. In *Handbook of cloud computing* (pp. 3–19). Springer. doi:10.1007/978-1-4419-6524-0_1

Gajdzik, B., & Grabowska, S. (2018). Leksykon pojęć stosowanych w przemyśle 4.0. *Zeszyty Naukowe. Organizacja i Zarządzanie/Politechnika Śląska*, (132), 221-238.

Gil-Vilda, F., Yagüe-Fabra, J. A., & Sunyer, A. (2021). From Lean Production to Lean 4.0: A Systematic Literature Review with a Historical Perspective. *Applied Sciences (Basel, Switzerland)*, *11*(21), 10318. doi:10.3390/app112110318

Haak, R. (2006). Implementing process innovation—the case of the Toyota production system. In *Management of Technology and Innovation in Japan* (pp. 185–203). Springer. doi:10.1007/3-540-31248-X_9

Helmold, M. (2020). *Lean management and Kaizen*. Springer International Publishing.

Hüttmeir, A., De Treville, S., Van Ackere, A., Monnier, L., & Prenninger, J. (2009). Trading off between heijunka and just-in-sequence. *International Journal of Production Economics*, *118*(2), 501–507. doi:10.1016/j.ijpe.2008.12.014

Jackson, T. L. (1996). *Implementing a lean management system*. CRC Press. doi:10.4324/9781482278071

Javaid, M., Haleem, A., Singh, R. P., Rab, S., Suman, R., & Khan, S. (2022). Exploring relationships between Lean 4.0 and manufacturing industry. *The Industrial Robot*, *49*(3), 402–414. doi:10.1108/IR-08-2021-0184

Junior, M. L., & Godinho Filho, M. (2010). Variations of the kanban system: Literature review and classification. *International Journal of Production Economics*, *125*(1), 13–21. doi:10.1016/j.ijpe.2010.01.009

Jurík, L., Horňáková, N., & Domčeková, V. (2020). The application of smed method in the industrial enterprise. *Acta Logistica*, *7*(4), 269–281. doi:10.22306/al.v7i4.189

Kolberg, D., & Zühlke, D. (2015). Lean automation enabled by industry 4.0 technologies. *IFAC-PapersOnLine*, *48*(3), 1870–1875. doi:10.1016/j.ifacol.2015.06.359

Kulkarni, P. C., & Lahiri, G. (2014). Improving productivity using SMED. *Journal of Manufacturing Engineering*, *9*(4), 253–258.

Levinson, W. A. (2002). *Henry Ford's Lean Vision. Enduring Principles from the First Ford Motor Plant*. Productivity Press.

Liker, J. K. (2004). *The Toyota Way. 14 Management Principles from the World's Greatest Manufacturer*. McGraw Hill.

Liker, J. K., & Convis, G. L. (2012). *Toyota way to lean leadership: Achieving and sustaining excellence through leadership development*. McGraw-Hill Education.

Liker, J. K., & Meier, D. (2006). *Toyota way fieldbook*. McGraw-Hill Education.

Lin, C. J., Chen, F. F., & Chen, Y. M. (2013). Knowledge kanban system for virtual research and development. *Robotics and Computer-integrated Manufacturing*, *29*(3), 119–134. doi:10.1016/j.rcim.2012.04.020

Lippolt, C. R., & Furmans, K. (2008). Sizing of heijunka-controlled production systems with unreliable production processes. In *Lean business systems and beyond* (pp. 11–19). Springer. doi:10.1007/978-0-387-77249-3_2

Lizak M. (2016). Methods of measuring the effectiveness of Lean Management. *Production Engineering Archives*, *13*(4), 31-34.

Mayr, A., Weigelt, M., Kühl, A., Grimm, S., Erll, A., Potzel, M., & Franke, J. (2018). Lean 4.0-A conceptual conjunction of lean management and Industry 4.0. *Procedia CIRP*, *72*, 622–628. doi:10.1016/j.procir.2018.03.292

Monden, Y. (1994). *Adaptable Kanban System Maintains Just-In-Time Production*. Springer. doi:10.1007/978-1-4615-9714-8_2

Monden, Y. (2011). *Toyota production system: an integrated approach to just-in-time*. CRC Press.

Ohno, T. (1988). *Toyota Production System. Beyond Large-Scale Production.* Productivity Press.

Ohno, T., & Bodek, N. (2019). *Toyota production system: beyond large-scale production*. Productivity Press. doi:10.4324/9780429273018

Pacana, A., & Czerwińska, K. (2020). Improving the quality level in the automotive industry. *Production Engineering Archives*, *26*(4), 162–166. doi:10.30657/pea.2020.26.29

Peças, P., Faustino, M., Lopes, J., & Amaral, A. (2022). Lean methods digitization towards lean 4.0: a case study of e-VMB and e-SMED. *International Journal on Interactive Design and Manufacturing (IJIDeM)*, 1-19.

Pegels, C. C. (1984). The Toyota Production System— Lessons for American Management. *International Journal of Operations & Production Management*, *4*(1), 3–11. doi:10.1108/eb054703

Pellegrini, S., Shetty, D., & Manzione, L. (2012). *Study and implementation of single minute exchange of die (SMED) methodology in a setup reduction kaizen* [Doctoral dissertation]. University of Hartford.

Pereira, A. C., Dinis-Carvalho, J., Alves, A. C., & Arezes, M. P. (2019). How industry 4.0 can enhance lean practices. *FME Transactions*, *47*(4), 810–822. doi:10.5937/fmet1904810P

Pietraszek, J., Radek, N., & Goroshko Andrii, V. (2020). Challenges for the DOE methodology related to the introduction of Industry 4.0. *Production Engineering Archives*, *26*(4), 190–194. doi:10.30657/pea.2020.26.33

Rosa, C., Silva, F. J. G., Ferreira, L. P., & Campilho, R. D. S. G. (2017). SMED methodology: The reduction of setup times for Steel Wire-Rope assembly lines in the automotive industry. *Procedia Manufacturing*, *13*, 1034–1042. doi:10.1016/j.promfg.2017.09.110

Sanders, A., Elangeswaran, C., & Wulfsberg, J. P. (2016). Industry 4.0 implies lean manufacturing: Research activities in industry 4.0 function as enablers for lean manufacturing. *Journal of Industrial Engineering and Management*, *9*(3), 811–833. doi:10.3926/jiem.1940

Schmidt, R., Möhring, M., Härting, R. C., Reichstein, C., Neumaier, P., & Jozinović, P. (2015). Industry 4.0 - potentials for creating smart products: empirical research results. In W. Abramowicz (Ed.), *Business Information Systems. BIS 2015. Lecture Notes in Business Information Processing* (Vol. 208, pp. 16–27). Springer. doi:10.1007/978-3-319-19027-3_2

Shingo, S., & Dillon, A. P. (2019). *A revolution in manufacturing: the SMED system*. Routledge. doi:10.4324/9781315136479

Simões, A., & Tenera, A. (2010). Improving setup time in a Press Line–Application of the SMED methodology. *IFAC Proceedings Volumes*, *43*(17), 297-302.

Ślusarczyk, B. (2019). Potencjalne rezultaty wprowadzania koncepcji Przemysłu 4.0 w przedsiębiorstwach. *Przegląd Organizacji*, (1), 4–10. doi:10.33141/po.2019.01.01

Spear, S. J. (2004). Learning to lead at Toyota. *Harvard Business Review*, *82*(5), 78–91. PMID:15146738

Stadnicka, D. (2015). Setup analysis: Combining SMED with other tools. *Management and Production Engineering Review*, *6*(1), 36–50. doi:10.1515/mper-2015-0006

Sutherland, J., & Bennett, B. (2007). The seven deadly wastes of logistics: applying Toyota Production System principles to create logistics value. *White Paper*, *701*, 40-50.

Ulutas, B. (2011). An application of SMED Methodology. *International Journal of Industrial and Manufacturing Engineering*, *5*(7), 1194–1197.

Ustundag, A., & Cevikcan, E. (2018). *Industry 4.0: managing the digital transformation*. Springer. doi:10.1007/978-3-319-57870-5

Vaidya, S., Ambad, P., & Bhosle, S. (2018). Industry 4.0 - a glimpse. *Procedia Manufacturing*, *20*, 233–238. doi:10.1016/j.promfg.2018.02.034

Valamede, L. S., & Akkari, A. C. S. (2020). Lean 4.0: A new holistic approach for the integration of lean manufacturing tools and digital technologies. *International Journal of Mathematical, Engineering and Management Sciences*, *5*(5), 851–868.

Vieira, A. M., Silva, F. J. G., Campilho, R. D. S. G., Ferreira, L. P., Sá, J. C., & Pereira, T. (2020). SMED methodology applied to the deep drawing process in the automotive industry. *Procedia Manufacturing*, *51*, 1416–1422. doi:10.1016/j.promfg.2020.10.197

Wada, K. (2020). *The Evolution of the Toyota Production System*. Springer. doi:10.1007/978-981-15-4928-1

Wilson, J. M. (1995). Henry Ford¢s just-in-time system. *International Journal of Operations & Production Management*, *15*(12), 59–75. doi:10.1108/01443579510104501

Wolniak, R. (2014). Relationships between selected lean management tools and innovations. *Zeszyty Naukowe. Organizacja i Zarządzanie/Politechnika Śląska*, (75), 157-166.

Womack, J. P. (2007). Moving beyond the tool age. *Manufacturing Engineer*, *86*(1), 4–5. doi:10.1049/me:20070101

Womack, J. P., & Jones, D. T. (1996). *Lean thinking: Banish waste and create wealth in your corporation*. Simon & Schuster.

Womack, J. P., Jones, D. T., & Roos, D. (1990). *The Machine that Changed the World: The Story of Lean Production*. Harper Collins Publishers.

Yang, C. C., & Yang, K. J. (2013). An integrated model of the Toyota production system with total quality management and people factors. *Human Factors and Ergonomics in Manufacturing & Service Industries*, *23*(5), 450–461. doi:10.1002/hfm.20335

Chapter 8
Modelling of an Automatic Gearbox Using AUTOSAR Standard

Cristian-Victor Greiner
Technical University of Cluj-Napoca, Romania

Camelia Avram
Technical University of Cluj-Napoca, Romania

Adina Astilean
Technical University of Cluj-Napoca, Romania

ABSTRACT

This paper presents the advantages of modelling an application destined for automotive using automotive standard architecture (AUTOSAR). This standard is structured in layers and is trying to make the software application independent from the microcontroller unit (MCU) specifications. By structuring an application in this way, it reduces the time and the cost of developing new ones for a different microcontroller or for creating new applications with a similar purpose for the same microcontroller. Also, the diagnosis for the errors is improved a lot, because it provides mechanisms to detect them, and, having a very structured form, it is easy to find them in comparison with the older procedures used for the soft-ware development that are different from one producer to another. This standard architecture helps to get better results in software development and embedded systems for the automotive area. Here is presented a primitive implementation for an electric automatic gearbox that can be developed more when new features are required.

DOI: 10.4018/978-1-6684-5606-4.ch008

INTRODUCTION

The functionality of vehicle guidance systems is now the focus of research and development for autonomous vehicles. Several experimental vehicle demonstrations have demonstrated the outstanding capabilities described above, with the most recent ones listed first. (Reschka, 2016)

As an illustration, the drive on the Bertha-Benz route completed by the Karlsruhe Institute for Technology and Daimler AG (Urmson, 2012 & Reschka, 2016), the Stadtpilot project of the Technische Universität Braunschweig (Nothdurft 2011 & Wille 2010), the operations of Google Inc. (Chatham, 2013; Reschka, 2016; Urmson, 2012), the BRAiVE Research Institute and the VIAC Project of the VisLab Institute of the University of Parma (Bertozzi, 2013 & Broggi, 2013), the research activities of the Collaborative Research Centre 28 of the German Research Foundation (DFG) (Stanek, 2010; Stiller, 2007; Kammel, 2008 & Thuy 2008) and the results of the DARPA Urban Challenge (Singh, 2008).

A safety driver was always present in the experimental vehicles on public roads and in traffic to keep an eye on the technical system. This person was required to step in if a technical issue developed, rendering the current scenario outside the scope of the vehicle or if a different circumstance called for it.

According to [20], the recommended test drives on public highways are categorised as semi-automated due to the technical system's requirement for constant monitoring. Future vehicle guiding strategies with increased levels of automation will strive to operate autonomously in every circumstance without human supervision.

Therefore, a safety concept covering the many stages of the development process, such as the specification, design, development, and functional tests, is needed when developing vehicle guiding systems. Additionally, the system must have safety components that can reach or try to maintain a so-called safe condition.

Automated vehicles (AVs) are automobiles in which at least one aspect of driving control, such as steering or speed control, operates independently of the driver. Avs use a variety of sensors to acquire data.

Assisted driving is a field that is growing very fast nowadays. Most majority of car constructors are trying to improve the safety of the drivers and to make driving to be more accessible.

The car's gearbox is one of the first parts of a vehicle which was shifted from manual to automatic. This happened for the safety of the drivers and users but also in terms of quality because of how components.

Actions to extend the engine's life and that are made by mechanical or electrical self-controlled systems will always be the same, no matter the environmental factors, like human actions, which are always influenced by external factors. So that way, the parts of the system involved in the activity will be very well preserved. Also, by using an automatic gearbox, the driver has fewer operations, acting the clutch pedal and switching the gear speed. In that way, he can pay more attention to the traffic and prevent in a better way an accident.

Nowadays, an automatic gearbox is way different from the first one. It is controlled more by the electrical components than the older ones controlled by hydraulic systems (Song, 2020). The actioning of the modern automatic gearboxes is also influenced by other factors measured by sensors, like ambient temperature and environment, the pressure in the wheels etc., which are processed in the Electric Control Unit (ECU) and transmitted to the gearbox.

To facilitate the development of the ECUs, the software developers that work in the automotive area must use a unique architecture to improve the quality of the electrical parts of a car and to make communication easier between multiple users of the products.

The most used software architecture for automobile development is AUTOSAR. The architecture came out in 2003 and since then is growing in the number of users and terms of quality because of how it is structured. This type of architecture helps improve how the code is developed and implemented. Having an open and standardised architecture for controlling the electronic parts of an automobile allows software developers to use component-based software in many different applications applicable to multiple products. Car producers use this standard more frequently to get into fully autonomous driving cars.

The model of the software application of an automatic gearbox presented in this paper represents an excellent start to developing better models that can be used in the future. It is customised for the STM32F407 microcontroller and is commanded using pushbuttons instead of the shift lever and a potentiometer for the power (gas) pedal. Using those external devices, the simulation can reproduce the behaviour of an actual gearbox.

The program uses AUTOSAR layers to make the information transition from the lower levels, more dependent on the microcontroller structure, to the upper levels, independent of the microcontroller specification (Autosar). Other models are not divided into layers, so the operations on the microcontroller registers are implemented in the same place with the integration of the interfaces required for the projects. This may lead to a complicated structure, be hard to debug and requires high costs and time to be adapted for other uses.

This chapter presents an early-stage implementation for an electric automatic gearbox using a microcontroller, external components representing actuators and related software tools. This model can be developed more when new features are required.

The first chapter presents the actual studies about the electric automatic gearboxes and embedded systems in automotive and AUTOSAR methodology and structure.

The second chapter discusses how the application is developed following the architecture layers. In the end, the results and some future improvements are mentioned.

The driver power on the ECU. Then it selects the gear speed, i.e., D, R, P, N, by pressing push buttons. To control the rate, it uses a potentiometer, which replaces the pedals of a car. The movement of a servomotor that changes its angle using a PWM signal illustrates the speed. Also, a 7-segment display shows when the gear speed or the rate level changes.

This paper aims to present the advantages of using AUTOSAR to develop embedded systems for automotive based on a concrete model: the simulation of an electrical automatic gearbox by using an STM32F407 microcontroller and AUTOSAR Architecture. To simplify the gearbox model, the essential functions of a gearbox are implemented, processing the driver's actions, and transmitting them to the engine through ECU. The operations realised by this model try to simulate the ones recognised by a natural gearbox system by taking the information transmitted from the driver, i.e., accelerating, braking, changing the gear speed, processing it and sending the proper commands to the actuators.

BACKGROUND

In the last decades, the automotive industry shifted to automatic control. The first subject taken into consideration was the automatisation of the gearbox. It stood out among the first because it increases the driver's attention to the road and reduces the energy consumption and usability of the transmission components. All the mechanical, hydraulic, or electric actions performed by a control system are more efficient than human actions.

The gearbox models can be divided into two types of transmission type: single-speed and multi-speed (STMicroelectronics).

The first models of automated gearboxes, called Automated Manual Transmission (AMT) gearboxes, used electrohydraulic or electromechanical actuators. They were efficient, simple and had a low manufacturing and maintenance cost. Still, a disadvantage is that the speed shift is not smooth because the torque is interrupted during the shifting. Inverse Automated Manual Transmission (IAMT) has an extra clutch as a synchroniser. Those are multi-speed models.

Another improvement for multi-speed models came in 2003 when Dual-Clutch Transmission (DCT) was released, bringing a smoother shift by controlling two clutches simultaneously; when one is decoupled, the other is engaged in the shifting operation.

The Continuously Variable Transmission (CVT) and Infinitely Variable Transmission (IVT) enable the gear ratio to vary continually from the minimum to the maximum percentage, so in that way, the motor works at its highest efficiency. The difference between these two is that IVT can reduce the gear ratio to zero, but this means adding a fixed percentage and a planetary gear set, which is expensive, so the IVT does not bring an improvement significant enough to be considered a better model than CVT. Those two models are of single-speed type.

The Magnetic Gear Transmission (MGT), a multi-speed model, replaces the classical model with teeth with permanent magnets. This model is attractive because it is contactless, so it does not need lubrication, but it is expensive due to its large number of draws and low efficiency.

The multi-speed models require more operations for design and optimisation than single-speed models because the gear ratio, the trade-offs between range, low-speed acceleration (launching), grade ability, and high-speed passing must be considered when modelled. Also, they present more losses, e.g., oil, bearings, and even teeth; that way, the power decreases. Noise, vibrations, and harshness represent other drawbacks for multi-speed models.

Electric vehicles nowadays use single-speed gearbox models. So, even if CVT and IVT are more expensive and less efficient, they are the best option for now.

Some studies are trying to improve the single-speed gearboxes to operate at two speeds (Shahid, 2016). This change will bring more power to the car's engine and consume less energy. This process implies determining the mechanical strength based on the electric motor's torque and speed. The gear ratio and the optimal shifting speed are chosen based on rate results. These operations improve the engine and the inverter, impacting energy consumption.

The transition to electric vehicles led to the development of embedded systems in the automotive area. These systems are related to the ECU, are crucial for the automobile's performance, and are considered the heart of the vehicle's electronic system (Autosar).

An embedded system runs independently from human actions and accomplishes real-time operations. To complete all the requirements of an ECU, they should have high speed, low power consumption, and be reliable for an extended period.

The automotive embedded systems contain (Autosar), Figure 1:

- Sensors – capture the information from the environment or the automobile system
- CPU (controller) – processes the information received from the sensors, makes decisions based on it and generates output signals on the actuators.
- Memory – stores the necessary information.
- Actuators – perform actions based on the CPU outputs.

Figure 1. Automotive Embedded System structure

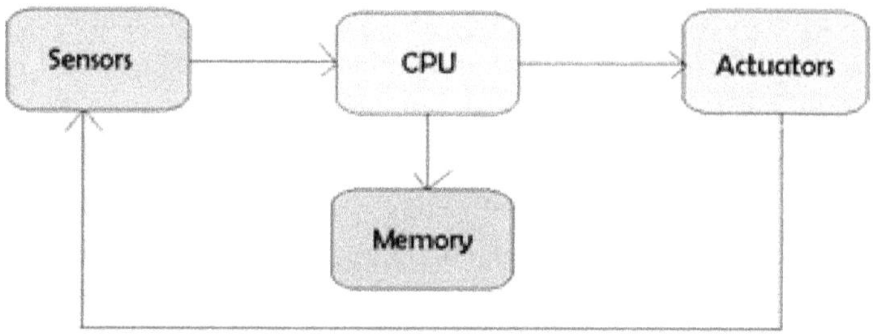

To be interoperable, these systems must be modelled in a unique language. Different Original Equipment Manufacturers (OEM) have agreed to some unrelated software components, but AUTOSAR brought a fundamental structure for the automotive applications.

In a car, embedded systems are used for a variety of tasks, including (Autosar):

- Fuel injection and combustion controller devices.
- Event data recorders.
- Anti-lock braking system.
- Adaptive cruise control.
- Automatic parking.
- Night vision.
- Navigational systems.
- Climate control.

Because ECU realises many operations, most modern ECUs use multicore systems. This means that in a system, more processors perform different actions. An important aspect must be followed in the scheduling and synchronising of the processes to maintain the real-time characteristic.

The biggest problem when a system use multiprocessors are the timing and the synchronisation (Kanjan, 2008). The best solution to fix this issue is to check the order and duration of these processes. This action is called Task Scheduling and implements the order of the tasks in the existing gaps (the available processor time). The tasks have different priorities: high, low and background. The background ones are realised only when there is no "low" task and a "low one" precedes a "high one" every time.

To check and visualise the order of the tasks there are two ways:

- Online – the execution is read in real-time and compared with a fixed schedule. In this way, the resources are fully exploited.
- Offline – read the recorded traffic from the multiprocessor and compare it with a fixed schedule.

In this way, the errors are detected very fast and allowed to solve without human interaction. In this way, the system gains better quality.

Most embedded systems are Service Oriented Architecture (SOA) because it provides an efficient and flexible software design paradigm for systems (Campbell, 2020). These SOA systems establish an efficient and flexible connection between the ECU systems to perform a specific job. SOA is implemented following the AUTOSAR methodology to uniform the construction, so most possible issues are avoided.

Automotive Open System Architecture (AUTOSAR) is an open and standardised automotive software architecture (Autosar). It brings the interfaces between application software and vehicular functions in a regulated form to establish a common Electric Control Unit (ECU) architecture for all the users.

Before the release of this architecture, the ECU software was developed by different OEMs, which could not be used between producers because they were not standardised. If the OEM were switching to a new supplier, the transition would be challenging, taking a very long time to understand the original structure, and the costs would be very high.

The central concept of AUTOSAR is to decouple the application from the hardware parts. This is realised through a virtual functional bus (VFB). Dedicated ports make the communication, so in that way, the lower-level parts do not have a significant influence in developing the software part. This advantage is that both parts, hardware and software, can expand independently.

This architecture is based on a layered structure, which distinguishes between the main software parts: The application Layer, Runtime Environment (RTE) and Basic Software (BSW). The applications of the automotive interface with the essential software via RTE. A detailed AUTOSTAR architecture is presented in Figure 2.

Figure 2. Detailed AUTOSAR layers (Autosar)

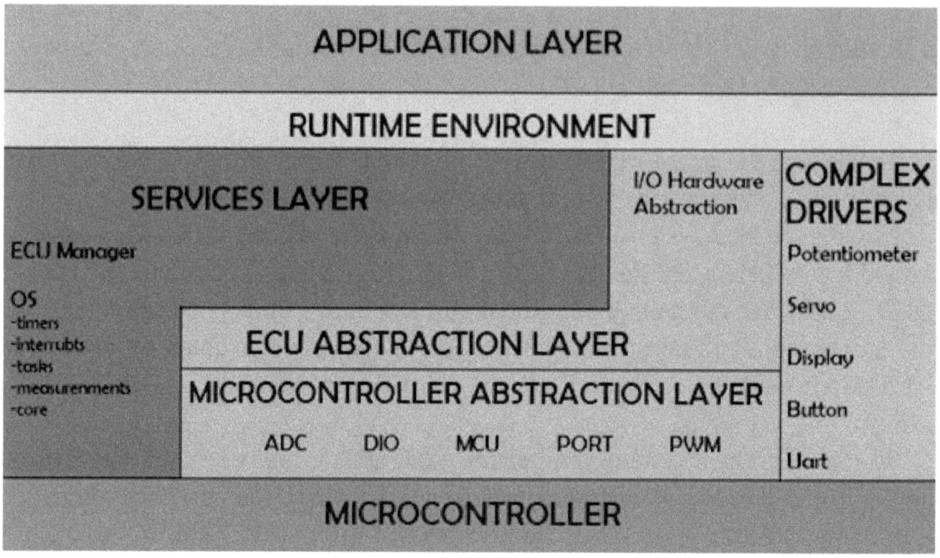

CONSTRUCTION OF THE GEARBOX

The Hardware of the Gearbox

The Microcontroller

For the development of this automatic gearbox, the used microcontroller is an STM32F407, with a processor of Cortex-M4 core that runs at 168 MHz. This microcontroller provides timers with pulse width modulation (PWM) control, analogue to digital converters (ADC), and digital inputs/outputs ports (DIO) and supports some communication protocols, like UART. It also contains multiple timers configured to operate the application in real-time. These features are handy for the application.

Due to the specification of the microcontroller, the application can be adjusted for new requirements, like processing data received from various sensors. In that way, the application can be extended to improve the actual model of the gearbox. To add new features to the project, no changes should be made to the existing structure to configure the controller registers, which are necessary for the lower levels of the code and to create the communication interfaces with the application in the higher levels.

The pins/ports, channels and registers that need to be used are for the communication between the microcontroller and external devices and to configure the MCU properties

Table 1. Used pins, ports, channels, and registers

Scope	PORTS	Channel(s)	Register(s)	Description
ADC	Port A	1,4	ADC1/2_CR1 ADC1/2_CR2 ADC1/2_SMPR2 ADC1/2_SQR1	Used to convert the analogue data
DIO	Port A Port C Port D Port E	0, 2, 7 6 … 12 8, 9, 10, 11 7 … 13	GPIOA GPIOC GPIOD GPIOE	Used to read and write digital information
MCU	-	-	FLASH_ACR RCC_APB1ENR RCC_APB2ENR PWR_CR RCC_CR RCC_PLLCFGR RCC_CFGR	In those registers for the reset and clock control and the flash memory
PWM	Port B	2	TIM2_PSC TIM2_ARR TIM2_CR TIM2_CCER TIM2_CCMR TIM_UG	Used to set and read the PWM frequency and duty cycle for timer 2
	Port B	3	TIM3_PSC TIM3_ARR TIM3_CR TIM3_CCER TIM3_CCMR TIM_UG	Used to set and read the PWM frequency and duty cycle for timer 3
Port	Port A Port B Port C Port E Port D	6 … 12 7 … 13 8 … 11	GPIO_OSPEEDER GPIO_MODER GPIO_PUDR GPIO_MODER GPIOA GPIOB	Used to enable the clocks pin mode, direction, output, slew rate
UART	UART dedicated ports	UART channels	USART1_CR UART1_BRR USART1_DR	Used to configure the UART protocol

and PWM module. The registers and channels configuration can be found in the datasheet and the microcontroller reference manual (STMicroelectronics)(see Table 1).

External Devices

The external devices are:

1. **Servomotor SG90**: it is used to indicate the actual speed set in the gearbox.

It replaces the speedometer. It can also be seen as the actuator of the gearbox. Other servomotors require unique adaptation and are helpful only for a specific scope (Ghadge, 2018). Because of its standard construction and the possibility to use a significant and extensive of libraries, it is straightforward to implement the driver for it.

2. **7 Segment Display**: to display the position in which the gearbox is situated: N, P, R or D, with the related steps regarding the car's speed.

Even if LCDs, which are often used (Shahid, 2016), are more adaptive to ambient light, the LED display presents a modular structure and is easier to adapt for different purposes. The driver for the segment display is implemented in a lower layer, and if more modules are added, it can be called for every other module, depending on its scope.

3. **Potentiometer**: its scope is to set speed by modifying its resistance and sending a signal with different values to the processor. It is used instead of the power (gas) pedal.

The one used in this project has one kΩ. The range in which the potentiometer operates is not very important because the layered structure allows the use of any potentiometer. The only thing that must be modified if a different potentiometer is used is scalability, a value defined in a lower layer. Without using the architecture, it is required to alter also how the data received from the potentiometer is transmitted.

4. **Push Buttons**: Four buttons are used to select the position of the gearbox state: N, P, D and R. They represent the shift lever of the gearbox and are chosen because it is easier to operate on them.

Most gearbox models use a lever (Shen, 2021). Nevertheless, on a lever, sometimes, the user must pass through all the positions to get in the desired one, so, by mistake, they set the wrong speed gear. Using buttons reduces the chance of making a similar mistake, and the shift is instant. Because of that, a system that prevents hazardous changes is provided.

5. **Resistor:** (for the display anode), wires to connect the external devices to the unit, breadboard, and cable to power the circuit.

The connections on the board are made due to the requirements of the application and to the port's configuration of the microcontroller, found in the datasheet (Shen, 2021), as follows (presented in Figure 3):

- The servomotor: to the power line, to the ground and to the A1 pin to control its rotation angle.
- The potentiometer: to the power line, to the ground and to the A4 pin to read its value.
- The 7-segment display: the anode to the power line with the resistor between, the cathode to the ground and the segments to the digital I/O pins E 7,8,9,10,11,12,13 pins.
- The buttons: to the power line and the corresponding D8,9,10,11 pins.

Figure 3. Circuit setup

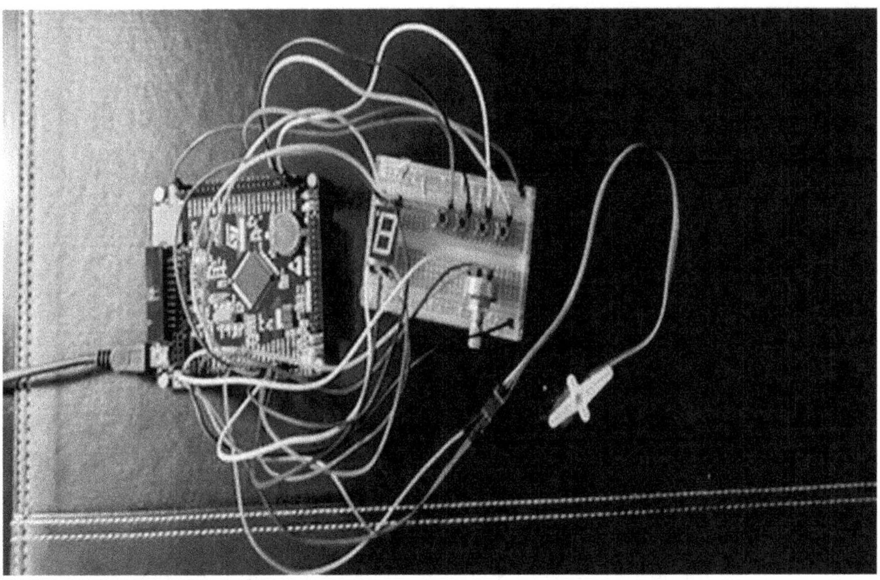

Software Application Development

Some rules are followed to implement an application using the AUTOSAR methodology (Autosar). These rules help to have a clear structure of the code. In that way, a differentiation between the physical data, e.g., signals and software data, reduces the chances of altering the information.

The Layered Structure Using AUTOSAR

The application is structured regarding the six main layers: RTE, Services, ECU Abstraction, Microcontroller Abstraction (MCAL) and Complex Drivers.

The Microcontroller Abstraction layer (MCAL), Complex Drivers layer and Services layer are directly related to the microcontroller configuration and performances, so those aspects are considered when implemented.

The ECU abstraction layer is independent of the MCU but dependent on the ECU because it contains the interfaces between the drivers implemented in the lower layers and the application.

The RTE layer can be considered the most important one because here are described the interfaces of the Virtual Function Bus (VFB) and implement the modules to enable the communication and schedule of the software components. VFB is a concept that describes the communication mechanism between the members of the system (Autosar).

The application layer is the highest one and is the farthest one from the physical components' abstraction. This layer configures the automatic gearbox to project the control components and the communication of the servomotor with the ECU through the user interface.

DEVELOPING THE SOFTWARE APP

Templates and Libraries

Following the standardised architecture of AUTOSAR is mandatory to respect some strict guidelines regarding the templates and libraries used in the project. This makes it easier to understand the implementation, debug it and, if needed, innovate the model. Also, converting the code for a different MCU requires less effort.

An advantage in comparison with other architectures used for automotive software development, like the ones which are semiautonomous decentralised and less organised (Kanajan, 2008), is that the AUTOSAR standard imposes to follows some well-defined templates. Those templates are structured so that all the code users familiarised with the standard can easily update, modify, or adapt the code.

These parts of code are not considered proper layers because they contain general information required for the application development and are also already provided by the producer.

The templates are added to the project only to suggest how the files must be structured and documented.

The inclusions and macro definitions should be declared first in all the files. After describing global data types, global variables and global constants are written. The functions are defined and implemented at the end of the file.

Also, all the files include a brief description of their scope and short definitions or comments for the variables, structures (including their elements) or functions.

In that way, when there is needed to add or adjust some values or procedures, it is easy to find them, so the time spent on this work is reduced.

Std stands for Standard libraries. The compiler abstraction is implemented in the AUTOSAR platform-dependent types and symbols and the AUTOSAR standard data types.

Avoiding using the libraries provided by the programming language, like "stdio" or "stdin", is a significant advantage because the code can be converted to a new programming language very quickly, and it does not need adaptation for every data type.

This way, also it is reduced the occupied memory space because the data types' size is set regarding the project requirements.

Complex Drivers' Layer

The Complex Drivers are the first AUTOSAR layer that is implemented. Here are the direct connections between the microcontroller and the RTE drivers with a specific purpose functionality that is not specified within AUTOSAR standard. The external devices used in the application interfaces are implemented here for the button, potentiometer, display, and servo motor. Also, the synchronous/asynchronous transmission UART protocol is established here to enable communication between the microcontroller and the other components.

The complex drivers used for the automatic gearbox model are:

1. **The Button Driver** – here, the DIO (digital input-output) channels are mapped to connect the buttons with the microcontroller.
2. **The Display Driver** – where the port configurations of the 7 Segment Display are defined to the microcontroller. Also, the functions that show and erase the values on the display are provided in this driver.
3. **The Potentiometer Driver** – the potentiometer gives an output of an analogue signal, and the data transmitted must be converted into a digital signal to be processed. So, in this module are defined the procedures to process the data through the ADCs' channels of the MCU.
4. **The UART Driver** – it is a communication protocol between devices. The acronym comes from Universal Asynchronous Receiver-Transmitter. Some implementations design the I2C protocol (Campbell, 2020) for communication.

Still, this system is not offered by all microcontrollers, so a transaction to another MCU is hard to realise if this protocol is used. The UART protocol uses two signals: Transmitter and Receiver signal. The controlling bus sends data in a parallel form to the transmitting UART. From here, the data is sent serially to the receiving UART, which delivers the information parallel to the receiver. Most microcontrollers provide this communication protocol, configured very simply (Pena, 2020).

5. **The Servomotor Driver** – here are configured the connection for the servomotor on the MCU and the procedure to set the angle of the servomotor and the duty cycle value.

The servo controller takes the place of the speedometer. The maximum admitted speed configured for this gearbox is 140 km/h. Still, to avoid variations on the limits, the servo will work between 20° and 160°, so the duty cycle values must be determined for these angles. The following formulas are used:

$$SERVO\ 20\ DEGREES = (SWEVO\ MIN\ DUTY) + 338(1\Delta = 16.849) \tag{1}$$

$$SERVO\ 160\ DEGREES = (SWEVO\ MIN\ DUTY) + 2703(20\Delta = 2703) \tag{2}$$

The formula computes the value of the duty cycle:

$$DutyCcl = \frac{((SERVO\ 20\ DEGREES) * (SERVO\ MAX\ ANGLE - us\_Angle)) + ((SERVO\ 160\ DEGREES) * us\_Angle)}{SERVO\ MAX\ ANGLE} \tag{3}$$

This way, if more devices of the same type but with different purposes are used in the application, they are configured in this lower level. Depending on the application's requirements, they can be called in the upper levels.

Another advantage of this structure is that it hides the configuration of more devices of the same type but with different purposes used in the application; they are configured in this lower level of the application and can be called in the upper levels depending on the application's requirements of the device from the software application. So, if there are errors in the software application, the chances of affecting the physical devices decrease significantly compared to the classical way of implementation, where the devices are configured directly where they are used.

MCAL Layer

In this layer, the data that is read or written on the MCU is abstracted and mapped on the memory. Because of that, the upper layers are entirely independent of the MCU. This represents a significant advantage of the standard. If a project must be implemented on a different MCU, all the other layers can remain unchanged except the MCAL layer. This brings an excellent benefit to the product development cost and time.

This part makes the drivers more well-defined by the AUTOSAR standard, making the configuration easier.

The drivers developed here are:

1. ADC (Analog to Digital Converter) driver [13], [14] - it is implemented to process the analogue signals that the MCU reads. Usually, most external components use analogue signals, but to be processed better, they need to be converted to a digital signal.

The conversion is done after the status of the ADC channel is checked. If it is not idle or busy, the conversion is initialised by setting the masks for the ADC registers. Then, the ADC channel is selected, and the read or write values are inserted in the regular sequence and transmitted to be processed through a buffer.

2. DIO driver (Autosar) - the digital Input and Output ports, channels and registers are mapped. Also, the read and write functions from these ports are provided in this part. It is usually a synchronous and unbuffered operation. These functions define the channels or the port's behaviour. Read functions store the level of the interrogated bit or port (sets of bits) and return its value, high or low, depending on if it is a 0 or 1 value.
3. MCU driver (Autosar) – The basic microcontroller operations are implemented here. The main functionalities provided by this module are the PLL (phase-locked loop) and MCU clock distribution, RAM section initialisation, the configuration of the MCU-dependent control bits, reduced power mode and reset function (from the software or the hardware).

The initialisation is accomplished through linker symbols. The linkers define the flash start address and RAM start and end addresses for the .data section. Here are the RAM start and end addresses for the bass section and CCM RAM addresses where the stack head and tail are placed. The stack grows descending, so the stack head address is higher than the tail address.

4. Port driver (AUTOSTAR) - This module provides the initialisation for the whole port structure of the microcontroller. The main functionalities of the port pins are In-put-Output actions, ADC, SPI, SCI, and PWM. This configuration depends on the microcontroller and ECU and sets the masks for the referenced configuration table.
5. PWM driver (Autosar) – it desires the functionality of the PWM channels. The module contains definitions and instructions to initialise and control the microcontroller PWM stage. The pulse width variation is guaranteed through the duty cycle and the signal period time. The values are manipulated by configuring the PWM and Timers registers.

The duty cycle value is written on the PWM channel by setting the channel address to the value of a pointer which is calculated by the formula:

$$PWM\ DutyCycle = (PWM\ Frequency{+}1{*}DutyCycle) \gg 15 \qquad (4)$$

>> is the right shift bit operator (the value is shifted 15 bits to the right to be written correctly in the PWM register).

A method to configure the PWM for a servomotor is to implement it using multiple software, like MATLAB and Proteus (Haidar, 2013), but this requires more resources, knowledge, and time. This procedure does not represent advantages and is also harder to debug the entire application.

Because the PWM module is configured here and independent of the scope used, it represents an advantage compared to other architectures. In different architectures, the PWM must be configured whenever it is used.

Also, suppose the application must be extended, and it is necessary to use these drivers for new purposes. In that case, they have only to be adjusted for the new usages, but this will not affect the initial configuration.

ECU Service Layer

The ECU Abstraction layer makes the upper software layers independent of the ECU hardware layout. It is independent of the microcontroller but still dependent on ECU hardware.

In this layer are provided with the interfaces with the MCAL layer and with external device drivers. Access to the peripherals and devices, included or not on the microcontroller, is made through this module. The API for interfacing with the microcontroller (ports, pins, interface types) is implemented here.

The ECU Abstraction layer offers uniform access to all functionalities of an ECU, such as communication, memory, or I/O.

An implementation to configure the ECU uses FPGA (Field Programmable Gate Arrays) circuits (Cho, 2019). This requires extra components and configurations for the communication protocol, i.e., Zipwire. The project must be reconfigured if the microcontroller does not support the connection with the FPGA or the protocol is not delivered. The implementation using the layered structure does not require any other components, and it uses only the drivers, protocols, and communication channels available on the microcontroller configuration.

The I/O Hardware Abstraction is needed for this project to transfer the data to and from the MCU to the upper layers (Autosar).

The I/O Hardware Abstraction module is an interface for the signal path between the MCU-dependent and independent layers. In this module, static abstraction and inversion occur, respecting the physical representation of the values at the inputs/outputs of the ECU hardware.

To respect the standard requirements for the I/O Hardware Abstraction, the following services shall be provided: the values need to be within a static range for each signal, services to read input and output voltages and current, services to update several outputs, synchronous signal access functions simultaneously.

In this module, all failure short circuits to the ground, open circuits, failure overload or over temperature are detected.

Services Layer

The Service layer is the first layer completely independent of the microcontroller and ECU hardware. Here are the services for hardware resources management, network, memory management and bus communication for the application layer. Also, the operating system is implemented in this layer.

This module improves the communication between the software application and the MCU. In this way, the application modelling has no restrictions regarding the hardware requirements. The other software architectures are poorly designed and need many adaptations for all the layers up to the application layer.

For the automatic gearbox application designed in this project, the ECU State Manager and the Operating System implementations are imposed (Autosar).

The ECU States Manager, abbreviated EcuM, handle the ECU states, like the wake-up or sleep events and their transitions. If the implementation follows the standard rules and is done correctly, the power consumption is reduced, and the energy of the ECU is managed inefficiently.

All the mechanisms accomplished in the operating system are configured in the OS module, like the interrupts, measurements, tasks, or timers. Here are the global timing values, like periodicity, recovery time, and the IDs for the timing tasks. The tasks can be of three types: fast, slow or background.

For the OS timer are defined the conversions from the international time units to OS timer ticks are. The OS timer configurations for the current time and their initialisation are described. In this section are configured the acceptable runtime limits. Those limits are used for timing measurements. The Core part defines the types used in the scheduling algorithms. The OS scheduling algorithms are implemented using the definitions of the state of the fast tasks and the schedule table.

RTE Layer

The RTE, Run Time Environment, interfaces, and controls all the communication between the application and the BSW (essential software or lower layers). Because of that, it can be considered the essential layer of the standard. The communication is made via VFB.

The RTE code is generated automatically according to the ECU configuration. No line should be written or modified from the generated code. The RTE Generator creates the API functions that manage the communication between software components and BSW. This type of communication is convenient and secure because if the instructions are followed when the generator is used, there are no chances of getting errors in the code.

Another procedure to communicate between ECU and software components is using CAN and LIN busses (Daimi, 2016), but those protocols are for low and medium-speed applications. Instead, communication using the VFB is also very suited for high-speed applications.

Application Layer

The Application layer, also called the software component, is the highest layer of the standard. It is connected to the lower levels through the RTE layer and is entirely independent of the ECU and microcontroller. This layer can be seen as the application interface with the user.

The software component can be divided into two parts: the sensor software component and the actuator software component. The sensor component takes data from the sensors and transfers it to other components through the I/O stack. The actuator component must state the state of an actuator on an ECU.

To develop this layer shall be taken in consideration the sensors and actuators used in the application. In this case, there is an actuator, the servomotor. To control the servomotor, the duty cycle value must be set. Based on the adjustments made by the users to the potentiometer, a new value is sent to the MCU through the RTE. The new duty cycle is computed related to the received information. Using the ECU Abstraction layer, the command is transmitted to the servomotor, which changes its angle and to the display that shows the required value.

The code structure is presented in Figure 4.

Figure 4. The code structure

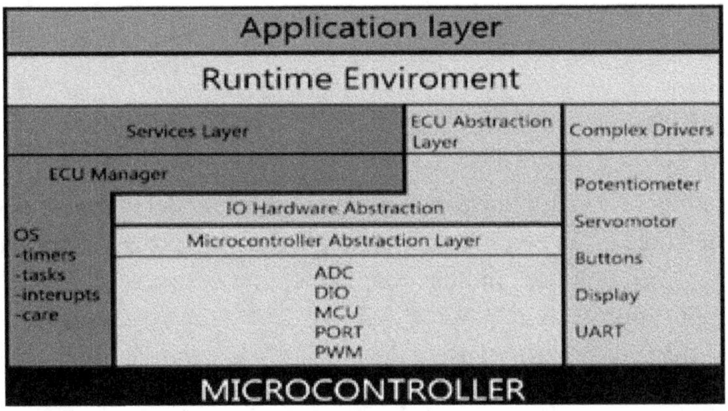

RESULTS

The methodology of AUTOSAR is followed to develop the coding part for embedded systems in automotive. This standardised structure is implemented with layers dependent on the MCU (microcontroller unit) and ECU (electric control unit) in the lower levels and independent layers on the higher levels in the software part.

The results are the ones expected. The application works in the desired parameters: the servo motor moves when the potentiometer is operated, and the display shows the correct gear speed. There are no fluctuations from the normal parameters because all the potential disturbing factors were considered, and the code was implemented in that way, and no fluctuations can occur.

The time response to the commands is terse and negligible. This is due to the processor speed, which is adequate for this application, and the operations done on it do not take long because they are primarily its operations. The way the data flow is transmitted and the way the code is structured and easy to process because, in the lower levels, the information is seen as signals and in upper levels, users' as binary values. So, the time factors do not have a significant influence on the way the application works.

The application is straightforward to be operated because the command components are the buttons and the potentiometer, which are intuitive. Any user can understand how it works, even if it is the first time it operates an application.

Also, there is a slight chance of errors in the application, but it can be fixed easily if an error occurs. If it is a physical error, it is probably of weak connections, so the jumpers must be adjusted, or a component was connected wrong. However, by checking the correct way, they need to be associated. Also, if the error is due to the software component, it can be easy to detect and fix because of the structure of the code and the imposed standards.

CONCLUSION

The application, by its simplicity, creates an excellent model to develop better ones. The main features of an electric automatic gearbox are provided here, i.e., ADC, DIO, PWM configurations, and the communication between MCU, ECU and the software application.

Because the code is realised using the AUTOSAR standard, it can be transferred to work on other microcontrollers only by changing the code in the lower layers, or it can be modified for different applications on the same microcontroller by adding new instructions in the upper layers.

An improvement that can be made to this project is to add more sensors to the system. These sensors can collect information from the environment and limit the maximum speed depending on how safe the road is, the weather, or how users other components of the car. In this way, the driver and the passengers are in safer conditions, and the life of the car's components will be longer.

For example, if it is rainy weather, check the humidity and temperature, the pressure of the wheels is lower than the average value, and the direction system presents a warning, the speed limit should be lower than in normal conditions. The microcontroller contains a humidity and temperature sensor, Am2320, and a luminosity sensor, Tsl2561, so it is easy to provide these features.

The second improvement of this application is to bring a more user-friendly interface. In that way, the users can operate easier. For example, a screen that shows all the parameters shown by the servomotor by the 7-segment display and the actual speed.

The last adjustment that can be made to the standard is to add standard drivers for the devices used a lot in automotive applications. For example, the potentiometer is an electrical component used a lot in every electric circuit, not only in automotive but also in some microcontrollers, that can be developed to make the implementation easier.

REFERENCES

AUTOSAR. (2016). *Specification of PWM Driver.*

AUTOSAR (2017). AUTOSAR Layered Software Architecture. *Autosar*, vol. *4*, 163.

AUTOSAR. (2017). *General Requirements on Methodology and Templates*. Autosar.

AUTOSAR. (2017). *Requirements on MCU Driver*. Autosar.

AUTOSAR. (2017). *Requirements on Port Driver*. Autosar.

AUTOSAR. (2017). *Specification of ADC Driver*. Autosar.

AUTOSAR. (2017). *Specification of DIO Driver*. Autosar.

AUTOSAR. (2017). Specification of Operating System. *System*.

AUTOSAR (2017). Virtual Functional Bus. Autosar.

AUTOSAR. (2018). Requirements of I / O Hardware Abstraction, pp. 1–29. Autosar.

AUTOSAR. (2018). *Specification of Port Driver*. Autosar.

AUTOSAR. (2018). Requirements on Operating System. *System*.

AUTOSAR (2019). Specification of ECU State Manager. Autosar.

AUTOSAR (2020). Requirements on PWM Driver. Autosar.

Bertozzi, M., Broggi, A., Coati, A., & Fedriga, R. I. (2013). A 13,000 km Intercontinental Trip with Driverless Vehicles: The VIAC Experiment. *Intelligent Transportation Systems Magazine*, *5*(1), 28–41. doi:10.1109/MITS.2012.2225651

Broggi, A., Buzzoni, M., Debattisti, S., Grisleri, P., Laghi, M. C., Medici, P., & Versari, P. (2013). Extensive Tests of Autonomous Driving Technologies. *IEEE Transactions on Intelligent Transportation Systems*, *14*(3), 1403–1415. doi:10.1109/TITS.2013.2262331

Campbell, S. Basics of the I2C Communication Protocol. Retrieved from https://www.circuitbasics.com/basics-of-the-i2c-communication-protocol/

Chatham, A. (2013). Google's Self Driving Cars: The Technology, Capabilities, Challenges. *Embedded Linux Conference*, Linux..

Cho, K., Kim, J., Choi, D. Y., Yoon, Y. H., Oh, J. H., & Lee, S. E. (2021). An FPGA-based ECU for remote reconfiguration in automotive systems. *Micromachines*, *12*(11), 2021. doi:10.3390/mi12111309

Daimi, K., Saed, M., Bone, S., & Robb, J. (2016). *Securing Vehicle's Electronic Control Units*, (c), 29–34.

Ghadge, B., Metha, G., and Kulkarni, A. (2018). Automated Manual Transmission Using Servo Motors for Sequential. *International Journal of Innovative Research in Science, Engineering and Technology*, 7767–7772. doi:. doi:10.15680/IJIRSET.2018.0707025

Haidar, A. M. A., Benachaiba, C., & Zahir, M. (2013). Software interfacing of servo motor with micro-controller, the *J. Electr. Syst.*, *9*(1), 84–99.

Kammel, S., Ziegler, J., Pitzer, B., Werling, M., Gindele, T., Jagzent, D., Schröder, J., Thuy, M., Goebl, M., von Hundelshausen, F., Pink, O., Frese, C., & Stiller, C. (2008). Team AnnieWAY's autonomous system for the 2007 DARPA Urban Challenge. *Journal of Field Robotics*, *25*(9), 615–639. doi:10.1002/rob.20252

Kanajan, S., Pinello, C., Zeng, H., and Sangiovanni-Vincentelli, A. (2008). Between Centralized versus Decentralized Automotive Architectures Using a Virtual Integration Environment. *Proceedings of the Design Automation & Test in Europe Conference*, *1*, 117. . doi:10.1109/DATE.2006.243895

Nothdurft, T., Hecker, P., Ohl, S., Saust, F., Maurer, M., Reschka, A., & Böhmer, J. R. (2011). Stadtpilot: First fully autonomous test drives in urban traffic. *International Annual Conference on Intelligent Transportation Systems (ITSC)*, pp. 919-924. IEEE. 10.1109/ITSC.2011.6082883

Peña, E., & Legaspi, M. G. (2020). UART: A Hardware Communication Protocol Understanding Universal Asynchronous Receiver/Transmitter, Visit Analog., 54(4).

Reschka, A. (2016). *Safety Concept for Autonomous Vehicles*. In M. Maurer (Ed.). Autonomous Driving. doi:10.1007/978-3-662-48847-8_23

Shahid, M., Gupta, H., & Tamang, J. S. (2016). Digital Speedometer with Password Enabled Speed Limiting Feature. *International Journal of Trend in Research and Development*, *3*(3), 513–517.

Shen, W., Zhang, Q., Chen, Z., Mao, W., & Li, Y. (2021). Testing and analysis of automotive gearshift performance based on gear shift analysis. *Eng. Reports*, *3*(5), 1–12. doi:10.1002/eng2DOI324

Singh, S. (2008). *Special Issue on the 2007 DARPA Urban Challenge Part I* (Vol. 25). Wiley Subscription Services, Inc.

Singh, S. (2008). *Special Issue on the 2007 DARPA Urban Challenge Part II* (Vol. 25). Wiley Subscription Services, Inc.

Singh, S. (2008). *Special Issue on the 2007 DARPA Urban Challenge Part III* (Vol. 25). Wiley Subscription Services, Inc.

Song, X. (2020). Design and analysis of automatic transmission for Ravigneaux transmission with four-speed. *Journal of Physics: Conference Series, 1676*(1), 2020. doi:10.1088/1742-6596/1676/1/012184

Stanek, G., Langer, D., Müller-Bessler, B., & Huhnke, B. (2010). Junior 3: A test platform for Advanced Driver Assistance Systems. *Intelligent Vehicles Symposium (IV)*, (pp. 143-149). IEEE. 10.1109/IVS.2010.5547997

Stiller, C., Färber, G., & Kammel, S. (2007). Cooperative Cognitive Automobiles. *2007 IEEE Intelligent Vehicles Symposium (IV)*. Istanbul, Turkey. 10.1109/IVS.2007.4290117

STMicroelectronics. (2022). *STM32F405xx, STM32F407xx Datasheet, 176*. ST Microelectrons. https://www.st.com/en/microcontrollers-microprocessors/stm32f407vg.html

STMicroelectronics. (2017). *Reference manual stm32f407 advanced ARM-based 32-bit MCUs*. ST Microelectronics. https://www.st.com/content/ccc/resource/technical/document/reference_manual/3d/6d/5a/66/b4/99/40/d4/DM00031020.pdf/files/DM00031020.pdf/jcr:content/translations/en.DM00031020.pdf

Thuy, M., Goebl, M., Rattei, F., Althoff, M., Obermeier, F., Hawe, S., Nagel, R., Kraus, S., Wang, C., Hecker, F., Russ, M., Schweitzer, M., Leon, F.P., Färber, G., Buss, M., Diepold, K., Eberspächer, J., Heißing, B., Wünsche, H.-J. (2008). Kognitive Automobile - Neue Konzepte und Ideen des Sonderforschungsbereichs/TR28. 3. *Tagung Aktive Sicherheit durch Fahrerassistenz. Garching b.* München, Germany.

Urmson, C. (2012). Realizing Self-Driving Vehicles. *Intelligent Vehicles Symposium (IV)*. IEEE.

Wille, J. M., Saust, F., & Maurer, M. (2010). Stadtpilot: Driving autonomously on Braunschweig's inner ring road. *Intelligent Vehicles Symposium (IV)*, (pp. 506-511). IEEE. 10.1109/IVS.2010.5548034

Chapter 9
Analysing Roles of I4.0 Technologies in the Lean-Green Paradigm

Ram Prasad K.
https://orcid.org/0000-0001-6225-7299
Sri Venkateswara College of Engineering, India

Nishal M.
https://orcid.org/0000-0003-1771-4678
Sri Venkateswara College of Engineering, India

ABSTRACT

In the recent trend, many manufacturing industries are looking to develop and optimise their operational excellence to match the raising complexity of integrating lean concept and Industrial 4.0 (I4.0). Through literatures of previous researchers, the authors can state that the lean principle and concept are the backbone for the industrial operational excellence which has been the primary objective across all sectors. Industry 4.0 has numerous technologies advanced to back up the process optimisation and supplement need for greener environment in industries. In this chapter, the study primarily focusses on exploring and identifying the best suited Industry 4.0 technologies, which can enhance lean and green paradigms in industry through which a clear pathway can be created for smooth transfer of technology within a system. Also, the authors have discussed the enhancement of lean tools by application of Industry 4.0 technologies and have developed a relationship matrix between Industrial 4.0 technologies and lean practices.

DOI: 10.4018/978-1-6684-5606-4.ch009

INTRODUCTION

Industry 4.0 has made its debut over the manufacturing sector which is to be said as digital production or smart industry. Over with the help of the different types of techniques available are integrated within a process to address and optimise the process Industry 4.0 also called as I4.0, the fourth industrial revolution emerging over the manufacturing sectors by creating smart network with machines, products, people, components, and information technology to integrate with the value chain of the system to have a smart factory. Thus, both the ways are states to improve the value chain of the system and achieve operational excellence and shows continuous upgrade and development changes. This shows that the Lean tools and Industry 4.0 having mutual connection in their goal to achieve operational excellence and reduce wastages within the system. The lean concepts basic approach is to standardise the process, induce the idea for continuous improvement and increasing the endowing of the workers on the shop floor (Shrouf et al., 2014). The fourth industry revolution laying path to Industry 4.0 to have a different approach to solve the arising complexity and improving the output. These approach mainly with respect to the digital technologies and assessing each process parameters to study the root cause which affects the operational excellence of a process (Bauters et al., 2018). In recent years industries are seeking to optimise have to understand on how to incorporate the traditional lean concepts and Industry 4.0 (Shrouf et al., 2014). There are several studies going on how to incorporate both the ways rather independently or sequentially. In this paper we have identified different types of lean tools with the appropriate definition and industry 4.0 technologies on how it enhances the lean tools. The relationship established between the lean tools and I4.0 techniques allows the industries to integrate application of lean management and I4.0 to reach next level of operational excellence (Shrouf et al., 2014).

2.0 LEAN

Toyota Production system (TPS), which was later known by the name of Lean Production System LPS primarily aims at elimination of activities that are non-value added from company's value chain which will help in reducing operating cost (Skalli et al., 2022). Key important concept of LPS, is customer-centric aspects which were identified to be requiring key focus. Its effect can be seen in all areas of complex, pro-quality management activities in an enterprise (Sommer, 2015).The system hence developed can render products with respect to changes in demand of customers with minimal wastages (Bauters et al., 2018)[6].

TPS (Toyota Production System) known as pioneer in implementing lean concepts have been using SLIM (Sales Logistics Integrated Management) system wherein all information collected from the entire value chain are used for creating a link between the sales channels and the supply chain. The information thus received will not be hidden in computer systems but will be visualized on tweeter-high screens (Kanban). Additionally, during product development phases Toyota relies on many digital systems for its effective and efficient functioning. Some them include utilising plenty of digital know-how databases and simulation tools for product design and process design (including digital assembly workability tools)

(This example is given as additional information for the reader in the context of I4.0 in lean)

2.1 Principles of Lean Manufacturing (LM)

Researchers have found a substantial improvement in performance of manufacturing industry with the development and implementation of LM. It has helped industries to operate at a higher efficiency and be competent in the changing market (Mrugalska & Wyrwicka, 2017). The ease of lean implementation has been given by a systematic framework which comprises of 5 key Lean principles. The 5 key principles listed in the table below are the key lean principles focussing on identification of value added and non-value-added components in a process flow.

Table 1. Key principles of lean

Lean Principles	Principle functions
Define Value	Identifying customer requirements for a specific product and determining how much a customer is willing to spend for the service or product.
Identify value stream	Entire product lifecycle are to be prepared which can help production team to identify procedure or steps that do not add value to the product, thereby the production team can understand entire product life cycle
Create smooth value flow	To smoothen the value flow, any steps/ Procedure which do not add value to the product are eliminated to smoothen the value flow. The objective is to allow raw material to flow through the process without any interruption and deliver the products to end-user smoothly.
Implement pull based production	Pull-based production approach is demand driven. The entire supply chain has to be managed with great flexibility as production of goods will only take place upon receiving an order from the customer.
Strive for excellent	Objective is to perform continuous improvement by constantly reviewing the process to remove non-value-added steps.

To improve the effectiveness of the lean approach, many LM tools have been developed to assist the industry to achieve lean. Selection of lean tools is highly critical to building the industry's confidence in implementing lean practices. Some of the lean tools exist in different names and overlap with other tools, for example, process mapping is also known as value stream mapping. Based on extensive literatures some 25 lean practices have been listed below which are used commonly in industries

Table 2. Lean practices

S.No	Lean Practices	Definition
1	5S principle	To effectively optimise work area by eliminating the waste resulting in poor organisation of work
2	Andon	Visual feedback system in plant floors indicating the production status, acts as real time communication tool
3	Bottleneck analysis	Analysing the processes limits and overall throughput, to identify the weak link and improve them
4	Continuous flow	To have a effective continuous flow in manufacturing process by eliminating waste
5	Gemba	Philosophy reminding to go out to the shop floor for understanding in deep about manufacturing issues first hand
6	Heijunka	Scheduling production in smaller batches leading to reduced lead time and inventory
7	HoshinKanri	Align the strategy of the company with the middle management and with the shop floor to achieve the company's goal
8	Jidoka	Partial automation of the process to assess the quality issues by a worker in multiple station
9	Just In Time (JIT)	Based upon demand of the customer the products are pulled for production
10	Kaizen	Strategy, where the employee looks and identify areas for improvement and optimisation
11	Kanban	This is a system which regulates flow of goods based upon the need and demand
12	KPIs (Key Performance Indicators)	Designing metrics to be aligned with the top level management and act as critical drivers of behaviour
13	Muda	Within a manufacturing process identifying any activities which doesn't have any value from the customer perspective
14	Overall Equipment Effectiveness	It is a framework to measure the productivity of a process with respect to different categories
15	PDCA (Plan, Do, Check, ACT)	It is to act upon methodology to implement different improvement with a sequential steps which are repeated for optimisation
16	Poka-Yoke	A system to identify the error within the process and prevents in the production area to achieve zero defects

continues on following page

Table 2. Continued

S.No	Lean Practices	Definition
17	Root cause analysis	Methodology to resolve the problem occurred earlier and to follow down to identify the underlying problem which triggered it
18	Single-Minute Exchange of Dies	Its main purpose to reduce the time of the change over and to eliminate non-essential operation during the operation
19	Six Big Losses	Breakdowns, Setup, Small stops, reduced speed, start-up rejects and production reject are major categories of six big losses and to provide a framework to resolve these common problems creating wastage in a process
20	SMART Goals	Specific Measurable Attainable Relevant and Time-Specific to ensure to align with the goals to be effective
21	Standardized work	In order to capture the best practice documentation of the manufacturing process is necessary and it helps to standardize
22	Takt Time	To fix a pace for production which aligns the production with the customer demand for optimised scheduling
23	Total Productive maintenance	To maximise the operational time of the machine within a process by focussing on proactive maintenance planning
24	Value stream mapping	To visualise entire flow of production, shows the current state of processes and highlights the areas for improvement. It exposes the waste in the process and allows to road map the improvements
25	Visual Factory	these are visual indicators display and controls through the entire plant to have better flow of information and communication

3.0 GREEN MANUFACTURING: PRINCIPLES

In order to achieve a healthy environmental performance in manufacturing, Anastas and Zimmerman (2003) proposed the 12 Principles of Green Engineering which stresses on the need to evaluate input and output of energy and material to be non-hazardous inherently and have higher product lifecycle as well. Helu and Dornfeld (2013) then modified those 12 principles to a simplified framework that consists of 5 principles of GM which are listed in the Table 3.0 below. All the principles exhibit a strong emphasis on energy and environmental emission issue which are the primary factors to be considered for green approach.

P1 takes environmental impact into consideration as the impact may have resulted from the process itself. In P2, Vertical refers to system varying level of detail from the enterprise down to the process while horizontal refers to the system at the same level of detail. This approach is important as environmental impact can occur depending on the level of detail. P3 stresses on the need to identify harmful input and output to be replaced with material that has a lower impact thorough recycle, reuse and remanufacture. P4 emphasizes on importance of net resources to be zero so that resources may be used at a rate equal to the rate of replenishment in the environment. P5 suggested that temporal effect is time-based and environmental impact should be considered in the design stage to allow better ability to consider for an alternative in reducing the future effect.

Table 3. Green principles

S.No	Green Principles
1	A comprehensive systems approach must be used to evaluate and improve manufacturing process from a green perspective (P1)
2	The system should be thoroughly viewed across both the vertical and horizontal directions (P2)
3	Harmful input and output of the system to the environment and humans should be reduced or removed (P3)
4	Net resource use should be lowered. (P4)
5	Temporal effect on the system should always be considered (P5)

3.1 Green Tools

There are multiple tools that helps company's objective of reducing pollution and environmental emissions for a green manufacturing (Anastas & Zimmerman, 2003). Researchers find that 80% of the economic, social, and environmental impact is determined during product or process design (Hallam & Contreras, 2016). Design for Environment (DfE) identifies and designs the product based on the environmental impact of a product throughout the life cycle of the product. The life cycle assessment (LCA) of a product is relatively important at the initial design stage. LCA analyses the potential environmental impact throughout the entire life cycle of a product from raw material, production, use and disposal (Chen & Lin, 2017).

GE digital – *a subsidiary of General Electric has developed software called* **Proficy Smart Factory- Manufacturing Execution Systems (MES)**, *a suite of on-premise and cloud solutions. Through integration of data across industries, Industrial Internet of Things (IIoT), Machine learning and predictive analytics, it brings together the digital world with the physical world of manufacturing, The MES provides lean solutions which helps industries to transform manufacturing business through insights and can deliver holistic performance management for today's connected enterprise.*

(This example is given as additional information for the reader in the context of I4.0 in lean)

One or more of the following points will be addressed when companies look for CP: conserving raw materials, water, and energy; eliminating toxic and dangerous raw materials; reducing the quantity and toxicity of emissions and wastes at source during the production process. Eco-Label and Eco-Design are few techniques which are commonly imparted in EMS for industries to meet environmental standards. Eco-labelling is a method of environmental performance certification that is practiced around the world which uses an eco-label to identify products or services that are proven to be environmentally preferable within a specific category. Eco- design consists of integrating environmental protection criteria over a service or a product's lifecycle to anticipate and minimize negative environmental impacts.

4.0 LEAN-GREEN: AN INTEGRATED APPROACH

Different authors have addressed the relation between Lean and Green manufacturing. Many researchers find that Lean and Green manufacturing can be seen as compatible or complimentary initiatives because of their joint focus on waste reduction, efficient use of resources, and emphasis on satisfying customer needs, at the lowest possible cost (Khanchanapong et al., 2014). With their focus on reducing waste and inefficiency, the management practices of both are synergetic (Kolberg & Zühlke, 2015). Hence, by expanding Lean theory to consider environmental wastes as an 8th form of waste, green manufacturing programs can maximize their gains by addressing to specific pollution prevention activities (Deif, 2011). Lean and Green manufacturing also share the goal of enhancing performance indicators, as both approaches seek to improve quality and time as well as to reduce costs while generating value. The use of green manufacturing helps reduces material wastes and energy consumption which diminishes production costs and improves production time (Kolberg & Zühlke, 2015). It will also improve the quality of the production process which will in turn impact product quality. Similarly, the main goal of a Lean manufacturing system is to produce products of higher quality at the lowest possible cost and in the least time by eliminating wastes (Shrouf et al., 2014).

There is an overlapping between Lean manufacturing and Green manufacturing based upon some common attributes (Bonilla et al., 2018). Those are people and system, waste reduction models, reducing lead time, delivery on time, KPI and services level common tools and practices stating that Lean and Green shares a common approach in eliminating and reducing waste within a system (Abualfaraa et al., 2020). Lean is to maximize the output through cost reduction while Green assesses the environmental impact and risks associated to improve the ecological efficiency of any organisation (Bonilla et al., 2018). Thus, Lean utilizes through resource utilization by frequent replenishment but green tries to optimize the replenishment frequency to reduce the environmental footprint (Walton et al., 1998). Thus, integrating Lean and Green to increase the operational performance as well as improve ecological impact will lead to sustainability of the organization's future.

The International Food and Agriculture Organization (FAO) *developed eco-labels for fish and seafood that are harvested or raised in a sustainable manner. The* **Federal Trade Commission (FTC)** *has created its Green Guides to help ensure that marketing claims regarding the environmental attributes of products are truthful and substantiated. Few of its recent labelling includes standards for electronics and building materials (such as furniture, carpet and paint). Other examples include the* **Japanese Eco Mark, International Energy Star, USA Green Seal and UK BREEAM**

(This additional information is given to the reader in the context of I4.0 for sustainability)

5.0 RELATIONSHIP BETWEEN LEAN, I4.0 AND GREEN

The purpose of the conceptual framework presented in Figure 1, is to establish relationships between Industry 4.0, lean manufacturing, performance, and environmental factors. The four relationships in the framework are described as follows: (a) Industry 4.0 technologies can support and further develop well-known lean manufacturing practices, that is, Industry 4.0 supports lean manufacturing. (b) Established lean manufacturing systems exert facilitating effects on Industry 4.0 implementations, that is, lean manufacturing supports Industry 4.0. (c) The changes imposed on the production system by the integration of Industry 4.0 and lean manufacturing affects different performance dimensions of the system, that is, it illustrates the performance implications of an Industry 4.0 and lean manufacturing integration. (d) Based on similar studies, it is likely that environmental factors influence the potential to integrate Industry 4.0 and lean manufacturing, as well as the resulting performance of such integration (Fercoq et al., 2013), that is, it depicts the effect of environmental factors on an Industry 4.0 and lean manufacturing integration (Wagner et al., 2017).

Figure 1. Conceptual framework for relationships between I4.0, Lean and Green

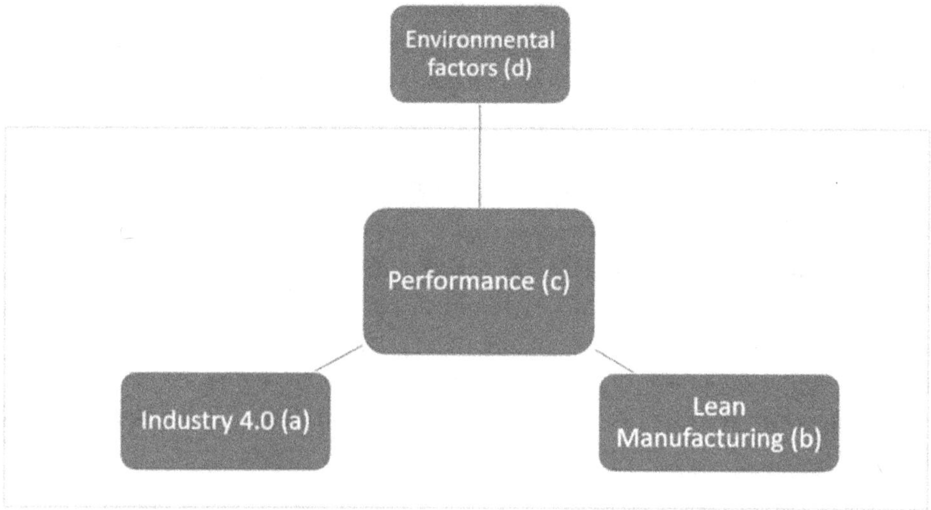

6.0 INDUSTRY 4.0

The Industrial revolution started with mechanization, steam power and weaving followed with the mass production, developing assembly line and utilizing electrical energy. It is applying the concepts of cyber physical system with the internet and future oriented technologies with the improved interaction between human and the machine (Womack & Jones, 1997). This states to link the production system, supply chain, warehouse, marketing, logistics and customer demand ensuring the creation of better visibility over the organisation (Cardinali & De Giovanni, 2022) (Carvalho & Cruz-Machado, 2011).Technological advancement like cyber physical system, internet of things, autonomous robots, cloud computing, big data, analytics, 3D printing, augmented reality, cyber security and others are the ones powering the fourth industrial revolution in the production industry. Currently, the information is communicated through the device level from sensing the environment and communicating it, but also in digest the information sent from the other devices (Cooney, 2002). Furthermore, the sensors are deployed at higher rate as it is small, lower weight. The data analysis with the adapted parameter from the new situation is considered and based upon the new parameter inputs new decision model is created. This is an important section as it integrates with all the functionality, data structure and streamlines the top layer application (Vogel-Heuser et al., 2017).This allows sharing information along the entire or specific system, having a unified platform and through big data analysis the patterns are identified. Thus, how it shows that industry 4.0 is mostly to be next level upgraded of the lean concepts below the table shows a set of categories the lean principles trying to address and how industry 4.0 could act as the next generation enabler.

Bosch Rexroth, *an Automation Technology Business Unit of Robert Bosch developed a Manual Production Systems which goes beyond simple lean cell design to view lean as a plant wide process. It has networking between things and independent machine-to-machine communication as its core and is commonly referred as Industry 4.0 and Web 3.0, or jointly as "The Internet of Things and Services." They have also developed a plant for control systems and linear motion technology which are digitally equipped with new manufacturing processes. It harmonizes real-time production using machine data from a variety of sources in the manufacturing environment, gives it a clear structure, and presents it to workers on their mobile devices*

Table 4. Lean with Industry 4.0- What is the link?

	Lean Manufacturing	Industry 4.0
Flexibility	To reduce change over time to enable multiple production of different products in single manufacturing line	Incorporate sensors and software to automatically trigger to sense products and instantly use the necessary program without stopping the process
Inventory Reduction	To reduce the waste which includes inventory cost and produce Just In time	This can be done with the help of real time data provided to trigger ordering for parts/raw material
Quality	To reduce defects with the help of self-inspection tools.	With real time monitoring and data driven analytics to resolve the root cause
Production planning	Shop floor management and other process to enhance the production change and optimise production plan	With the help of data through the value chain, specific plan can be induced. This can be done in real time to enhance the production
Productivity	Opt for continuous improvement in a different aspect of process	Real time data identify root cause problem and validates improvements at a faster rate
Safety	With the help of visual aids and signals it is done	Sensors can be effectively utilized to initiate protocols
Machine downtime	Incorporates preventive maintenance with the help of maintenance logs	With the help of real time data sets the preventive maintenance can be levelled up to predictive maintenance
Data driven innovation	Collection and analyzing customer review and incorporating to drive product innovation	Data analytics helps to process the collected data and with the help of sensors for product performance fine tuning can meet the expectation of the customer.

7.0 LINKING LEAN AND INDUSTRY 4.0

As industry 4.0 is going to be the future of industries, linking them with lean seems to be the need of the hour for all companies. The link between Industry 4.0 and Lean is shown in Table 4.0. Lean manufacturing focuses on eliminating all kinds of waste in the production process by identifying any unnecessary activities, streamlining the process, and creating standardised routines. Simple machines and workstations with low levels of complexity facilitate automation and digitalisation of the manufacturing process (Durakbasa et al., 2016). Lean manufacturing has led to some researchers claiming that a lean implementation necessarily must be seen as a prerequisite for a successful Industry 4.0 transformation (Leong et al., 2019). From cases reported in the literature, they find that increased flexibility is the most common reported performance benefit, followed by improved productivity, reduced cost, reduced delivery time, and improved quality (Bauer et al., 2018). Regarding the performance impacts of combining lean manufacturing with AMTs, the synergistic performance impact of such integration motivates the joint optimisation of the two rather than optimising either resource alone (Groger et al., 2016). To distinguish among different environments, internal and external environmental factors that can influence the organisation should be mapped. Thus, an environmental factor is defined as an identifiable element in the environment that influences the organisation's operations. In addition to the moderating effect on performance, environmental factors tend to influence the applicability and implementation approach of improvement programmes (Mayr et al., 2018). However, the extent to which lean principles are suitable for non-repetitive environments has been questioned (Lucantoni et al., 2022). The lean practices and methods developed for mass production do not usually fit these environments, which tend to experience major difficulties when seeking to implement lean practices. Similarly, for Industry 4.0, it is argued that environmental factors will have a significant impact on the applicability of Industry 4.0 (Sony, 2018). Through a multiple case study, find that companies with repetitive production systems on a general basis should have an easier transition to Industry 4.0 than non-repetitive production systems. Other researchers claim that only big enterprises will be able to reap the benefits from Industry 4.0 and that small and medium-sized enterprises (SMEs) can quickly become the victims of Industry 4.0 (Mayr et al., 2018). Smaller enterprises will suffer because of the high investments needed, and the increased flexibility introduced by Industry 4.0 will allow bigger enterprises to steal market shares for customised products, a market segment now usually dominated by SMEs

7.1Cyber Physical System

Though companies have been able to lower cost drastically using lean, increased need to respond for changing customer demand has pushed companies to move further with lean concepts. Impact of digitalization on lean methods for improving productivity is shown in figure below. Researches emphasized the impacts of CPS's in industrial services which can pave way to seven affordances: 1. Engineering improved equipment with the leverage of data collected, 2. Optimization of equipment operations, 3. Remote control and management of equipment, 4. Predictability to service activities, 5. Remote diagnostics and replace field service activities, 6. Empower and optimize field service and 7. Information and data-driven services (El Jaouhari et al., 2022).

CPS with JIT

Material movement tracked via sensor networks has enabled direct material flow from warehouse to machines which has eliminated the need of buffers in shop floor (Sommer, 2015). Based on statistical data and comparing it to a digital model of a complete process created by the CPS, Through CPS, quantity of material required could be predicted through statistical data which would improve process reliability and traceability.

Example: *A smart lean automation engine enabled by CPS technologies (SLAE–CPS), based on analysis of Jidoka functions and the smart capacity of CPS technologies, is widely used for providing an integrated and standardized approach to design and implement a CPS-based smart Jidoka system. It works by converting heterogeneous physical data into uniform services for subsequent abnormality*

7.2 Internet of Things and Industrial Internet of Things in Lean Environments

A global logistics model for transportation in combination with Industrial Internet of Things (IIoT) technology and I4.0, allows a fully autonomous global supply chain. By using Lean six sigma approach, the process flow is optimized and efficiency is increased overall. Through IIOT supported network connection, the model provides real time data about machines and operations, via connection of production flow and supply chain.

7.3 Big Data and Data Analytics Role for Lean Tools Enhancement

Wagner et al. (2017) supported the potential of using Big Data technology and data analytics that enables real-time visualization of results using RFID technology. Mrugalska (2017) stated the principle First in First Out (FIFO) logic which determines safety inventory, based on Big Data model For live data acquisition from all lines in the production, KPI needs to be identified and traced by the network supported by a cloud solution. With standardized data formats becoming obsolete, a real-time data exchange can facilitate improved data processing, reducing waiting and operation times during product development. With vertical integration in smart manufacturing environment, it can promote and manage continuous improvement through the whole product life cycle.

7.4 Virtual and Augmented Reality (VR & AR)

Virtual Reality (VR) technology combined with CPS provides real-time data to create virtual VSM, which is one of the core lean practices. Virtual VSM allows stakeholders to connect in a virtual model, observing and mapping current and future state of processes, without the need of understanding the conventional VSM symbols (Ferro et al., 2017). Kolberg and Zuhlke (2015) recommended the use of AR and CPS-based wearable devices that provide information to operators about cycle time and tasks to perform via AR, to support JIT production. In addition, the wearable devices will also receive failure information and display it in real-time to operators. Moreover, these technologies can represent a product true to scale, improving development activities and making processes more intuitive.

Knowledge sharing*: PepsiCo along with a university has developed a simulation software which is built using Unity3D which has scripting in C and Java Script. This software emulates running of a manufacturing cell within a Lean environment to enhance training and educate personnel through simulating a functioning manufacturing cell. The software displays potential Lean wastes and problems such as bottle necking and overproduction. There is also a concept developed called 'Gemba VR' wherein students can access areas and views that might be unavailable during a field trip, such as clean rooms and close-up views of machinery.*

7.5 Autonomous and Collaborative Robotics for Flexible Manufacturing Systems

To work in flexible environment, responding to unpredictable changes and providing efficient, reliable and predictable path-based navigations. However, robots are flexible enough to react fast to obstacles and persons, avoiding them and blocking their way, meeting the safety challenges of robot fleets. Durakbasa (2016) pointed out sensor technology and Multifunction Intelligent Measurement Robots can assist the flexile implementation of automation in process control and quality assurance.

7.6 Video-based Models and 3D

Bauters et al (2018) focused their work on a video-based system for automatically analyse manual assembly work tasks through a 3D-model. This system captures information about the way tasks are performed by the operator, being able to detect anomalous events that are linked with video data for further analysis. The collected information is useful for continuous improvement processes and the identified best practices are used for standard work instructions and information sharing within the company.

7.7 Simulation and Digital Twin

Mayr et al. (2018) suggested that digital twin concept supported by simulation technologies enables dynamic VSM, which gives real-time replication of the whole manufacturing system, and thereby enabling access to updated information which gives more predictable and reliable planning strategies. Ferro et al. (2017) carried out a survey with the aim of analysing the integration of Discrete Event Simulation in operations management tools, such as, MES, ERP, RFID, core manufacturing simulation data and e-Kanban.

7.8 3D Printing

Chen and Lin (2017) presented a discussion about 3D printing technology which facilitates the achievement of lean manufacturing principles, like small batch production. Since this technology allows print-on-demand production systems, the lead time is decreased and efficiency of logistics is enhanced as it supports pull systems. Rauch et al. (2016) supported that the use of additive manufacturing technologies, such as 3D Printing, heightens smart product development processes and reduce wastages to a greater extent. Also, this technology is useful to produce complex parts, which cuts down setup times, enabling the one-piece flow production.

***Knowledge sharing**: GE Additive, and the Dubai Future Foundation with a combined expertise created a micro-factory to accelerate additive design and digital manufacturing technologies in the UAE. Anatomics, an Australian maker of customized surgical implants successfully implanted a titanium sternum and ribcage in a living patient, having designed and manufactured the bones technology. They claimed that with this adoption of 3D printing, they have slashed the cost of their patient-specific products by 30 to 50 percent through material waste reduction and tooling costs.*

Though the implications of technologies in lean and green concepts are exceedingly large, some technologies which has strived greater importance in I4.0 technologies are discussed above. Fig 2, depicts the usage of those technologies which has facilitated the supply chain process in an industry. Their utilization to support and lean and green methods are discussed in the chapters to follow.

Figure 2. Technologies which support supply chain process

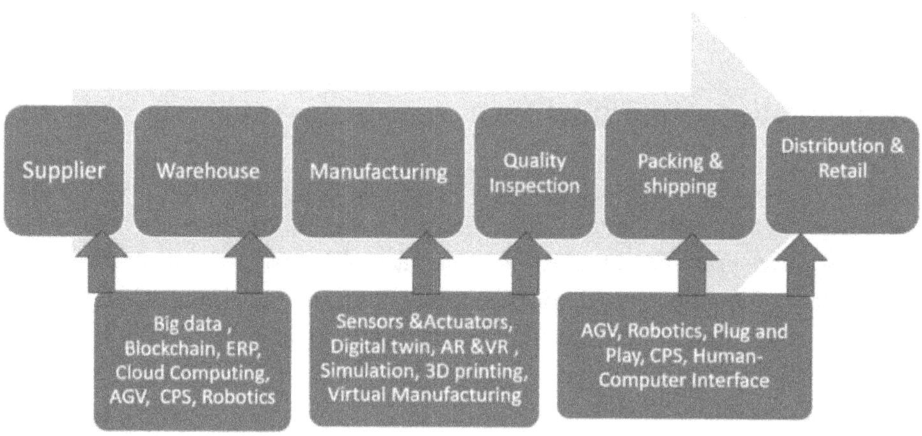

8.0 INDUSTRY 4.0 FOR A GREENER & SUSTAINABLE DEVELOPMENT

Digitization of manufacturing processes offers wide opportunities for energy saving. Shrouf and Miragliotta (2014) describe various benefits that can be obtained by IoT adoption and integration between real-time data and the company's information technology tools and platforms, in order to improve energy efficiency. The application of optimization software tools has resulted in energy savings, and reduces up to 30% of the consumption for real industrial robot trajectories. In addition to improving energy efficiency utilizing the optimization of a single machine or the whole manufacturing process, there exists the possibility of smart energy allocation promoted by the horizontal integration of factories and enterprises. Optimization algorithm helps in energy saving for production management by optimizing total energy consumption with a big data processing platform (Bortolini et al., 2016) Industry 4.0 provides continuous support through resource management due to the detailed information availability on each point of the production process (Bai et al., 2022). Accordingly, the monitoring of real-time data enables the awareness of resource consumption and responsive production management. Besides this, the emergence of novel technologies can improve material savings, as is the case for additive manufacturing, known as 3D printing (Wyrwicka & Mrugalska, 2015). Additive manufacturing creates products layer-by-layer, it is undoubtedly more resource efficient and less wasteful than traditional subtractive methods due to its ability to reuse waste material (Netland, 2016). The technology is promising since a variety of polymers, metals, ceramics, and composites can be used. Though the first applications of it were in the area of rapid prototyping and then tooling, they are now increasingly being used for direct manufacturing (Netland, 2016). In addition, 3D printing does not require ancillary, sustainability-impacting cutting fluids, casting release compounds or forging lubricants and can influence maintenance, logistics and contribute to the flexible nature which are necessary for on-demand customized products. On-demand customized products, an extended version of JIT and one of the drivers of Industry 4.0 development, enables two approaches regarding its impact on environmental sustainability (Testi, 2019). The more pessimistic approach relies on the thinking that the easy availability of customization may foster the need to possess more objects, feeding a short-term hedonism, a sense of ephemeral happiness. On the other hand, the customized product may eliminate undesired or unneeded functionality for end users (Silvestri et al., 2022). Industry 4.0 can also foster disruptive business models where not products but functionalities, maintenance and services will be offered to consumers (Kim & Kara, 2012). These new business models can extend the life-cycle of products, since new functionalities could be added in a modular way without replacing the whole device. Summarizing all the literatures from various researchers, an overview of I4.0 elements which have a positive impact on environmental sustainability is presented in Table 5.0 below,

9.0 RESEARCH GAP

The above literature study clearly shows that the lean concepts have been the back bone for the manufacturing industries to optimise their process in various ways. It is

Table 5. Impact of I4.0 elements on environmental sustainability

I 4.0 elements	Possibilities	Flow of materials & energy
IOT and CPS	Vertical Integration	Availability of reliable data about materials and energy flows
	Horizontal Integration	Availability of reliable data about material consumption and energy along the life cycle
Big data	Optimization of material consumption/eco-efficiency	Less material flow in manufacturing
	Optimization of energy consumption/eco-efficiency	Less energy flow in production
	Predictive / Remote maintenance	Less energy flow
Additive Manufacturing	Prototyping	Decreased material flow, resulting in less wastage of material
	Part / Final product manufacturing	No cutting fluids or lubricants, resulting in less energy flow
On-demand production (JIT 4.0)	Elimination of the undesired functionalities of product	Reduced material and energy flow
	Disruptive business model/ functionality and service	Increased life cycle of product and decreased End-of-life products

also evident that the current technologies are also growing at a faster rate and have also been proved to be very essential during this competitive world. Having heard of so many industries being leaped with the technology transfer and with supporting cases of success by their side, it has been clear that they are not to be side lined. With that there are also some cases of leading major industries experiencing a setback during the technology transfer, as there is not a clear set of guidelines about how to incorporate technologies in the prevailing setup to achieve the desired outcomes in this challenging environment. Initially, focus is majorly towards identifying the lean tools with their importance on how they are specifically used to enhance a particular area and then based on various literatures, the different industry 4.0 technologies with its strong suit and the best fit work areas for optimisation are identified which could help the industries entering the era of the fourth revolution to set a path for incorporating the appropriate technologies at required areas for optimisation.

10.0 METHODOLOGY

On numerous occasions, it has been proven in the research field that, a detailed literature review will give the best suited possible solution. Thus, in this paper with the help of various researches, lean and green paradigm concepts have been gone through to affix them with Industry 4.0 technologies for appropriate usage. Various current researches point out that the industry 4.0 technologies have been unique and have been excellent in enhancing the decision making with real time data and processing. In today's competitive world, many big companies have started to integrate the technologies but to cope up with them other industries must converge and start to integrate new technologies. This sudden transition and desperate attempts may lead to ruining of entire system. Thus, through literature review, the best suited technologies to enhance lean and green paradigms are appropriately identified to help industries create a notion on which technology to incorporate for them to get the better out of it.

11.0 INDUSTRY 4.0 TECHNOLOGIES ENHANCING LEAN & GREEN

The lean and green tools selected based on literatures, can be enhanced with the application of emerging technologies, which has a greater impact on productivity and environment and thereby enabling greener manufacturing. The matrix shown in Table 6.0, illustrate which I4.0 tools can be utilized to support the analysed lean and green methods.

12.0 RESULT AND DISCUSSION

Establishing the relationship with Industry 4.0 technology and lean tools & concept can coexist and support each other (Kolla et al., 2019). Accordingly, Vogel-Heuser et al, rejected that there exists a contradiction between I4.0 and LM (Shrouf et al., 2014). In addition, existing barriers in lean implementation can be dealt with commitment towards I4.0 (Khanchanapong et al., 2014). Also, the relationship and how Industry 4.0 enhances the lean tools proves fact that there exists a general compatibility of Lean and Industry 4.0 together. The Impact of digitalization on lean methods has given industries a never-ending saturation point for long-term productivity. This perspective can be attributed to similarities concerning targets, like the reduction of complexity and lean principles as a common ground. Based on extensive literatures and reasonable assessments of the authors, various I4.0 tools has been listed in the Table, which gives a clear insight about Industry 4.0 tools that can be utilized to support lean methods. With respect to that we can state that establishing the relationship will be the pathway to development of lean tools integrated with the industry 4.0 technologies. These inferences have further lead to tools which have been discussed below.

Table 6. Relationship matrix between Lean & Green practices with Industry 4.0 technologies

S. No	Industry 4.0 Technologies Lean – Green Practices	Cyber Physical System	Robotics	Augmented Reality	Virtual Manufacturing	Big Data	Block Chain	Cloud Computing	Internet Of Things	Horizontal & Vertical Integration	Additive Manufacturing	Simulation	Digital Twin	Optimization Algorithms	Sensors & Actuators	Real-Time Computing	Machine Learning	Plug And Play	Automated Guided Vehicles	Digital Object Memory	Human-Computer Interaction	Video Based And 3d Models
1	5s Principle		X	X	X			X						X			X			X	X	
2	Andon	X	X		X							X	X								X	
3	Bottleneck Analysis		X	X	X				X		X				X		X				X	
4	Continuous Flow	X	X	X	X	X	X	X	X			X		X	X	X			X			X
5	Gemba			X		X			X				X				X					
6	Heijunka					X		X	X						X						X	
7	HoshinKanri					X		X	X			X					X					
8	Jidoka	X	X												X							
9	Just In Time (Jit)		X			X			X	X							X		X	X		
10	Kaizen			X	X	X	X	X		X						X					X	
11	Kanban	X		X	X	X							X						X		X	
12	Kpi	X				X	X					X										X
13	Muda	X	X	X	X	X		X	X			X		X					X			X
14	OEE									X	X						X				X	
15	Pdca		X				X								X		X				X	
16	Poka-Yoke			X	X			X									X				X	
17	Root Cause Analysis					X				X				X			X			X		
18	Smed			X	X						X		X					X		X		
19	Six Big Losses	X				X	X	X	X										X			
20	Smart Goals			X	X						X	X	X	X				X				X
21	Standardized Work	X	X	X	X	X		X						X	X	X						X
22	Takt Time			X	X	X	X			X												
23	Total Productive Maintenance		X	X	X	X		X	X					X	X			X		X	X	
24	Value Stream Mapping			X	X	X	X	X				X	X			X	X				X	
25	Visual Factory	X				X	X	X					X	X		X		X			X	X
26	LCA				X	X						X		X			X				X	X
27	DfE				X			X			X					X	X			X		
28	MRP						X				X			X			X					
29	CP		X			X		X								X				X		
30	Eco-Label														X		X			X	X	
31	EMS	X				X	X		X						X						X	
32	Eco-Design	X									X	X		X	X					X		

Just-In-Time/Just-In-Sequence 4.0

Automated guided vehicles (AGV) assist in material supply to workstations in accordance to the requirements, rerouting in alternate path in case of obstacles and minimizing the possibilities of empty trips (Lucantoni et al., 2022). A digital object memory, storing every necessary information, in combination with condition monitoring navigates AGV efficiently (Bortolini et al., 2016). Furthermore, Auto-ID technology, such as RFID, assists real-time material tracking in value chain and continuous stock monitoring which helps in maintaining reduced inventory levels (Ferro et al., 2017) (Mrugalska & Wyrwicka, 2017). The JIT/JIS 4.0 method additionally applies big data and data analytics techniques for analysing detailed real-time process information by providing insights into parameters. It helps in identifying trends and arriving at rules for the production system (Netland, 2016). Mainly, data analysis has the potential to contribute to an improved system performance of the whole supply chain (Testi, 2019).

Heijunka 4.0

Some I4.0 tools like data analytics enhances forecast quality and planning. The results aids in stabilizing planning schedule, as it gives an in-depth analysis of market using historical data (Bortolini et al., 2016) (Mayr et al., 2018). Some software tools like AnaPro levels the production program automatically based on specification, technological process, workplace, and sales (Ojha, 2022). In heijunka 4.0, planning is automated and short-dated adjustments can be integrated with reduced effort for production levelling.

Kanban 4.0

Through simulation methods or a virtual real-time representation of physical objects based on a CAD model (digital twin), a new Kanban loop can be integrated into the existing production flow effortlessly. Additionally, external changes can be included while the system refreshes parameters autonomously (Ferro et al., 2017). By applying Auto-ID, a constant monitoring of work allows a comparison of target and actual values to remove unnecessary stock (Khanchanapong et al., 2014).

Value Stream Mapping 4.0

VSM enhances the transparency of the material and information flow within the value chain to minimize the lead time (Nishal et al., 2021). applying Auto-ID enables the instant localization of objects, big data and data analytics facilitate the consolidation of information. Consolidated key performance indicators enable decision making based on facts (Mayr et al., 2018). By deploying human-computer interaction (HCI) devices which allow receiving information, trigger actions and control processes (e.g. tablet, smartphone, and head mounted displays) information becomes remotely retrievable for stakeholders. Machine learning and data analytics support the creation of a value stream design. Target states are generated automatically and validated before implementation. Besides, the effort to carry out VSM is reduced and decisions are based on real time data.

Total Productive Maintenance 4.0

The combination of virtual representation technologies like virtual reality (VR) and augmented reality (AR) as well as head-mounted displays facilitates training as well as maintenance instructions in a more responsible way (Ojha, 2022). As maintenance typically involves non-recurring and context sensitive activities, interaction with maintenance experts becomes crucial. By displaying virtual elements operators can be guided remotely (Pereira et al., 2019). Unlike conventional Corrective Maintenance (CM), predictive analytics uses complex algorithms to predict defects based on large data sets (big data). Plug and play allows the autonomous integration of a technical system based on a modular design and a service-oriented architecture. Thus, production plants can easily be adapted and customized. More precisely, hardware-in-the-loop simulation enables testing of real PLC code on real controls against a simulated plant model.

Single Minute Exchange of Die 4.0

While I4.0 provides a considerable potential for optimizing digital activities, physical setup times generally remain (Leong et al., 2019). Apart from AR and plug and play, additive manufacturing (AM) is expected to achieve the highest impact on setup time. Because AM processes are not product-specific, varying work-pieces can be produced with minimum setup times. Times for selection, search and adjustment of tools and workpieces are omitted. Nevertheless, small adaption, temperature adjustments and cleaning operations will still incur. Hence, it can be argued that SMED can also be applied to AM.

Visual Management 4.0

RFID can be used for indoor navigation, however, compared to Wi-Fi or Bluetooth, it is not commonly installed on smart phones and tablets (Nishal et al., 2021). Unlike traditional andon lamps Human- computer Interface (HCI) devices like tablets, smart phones, head-mounted displays, and smart watches enable a targeted notification for users. Hence, notifications are displayed in real-time regardless of the distance between operator and machine (Helu & Dornfeld, 2013) (Kolla et al., 2019). For digital andon boards, several suppliers provide solutions to visualize complex data and processes in real-time. Retrieving this information from mobile devices supports a location independent access and use.

Poka-Yoke 4.0

Auto-ID ensures the correct identification and assignment. A digital product memory allows requesting required components and helps to identify incorrect deliveries. This prevents adding value to defective parts (Kolla et al., 2019). By using smart sensors and machine learning, machines can automatically adjust to irregularities to ensure optimal product quality (Rauch et al., 2016). Eventually, AR and head-mounted displays, as well as RFID readers can be used to achieve zero-error picking (Wyrwicka & Mrugalska, 2015).

Digital Twin Enables Dynamic VSM

The integration of a digital twin replicating the whole manufacturing system is promising as it links the existing system in real-time to a digital reflection. In turn, this reflection can be used to build a value stream map based on real-time information instead of using stochastic models. This allows overcoming the static character of VSM as dynamic changes are considered. Hence, detailed planning becomes more predictable and reliable.

13.0 CONCLUSION

The above established relationship of various lean & green tools with emerging technologies will be helpful for further research in exploring them in real time cases. With current market demand fluctuating to a greater extent, I4.0 promises to cope with it by a superior levelled production in LM and GM. Eventually, the increased flexibility through I4.0 helps to subsist with the rising complexity. Associated with the beginning of the fourth industrial revolution, I4.0 depicts the recent trend in Information and Communication Technologies (ICT) which has gained significant importance in manufacturing industries. This study has led to development of new tools with respect to lean and green concepts for integration with Industry 4.0 technologies. This will enhance the operational excellence and also to enhance the Green-Lean concept. These future tools will assess the given situation not only to optimise economically but also the environmental impact as well, allowing enhancement of operational sustainability.

REFERENCES

Abualfaraa, W., Salonitis, K., Al-Ashaab, A., & Ala'raj, M. (2020). Lean-green manufacturing practices and their link with sustainability: A critical review. *Sustainability*, *12*(3), 981. doi:10.3390u12030981

Anastas, P. T., & Zimmerman, J. B. (2003). *Peer reviewed: Design through the 12 principles of green engineering*. Academic Press.

Bai, C., Orzes, G., & Sarkis, J. (2022). Exploring the impact of Industry 4.0 technologies on social sustainability through a circular economy approach. *Industrial Marketing Management*, *101*, 176–190. doi:10.1016/j.indmarman.2021.12.004

Bauer, H., Brandl, F., Lock, C., & Reinhart, G. (2018). Integration of Industrie 4.0 in lean manufacturing learning factories. *Procedia Manufacturing*, *23*, 147–152. doi:10.1016/j.promfg.2018.04.008

Bauters, K., Cottyn, J., Claeys, D., Slembrouck, M., Veelaert, P., & Van Landeghem, H. (2018). Automated work cycle classification and performance measurement for manual work stations. *Robotics and Computer-integrated Manufacturing*, *51*, 139–157. doi:10.1016/j.rcim.2017.12.001

Bonilla, S. H., Silva, H. R., Terra da Silva, M., Franco Gonçalves, R., & Sacomano, J. B. (2018). Industry 4.0 and sustainability implications: A scenario-based analysis of the impacts and challenges. *Sustainability*, *10*(10), 3740. doi:10.3390u10103740

Bortolini, M., Ferrari, E., Galizia, F. G., & Mora, C. (2016). A reference framework integrating lean and green principles within supply chain management. International Journal of Social, Behavioral, Educational, Economic. *Business and Industrial Engineering*, *10*(3), 859–864.

Cardinali, P. G., & De Giovanni, P. (2022). Responsible digitalization through digital technologies and green practices. *Corporate Social Responsibility and Environmental Management*, *29*(4), 984–995. doi:10.1002/csr.2249

Carvalho, H., & Cruz-Machado, V. (2011). Integrating lean, agile, resilience and green paradigms in supply chain management (LARG_SCM). *Supply Chain Management*, 27–48.

Chen, T., & Lin, Y. C. (2017). Feasibility evaluation and optimization of a smart manufacturing system based on 3D printing: A review. *International Journal of Intelligent Systems*, *32*(4), 394–413. doi:10.1002/int.21866

Cooney, R. (2002). Is "lean" a universal production system? Batch production in the automotive industry. *International Journal of Operations & Production Management*, *22*(10), 1130–1147. doi:10.1108/01443570210446342

Deif, A. M. (2011). A system model for green manufacturing. *Journal of Cleaner Production*, *19*(14), 1553–1559. doi:10.1016/j.jclepro.2011.05.022

Durakbasa, N. M., Bauer, J. M., Bas, G., & Kräuter, L. (2016). Novel Trends in the Development of Autonomation and Robotics in Metrology for Production in the Future. *IFAC-PapersOnLine*, *49*(29), 6–11. doi:10.1016/j.ifacol.2016.11.057

El Jaouhari, A., Arif, J., Fellaki, S., Amejwal, M., & Azzouz, K. (2022). Lean supply chain management and Industry 4.0 interrelationships: the status quo and future perspectives. *International Journal of Lean Six Sigma*, ahead-of-print.

Fercoq, A., Lamouri, S., Carbone, V., Lelièvre, A., & Lemieux, A. A. (2013). Combining lean and green in manufacturing: a model of waste management. *IFAC Proceedings Volumes, 46*(9), 117-122. 10.3182/20130619-3-RU-3018.00164

Ferro, R., Ordóñez, R. E. C., & Anholon, R. (2017). Analysis of the integration between operations management manufacturing tools with discrete event simulation. *Production Engineering*, *11*(4), 467–476. doi:10.100711740-017-0755-2

Groger, C., Kassner, L., Hoos, E., Konigsberger, J., Kiefer, C., Silcher, S., & Mitschang, B. (2016). The data-driven factory. *ICEIS*, *2016*, 40.

Hallam, C. R., & Contreras, C. (2016, September). The interrelation of Lean and green manufacturing Practices: A case of push or pull in implementation. In *2016 Portland International Conference on Management of Engineering and Technology (PICMET)* (pp. 1815-1823). IEEE. 10.1109/PICMET.2016.7806669

Helu, M., & Dornfeld, D. (2013). Principles of green manufacturing. In *Green Manufacturing* (pp. 107–115). Springer. doi:10.1007/978-1-4419-6016-0_5

Khanchanapong, T., Prajogo, D., Sohal, A. S., Cooper, B. K., Yeung, A. C., & Cheng, T. C. E. (2014). The unique and complementary effects of manufacturing technologies and lean practices on manufacturing operational performance. *International Journal of Production Economics*, *153*, 191–203. doi:10.1016/j.ijpe.2014.02.021

Kim, S. J., & Kara, S. (2012). Impact of technology on product life cycle design: Functional and environmental perspective. In *Leveraging Technology for a Sustainable World* (pp. 191–196). Springer. doi:10.1007/978-3-642-29069-5_33

Kolberg, D., & Zühlke, D. (2015). Lean automation enabled by industry 4.0 technologies. *IFAC-PapersOnLine*, *48*(3), 1870–1875. doi:10.1016/j.ifacol.2015.06.359

Kolla, S., Minufekr, M., & Plapper, P. (2019). Deriving essential components of lean and industry 4.0 assessment model for manufacturing SMEs. *Procedia CIRP*, *81*, 753–758. doi:10.1016/j.procir.2019.03.189

Leong, W. D., Lam, H. L., Ng, W. P. Q., Lim, C. H., Tan, C. P., & Ponnambalam, S. G. (2019). Lean and green manufacturing—a review on its applications and impacts. *Process Integration and Optimization for Sustainability, 3*(1), 5-23.

Lucantoni, L., Antomarioni, S., Ciarapica, F. E., & Bevilacqua, M. (2022). Implementation of Industry 4.0 Techniques in Lean Production Technology: A Literature Review. *Management and Production Engineering Review*.

Mayr, A., Weigelt, M., Kühl, A., Grimm, S., Erll, A., Potzel, M., & Franke, J. (2018). Lean 4.0-A conceptual conjunction of lean management and Industry 4.0. *Procedia CIRP*, *72*, 622–628. doi:10.1016/j.procir.2018.03.292

Mrugalska, B., & Wyrwicka, M. K. (2017). Towards lean production in industry 4.0. *Procedia Engineering*, *182*, 466–473. doi:10.1016/j.proeng.2017.03.135

Netland, T. H. (2016). Critical success factors for implementing lean production: The effect of contingencies. *International Journal of Production Research*, *54*(8), 2433–2448. doi:10.1080/00207543.2015.1096976

Nishal, M., Prasad, K. R., Balaji, T. K., & Kalaivanan, K. (2021). Retrofit of two way holding chuck to improve process efficiency and resource management. *Materials Today: Proceedings*, *46*, 9697–9701. doi:10.1016/j.matpr.2020.08.024 PMID:33014714

Ojha, R. (2022). Lean in industry 4.0 is accelerating manufacturing excellence–A DEMATEL analysis. *The TQM Journal*. Advance online publication. doi:10.1108/TQM-11-2021-0318

Pereira, A. C., Dinis-Carvalho, J., Alves, A. C., & Arezes, P. (2019). How Industry 4.0 can enhance lean practices. *FME Transactions*, *47*(4), 810–822. doi:10.5937/fmet1904810P

Rauch, E., Dallasega, P., & Matt, D. T. (2016). Sustainable production in emerging markets through Distributed Manufacturing Systems (DMS). *Journal of Cleaner Production*, *135*, 127–138. doi:10.1016/j.jclepro.2016.06.106

Shrouf, F., Ordieres, J., & Miragliotta, G. (2014, December). Smart factories in Industry 4.0: A review of the concept and of energy management approached in production based on the Internet of Things paradigm. In *2014 IEEE international conference on industrial engineering and engineering management* (pp. 697-701). IEEE.

Silvestri, L., Gallo, T., Silvestri, C., & Falcone, D. (2022, March). Integration of Lean Manufacturing in Industry 4.0: An overview of tools and applications. In *2022 2nd International Conference on Innovative Research in Applied Science, Engineering and Technology (IRASET)* (pp. 1-5). IEEE.

Skalli, D., Charkaoui, A., & Cherrafi, A. (2022). The Integration of Industry 4.0 in Operations Management: *Toward Smart Lean Six Sigma. In International Conference on Digital Technologies and Applications* (pp. 3-11). Springer.

Sommer, L. (2015). Industrial revolution-industry 4.0: Are German manufacturing SMEs the first victims of this revolution? *Journal of Industrial Engineering and Management*, *8*(5), 1512–1532. doi:10.3926/jiem.1470

Sony, M. (2018). Industry 4.0 and lean management: A proposed integration model and research propositions. *Production & Manufacturing Research*, *6*(1), 416–432. doi:10.1080/21693277.2018.1540949

Testi, D. (2019). *A statistical research on the impact of lean and industry 4.0 on companies in northern Italy*. Academic Press.

Vogel-Heuser, B., Bauernhansl, T., & Ten Hompel, M. (2017). Handbuch Industrie 4.0 Bd. 4. *Allgemeine Grundlagen, 2*.

Wagner, T., Herrmann, C., & Thiede, S. (2017). Industry 4.0 impacts on lean production systems. *Procedia CIRP*, *63*, 125–131. doi:10.1016/j.procir.2017.02.041

Walton, S. V., Handfield, R. B., & Melnyk, S. A. (1998). The green supply chain: integrating suppliers into environmental management processes. *International Journal of Purchasing and Materials Management, 34*(1), 2-11.

Womack, J. P., & Jones, D. T. (1997). Lean thinking—Banish waste and create wealth in your corporation. *The Journal of the Operational Research Society, 48*(11), 1148–1148. doi:10.1057/palgrave.jors.2600967

Wyrwicka, M., & Mrugalska, B. (2015, September). Barriers to eliminating waste in production system. In *Proceedings of the 6th international conference on engineering, project, and production management* (pp. 354-363). 10.32738/CEPPM.201509.0035

Chapter 10
Lean Healthcare:
A Guide to Use Statistical Quality Tools in the Lean Healthcare Context

Gozdem Dural-Selcuk
Social Sciences University of Ankara, Turkey

ABSTRACT

Lean thinking is a phenomenon that originated in the production sector; nevertheless, it has been warmly welcomed by the service industry. Healthcare practitioners are also keen to benefit from that notion being aware of the potential contributions that lean operations would bring in their field. Healthcare operations have much in common with the production sector, yet it has its own characteristics which ought to be handled separately. This chapter is dedicated to providing a guideline for healthcare practitioners to apply statistical quality control tools within a correspondence to four main components of lean thinking: problem detection, process redesign, process reliability and sustainability, and continuous improvement. By this means, practitioners will be able to start their own journey in the world of lean healthcare systems through substantial statistical tools as well as systems thinking.

INTRODUCTION

Lean thinking is a philosophy that one can adopt and interiorize with time. It takes time for organizations to change and transform (Sartal, Llach, & León-Mateos, 2022). The transformation to a lean hospital is an issue of quality improvement. The modern way of defining "quality" is associated with "elimination of waste" and statistically speaking "reduction of variation" (Montgomery, 2004), that can

DOI: 10.4018/978-1-6684-5606-4.ch010

eventually be linked with the value of statistical tools for quality improvement. The challenge is the volatile environment where the organizations are operating. Therefore, quality improvement is not a one-hit wonder, on the contrary, it is an ongoing battle of doing good in any circumstances, which highlights the fact that one of the main principles of quality is "continuous improvement"(Wickramasinghe et al., 2014). Adoption of continuous improvement would lead an organization to keep its operations sustainable in medium to long-run. The practicality of continuous improvement obviously requires knowledge of statistical quality control tools, of which the roots go back to 1920s with Schewart control charts and the evolution of this field has dominantly been in production environment.

The literature highlights the scarcity of resources regarding the application of contemporary statistical tools for quality improvement in healthcare services (Antony, Sunder M, Sreedharan, Chakraborty, & Gunasekaran, 2019). The majority of quality improvement applications in healthcare context covers the use of qualitative tools, whereas statistical counterparts (i.e. 6sigma, SPC) are located towards the end of the list (Akmal, Greatbanks, & Foote, 2020). It is also emphasized that the main challenge in the implementation of statistical quality improvement tools in healthcare services is down to inadequate knowledge (Antony, Palsuk, Gupta, Mishra, & Barach, 2018; Winner, Reinhardt, Benishek, & Marsteller, 2022). Healthcare practitioners are in an obvious need for clear-cut instructions to construct their road maps towards lean systems. This particular fact constitutes the rationale of this book chapter. It presents a guide for the reader to explore how to apply statistical quality control tools in order to enable the transformation to lean healthcare systems and keep it sustainable.

The chapter presents a comprehensive understanding of a lean implementation process starting from a problem detection phase through taking action to solve it, then improve it, afterwards sustain and monitor the improvement with statistical quality tools in a healthcare setting. In other words, it informs readers about the scientific base of lean thinking via statistical tools, so that, they can make informed decisions over facts and data. The chapter is further nourished with example applications and short cases for a better understanding. Different than production environment, lean healthcare does not only focus on efficient operations, but it also aims at effective health outcomes. Thus, lean transformation in a healthcare system is a bipartite problem. The complex structure of healthcare systems makes it even more difficult to manage the situation in such a way that a change in one specialty may have unforeseen spill-over effects on other departments (Joosten, Bongers, & Janssen, 2009). In that respect, lean healthcare implementation urges the practitioners to apply systems approach. There have been studies that reveal the beneficiary of joint application of lean and system approaches (Demirli et al., 2021; Wickramasinghe et al., 2014; Lima, Dinis-Carvalho, Souza, Vieira, & Gonçalves, 2021). Hence, the reader is also introduced to the concept of systems thinking, so that, they could avoid potential sub-optimal implementations and keep track of multiple and mostly contradictive objectives.

In the following parts of the chapter, first background information about lean healthcare applications is presented. Motivation and benefits of lean healthcare, methodologies and tools are mentioned and the contribution of the chapter is emphasized. Afterwards, a handbook on statistical quality tools that could particularly be used in transformation towards lean healthcare services is given. In this section, statistical quality improvement tools are introduced within the context of 4 main components of lean thinking (Mazzocato, Savage, Brommels, Aronsson, & Thor, 2010): Problem Detection, Process Redesign, Assure Process Reliability & Sustainability and Continuous Improvement. Under each component, corresponding statistical tools will be explained and demonstrated with specific examples and cases from healthcare services. Also, role of systems thinking and simulation in healthcare services is mentioned in process redesign. The chapter is finalized with conclusion, where findings, limitations, future directions are mentioned.

LEAN THINKING IN HEALTHCARE

The origin of lean thinking dates back to 1950s with Toyota Production Systems. The goal was to streamline the operations so that throughput rates are increased and any potential waste in production is eliminated. With the launch of Industry 4.0, it has been recognized that lean systems are far beyond productivity and deemed as a contemporary tool for sustainability. The concerns in the new era have been evolved to creating systems that are productive as well as environmental friendly and caring for people. Sustainability has three main branches that are people, planet and profit. For instance, lean approaches have recently been consulted for economic sustainability (Awad, Hashem, & Naguib, 2022), green manufacturing (Afum, Li, Han, & Sun, 2022) and improvement of social reputation (Afum et al., 2022). In the rest of this section, it is focused on lean thinking in detail and its link to healthcare management.

Lean thinking is an approach that aids organizations to create maximum possible value in a system through the most possible efficient set of operations. The building block of lean system is the "value" that is defined by customers. Activities that do not add value from a customer point of view are basically denoted as "waste". Hence, lean thinking can be defined as the art of enhancing value by eliminating waste under limiting conditions.

Five main principles of lean are listed as value, value stream, flow, pull and perfection (Inozu, Chauncey, Kamataris, Mount, & Novaces, 2011). One first needs to define value and then polish the value stream so that wastes are eliminated. This would create a process with an uninterrupted flow. In parallel, lean systems promote pull approach, where the flow of a process is first triggered by customer demand. Lastly, lean systems seek for perfection through continuous improvement. This is a general definition that is applicable to any system. However, focus of this chapter will be on healthcare services. In that respect, definition of lean systems ought to be re-done in the context of healthcare services.

Key performance indicators of a healthcare institution are being safe, effective, patient-centered, timely, efficient and equitable (Wickramasinghe et al., 2014). Thus, lean healthcare systems should improve patient flow, decrease potential wastes, but at the same time, it should keep track of patient safety and patient health outcomes as well as patient equity. A recent study emphasizes the importance of lean management by referring to new surgical pathways that are safer (Bolcato, Rodriguez, & Aprile, 2022). Another study addresses lean layout design for agile use of the resources in an intensive care unit (Romano, Falegnami, Cagliano, & Rafele, 2022) . It has also been mentioned in literature how lean management have been used to divert backlogged demand in post-COVID period in a hospital in England (Smith & Bayliss, 2022). These recent examples highlight the prominence of lean thinking in healthcare context with a common goal of serving people in a better way with scarce resources. Developed countries encounter increasing burden of ageing population along with their enhanced needs for continuous healthcare support. This fact paves the way for innovative approaches to healthcare services so that the quality of service can be increased, yet, economic constraints are still kept under tight budgets. Hence, lean thinking could be the right answer to the challenges that healthcare service providers are currently facing with. In the succeeding sub-chapter, lean healthcare concept is given in detail with its main motivations, benefits and key success measures.

Motivations, Benefits, and Success Measures

Key driver of lean implementation is to achieve efficient systems that create maximum possible outcomes with less amount of effort and resources, concurrently keeping the customers happy with the highest possible value of the end product. When it comes to lean healthcare, the target of high value would be replaced as healthy & happy patients. Accordingly, top two motivations of lean healthcare studies are reported as overcrowding and patient dissatisfaction, followed by low quality of care and efficiency (Tiso, Crema, & Verbano, 2021). As a response, objectives of lean healthcare is set as waiting time and Length of Stay (LoS) reduction; patient flow improvement; enhancement of quality and safety of care and patient satisfaction; followed by other efficiency improvements and time reductions (Tiso et al., 2021).

Table 1 expands on motivation, waste type and performance measure examples that are elaborated from relevant literature.

Table 1. Motivations, wastes and performance measures

Motivation/objective	Serving for higher number of patients with limited resources, better health outcomes, higher quality of care, patient safety and equity
Waste Type	Search for information, patient waiting times, prolonged LoS, over processing, defects, unnecessary movements, unnecessary transportation of patient/material, inventory, unnecessary tasks/activities
Performance Measure	Patient health outcomes, health personnel utilization, health personnel satisfaction, patient satisfaction, patient throughput (journey) time, cost reduction

(Source: Own elaboration from relevant literature.)

With an effort on lean healthcare, organizations enhance patient satisfaction, gain competitive advantage, improve process and operational efficiency, enhance service quality, standardize and streamline processes, reduce delays and operational time, eliminate waste/non-value adding tasks, reduce staff and administrative inefficiencies.

Methodologies and Tools Used

There exist various methodologies and frameworks proposed for the implementation of lean healthcare; e.g. (Al-Balushi et al., 2014; Demirli et al., 2021; Martins Drei & Sérgio de Arruda Ignácio, 2022). Most are context specific, but it can be generalized with the following steps (adopted from Mortimer et al., 2018):

Step 1: Set the goals
Step 2: Study the system
Step 3: Design of the improvement effort
Step 4: Measure impact and value
Step 5: Check for sustainability and continuous improvement options

In the light of these steps of actions, four change mechanisms are recorded (Mazzocato et al., 2010) and they are adopted and visualized as in Figure 1.

In problem detection phase, current processes are scrutinized and potential problem areas and root causes are detected. In the succeeding phase, process redesign, an improved new process flow is proposed for higher effectiveness and efficiency. In the next phase, it is advised to focus on process reliability & sustainability such that proposed system is able to detect and fix errors and keep the process under absolute

Figure 1. Change mechanisms in lean implementation

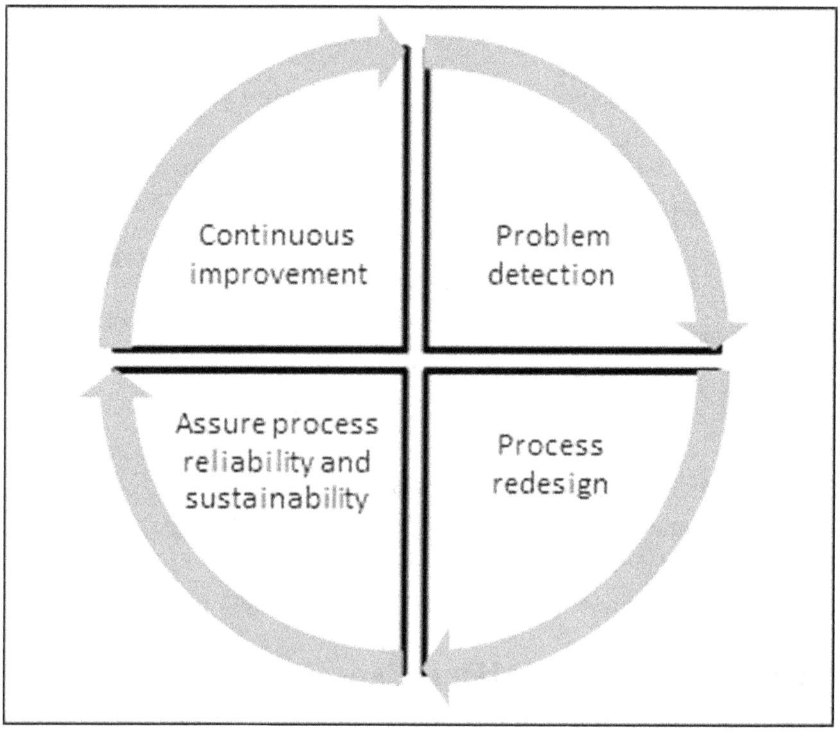

control in the medium to long-run. Last phase, continuous improvement, refers to systematically problem solving and continual improvement.

There are various tools used in each phase of the lean implementation. Recent studies (de Barros et al., 2021; Lima et al., 2021; Santos, Reis, Souza, Santos, & Ferreira, 2020) report on tools, their use cases and use frequencies. Lima et al., 2021 lists lean tools under five categories: Diagnosing tools and problem solving, workspace organization and visual management, continuous improvement, production flow and complementary management approaches; where majority of the tools are listed under the first two categories. Most commonly used tools are declared as DMAIC (Define-Measure-Analyze-Improve-Control), VSM (Value Stream Mapping), SIPOC (Suppliers-Inputs-Process-Outputs-Customers), Ishikawa Diagram, 5S (Sort-Set in order-Shine-Standardize-Sustain), spaghetti diagram, Pareto analysis (de Barros et al., 2021). As it is obvious from the list of commonly used lean tools, there is a domination of qualitative tools in the field, whereas analytical and quantitative tools are underrepresented (Santos et al., 2020). Simulation, control charts and data mining only constitutes 5.3%, 2.4% and 0.5% of the studies in lean healthcare literature respectively (Santos et al., 2020). Among all, VSM has been the number one lean implementation tool in healthcare.

Interested reader is referred to a report by Marin-Garcia et al., (2021) on the role of value stream mapping in healthcare services and also to a detailed guide on how to apply VSM in healthcare setting (Henrique et al., 2015). VSM finds a great variety of application areas within healthcare setting along with some other lean tools. These application areas are mentioned below in detail.

Application Areas

There have been different studies that focus on transformation to lean hospitals, however, majority of them are limited to a restricted area in a hospital. Table 2 is a summary of application areas encountered in the relevant literature. Note that this table is designed to give reader a general idea about application areas, but it may not provide a complete list of them.

Table 2. Application areas of lean healthcare

Application Areas	Example Studies
Entire hospital operations	(Zdęba-Mozoła, Rybarczyk-Szwajkowska, Czapla, Marczak, & Kozłowski, 2022)
Medical clinic entry system	(Martins Drei & Sérgio de Arruda Ignácio, 2022)
Patient care in an oncology day hospital	(Garcia-Sabater, Marin-Garcia, Vidal-Carreras, Garcia-Sabater, & Marin-Garcia, 2022)
A primary care center	(Morell-Santandreu, Santandreu-Mascarell, & Garcia-Sabater, 2021)
Emergency department	(Tiso et al., 2021)
Medicine clinic	(Fisher, Ding, Hochheiser, & Douglas, 2016; Rocha & Vasconcelos, 2021)
Discharge process	(Peimbert-García, Gutiérrez-Mendoza, & García-Reyes, 2021)
Operating room cleaning process	(Claudio, Cosgriff, Nino, & Valladares, 2021; Nino, Claudio, Valladares, & Harris, 2020)
Inpatient care	(Zepeda-Lugo et al., 2020)
Outpatient care	(Tlapa et al., 2020)

(Source: Own elaboration from relevant literature.)

A wide variety of healthcare sub-systems are studied in the lean literature, nevertheless, applications in the areas of home care, community care and primary care are less mentioned (D'Andreamatteo, Ianni, Lega, & Sargiacomo, 2015).

Another striking point that can be interpreted from application areas is the fact that current approaches are limited to restricted impact areas and they do not cover a comprehensive healthcare system at local, regional or national level.

Research Gaps

Throughout the chapter, some gaps in the literature are mentioned. Hereby, they are elaborated further in a comprehensive way. There is an obvious fact that quantitative/analytical tools are underrepresented in lean healthcare literature (Santos et al., 2020) and SPC is listed among the least preferred lean tools despite its promising nature for the field (Akmal et al., 2020). On the other hand, it is highlighted that the main reasons that hinder organizations from conducting successful lean projects are lack of knowledge about lean implementation (Régis, Santos, & Gohr, 2019), lack of empirical evidence and assessment methodology (Antony et al., 2019). Antony et al. (2018) also addresses that the key challenges against lean implementation are inadequate knowledge of six sigma, limited understanding of statistics and lack of awareness of six sigma benefits.

Another major stream of research gap is focused on the fragmented nature of current studies (Borges, Tortorella, Rossini, & Portioli-Staudacher, 2019). Most studies are done on departmental basis and unless a systems approach is implemented, it comes out to be transferring waste from one place to another but not eliminating it (Akmal et al., 2020).

In the light of the findings presented by relevant literature, this book chapter aims to fill in two key research gaps:

Gap 1: Implementation of statistical quality tools in lean healthcare.
Gap 2: The role of systems approach for lean healthcare.

A GUIDE TO USE STATISTICAL QUALITY TOOLS FOR LEAN HEALTHCARE

Quality is inversely proportional to variability. (Montgomery, 2004)

Quality improvement is the reduction of variability in processes and products. (Montgomery, 2004)

Life is a random walk. Anything and everything contains a natural variability and it creates an unavoidable randomness. Random inputs come along with random outputs and if the level of randomness is not taken under control, results may appear to be in undesired and/or unpredictable ranges. If that is the case, one can talk about poor quality. The underlying reason is that higher quality standards are explained with standardized outputs that fit to specifications within predetermined ranges with an acceptable level of confidence. That being said, two statements of Montgomery that is quoted above and links quality and variability are very well accepted.

Besides natural and unavoidable variability, there could be some other facts that could increase the variability in processes or systems. The latter ones are the factors that can be eliminated for higher levels of quality and those are the ones that are, in other words, defined as "waste". The elimination of waste in processes would pave the way for systems with lower variability and higher level of quality in return. Hence, the ultimate aim of lean systems being the elimination of waste is said to be equivalent with statistical quality improvement through reduction of variability.

In this chapter, principles of statistical quality control tools presented by Montgomery (2004) are adopted. The use of these statistical quality control tools in lean healthcare context are discussed and displayed with examples where it is possible. The presentation of the tools is done under four categories that are the four main change mechanisms of lean implementation.

Problem Detection

The change mechanism of lean healthcare transformation starts with problem detection. First action is to find potential problem areas through the use of some specific statistical tools so that next phases of transformation would be guided accordingly.

Stem-and-leaf Diagram and Histogram

The process of lean implementation starts with data collection and/or analyzing available data. The first ever step should be getting familiar with the data on hand. The best way to know your data is to get an idea about its distribution regardless of the fact that it is discrete or continuous. Two basic visualization tools used to describe data are stem-and-leaf diagram and histogram. Both graphing tools give information about the central tendency and dispersion of data. The main difference of stem-and-leaf diagram is that it gives the user the opportunity to keep track of individual data points, whereas histogram puts data points into mutually exclusive and collectively exhaustive discrete class intervals, so that, the user loses the track of individual data points while being able to follow the frequencies of class intervals. Stem-and-leaf diagrams are found to be suitable for data sources that are relatively small in size and histograms are found to be suitable for large size data.

By using these two data visualization tools, one can get an initial insight whether the distribution of data points out a problem.

Table 3 represents patient time spent in an emergency department in minutes.

Table 3. Time in Emergency Department Data (in minutes)

No	Time in ED	No	Time in ED	No	Time in ED	No	Time in ED
1	180	26	237	51	232	76	161
2	164	27	239	52	185	77	190
3	125	28	240	53	239	78	69
4	119	29	186	54	168	79	126
5	217	30	246	55	163	80	72
6	205	31	75	56	223	81	162
7	176	32	198	57	264	82	385
8	116	33	80	58	234	83	238
9	190	34	206	59	235	84	84
10	190	35	72	60	230	85	208
11	147	36	175	61	240	86	67
12	195	37	238	62	224	87	30
13	211	38	95	63	129	88	115
14	237	39	172	64	216	89	96
15	194	40	475	65	226	90	94
16	75	41	238	66	30	91	76
17	191	42	165	67	103	92	225
18	239	43	167	68	98	93	203
19	240	44	239	69	176	94	212
20	239	45	209	70	95	95	204
21	195	46	158	71	199	96	116
22	227	47	227	72	170	97	101
23	84	48	238	73	139	98	55
24	183	49	186	74	200	99	237
25	237	50	164	75	58	100	116

Figure 2 and Figure 3 tell that time spent in an emergency department do not have a symmetrical distribution but it is right skewed. There are some outliers observed at 260, 380 and 470 minutes. The most frequent patient time spent in emergency department fits in two class intervals which are 150-160 and 200-240 minutes. Data concentration in two particular class intervals may refer to a threshold value imposed by national and/or local authorities such that patients should not spend more than 4 hours in emergency departments. They should either be discharged or admitted to a hospital bed if they need. Such an enforcement may push healthcare practitioners to discharge patients earlier than they need, which eventually may cause poor health outcomes. Another point that this graph highlights is the huge dispersion in patient waiting times. This fact addresses the existence of an unstandardized service for patients. This emergency data example highlights that even these two basic graphing tools that are used for descriptive statistics can draw an attention to a potential problem area that ought to be scrutinized further.

Figure 2. Stem-and-leaf diagram example

Stem-and-Leaf Display: Time in ED

```
Stem-and-leaf of Time in ED  N  = 100
Leaf Unit = 10

  2    0  33
 19    0  55667777788899999
 31    1  001111122234
(28)   1  5666666667777788888999999999
 41    2  00000001111222222333333333333333334444
  3    2  6
  2    3
  2    3  8
  1    4
  1    4  7
```

Check Sheet

Check sheets are mainly used for investigating the root causes of a problem area. In particular, check sheet lists the causes that resulted in an unwanted/non-confirming situation in the outcome and covers the number of occurrences of a specific reason on a time-line. Table 4 is a representative example to display the causes that has led to dissatisfied patients in a hospital. Data has been recorded on a weekly basis for a two-month period.

Figure 3. Histogram example

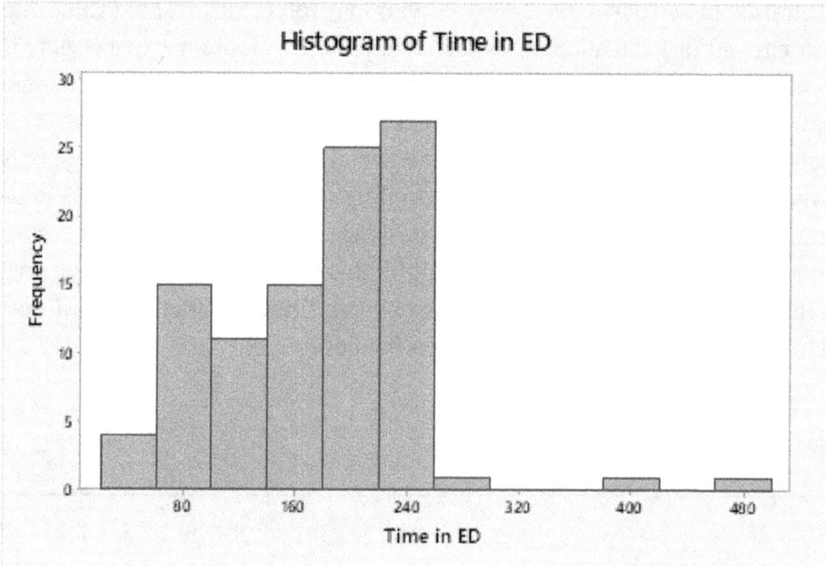

Table 4. Check sheet example

	January 2022				February 2022				
Reason for Dissatisfaction	**W1**	**W2**	**W3**	**W4**	**W1**	**W2**	**W3**	**W4**	**TOTAL**
Administration									
Unfriendly staff	2	1	3	2	0	1	2	2	13
Long triage time	8	10	15	13	12	8	9	11	86
Complicated forms	2	1	1	4	2	3	1	0	14
Care and treatment									
Medication error	1	0	2	1	0	2	1	1	8
Wrong diagnosis	2	0	0	0	1	2	1	0	6
Long waiting time	5	7	6	8	9	4	7	10	56
Unfriendly medical staff	2	4	3	0	1	1	2	1	14
Communication with nurses	1	2	1	0	0	0	1	1	6
Inadequate number of nurses	2	5	6	2	3	3	4	5	30
Physical conditions									
Inadequate space in waiting area	7	10	12	4	4	5	7	3	52
Inadequate medical infrastruture	0	0	1	2	1	0	0	2	6
Uncomfortable in wards	0	2	1	0	0	1	1	0	5
Location of hospital	2	3	2	1	7	3	2	0	20
TOTAL	34	45	53	37	40	33	38	36	316

Pareto Analysis

Elimination of any reason that resulted in a dissatisfaction is crucial, yet, resources are always limited and it is required to prioritize the tasks and concentrate on the ones that would create relatively higher impacts under limiting conditions. Pareto principle states that majority of the problems stem from minority of the reasons. In that respect, it is important to find the correct minority of indicators that create the majority of the unwanted outcomes. A rule of thumb magnitude to describe minority and majority is accepted as 20-80 rule, that is, 20% of the reasons constitutes 80% of the outcomes.

As an example, a Pareto analysis is conducted in Figure 4 by using the data given in Table 4 about reasons of patient dissatisfaction.

Figure 4. Pareto analysis example

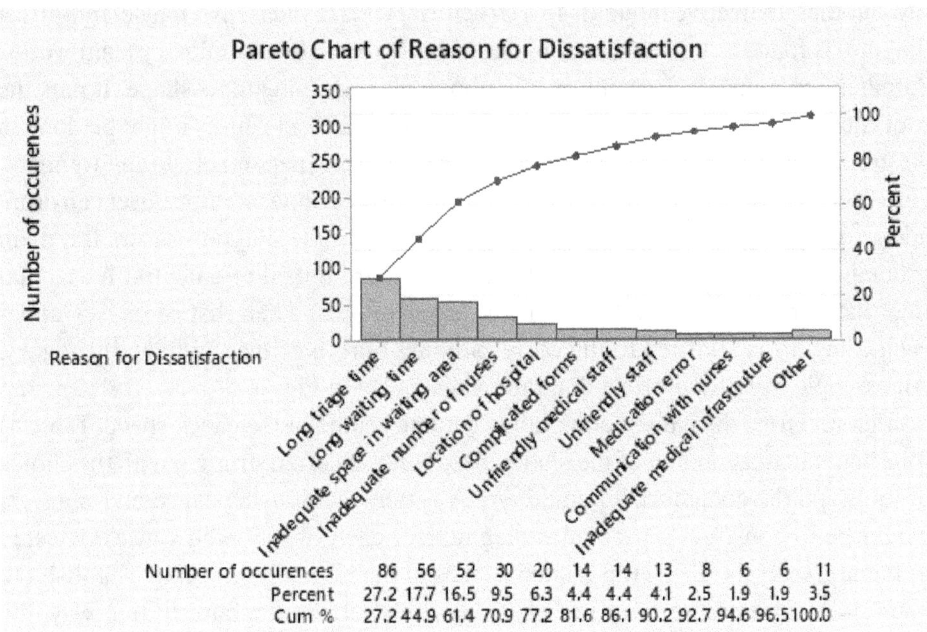

In Pareto analysis, causes are listed with a descending order of occurrences and a frequency diagram is constructed with an additional axis on the right hand-side that shows the cumulative frequencies. Pareto chart indicates that top three reasons of patient dissatisfaction are long triage time, long waiting time and inadequate space in waiting area. Along with these three reasons, quality managers are also advised to address patient complaints about inadequate number of nurses and location of hospital. These five complaints constitute 77.2% of the entire patient dissatisfaction. This is a limited analysis that is done with frequency data only. A further analysis might be done accounting for dissatisfaction levels. In such a case, additional data is needed on the level of patient dissatisfaction due to each particular reason. It would be possible that a patient gets effected by medical errors deeply but would not care about hospital location in the same manner, or vice versa. By doing so, Pareto analysis would yield different results such that a less frequently occurring complaint may become among the top rated reasons for patient dissatisfaction due to its higher impact level.

Cause-And-Effect Diagram

Cause-and-effect diagram is a brainstorming tool that uncovers the root causes of a problem area. It eases the communication among problem owners and aids them to present their collective thoughts in a structured way. In that sense, cause-and-effect diagram is found to be very beneficial especially for multi-disciplinary team works. Another common way to call it is "fish-bone diagram" due to its shape. It puts the root causes in categories. A generic categorization of root causes might be done in six groups: machines, materials, methods, measurement, personnel and environment. However, depending on the nature of the problem area under scrutiny, user can drop/add existing/new categories as needed. The head of the diagram shows the main problem area, where main categories of causes are linked to a central horizontal line that comes out of the box of main problem area. Then, list of causes under each category is attached to the corresponding branch of that particular category. An example cause-and-effect diagram is displayed in Figure 5.

Figure 5 uses the patient complaints data presented in the check sheet (Table 4) for a better understanding of the reader, because users often struggle with the choice of tools and the coherence among them. A better way of using cause-and-diagram would be to construct a particular diagram for each of the main causes detected in Pareto Analysis. Thus, top ranked causes in Pareto analysis would establish the main problem area (i.e. head) of each cause-and-effect diagram. In that way, the main problem area of patient dissatisfaction would be peeled into its layers with consecutive cause-and-effect diagrams. For instance, long triage and long waiting times were among the most frequent complaints. Let's define the main problem area as "long patient waiting time" and uncover its root causes with a new cause-and-effect diagram (Figure 6). With the new root causes listed in Figure 6, quality managers could opt for additional data collection process from internal sources such that they can understand which item is the main cause that lengthens patient waiting times. This step-wise and iterative approach would bring the quality people to the point where they could take corrective actions in the right direction in an effective way. Without those analysis, actions taken to improve quality would be some random acts with random and/or unintended outcomes.

Figure 5. Cause-and-effect diagram example-I

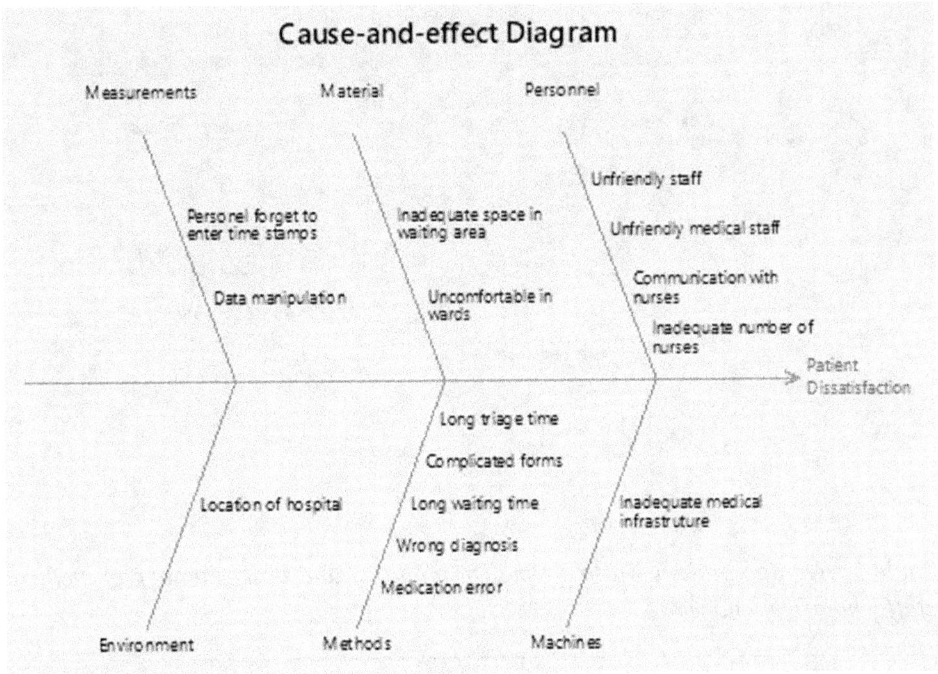

Scatter Diagram

Scatter diagrams are used to quantify and/or validate a relationship between two variables. Even if scatter diagram shows a positive/negative relationship between the two, user is advised to first check the conceptual causality between the variables in order to avoid deceive results. Following the previous healthcare examples, let's assume that an expert is questioning whether patient waiting time is effected by the number of staff who are in charge at that particular day. She claims that if too many nurses or doctors take a leave in the same or overlapping periods, time to serve patients with limited number of staff will be longer. Figure 7 illustrates scatter diagram of number of medical staff in charge versus average patient waiting time of which data is presented in Table 5.

Figure 6. Cause-and-effect diagram-II

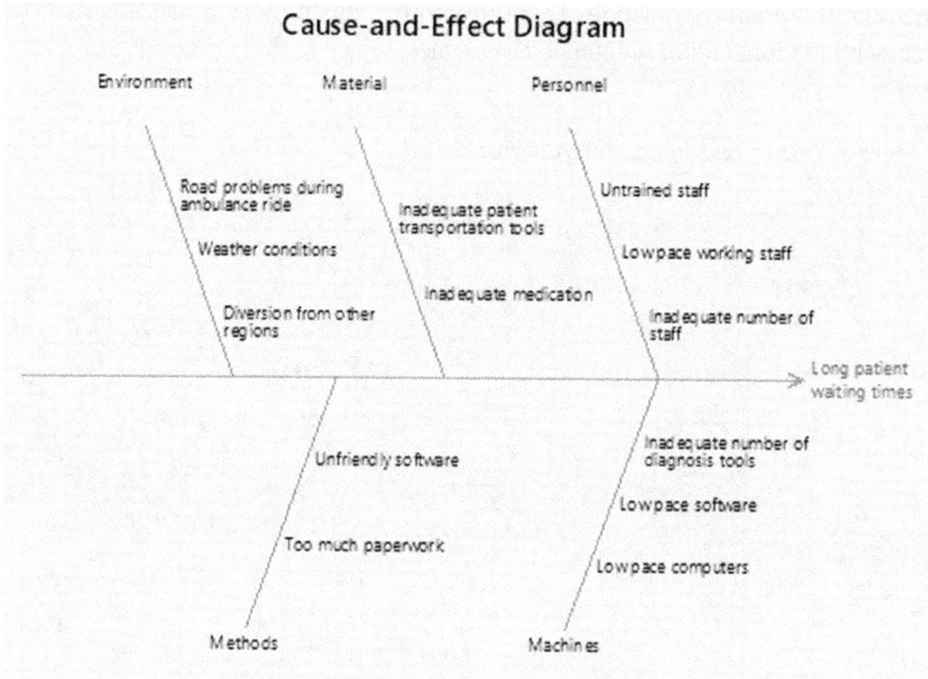

Table 5. Average patient waiting time (in minutes) and daily number of medical staff who are in charge

Days	Number of Medical Staff	Average Patient Waiting Time	Days	Number of Medical Staff	Average Patient Waiting Time	Days	Number of Medical Staff	Average Patient Waiting Time
1	45	50	11	42	72	21	55	81
2	40	75	12	45	82	22	43	56
3	42	75	13	50	34	23	45	67
4	43	72	14	40	43	24	45	66
5	50	30	15	41	45	25	38	63
6	38	90	16	41	68	26	37	85
7	37	80	17	42	67	27	38	67
8	36	75	18	42	66	28	45	56
9	40	67	19	43	62	29	43	60
10	43	69	20	50	20	30	44	58

Figure 7. Scatter diagram example

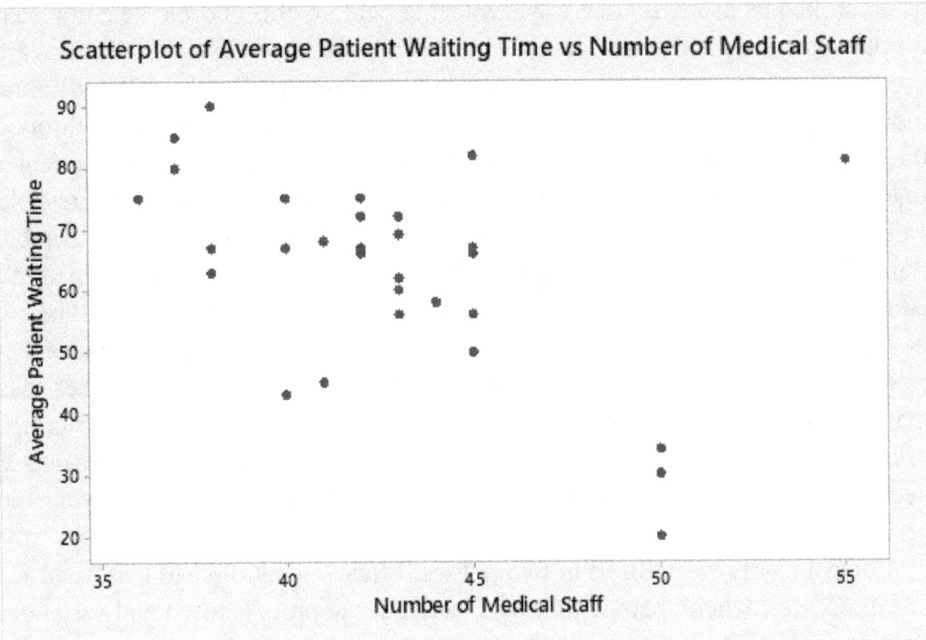

Figure 7 depicts that average patient waiting time tends to increase with decreasing number of medical staff. However, the user should always keep in mind that findings of scatter diagrams could be deceptive and one should be careful about two points: 1- check conceptual causality; 2- search for potential third variables that could also be effecting the outcome measures. For instance, in this example, before making a judgement one needs to be sure that the waiting time increase is only up to inadequate number of staff but not peak demand levels or any other potential cause occurring at that time.

Statistical Process Control Charts

Statistical Process Control (SPC) Charts are a major topic in statistical quality control and it is impossible to cover all the fundamentals of SPC in a single book chapter. With this book chapter, it is aimed to guide the readers who are familiar with the major principles of SPC about how to make use of this particular tool for lean implementations in healthcare context. Bare readers who are interested in learning SPC in depth are referred to Montgomery (2004).

As it is mentioned earlier in this chapter, any measurement has an inherited natural variability in itself and this yields an inevitable randomness. For the sake of quality improvement and/or control, focus is mainly on the random factors that can be controlled by users. By that way, avoidable random effects could be eliminated for the sake of more efficient, accurate and standardized processes. SPC charts are used to differentiate the source of randomness in a process. They are used as online monitoring tools, where intended measurements are periodically recorded through the time line on a graph constructed with upper and lower bound lines with a center line in between. Upper, lower bounds and center line tells the user about threshold values to get alarmed if s/he recognizes a data point that is outside the tolerable limits. If every data point fits within the limits, then the variation is called natural/ **common cause** variability, there is no need to get an alarm. If a data point falls below or above the tolerable limits, then the user should search for **assignable cause** that creates a possible to eliminate unintended variation in the process. Another case that triggers the user to search for assignable causes are potential trends, run-ups or run-downs, which are consecutive data points that are consistently increasing or decreasing. Such cases are also deemed as potential causes to increase avoidable variation.

Control charts are utilized in two phases. **Phase-I** control charts are used for new processes, where there is limited data about the process mean and variation, that is, no data exists for process lower and upper bounds. In such cases, sector standards, targets or specifications forced by customers can be used as control limits until adequate data is collected about the process itself. After one gets sure that the process is running with a compliance to its regular and desirable standards, control limits can be calculated with the process' own data and it is the time where the user can start to use the control chart as an online monitoring tool for quality control in **Phase-II**.

There are different SPC charts depending on the data type used. These are basically, SPC charts for variables and attributes. Commonly used SPC charts for variables are $\bar{X}$ and R charts. The former is a measure to track central tendency whereas the latter is to track the process variability. This two charts are advised to be interpreted together, because there could be cases where central tendency shifts without any change in variation or vice versa. In such cases, only one of the charts give an alert to the user to search for an assignable cause, i.e. shift in mean effects $\bar{X}$ chart and change in variation affects R chart only. There are variations of variable control charts depending on data availability such as $\bar{X}$ and s charts, where sample standard deviation (s) can be used to measure process data dispersion. In healthcare context, SPC charts for variables can be used to track any performance criteria that is measured on a continuous scale (e.g. waiting time to see a doctor, time to treatment, treatment time, time to admission, time to get operated, etc.) Below is an example for $\bar{X}$ and R charts for patient waiting time to see a doctor in an emergency department (Figure 8).

Each sample in Figure 8 represents average waiting time per week, i.e. average waiting time data is recorded daily and subgroups of 7 is used to calculate weekly averages. Upper bounds for $\bar{X}$ and R is set to 60 minutes with an assumption such that there is a national target of maximum 60 minutes on patient waiting times in emergency departments. $\bar{X}$ chart reveals that the hospital can comply with the target of 60 minutes, nevertheless there are some trends (i.e. between weeks 22-31, there are 5 consecutive points increasing and 5 consecutive points decreasing) that needs to be investigated as well as few points (week 22 and 32) that are so close to the upper bound. When it comes to examine R chart, few points that are very close to upper bound are observed. Note that upper bound for R chart is also assumed to be 60 minutes, where the maximum tolerable limit could be the difference between minimum level (zero waiting time) and the maximum threshold (waiting time of 60 minutes).

Figure 8. $\mathbf{\bar{X}}$ *and* **R** *chart example*

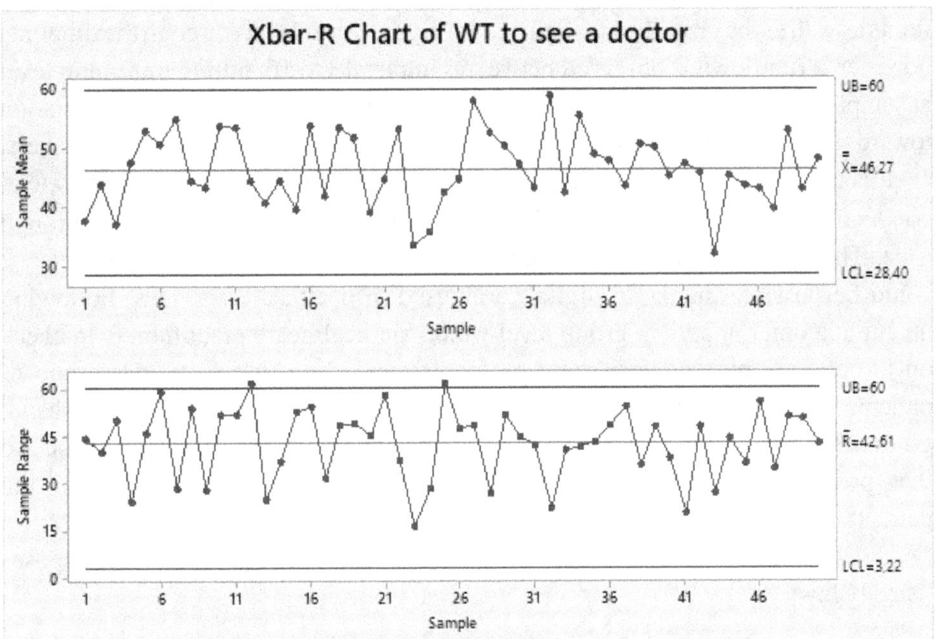

SPC charts for attributes are p and c charts. The former one is the SPC chart used for non-conforming proportions. For instance, if there is a threshold value set by national/local authorities on patient waiting time in an emergency department, p chart is used to keep control of proportion of patients who are recorded beyond the threshold. On the other hand, ***c*** charts are used to keep track of number of non-conformities in a particular time period, e.g. number of patients who are exceeding the threshold value of patient waiting time in a day.

There are few examples that utilizes SPC to have a control on health outcomes at patient and/or patient group levels (Flood et al., 2017; Lawson, Weekes, & Hill, 2018). In particular, control charts for attributes can be used to keep control of health outcomes of patients on a regular basis. For instance, assume that a healthcare institution launches a project to improve the health conditions of patients diagnosed with high blood pressure. In that case, p chart would be appropriate to control the proportion of patients under treatment whose blood pressure levels are observed to be within pre-specified medical limits. It can be discussed to use c charts as well; however, it would be misleading to work on the number of patients whose blood pressure levels exceed the limits, because numbers are under the influence of the size of the sample population which is a function of demand levels and dynamic in nature. Figure 9 depicts an example p chart for proportion of patients that exceed the threshold blood pressure levels recorded on a periodical basis. It shows a slight improvement in the care of patients diagnosed with high blood pressure, because the limits as well as the proportions slightly converge at lower levels through the timeline, however, a run-down is observed between samples 13 to 16, hitting minimum level at sample 16. This could be scrutinized whether there could be a data manipulation towards better health outcomes, which would eventually mislead the decision makers.

It is also possible to follow health outcomes at an individual patient level, e.g. conducting $\bar{X}$ and R charts analysis on individual's blood pressure levels through time. This seems to be a burdensome, number crunching procedure, however, it could be possible thanks to digital tools used in healthcare services. Following health outcomes at patient group level would aid healthcare practitioners to check on the effectiveness of healthcare protocols applied on that particular group of patient. Tracking health outcomes at individual patient level, on the other hand, gives the opportunity to follow patient's health condition on a continuous basis, so that, preventive actions could be taken timely depending on the situation of the patient.

To summarize, statistical control charts are advocated to be used for the purposes listed below:

- To keep track of key performance indicators of hospital operations.
- To keep track of health outcomes of particular patient groups.
- To follow health conditions of individual patients.

Figure 9. P Chart example

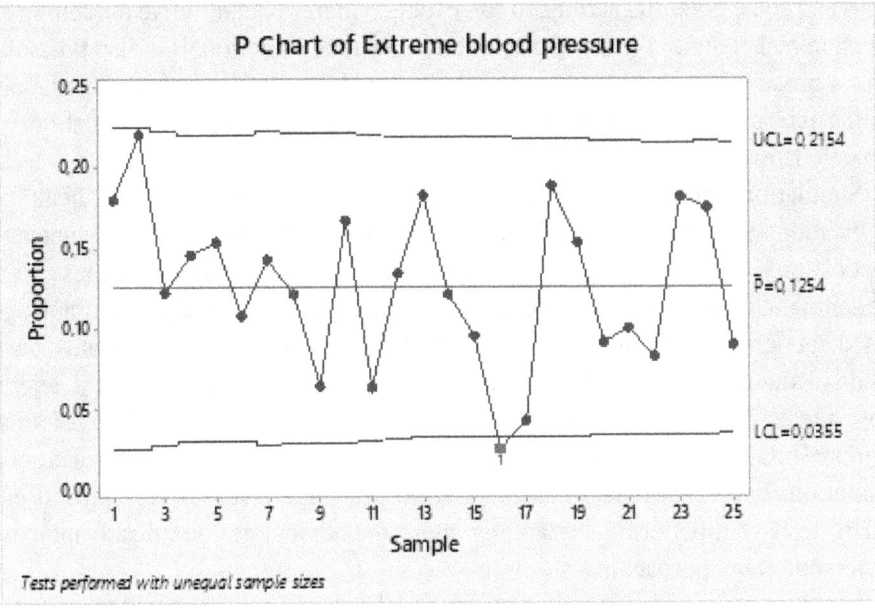

Process Redesign

In the preceding section, statistical quality tools that can be used in the phase of problem detection have been discussed. After main problem areas are defined, it is time to work on process redesign to eliminate problematic areas or at least make an improvement in the current situation. In this phase, tools to be used and the actions to be taken are linked to the nature of the problem defined in the previous phase. However, lean healthcare implementations are dominated by the use of value stream mapping and process flow diagrams to detect the actions that could be taken to re-design the process. As it has been discussed in the background section, these qualitative tools are criticized, because it provides a limited view point and they are restricted in the sense that they cannot provide decision makers with the required facts. As a remedy, simulation modelling could be used in order to run what-if analysis. By doing so, decision makers would be able to see the big picture, and test different scenario analysis and gather adequate data to comment on possible outcomes of planned actions. The offer of simulation modelling in that phase does not trivialize qualitative tools. Indeed, their use should be promoted to explore the current situation and ease the communication between modelers and healthcare practitioners. Hence, both approaches, qualitative and quantitative, are advised to be used in harmony.

Qualitative tools that cover the process flow information points out the problem areas and some potential actions to solve them; whereas quantitative modelling aids decision makers with facts and data before they take an action. It is also possible to have a broader view with system simulation modeling such that one can elaborate on the interplay of different sub-systems that are only studied in isolation with separate flow diagrams.

Simulation and systems modeling has found a fertile ground in healthcare applications and they are mainly used to evaluate the performance of innovative applications in the field (Dural Selcuk & Vasilakis, 2021). There are various systems modelling techniques such as discrete event simulation, system dynamics and agent based modeling. The choice of simulation modeling technique depends on the needs of the researcher and none of them is found to be superior to one another. Nevertheless, discrete event simulation and systems dynamics modelling is found to be more suitable for a macro-level approach to cover entire operations of a healthcare institution. Interested reader can be referred to Dangerfield (2016) and Pitt et al. (2016) to have a better understanding about the advantages and disadvantages of each modelling approach.

Example cases in healthcare context could be linked to the problem of patient waiting times. In order to lower down the waiting time; different actions could be taken such as increasing number of staff, changing the process flow, digitizing some of the manual processes, proposing a new layout to ease the movement or cut down transportation efforts, offering a new/alternative patient pathway. In this particular example, qualitative tools could be used to understand the flow of operations and point out the bottlenecks, then simulation models could be used to evaluate the alternative courses of actions looking at the tradeoff between their costs and potential beneficiary outcomes. Simulation approaches also help the user to comment on the robustness of the decisions taken, because it is also possible to incorporate uncertainty.

Besides simulation modelling, for very structured cases where it is possible to make simplifying assumptions, one can also opt for mathematical modelling tools to improve the current systems. Such models can be exemplified with scheduling problems, where utilization is maximized, patent waiting times are minimized. Another example could be models to decide optimal layout plans that minimizes the movements. This is a huge area to discover and interested reader is referred to the field of operations research modelling applied in healthcare services (Capan, Wu, Campbell, Mascioli, & Jackson, 2015).

Assure Process Reliability and Sustainability

After problem detection and process redesign, assuring process reliability & sustainability comes in the change mechanism of lean implementation. It is important to ensure that the changes offered for a better system is correctly implemented, kept sustainable and reliable through the time (Lawson et al., 2018; Mortimer et al., 2018). Any change offered in an organization is prone to internal and/or external resistance. Being that the case, extra effort is needed for its adoption and correct implementation. Besides qualitative tools like establishment of leadership mechanisms, Gemba walks and etc., it is highly recommended to again use data and facts to evaluate the status of the system in terms of reliability and sustainability.

After a process redesign is taken into action, it is found to be beneficial to put some short-term key performance indicators, that could be measured easily and motivate stakeholders to adopt the change with an eager to operate in a more efficient and/or effective way. For instance, assume that a new patient pathway is offered to better serve the community through an alternative virtual triage system such that initial evaluation of the patient is done virtually in an outer clinic. Then, they are referred to specialty clinic for further scrutiny if they need it. In that way, increasing demand is aimed to be managed in an efficient way, trying to create extra room in specialty clinics for those patients who are really in need of specialty care. This system eliminates the time that a specialist spends for non-value added task like administration and triage; and enable them to use their entire time with value added-tasks that are related to patient care only. In that case, showcasing practitioners how much time they have gained by not dealing with administration and triage and transferred to patient care would increase the appetize of them for the new application.

In parallel, statistical quality tools mentioned in problem detection phase would also be beneficial in assuring process reliability. A basic example is presented hereby with SPC charts. Remember the case with p chart in Figure 9. After you launch a new treatment program for the care of patients that are diagnosed with high blood pressure, you would expect that the proportion of patients who are recorded with blood pressures higher than the threshold value to decline. Thus, what is desired to be observed should look like the case presented in Figure 10, where the data points recorded after the program launch are marked with a circle. If the new treatment program's reliability is guaranteed as it is in this example, then SPC chart could be further used to ensure the program's sustainability in the future. That is, if the levels are kept under control all through the time, then there would be no case that gives an alarm unless an assignable cause occurs. If it happens so, the proposed system is expected to detect it in a short time and fix the situation.

Figure 10. p chart after intervention

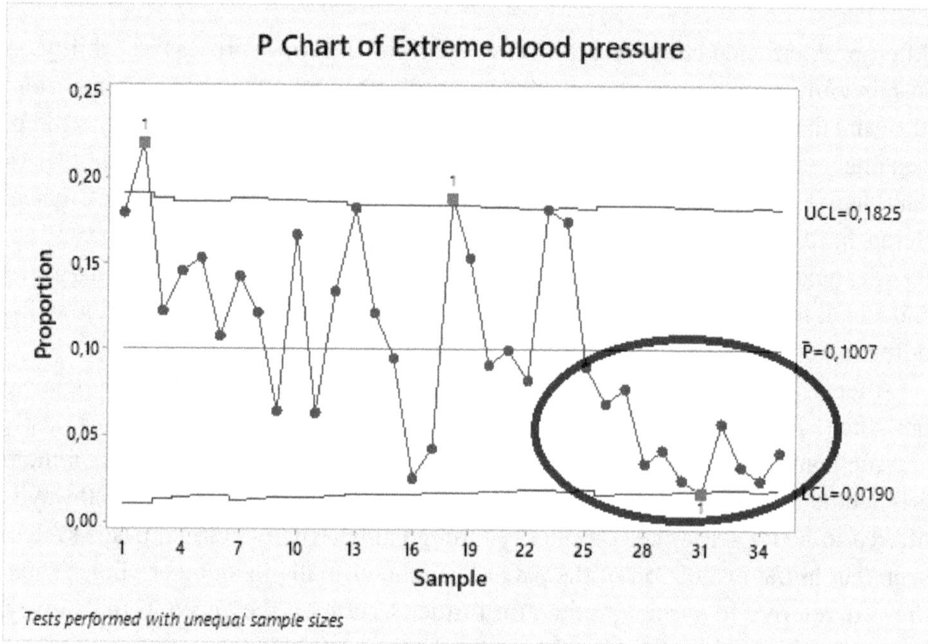

The use of SPC as a tool for quality assurance is summarized here one more time. They are used to:

- Detect assignable causes.
- Detect improvements after intervention programs.
- Control sustainability of improved systems in the medium to long run.

In addition to statistical tools, qualitative tools of VSM and process flow diagrams are found to be a good fit in this phase as well. As opposed to SPC chart, they are not advised to be used as a monitoring tool, but they can be used for less frequent periodical checks such as questioning whether the intervention has really worked (i.e. before/after analysis to test efficiency) and whether it still works after 6, 12, 24 months.

Continuous Improvement

Quality improvement is a never-ending story. Its main principle is assuming that there is always some room for further improvement. Even if data and facts seem to comply with the performance criteria, quality control engineers should look for better process and system designs and revise their criteria for higher standards. For an organization, lean healthcare is a life-long journey. Four change mechanisms of lean implementation are presented as a circle in Figure 1, meaning that an ending of each quality improvement project triggers a new beginning of a successive one. Also note that there may not exist clear-cut distinctions among the change mechanisms. The transition among them is mostly flu and iterative.

The cyclic approach of lean implementation urges an institution to reach a higher development level as the time goes on. For instance, think of a healthcare service provider and the story starts with the trivial concern of high demand levels against the backdrop of limited budgets. This particular need initiates a search for more efficient hospital operations management so that it does have a higher patient throughput without sacrificing patient health outcomes and patient satisfaction. From sustainability point of view, such a project cares for profit and people, i.e. two main categories in the Triple Bottom Line of sustainability. As the project goes further, managers are expected to care for environment (i.e. Planet, third leg of Triple Bottom Line) as well. The cornerstone of lean healthcare is creating value for patients (Mortimer et al., 2018). It can be defined as receiving timely and quality health service from a patient point of view; but at the same time, it is caring for upcoming generations such that they could have the same opportunities in the future as they do today. Hence, sustainability is interpreted in two perspectives. First, it is defined as the continuation of the proposed systems in longer terms. Secondly, it is taking care of all potential stakeholders that are getting affected from your actions.

All in all, sustainability (people, profit, planet) gains a great importance more than ever before and lean healthcare services have much to undertake in that sense. The principle of continuous improvement, that is going through change mechanisms of lean implementation in a cyclic manner with a sought for better, seems to play a key role for a sustainable future.

CONCLUSION

In this book chapter, reader is introduced to lean thinking in healthcare context. Key lean concepts are explained and associated with healthcare examples. The motivating factor for this chapter has been the underrepresentation of statistical quality tools in lean healthcare implementations and inadequate knowledge about them. In that respect, four main change mechanisms are determined for lean healthcare implementation as problem detection, process redesign, process reliability & sustainability and continuous improvement. Each change mechanism can be deemed as a phase in a quality improvement project. As opposed to the dominating trend towards qualitative tools in the field, this chapter has presented a handbook about the use of statistical quality tools in each phase. Additionally, the role of systems modeling and simulation in the field is also discussed.

As all the studies should have, this book chapter has also some limitations. Statistical quality tools are not limited to the ones mentioned in this chapter, however, the ones that are most commonly used and easy to apply are given priority. Establishing coherence among the tools is found to be challenging from a practitioner perspective. In that respect, it is aimed to provide a coherent understanding of statistical quality tools by using repetitive examples and cases. It is not claimed that this chapter is a perfect and complete guide for lean healthcare, but it creates a high awareness about a very important aspect of it. Herewith, it is intended to equip healthcare practitioners with a clear guideline during their transformation journey for lean systems. In the light of the examples presented, they could link the theory with their own example cases, get the right keywords and elaborate on them with a common understanding.

By aiding healthcare practitioners have a step in healthcare lean concept, it is envisaged to increase the awareness of healthcare practitioners about the actions they can do better. It does not matter whether it is a breakthrough innovation or a basic every-day issue, a single change can create an effect of a pebble threw into the water. The key phenomenon here is to address that healthcare practitioners have the potential to trigger big changes. Lean management requires long-term commitment and workforce training. Any attempt in this direction is found to be valuable. In this book chapter, it is aimed to improve analytical skill sets of healthcare service providers, so that, they will be able to question their routine operations and help reorganize and improve the daily flow. This would indeed be the beginning of a lean transformation story with empowerment and self-initiative.

In future studies, it could be beneficial to work on more comprehensive case studies, where complete real-life examples are explored. Furthermore, people are prone to illustrate success stories, nevertheless human beings learn more from failures and challenges. Accordingly, it would be advised to study lean healthcare implementations that have failed or not been sustainable in longer terms. Although telling people not to do is found to be counterintuitive, it would help them avoid potential repeating failures. By doing so, a common know-how in the field of lean healthcare could be disseminated.

REFERENCES

Afum, E., Li, Y., Han, P., & Sun, Z. (2022). Interplay between lean management and circular production system: Implications for zero-waste performance, green value competitiveness, and social reputation. *Journal of Manufacturing Technology Management, 33*(7), 1213–1231. doi:10.1108/JMTM-01-2022-0038

Akmal, A., Greatbanks, R., & Foote, J. (2020, June 1). Lean thinking in healthcare – Findings from a systematic literature network and bibliometric analysis. *Health Policy (Amsterdam), 124*(6), 615–627. doi:10.1016/j.healthpol.2020.04.008 PMID:32456781

Al-Balushi, S., Sohal, A. S., Singh, P. J., Al Hajri, A., Farsi, Y. M. A., & Al Abri, R. (2014). Readiness factors for lean implementation in healthcare settings - a literature review. *Journal of Health Organization and Management, 28*(2), 135–153. doi:10.1108/JHOM-04-2013-0083 PMID:25065107

Antony, J., Palsuk, P., Gupta, S., Mishra, D., & Barach, P. (2018). Six Sigma in healthcare: A systematic review of the literature. *International Journal of Quality & Reliability Management, 35*(5), 1075–1092. doi:10.1108/IJQRM-02-2017-0027

Antony, J., Sunder, M. V., Sreedharan, R., Chakraborty, A., & Gunasekaran, A. (2019, August 30). A systematic review of Lean in healthcare: A global prospective. *International Journal of Quality & Reliability Management, 36*(8), 1370–1391. doi:10.1108/IJQRM-12-2018-0346

Awad, M. M., Hashem, A., & Naguib, H. M. (2022). The Impact of Lean Management Practices on Economic Sustainability in Services Sector. *Sustainability (Switzerland), 14*(15), 9323. Advance online publication. doi:10.3390u14159323

Bolcato, M., Rodriguez, D., & Aprile, A. (2022). Guiding Principles for Surgical Pathways: A Tool for Improving Outcomes and Patient Safety. *Frontiers in Public Health, 10*, 869607. Advance online publication. doi:10.3389/fpubh.2022.869607 PMID:35462846

Borges, G. A., Tortorella, G., Rossini, M., & Portioli-Staudacher, A. (2019, May 24). Lean implementation in healthcare supply chain: A scoping review. *Journal of Health Organization and Management, 33*(3), 304–322. doi:10.1108/JHOM-06-2018-0176 PMID:31122116

Brailsford, S., & Hilton, N. (n.d.). *A Comparison of Discrete Event Simulation and System Dynamics for Modelling Healthcare Systems*. Academic Press.

Capan, M., Wu, P., Campbell, M., Mascioli, S., & Jackson, E. V. (2015). Using electronic health records and nursing assessment to redesign clinical early recognition systems. *Health Systems (Basingstoke, England), 6*(2), 112–121. doi:10.1057/hs.2015.19

Claudio, D., Cosgriff, V., Nino, V., & Valladares, L. (2021). An agile standardized work procedure for cleaning the operating room. *Journal of Industrial Engineering and Management, 14*(4), 701–717. doi:10.3926/jiem.3440

D'Andreamatteo, A., Ianni, L., Lega, F., & Sargiacomo, M. (2015, September 1). Lean in healthcare: A comprehensive review. *Health Policy (Amsterdam), 119*(9), 1197–1209. doi:10.1016/j.healthpol.2015.02.002 PMID:25737260

Dangerfield, B. C. (2016). System Dynamics Applications to European Healthcare Issues. *Operational Research for Emergency Planning in Healthcare, 2*, 296–315. doi:10.1007/978-1-137-57328-5_13

de Barros, L. B., Bassi, L. de C., Caldas, L. P., Sarantopoulos, A., Zeferino, E. B. B., Minatogawa, V., & Gasparino, R. C. (2021). Lean Healthcare Tools for Processes Evaluation: An Integrative Review. *International Journal of Environmental Research and Public Health, 18*(14), 7389. doi:10.3390/ijerph18147389

Demirli, K., Al Kaf, A., Simsekler, M. C. E., Jayaraman, R., Khan, M. J., & Tuzcu, E. M. (2021). Using lean techniques and discrete-event simulation for performance improvement in an outpatient clinic. *International Journal of Lean Six Sigma, 12*(6), 1260–1288. doi:10.1108/IJLSS-09-2020-0138

Dural Selcuk, G., & Vasilakis, C. (2021). Evaluating the sustainability of complex health system transformation in the context of population ageing: An empirical system dynamics study. *The Journal of the Operational Research Society*, 1–17. Advance online publication. doi:10.1080/01605682.2021.1992307

Fisher, A. M., Ding, M. Q., Hochheiser, H., & Douglas, G. P. (2016). Measuring time utilization of pharmacists in the Birmingham Free Clinic dispensary. *BMC Health Services Research, 16*(1), 1–7. doi:10.118612913-016-1787-6 PMID:27687973

Flood, D., Douglas, K., Goldberg, V., Martinez, B., Garcia, P., Arbour, M., & Rohloff, P. (2017). A quality improvement project using statistical process control methods for type 2 diabetes control in a resource-limited setting. *International Journal for Quality in Health Care, 29*(4), 593–601. doi:10.1093/intqhc/mzx051 PMID:28486632

Garcia-Sabater, P. I. ;, Marin-Garcia, J. J. ;, Vidal-Carreras, P. I., Garcia-Sabater, J. J., & Marin-Garcia, J. A. (2022). Applying Value Stream Mapping to Improve the Delivery of Patient Care in the Oncology Day Hospital. *International Journal of Environmental Research and Public Health, 19*(7), 4265. doi:10.3390/ijerph19074265

Henrique, D. B., Rentes, A. F., Godinho, M., Kleber, F., Esposto, F., Barberato Henrique, D., . . . Godinho Filho, M. (2015). *A new value stream mapping approach for healthcare environments*. doi:10.1080/09537287.2015.1051159

Inozu, B., Chauncey, D., Kamataris, V., Mount, C., & Novaces, L. L. C. (2011). *Performance improvement for healthcare: Leading change with lean, Six Sigma, and constraints management*. McGraw Hill Professional.

Joosten, T., Bongers, I., & Janssen, R. (2009). Application of lean thinking to health care: Issues and observations. *International Journal for Quality in Health Care, 21*(5), 341–347. doi:10.1093/intqhc/mzp036 PMID:19696048

Lawson, T., Weekes, L., & Hill, M. (2018). Ensuring success and sustainability of a quality improvement project. *BJA Education, 18*(5), 147–152. doi:10.1016/j.bjae.2018.02.002 PMID:33456825

Lima, R. M., Dinis-Carvalho, J., Souza, T. A., Vieira, E., & Gonçalves, B. (2021, March 20). Implementation of lean in health care environments: An update of systematic reviews. *International Journal of Lean Six Sigma, 12*(2), 399–431. doi:10.1108/IJLSS-07-2019-0074

Marin-Garcia, J. A., Vidal-Carreras, P. I., & Garcia-Sabater, J. J. (2021). The Role of Value Stream Mapping in Healthcare Services: A Scoping Review. *International Journal of Environmental Research and Public Health, 18*(3), 951. doi:10.3390/ijerph18030951

Martins Drei, S., & Sérgio de Arruda Ignácio, P. (2022). Lean healthcare applied systematically in a medium-sized medical clinic hospitalization. *Journal of Health Organization and Management, 36*(5), 666–689. Advance online publication. doi:10.1108/JHOM-05-2021-0194 PMID:35439404

Mazzocato, P., Savage, C., Brommels, M., Aronsson, H., & Thor, J. (2010, October). Lean thinking in healthcare: A realist review of the literature. *Quality & Safety in Health Care, 19*(5), 376–382. doi:10.1136/qshc.2009.037986 PMID:20724397

Montgomery, D. C. (2004). Intro to Statistical Quality Control 5th Edition with Minitab Student Release 14 Set. John Wiley & Sons.

Morell-Santandreu, O., Santandreu-Mascarell, C., & Garcia-Sabater, J. J. (2021). A Model for the Implementation of Lean Improvements in Healthcare Environments as Applied in a Primary Care Center. *International Journal of Environmental Research and Public Health, 18*(6), 2876. doi:10.3390/ijerph18062876

Mortimer, F., Isherwood, J., Wilkinson, A., & Vaux, E. (2018). Sustainability in quality improvement: Redefining value. *Future Healthcare Journal, 5*(2), 88–93. doi:10.7861/futurehosp.5-2-88 PMID:31098540

Nino, V., Claudio, D., Valladares, L., & Harris, S. (2020). An Enhanced Kaizen Event in a Sterile Processing Department of a Rural Hospital: A Case Study. *International Journal of Environmental Research and Public Health, 17*(23), 8748. doi:10.3390/ijerph17238748

Peimbert-García, R. E., Gutiérrez-Mendoza, L. M., & García-Reyes, H. (2021). Applying Lean Healthcare to Improve the Discharge Process in a Mexican Academic Medical Center. *Sustainability, 13*(19), 10911. doi:10.3390/su131910911

Pitt, M., Monks, T., Crowe, S., & Vasilakis, C. (2016). Systems modelling and simulation in health service design, delivery and decision making. *BMJ Quality & Safety, 25*(1), 38–45. doi:10.1136/bmjqs-2015-004430 PMID:26115667

Régis, T. K. O., Santos, L. C., & Gohr, C. F. (2019). A case-based methodology for lean implementation in hospital operations. *Journal of Health Organization and Management, 33*(6), 656–676. doi:10.1108/JHOM-09-2018-0267 PMID:31625821

Rocha, Í. J. A., & de Vasconcelos, C. R. (2021). Lean healthcare implications in an occupational medicine clinic. *International Journal of Lean Six Sigma, 12*(5), 973–991. doi:10.1108/IJLSS-05-2020-0056

Romano, E., Falegnami, A., Cagliano, A. C., & Rafele, C. (2022). Lean ICU Layout Re-Design: A Simulation-Based Approach. *Informatics (MDPI), 9*(2), 35. Advance online publication. doi:10.3390/informatics9020035

Santos, A. C., Reis, A. C., Souza, C. G., Santos, I. L., & Ferreira, L. A. F. (2020). The first evidence about conceptual vs analytical lean healthcare research studies. *Journal of Health Organization and Management, 34*(7), 789–806. doi:10.1108/JHOM-01-2020-0021 PMID:32945155

Sartal, A., Llach, J., & León-Mateos, F. (2022). Do technologies really affect that much? exploring the potential of several industry 4.0 technologies in today's lean manufacturing shop floors. *Operations Research, 22*(5), 6075–6106. Advance online publication. doi:10.100712351-022-00732-y

Smith, I. M., & Bayliss, E. (2022). Recovering staff, recovering services: Massive-online support for recovering a paediatric service using Lean and compassionate communication. *BMJ Open Quality, 11*(2), e001914. Advance online publication. doi:10.1136/bmjoq-2022-001914 PMID:35750350

Tiso, A., Crema, M., & Verbano, C. (2021). A framework to guide the implementation of lean management in emergency department. *Journal of Health Organization and Management, 35*(9), 315–337. doi:10.1108/JHOM-01-2021-0035 PMID:34558251

Tlapa, D., Zepeda-Lugo, C. A., Tortorella, G. L., Baez-Lopez, Y. A., Limon-Romero, J., Alvarado-Iniesta, A., & Rodriguez-Borbon, M. I. (2020). Effects of Lean Healthcare on Patient Flow: A Systematic Review. *Value in Health, 23*(2), 260–273. doi:10.1016/j.jval.2019.11.002 PMID:32113632

Wickramasinghe, N., Al-Hakim, L., Gonzalez, C., & Tan, J. (2014). *Healthcare Delivery in the Information Age Lean Thinking for Healthcare*. Retrieved from https://www.springer.com/series/8783

Winner, L. E., Reinhardt, E., Benishek, L., & Marsteller, J. A. (2022). Lean Management Systems in Health Care: A Review of the Literature. *Quality Management in Health Care, 31*(4), 221–230. doi:10.1097/QMH.0000000000000353 PMID:35180733

Zdęba-Mozoła, A., Rybarczyk-Szwajkowska, A., Czapla, T., Marczak, M., & Kozłowski, R. (2022). Implementation of Lean Management in a Multi-Specialist Hospital in Poland and the Analysis of Waste. *International Journal of Environmental Research and Public Health, 19*(2), 800. doi:10.3390/ijerph19020800

Zepeda-Lugo, C., Tlapa, D., Baez-Lopez, Y., Limon-Romero, J., Ontiveros, S., Perez-Sanchez, A., & Tortorella, G. (2020). Assessing the Impact of Lean Healthcare on Inpatient Care: A Systematic Review. *International Journal of Environmental Research and Public Health, 17*(15), 5609. doi:10.3390/ijerph17155609

Chapter 11
Trends in Lean Maintenance Implementation in Production Companies:
Research Results

Katarzyna Antosz
Rzeszow University of Technology, Poland

Małgorzata Jasiulewicz-Kaczmarek
Poznan University of Technology, Poland

José Carlos Sá
https://orcid.org/0000-0002-2228-5348
School of Engineering, ISEP, Polytechnic of Porto, Portugal

José Machado
https://orcid.org/0000-0002-4917-2474
University of Minho, Portugal

ABSTRACT

In this chapter, the authors highlight the benefits of using Lean Maintenance, showing and discussing obtained results from studying industrial companies and concluding about used tools and level of this concept implementation in their activity. For obtaining the base results for this work, surveys were used for research carried out in enterprises. Some questionnaires were sent to companies, in Poland, for being possible to acquire some data from their experience and results by using Lean Maintenance. As main achievements of this study, it can be concluded that levels of application of Lean Maintenance, and respective used tools, are different, when

DOI: 10.4018/978-1-6684-5606-4.ch011

analyzed by the type of company: small, medium, or large. In most companies, the employment level of maintenance services has not changed significantly due to the implementation of Lean Maintenance. Only in large enterprises and mostly with numerical machines, the employment level of maintenance services employees decreased. Large enterprises achieved the greatest benefits from the implementation of Lean Maintenance tools.

INTRODUCTION

Each enterprise tries to be competitive and tries to achieve higher profits by increasing productivity and meeting customer expectations in terms of the quality and price of the offered products. To improve the efficiency and effectiveness of implemented processes, enterprises are looking for new solutions and concepts. One of the most used process improvement concepts is Lean Manufacturing (Patel et al., 2021; Khalfallah et al. 2021; Maware et al., 2022). Lean Manufacturing in the age of industry 4.0 will have a large impact on waste reduction. This will result in an increase in production productivity in modern enterprises (Mostafa, et al., 2015; Lai, et al., 2019; Marttonen-Arola, et al., 2020).

Enterprises implementing lean constantly strive to eliminate waste (Yadav et al., 2020). In this context, the reliability of their production equipment is fundamental. Machine failures during production have a negative impact on the production schedule, and thus affect the timeliness and quality of deliveries to customers. In addition, they lead to financial losses by requiring overtime and rework from employees to compensate for production losses (Habidin, et al., 2018). Therefore, maintenance of production equipment is one of the functions of the company that can significantly contribute to an increased effectiveness and efficiency as well as customer satisfaction (Ball & Lunt, 2020; Bakri, et al., 2021; Antosz, et al., 2021). As such, the integration of maintenance and lean concept has a vital role in organizations. According to (Smith & Hawkins, 2004) "without a Lean Maintenance operation, Lean Manufacturing can never achieve the best possible attributes of Lean".

The aim of this work is to identify activities related to the implementation of lean maintenance tools and to assess the benefits of their implementation in manufacturing companies. The structure contains five sections, including this one. The second section shows the background of lean maintenance. In the third section the research methodology is described. Next, fourth section, the research results, concerning the lean maintenance implementation in the production companies, are discussed. Finally, the conclusions of the work are presented.

BACKGROUND

European standard EN 13306 defined "maintenance" as the "Combination of all technical, administrative and managerial actions during the life cycle of an item intended to retain it in, or restore it to, a state in which it can perform the required function (function or a combination of functions of an item which are considered necessary to provide a given service)". According to (Velmurugan & Dhingra, 2015) "maintenance is not just ensuring the healthiness of equipment in a facility but it also plays a crucial role in achieving organization's goals and objectives with optimum maintenance cost and maximum production. [...] and needs to be viewed as a strategic function in an organization."

For many years, maintenance was perceived as a technical function, the main task of which was to repair machines and devices, and the improvement activities focused on improving the repair technology. Lean Manufacturing shifted attention from improving maintenance from technical matters to the management side, which focuses on eliminating the causes of problems and making decisions about improvements, their implementation and assessment of effectiveness. In the literature, maintenance activities supporting the implementation of the lean manufacturing concept are referred to as lean maintenance. Ricky Smith (Smith, 2004) defined Lean Maintenance as a "proactive maintenance operation employing planned and scheduled maintenance activities through Total Productive Maintenance (TPM) practices, using maintenance strategies developed through application of Reliability Centered Maintenance (RCM) decision logic and practiced by empowered (self-directed) action teams using the 5S process, weekly Kaizen improvement events, and autonomous maintenance together with multi-skilled, maintenance technician-performed maintenance through the committed use of their work order system and their Computer Managed Maintenance System (CMMS) or Enterprise Asset Management (EAM) system"

Several studies focus on the effect of lean techniques on maintenance efficiency (Jasiulewicz-Kaczmarek, 2015; Hassan, et al., 2020; Shou, et al., 2020; Singha & Shenoy, 2022; Kose, et al., 2022). Such techniques include, in particular, the Total Productive Maintenance (TPM), 5S workplace organization system, kanban, kaizen, Value Stream Mapping (Mostafa, et al., 2015; Jasiulewicz-Kaczmarek & Saniuk, 2017; Duarte & Scarpin, 2022; Antosz, et al., 2020; Pombal, et al., 2019), in the research presented, which consisted in the implementation of some lean tools in maintenance management. They managed to improve the organisation of the consumables cupboard through the implementation of 5S, having also obtained a reduction in the time of location of consumable materials, to about 70%, through Visual Management. The use of kanbans allowed an improvement in stock control of about 30%.

Among lean tools, TPM can be regarded as the most frequently applied lean technique for improving maintenance process (Bataineh, et al., 2019; Xiang & Chin, 2021). Total Productive Maintenance (TPM) is a holistic approach to equipment maintenance with the goal of achieving near-perfect production processes. This concept focused on improving the working conditions of production equipment, reducing/eliminating failures, maintaining equipment at an optimal level of efficiency and reliability, and aimed at zero defects and zero accidents, with the involvement of operators, technical personnel and management (Habidin, at al. 2018; Tortorella, et al., 2021). Vaz et al. (2021), developed research through a structured survey, which was sent to 472 Portuguese companies, having obtained 84 valid answers, to assess the impact of TPM in five dimensions of operational performance, namely: quality, flexibility, productivity, safety and costs. This survey verified that "planned maintenance" and "education & training", are the practices with the highest degree of implementation in the Portuguese industry, exceeding 70% for both. Productivity was the dimension that demonstrated the greatest impact resulting from the implementation of TPM.

5S plays a key role in the overall implementation of TPM (Ribeiro, et al., 2019). The name of '5S' comes from five activities that begins with the letter 'S' – Seiri, Seiton, Seiso, Seiketsu and Shitsuke which are Japanese words. 5S helps organizations to identify visible and critical waste in the maintenance process and thus helps to establish a framework and action plan to successfully follow the lean maintenance road to continual improvement (Makwana & Patange, 2022).

Positive results of the implementation of lean maintenance tools can be found in various industries, such as the automotive industry, aviation industry, power plants, textile industry, and food industry among others (Hassan, et al., 2020; Arlinghaus & Knizkov, 2020). The results of the implementation indicate the universal nature of lean maintenance tools and the possibility of their application in various contexts and industries, increasing their importance as an approach to continuous improvement (Mkaka & Burduk, 2022). To assess the effectiveness of those improvements, companies used different indicators such as MTTR - Mean Time to Repair, MTBF (Mean Time Between Failure) and OEE (Overall Equipment Effectiveness) (Pinto, et al., 2019; de Jong & Beelaerts van Blokland, 2016).

RESEARCH METHODOLOGY

The paper presents the results of several years of research on the selected methods and tools of Lean Maintenance implementation. The implementation of the adopted research goals required the definition of a research procedure. It was carried out in several steps: development of a questionnaire containing survey questions, selection of enterprises to conduct the research, implementation of the research, preparation of research results, analysis of the obtained results and drawing conclusions.

Questionnaire surveys were used for research carried out in enterprises. The developed questionnaires made it possible to obtain data in the same form from all respondents. The research was attended by the representatives of middle and top management as well as employees directly responsible for the maintenance process. The research was carried out in the form of conjunctive closed questions, which contained a list of prepared, predetermined answers presented to the respondent, enabling the selection of more than one of the given possible answers. Additionally, other answers could be added, if they were not included in the prepared options. Qualitative and quantitative research methods were used to analyze the obtained results. The presented analysis made it possible to highlight the actual activities undertaken in the management of technical infrastructure with the use of Lean Maintenance methods and tools. The presented research was carried out in production companies in Poland over a period of several years: stage I - four years, and stage II – next three years. The main areas and scope of the conducted research are presented in Table 1.

Table 1. Areas and scope of the conducted research

Area of analysis	Scope of analysis
Implementation of the Lean concept	1. Goal of Lean implementation. 2. Implementing the Lean concept in the enterprise (implementation period). 3. Implemented Lean Manufacturing tools.
Analysis of the implementation of the TPM method on machines	4. The reasons why the company decided to implement the TPM method. 5. Activities carried out in the process of implementing TPM. 6. Problems that appeared in the process of implementing TPM in the enterprise.
5S method implementation analysis	7. 5S implementation areas. 8. Activities carried out in the process of implementing 5S. 9. Implementation of improvements at production work stands.
Indicators used to assess the effectiveness of Lean Maintenance	10. Using the OEE indicator. 11. Using the quality, efficiency and availability indicator of machines.
Benefits resulting from the implementation of Lean Maintenance in enterprises,	12. Changes in the value of the OEE indicator, the number of unplanned downtime and the number of failures after the TPM implementation.

The selection of areas and scope of the research was carried by the results presented in the work (Duran, et al. 2017).

CHARACTERISTICS OF RESEARCH OBJECTS

Structure of the Surveyed Enterprises

One hundred companies took part in the first stage (I), and fifty companies in the second stage (II) of the research. For the conducted research, a confidence level of 95% and a fraction size of 0.5 were assumed, which made it possible to estimate the measurement error at the level of 10% in stage I and 14% in stage II. The surveyed enterprises were classified according to the following criteria: organization size, production type, industry and company's situation. Among the analyzed enterprises, there were those that carried out several types of production or operated in several industries. The structure of the surveyed enterprises is presented in Table 2.

Among the analyzed enterprises, the smallest group were large enterprises (stage I - 46%, stage II - 52%) (Table 1). The next group were medium-sized enterprises (stage I - 27%, stage II - 32%). The surveyed companies were dominated by those from the metalworking industry (stage I - 22.77%, stage II - 26%), the aviation industry (stage I - 23.76%, stage II - 24%) and the automotive industry (stage I - 18, 81%, stage II - %). Most of them were private enterprises (stage I - 94%, stage II - 98%), with Polish capital (stage I - 44%, stage II - 23%) or with majority foreign capital (stage I - 44%, stage II - 25%). Unit production dominated among the surveyed enterprises (stage I - 28.44%, stage II - 28%) and small and medium-series production (stage I - 24.77%, stage II - 24% and stage I - 21.10%, stage II - 28%).

LEAN MANUFACTURING IMPLEMENTATION IN SURVEYED ENTERPRISES

The main goal of implementing the Lean Manufacturing philosophy in the enterprise is the elimination of waste (Womack & Jones, 2003). Removing sources of waste is effective when using the so-called lean manufacturing practices, which include:

- integrated flow of one product, low inventory levels and small production series produced just in time,
- preventing errors, not correcting them,
- production in a suction system according to the customer's current needs,
- work organization based on teamwork with flexible (universal) operators of machines and devices and a small number of supervising employees,
- recognizing the potential inherent in employees (they are a source of knowledge about production processes),

Table 2. Structure of the surveyed enterprises

Classification criteria	Stage I		Stage II	
	Number of enterprises	Percentage share [%]	Number of enterprises	Percentage share [%]
Size of the organization				
Micro	8	8	2	4
Small enterprise	19	19	6	12
Medium enterprise	27	27	16	32
Large enterprise	46	46	26	52
Total	**100**		**50**	
Production type				
Unit	31	28.44	14	28
Small	27	24.77	12	24
Medium	23	21.10	14	28
Large	19	17.43	8	16
Mass	9	8.26	2	4
Total	**109**		**50**	
		Industry		
Automotive	19	18.81	12	24
Aviation	24	23.76	14	28
Food	6	5.94	0	0
Chemical	6	5.94	2	4
Wood And Paper	8	7.92	1	2
Metalworking	23	22.77	13	26
Metallurgical	2	1.9	2	4
Other	13	12.87	14	28
Total	**101**		**58**	
The company's situation				
Difficult (small/ decreasing number of orders)	3	3	2	4
Stable (stable number of orders)	36	36	17	34
Development (increasing number of orders)	58	58	30	60
No answer	3	3	1	2
Total	**100**		**Total**	**100**

- continuous improvement in order to gradually eliminate non-added-value activities, unplanned downtime or process variability that are usually be referred to as waste,
- integrating the supply chain for production through close cooperation with suppliers of raw materials as well as distributors and recipients of products.

The essence of Lean Manufacturing can be summed up in the Latin sentence: *Primum non prodigere.* Avoiding waste is a source of success for enterprises using production management based on lean manufacturing (Antosz & Stadnicka, 2015). The primary goal of eliminating waste in the field of Lean Manufacturing is also declared by the analyzed enterprises (stage I - 86.44%, stage II - 83.93%) (Figure 1). It should be noted that in the second stage of the research, none of the analyzed companies indicated employment minimization as the primary goal of Lean Manufacturing.

Figure 1. Goal of Lean Manufacturing implementation in the surveyed enterprises

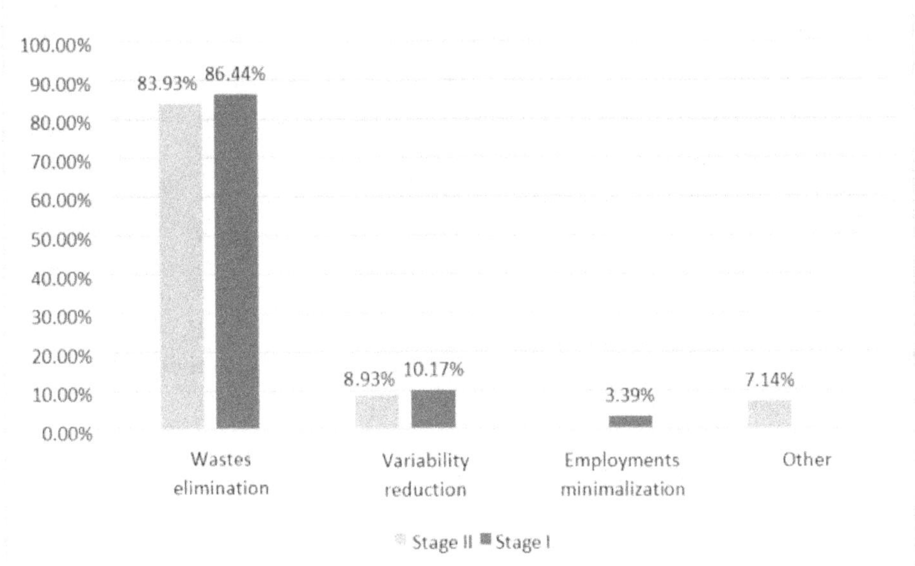

The analyzed enterprises identified different types of waste. The most common answers include non-conforming products (stage I - 64%, stage II - 40.59%), inventories (stage I - 45.54%, stage II - 66%) and unnecessary movements (stage I - 46.53%, stage II - 56%). It should be noted that the wastes also included those related to the operation of machines: i.e. too long changeovers (stage I - 25.74%, stage II - 52%) and machine failures (stage I - 44.55%, stage II - 48%). Redundant processes were indicated least often (stage I - 86.44%, stage II - 83.93%) and failure to use the inventiveness of employees (stage I - 86.44%, stage II - 83.93%).

In order to eliminate waste, more and more enterprises implement the Lean Manufacturing philosophy. Comparing the results obtained in the first and second stage of the research, it should be noted that the percentage of companies not implementing the Lean concept has changed significantly (stage I - 35.64%, stage II - 18%) - a reduction of over 17%, more companies planning implement it (stage I - 9.90%, stage II - 24%) - an increase of over 14%.

Enterprises that have identified types of waste, such as machine failures and long changeover times, plan to implement or have implemented various Lean manufacturing methods and tools related to the operation of machines and the improvement of workplace organization (Figure 2). Most of them in the second stage of the research implemented the 5S method - 9.80%, the Poka Yoke method - 7.35%, work standardization - 6.86%, the TPM method - 5.39% and the SMED (Single Minute Exchange of Die) method and OEE - 4.41%. The mentioned methods and tools were also indicated as planned for implementation by many companies. Enterprises implementing the Lean philosophy, in particular those that use methods and tools in the area of machine operation, were further analyzed in detail (68 enterprises).

MAINTENANCE STRATEGIES USED IN SURVEYED ENTERPRISES

The analyzed companies could use several maintenance strategies simultaneously. Therefore, for selected strategies Corrective Maintenance (CM), Preventive Maintenance (PM), Condition Based Maintenance (CBM), detailed actions based on the strategies assumptions have been defined:

- CM strategy - only failures elimination,
- PM strategy - inspections carried out during the warranty period, scheduled inspections performed by maintenance services, scheduled inspections and repairs carried out by maintenance services, assessment of the machine's condition by the operator before starting work,
- CBM strategy - continuous monitoring of the condition of selected machines (e.g. noise, vibration, temperature) and continuous monitoring of the condition of all machines (e.g. noise, vibrations, temperature).

Figure 2. Lean Manufacturing methods and tools implemented or planned for implementation in the surveyed enterprises

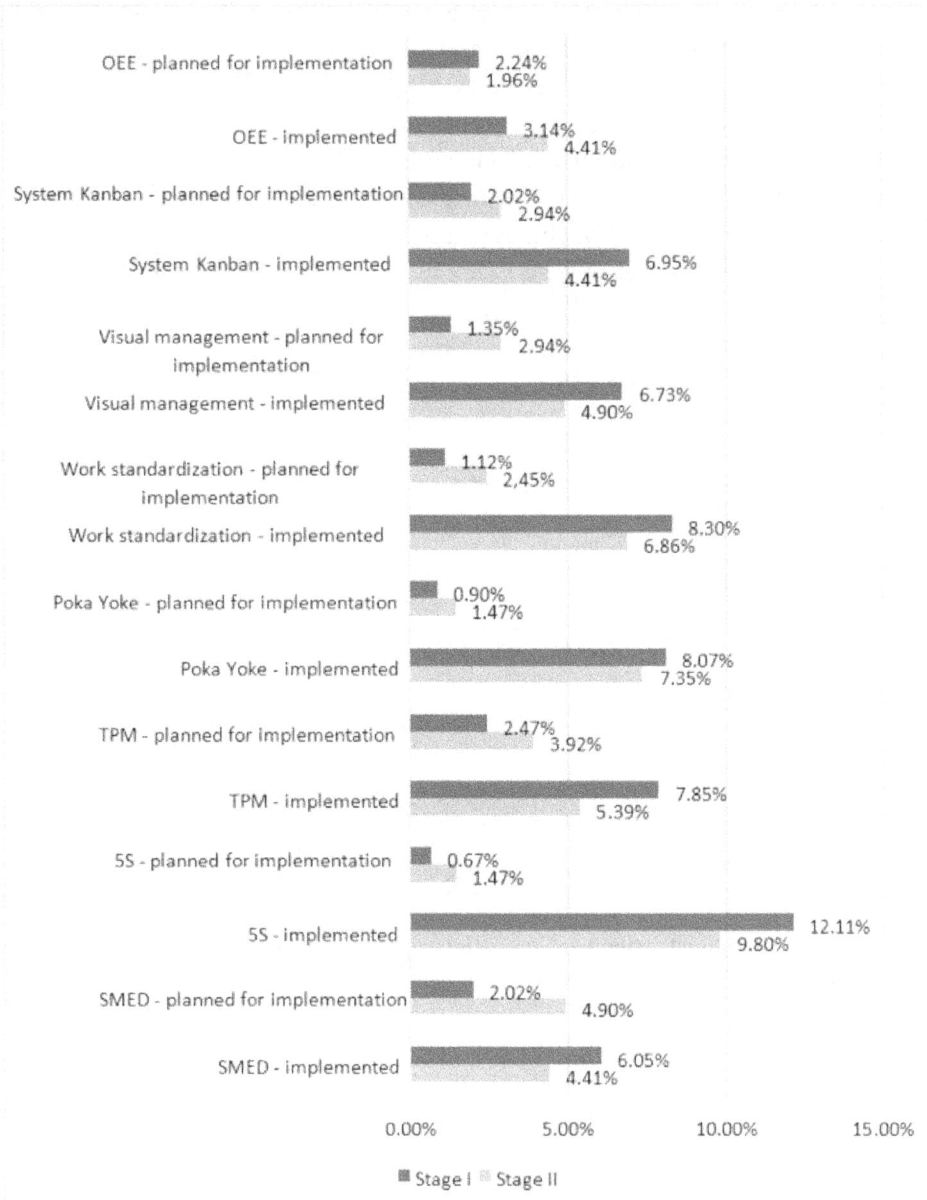

The conducted research shows that in enterprises the PM strategy is most often used. Among the specified activities, the operator's assessment of the machine's condition is most often carried out before starting work (stage I - 22.04%, stage

II - 24.09%), then scheduled inspections and repairs carried out by maintenance services (stage I - 19.68%, stage II - 20.44%) and scheduled inspections and repairs carried out by maintenance services (stage I - 19.68%, stage II - 20.44%). On the other hand, some enterprises use activities related to the CBM strategy: continuous monitoring of the condition of all machines (e.g. noise, vibration, temperature) (stage I - 6.02%, stage II - 5.84%) and continuous monitoring of the condition of selected machines (e.g. . noise, vibrations, temperature) (stage I - 8.84%, stage II - 5.11%). CBM is a high-cost strategy (Guizzi et al. 2009) and this is perhaps the main reason to change this strategy to a PM strategy. It was also noticed that enterprises apply the CM strategy less and less (stage I - 9.24%, stage II - 8.76%) (Figure 3).

Figure 3. Maintenance strategies used in surveyed enterprises

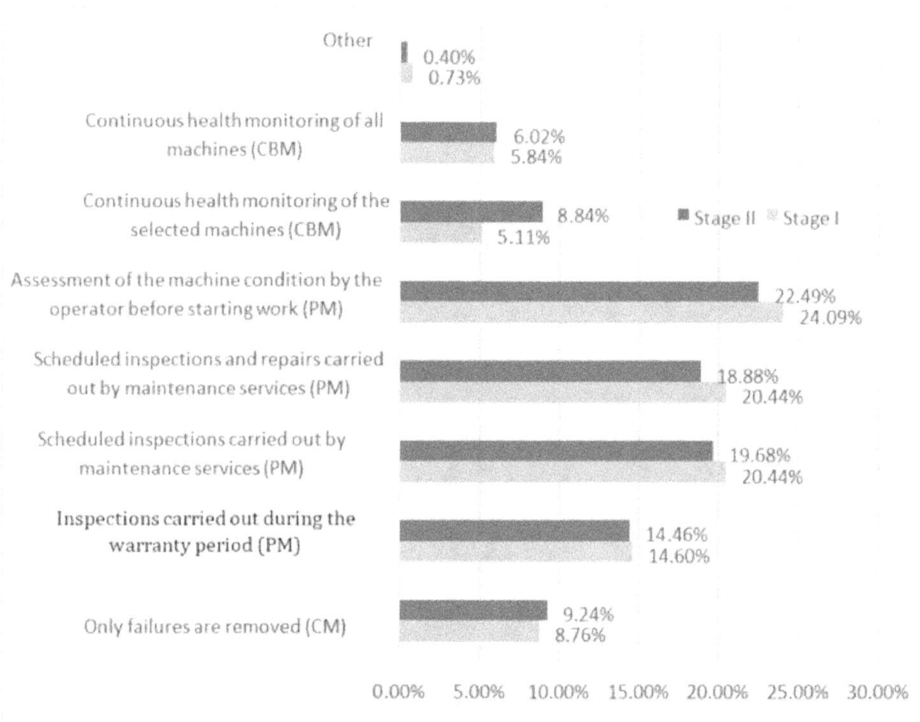

MAINTENANCE INFORMATION COLLECTED IN SURVEYED ENTERPRISES

Decisions concerning actions of maintenance strategy should be made on the based on the facts. Thus, it can be said that the efficiency of the technical infrastructure management process largely depends on the type and amount of information about the machines. Collecting the necessary information, making the right decisions at the right time and ensuring targeted action and response are constant challenges for the information system of an organization (AL Nawaiseh et al., 2022). If we are not aware of problems and where they occur, we cannot eliminate or prevent them. The conducted research shows that enterprises see the need to record data. Comparing the data obtained in stages I and II, it can be noticed that the percentage of companies that do not record this data is falling (stage I - 10.45%, stage II - 3.80%). These data are most often collected by maintenance department (stage I - 32.09%, stage II - 36.71%), less and less frequently at the workplace (stage I - 32.84%, stage II - 36.71%). Information systems are more and more often used to collect the data (stage I - 17.91%, stage II - 22.78%) and to machines maintenance - an increase by 4.27%.

The people most often responsible for collecting information are: maintenance workers and operators on the work stand. Different types of information about machines are collected in the analyzed enterprises. Data is collected both from individual workstations as well as from lines or production departments. They concern downtimes of machines, waiting time for service, spare parts for machines, efficiency and load of machines. Based on Figure 4 the information that is most often collected in enterprises is:

- the number of failures on individual machines (stage I - 18.21%, stage II - 18.72%),
- failure elimination time (stage I - 15.02%, stage II - 14 44%),
- machine load (stage I - 14.06%, stage II - 11.23%),
- machine efficiency (stage I - 11.09%, stage II - 13.90%).

More and more enterprises collect information on the number of failures on all machines (stage I - 7.03%, stage II - 9.09%) - an increase by 2.06%.

Figure 4. Type of collected information in the surveyed enterprises

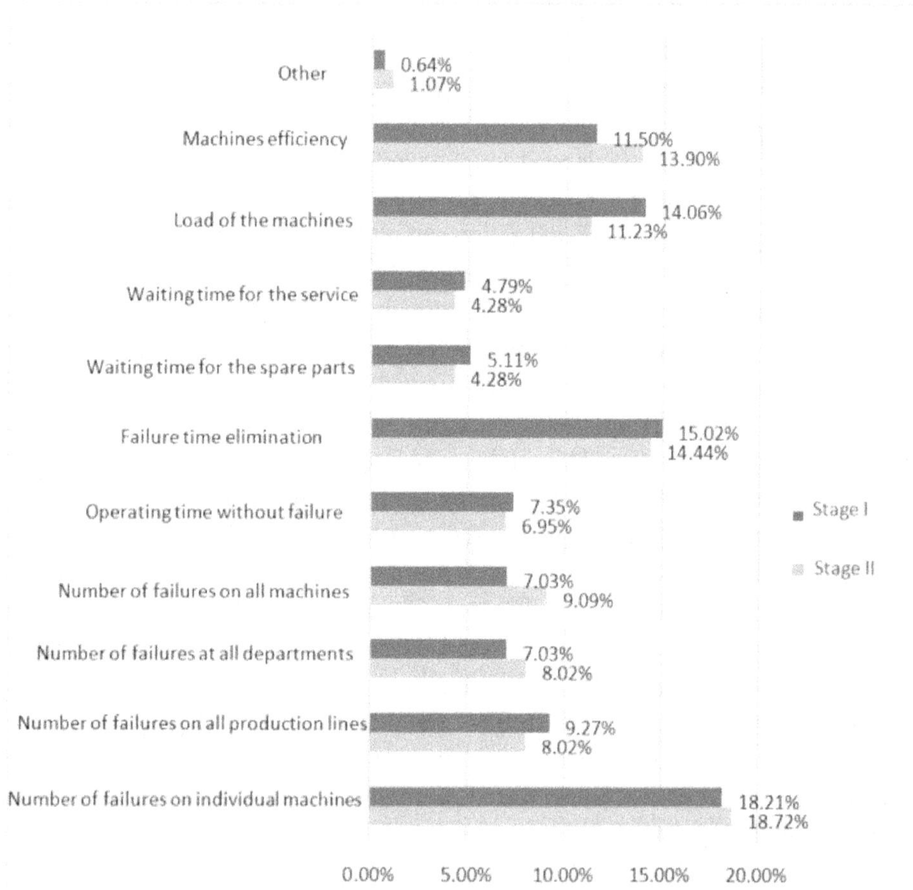

LEAN MAINTENENACE IMPLEMENTATION - RESEARCH RESULTS

TPM Method Implementation

According to the literature (Singh & Singh, 2020; Singh et al., 2018; Chaabane et al., 2021), one of the main reasons for implementing TPM in enterprises is to reduce the number of failures, and thus increase the efficiency of machines. The conducted research showed that a smaller number of enterprises decide to implement TPM (Figure 5).

Figure 5. Areas of TPM implementation in the surveyed companies

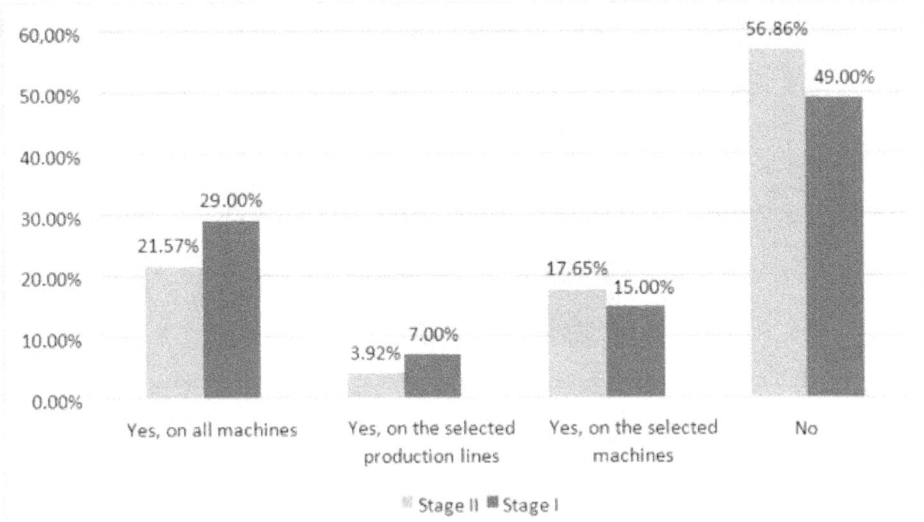

Although in many cases the effectiveness of TPM implementation is appreciated (Schindlerová et al., 2020). Potential of using TPM to increase the efficiency of production processes. In the anlayzed companies the percentage of enterprises that do not implement TPM decreased by 7.86% (stage II - 56.86%, stage I - 49%). Many enterprises implement TPM on all machines (stage II - 21.57%, stage I - 29%). The percentage of companies implementing TPM on selected production lines is also decreasing (stage II - 3.92%, stage I - 7.00%). On the other hand, the percentage of companies implementing TPM on selected machines is increasing (stage II - 15.00%, stage I - 17.65%).

The conducted research confirmed that many companies decided to implement TPM due to the high failure rate of machines (stage I - 30.36%, stage II - 27.27%) and the low technical condition of machines (stage I - 24.24%, stage II - 23.21%) (Figure 6). Especially in the second stage of the research, the main reason for the implementation of the TPM method was to establish TPM as a corporate standard (large enterprises) (Figure 6).

Among other reasons for the implementation of TPM, the companies mentioned:

- the need to improve the reliability and productivity of machines,
- the need to ensure continuity of production,
- work safety,
- as preventive measures,
- awareness that TPM supports meeting customer requirements,

Figure 6. Reasons TPM implementation in the surveyed enterprises

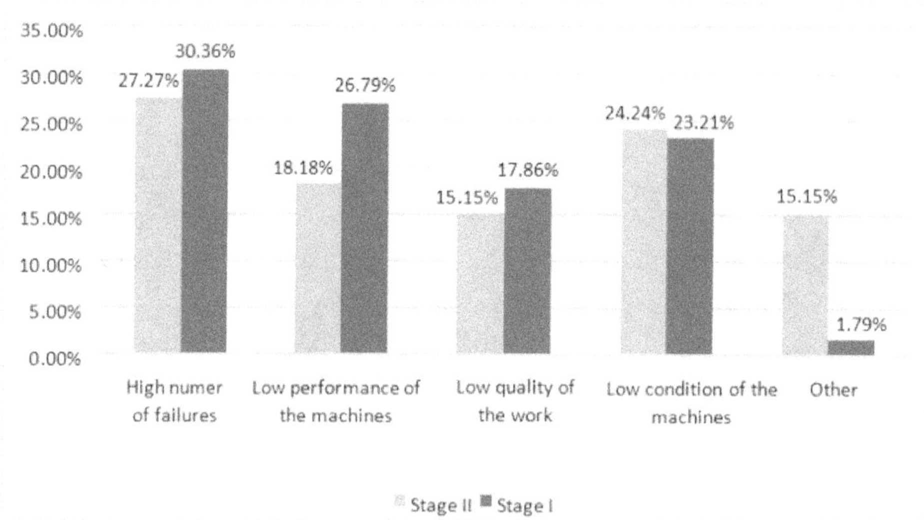

- the need to reduce the causes of failures,
- the need for better machine control,
- the need to improve processes.

The effectiveness of the implementation of the TPM method is influenced by the type of activities undertaken both during the implementation of TPM and in the subsequent operation of the company (Nakajima, 1989; Hooi & Leong, 2017). The conducted research has shown that companies, as part of the implementation of TPM, most often developed a maintenance schedule (stage I 12.50%, stage II 13.42%). In addition, the companies undertook the following activities:

- assessment of the technical condition of machines (stage I - 11.76%, stage II - 12.08%),
- development of the scope of autonomous maintenance (for the operator) (stage I - 10.36%, stage II - 11, 41%),
- development of the scope of preventive maintenance (for maintenance services) (stage I - 10.00%, stage II - 10.74%),
- TPM workshops in a selected pilot area (work stand, production line, etc.) (stage I - 8.93%, stage II - 9.40%) and others (Figure 7).

In addition, the conducted research have shown that more and more companies identify non-conformities on machines (stage I - 5.36%, stage II - 8.72%). More companies apply training for employees and evaluate machines in terms of meeting the safety requirements.

Figure 7. The activities during TPM implementation in the surveyed enterprises

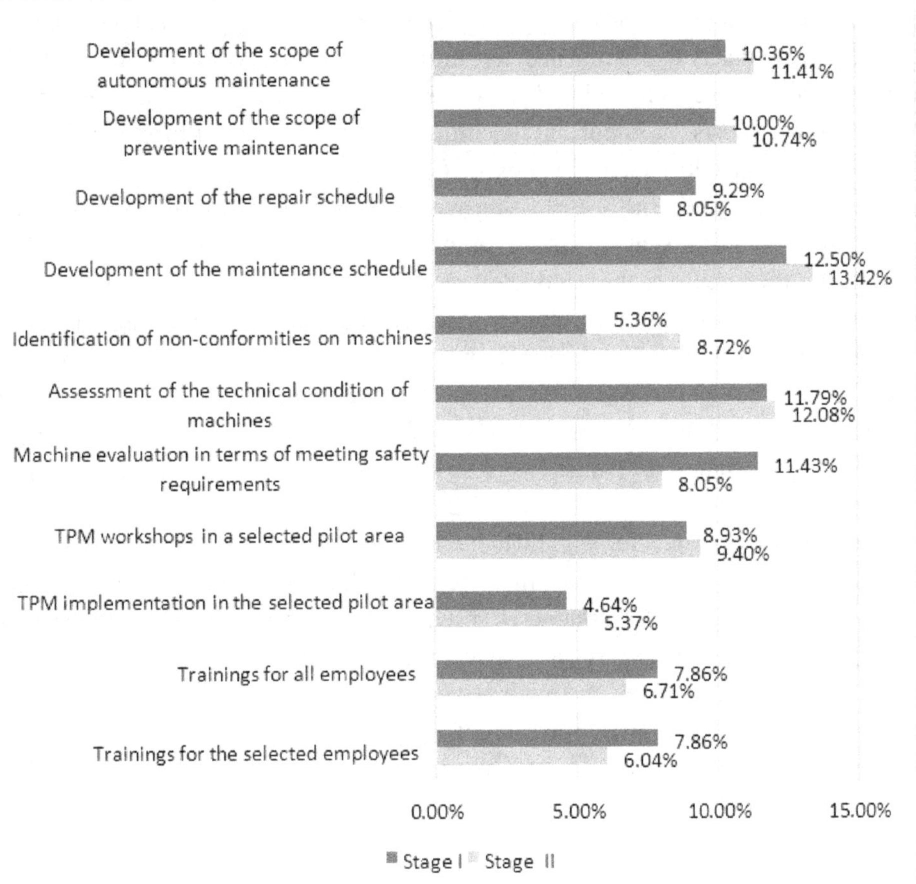

In the analyzed companies, many employees in various positions are involved in the process of TPM implementation. Both in the first and second stage of the research, the involvement of maintenance service employees did not change significantly (stage I - 16.89%, stage II - 16.98%). In the implementation of TPM in the analyzed companies was involved: production workers (stage I - 16.00%, stage II - 18.87%), line operators (stage I - 13.78%, stage II - 15.09%) and office workers (stage I - 2.67% stage II - 3.77%). However, a worrying phenomenon is the decline in the involvement of middle and top management employees: line managers (stage I - 11.11%, stage II - 10.38%) and representatives of the top management (stage I - 6.22%, stage II - 5, 66%). According to the assumptions of the Lean philosophy (Womack and Jones, 2003; Gelei, et al. 2015), they should motivate and support such activities with their attitude.

The implementation of the TPM method takes place gradually on individual machines operating in the enterprise. During its implementation, it is helpful to define the order of typing machines involved by TPM. For this purpose, a categorization is carried out, which is also useful in determining the scope of preventive and predictive maintenance, which is associated with additional costs. It may be justified to bear the associated costs for important machines and not to do so for machines in lower categories (Gopalakrishnan & Skoogh, 2018).

There are many criteria for evaluating machines and models for their categorization, which have been presented, among others, in the works (Marquez et al. 2009). Analyzing the results of the conducted research, it can be noticed that the number of enterprises categorizing machines is decreasing (stage I - 50%, stage II - 36%), which may be related to the decline in interest among enterprises in implementing the TPM method. Most often, the categorization of machines takes into account the following criteria: number of failures of machines (stage I - 21.32%, stage II - 22.81%), machine load (stage I - 19.85%, stage II - 22.81%) and the age of the machine (stage I - 12.50%, stage II - 12.28%). .

Another important element influencing the implementation of TPM is the categorization of spare parts (Bošnjaković, 2010; Antosz & Ratnayake 2019). When analyzing the results of the conducted research, it can be noticed that the number of enterprises categorizing spare parts are decreasing (stage I - 35.87%, stage II - 22%). As in the case of machines, the analyzed companies apply different criteria for the categorization of spare parts. The categorization of spare parts most often takes into account the following criteria: failure frequency (stage I - 21.62%, stage II - 25.00%), machine category (stage I - 16.22%, stage II - 20.00%) and delivery time (stage I - 23.42%, stage II - 22.50%). Another important evaluation criterion is the stock level (stage I - 13.51%, stage II - 17.50%) - an increase by almost 4% compared to the results from the first and second stage of the research. Many companies take into account the cost of the part when categorizing it (stage I - 19.82%, stage II - 12.50%) and the expiry date (stage I - 5.41%, stage II - 2.50%). In the case of spare parts, enterprises also used categorization models.

During the implementation of modern lean methods some problems can be observed. It is related not only to the ignorance of the rules, goals and techniques of implemented solutions, but also to employees' fears of something new, unknown. For many employees, introducing changes is very often associated with reducing employment. Many problems also appeared in the surveyed companies when implementing TPM. The most common problems that arose when implementing TPM were included in the surveyed companies: the inability to exclude the machine from the production process for the duration of TPM workshops (stage I - 13.01%, stage II - 19.54%) - an increase by 6.53%, employee resistance (stage I - 9.76%, stage II - 14.95%) - an increase by 5.19%, difficult to identify irregularities on the machine (stage I - 8.94%, stage II - 9.20%) and the lack of skilled people to remove irregularities on machines (stage I - 2.44%, stage II - 6.90%) - an increase by over 4%. When comparing the results obtained in the first and second stage of the research, it should be noted that several problems appear less frequently. These include: difficulties in adapting machines to health and safety requirements (stage I - 10.57%, stage II - 4.60%) - reduction by almost 6%, no availability of spare parts (stage I - 10.57%, stage II - 6.90%) - reduction by almost 4%, difficulties in defining the scope of autonomous maintenance (stage I - 8.13%, stage II - 4.60%) - reduction by 3.53%. The problem of the lack of involvement of the top management in activities related to TPM appears again.

Implementation of the 5S Method

The 5S method is the basis for the implementation of Lean Maintenance. It is a tool that does not require large financial outlays, allows to create and maintain high-quality jobs by shaping the correct organization of the work environment and constantly improving the organizational culture of the company (Antosz & Stadnicka, 2015). The method helps employees to get involved in the company's activities and in the process of continuous improvement, which translates into high productivity and efficiency of the organization. A well-organized workplace facilitates the process of eliminating waste in the enterprise. In addition, the use of the 5S method helps to improve the working atmosphere, increases employee satisfaction with the tasks performed and their integration into the company's activities, and improves the company's image.

Introduction of 5S practices into maintenance processes improves MTTR, which affects the efficiency of production equipment, increasing OEE (Figure 8).

The conducted research has shown that enterprises are more and more willing to implement this method. 36.08% of enterprises participating in the first stage of the research declared that they did not implement 5S, in the second stage only 28%. In the first stage of the research, only 15.46% of the companies were in the process of implementing the method, but in the second stage - 34%.

Figure 8. Relation between MTTR and OEE – example (Jasiulewicz-Kaczmarek & Saniuk, 2017)

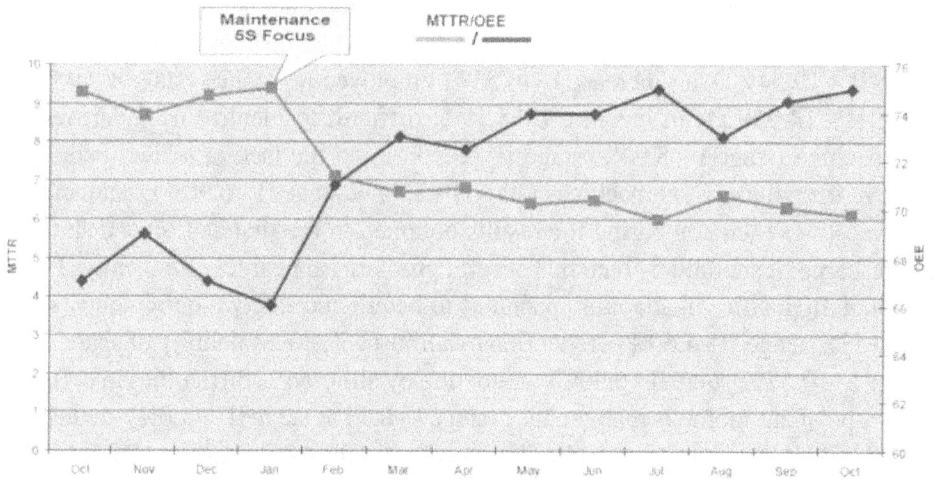

Many companies declare that they have implemented 5S in the entire enterprise (stage II - 10.14%, stage I - 18.80%), at all production positions (stage II - 14.49%, stage I - 23.31%), on all production lines (stage II - 8.70%, stage I - 12.78%) and in all departments (stage II - 10.14%, stage I - 12.03%). 5S is being implemented more and more often in selected departments (stage II - 10.14%, stage I - 4.51%), on selected production work stands (stage II - 17.39%, stage I - 8.27%) and selected lines production (stage II - 18.70%, stage I - 1.50%).

The main activity carried out during the implementation of 5S is training for selected employees (stage I - 21.62%, stage II - 31.82%) responsible for positions where this method is implemented (Figure 9). Additionally, many companies conduct 5S audits (stage I - 72.31%, stage II - 75.68%).

Workplace audit is the most important part supporting the 5S method. It enables the identification of deviations from the standards related to the work stand and determination of corrective actions in the case of non-compliance. Audits enable the identification of non-conformities and their elimination by designating and implementing appropriate actions, setting a deadline and assigning responsibility for them (Gupta, 2022; Randhawa & Ahuja, 2018).

The frequency of conducted audits varies significantly depending on the size of the company and the type of machines. In large, small and micro-enterprises, audits are most often carried out once a shift, and in medium-sized enterprises, once a month. Audits are most often carried out by specially selected 5S auditors (stage I - 38.71%, stage II - 50.00%) and representatives of the lowest management level

- masters (stage I - 22.58%, stage II - 16.67%). The results of the audits carried out are mainly used to set the corrective and preventive actions (stage I - 25.44%, stage II - 35.83%) and the process improvements (stage I - 28.07%, stage II - 29.23%).

Figure 9. Activities carried out during the implementation of 5S method in the surveyed enterprises

ASSESSMENT OF THE EFFECTIVENESS OF SELECTED LEAN MAINTENANCE METHODS AND TOOLS IMPLEMENTATION

An inseparable element of the assessment of the effectiveness of the selected Lean Maintenance methods and tools implementation is the use of various measures. Data obtained from measurements of specific indicators are the basic source of information about the necessity to take improvements actions.

One of the indicators recommended in the literature is the OEE indicator. This parameter is very important when assessing the machines effectiveness and implementing the TPM method. As the research conducted shows, OEE indicator it is not always used (Stadnicka & Antosz 2015).

The results of conducted research indicated that many of the analyzed enterprises still do not use the OEE indicator (stage I - 60.38%, stage II - 73.96%). This indicator for all machines is used by only a few percent of enterprises (stage I - 7.55%, stage II - 5.21%). The second stage of the research showed that this indicator is not most often used in medium-sized enterprises (stage I - 7.55%, stage II - 5.21%). On the other hand, using in micro-enterprises increased significantly (stage I - 10.26%, stage II - 5.88%). Moreover, the obtained results show that this indicator is not most often used in enterprises where unit production (stage I - 29.49%, stage II - 29.41%) and medium batch production (stage I - 23.08%, stage II - 29.41%) is used. Its applicability in mass production increased significantly (stage I - 8.97%, stage II - 2.94%). The OEE indicator is not most often used in enterprises from the aviation, metalworking and automotive industries (Stadnicka & Antosz 2015). On the other hand, all food industry companies participating in the second stage of the research declared their use (Figure 10).

Figure 10. Percentage of enterprises not using the OEE indicator

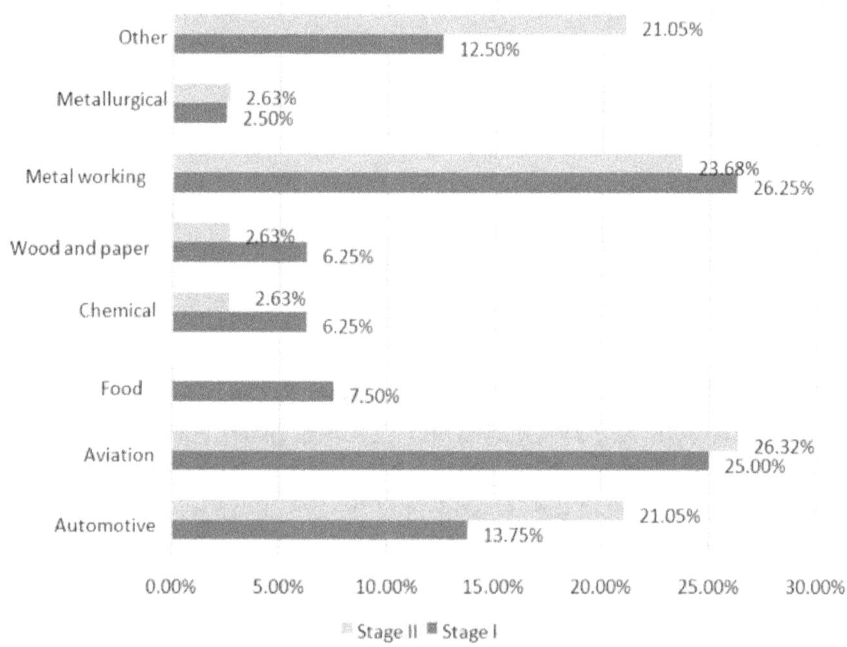

Another important issue in the area of the conducted research was to collect information on used indicators in enterprises, when the OEE indicator is not calculated. The survey questions concerned checking whether the machine quality, efficiency and availability indicator is being calculated and what Lean indicators for machines were additionally determined.

The quality indicator was defined as the number of conforming products to all products manufactured on the machine. Machine performance was defined as the number of products produced in relation to the number of products that could be produced on the machine in each time. The availability of the machine was considered as the actual working time in relation to the available working time at the position. Partial results of these studies for large enterprises are presented in the paper (Antosz & Stadnicka 2015).

Figure 11. Quality, performance, and availability index calculated in the surveyed enterprises

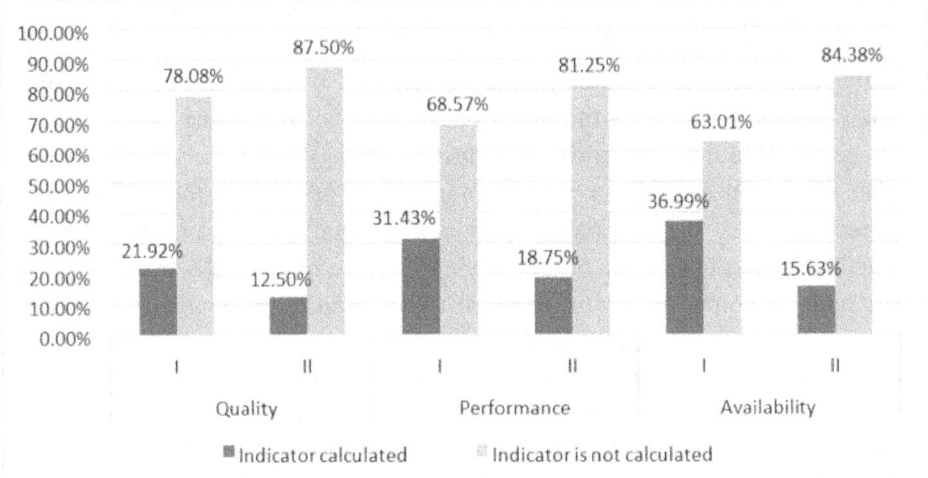

The obtained results indicate (Figure 11) that most companies do not calculate the quality, availability and performance indicators of machines.

Some of surveyed companies established additional Lean Maintenance implementation indicators, such as reducing the number of failures and increasing the degree of machine utilization (Figure 12).

BENEFITS OF IMPLEMENTING LEAN MAINTENANCE

Another important element of the conducted research was to obtain information about the types of benefits identified by enterprises after the implementation of Lean Maintenance tools. The research focused mainly on the benefits of implementing TPM, 5S.

The ongoing monitoring of the effects of TPM implementation is importance in assessing the effectiveness of TPM implementation in the enterprise. Many of the surveyed companies emphasize that the main effect is to reduce the number of unplanned downtime and breakdowns. Unplanned downtime is defined as any sudden shutdown of a machine from the production process. The most common cause of such a shutdown is a mechanical, electrical or electronic failure, which poses a risk to safety at the workplace and failure to maintain proper operating parameters. A failure was understood as any event reported in the failure book that required intervention (repair of a machine or device) by an employee of the maintenance services (Antosz & Stadnicka, 2015).

When analyzing the obtained results, it should be noted that in large enterprises, the implementation of TPM most often resulted in a reduction in the number of unplanned downtimes in the range of 10-30% - over 70% of the surveyed companies. In 5.88% of large enterprises, the reduction of unplanned downtime was over 50%. In most medium and small enterprises, a reduction of this indicator to 10% was noticed.

The effectiveness of TPM implementation looks similar in the analysis of the number of failures. In enterprises, the implementation of TPM most often resulted in a reduction in the number of failures in the range of 10-30% - over 50% of the surveyed large companies. Most medium-sized companies saw a reduction in this ratio to 10%. 100% of small companies participating in the second stage of the research declared a reduction in the number of failures by 100%.

Enterprises in the automotive industry most often indicated a reduction in the number of breakdowns by 10-30%. In 14.29% of the aviation industry enterprises in the second stage, the number of failures decreased by over 30% and by 50%. In metalworking, more and more companies recorded a reduction of this ratio below 10%. In other industries, the number of failures was set at 30-50%.

The greatest effects of using TPM in reducing the number of failures can be seen in enterprises with the majority of foreign capital.

One of the main elements of implementing the TPM method is the implementation of the 5S method. In the area of the research, information on the benefits obtained by enterprises was collected. All analyzed enterprises also noticed the benefits of implementing the 5S method. The most common benefits of implementing 5S are the improvement of work organization (stage I - 27.13%, stage II - 29.41%) and improvement of work safety (stage I - 18.18%, stage II - 33.33%). It is also important to shorten the duration of tasks (stage I - 16.92%, stage II - 14.29%) and improve the quality of production - reducing non-compliance (stage I - 12.31%, stage II - 11.76%).

The presented results indicate that large enterprises achieved the greatest benefits from the implementation of Lean Maintenance tools. In most of the analyzed areas, these benefits were greater than expected. The worst situation is in micro and small enterprises. In most of the analyzed areas, they did not achieve the expected benefits. For these companies, the same level of expected and achieved benefits is noticed only in the first stage of research in terms of increasing productivity and reducing the number of non-compliant products.

CONCLUSION

The main purpose of this work was to present the possibilities of improving the efficiency of maintenance by implementing the methods and tools of the Lean Maintenance concept. As part of the conducted research, the basic maintenance strategies in enterprises were analyzed and compared, as well as activities undertaken by enterprises as part of the implementation of selected methods and tools of the Lean Maintenance concept, and what results they achieve after their implementation.

Based on the research conducted in the enterprises and their results presented in this work, the following conclusions can be drawn. In enterprises, the PM strategy is most often used. This strategy applies to both numerical and conventional machines. The use of the CBM strategy for the types of machines owned is significantly decreasing.

Enterprises see the need to record machine data. Various types of information on machines are collected in the analyzed enterprises. Data is collected both at individual workstations, as well as on lines or production departments. The people most often responsible for collecting information are the maintenance worker, the master and the operator at the workplace. Moreover, all analyzed enterprises undertake actions aimed at minimizing unforeseen machine downtime. The presented results showed that in the case of large enterprises, the type of these activities practically did not change over several years. The analyzed enterprises identify various types of waste in the process of managing technical infrastructure. To eliminate them, more and more companies implement the Lean Maintenance philosophy. What's more, companies that have identified types of waste, such as machine failures, plan to implement or have implemented various Lean methods and tools related to the operation of machines and the improvement of the organization of workplaces. However, the number of enterprises implementing TPM is decreasing. Medium-sized enterprises most often give up the implementation of the TPM method. The results show that if a medium-sized enterprise decides to implement the TPM method, it only implements it on selected production lines. Small and large enterprises implement TPM mainly on selected machines.

The conducted research confirmed that most companies decided to implement TPM due to the high failure rate of machines. The most implemented TPM system is on all machines. Enterprises carry out various activities as part of the implementation of the TPM method. The presented results showed that in large enterprises the type of these activities practically did not change. Medium-sized enterprises slightly intensified their activities in the scope of developing a repair schedule and training selected employees. The situation in the case of small and micro enterprises has changed significantly.

In enterprises, many employees in various positions are involved in the process of implementing TPM. Additionally, the number of enterprises categorizing machines and categorizing spare parts is decreasing. The most common problems that arose during the implementation of TPM were the lack of competent people to remove irregularities on the machines and the lack of top management involvement in activities related to TPM.

Enterprises are more and more willing to implement the 5S method. However, more companies declare that they have implemented 5S throughout the enterprise. They notice the benefits of implementing this method and assess its effectiveness mainly by 5S audits. Most of the analyzed enterprises still do not use the OEE indicator. This indicator is not most used in medium-sized enterprises. However, it is most often used in enterprises where unit production is carried out, as well as in enterprises from the aviation, metalworking and automotive industries.

In most companies, the employment level of maintenance services has not changed significantly due to the implementation of Lean Maintenance. Only in large enterprises and mostly with numerical machines the employment level of maintenance department employees decreased. Finally, large enterprises achieved the greatest benefits from the implementation of Lean Maintenance tools.

The subject of the further research will be the analysis: how the industry 4.0 technologies have influence in changing the direction of implementation of Lean Maintenance and predictive maintenance in production companies.

REFERENCES

Antosz, K., Jasiulewicz-Kaczmarek, M., Paśko, Ł., Zhang, C., & Wang, S. (2021). Application of machine learning and rough set theory in lean maintenance decision support system development. *Eksploatacja i Niezawodnosc - Maintenance and Reliability, 23*(4), 695-708. doi:10.17531/ein.2021.4.12

Antosz, K., Pasko, L., & Gola, A. (2020). The use of artificial intelligence methods to assess the effectiveness of lean maintenance concept implementation in manufacturing enterprises. *Applied Sciences (Basel, Switzerland), 10*(21), 7922. doi:10.3390/app10217922

Antosz, K., & Ratnayake, R. M. C. (2016). Classification of spare parts as the element of a proper realization of the machine maintenance process and logistics - case study. *IFAC-PapersOnLine, 49*(12), 1389–1393. doi:10.1016/j.ifacol.2016.07.760

Antosz K. & Stadnicka D. (2015). Evaluation measures of machine operation effectiveness in large enterprises: study results. *Eksploatacja i Niezawodność - Maintenance and Reliability, 17*(1), 107-117. doi:10.17531/ein.2015.1.15

Arlinghaus, J. C., & Knizkov, S. (2020). Lean Maintenance and Repair Implementation-A Cross-Case Study of Seven Automotive Service Suppliers. *Procedia CIRP, 93*, 955–964. doi:10.1016/j.procir.2020.03.144

Bakri, A., Alkbir, M. F. M., Awang, N., Januddi, F., Ismail, M. A., Ahmad, A. N. A., & Zakaria, I. H. (2021). Addressing the issues of maintenance management in SMEs: Towards sustainable and lean maintenance approach. *Emerging Science Journal, 5*(3), 367–379. doi:10.28991/esj-2021-01283

Ball, P., & Lunt, P. (2020). Lean eco-efficient innovation in operations through the maintenance organisation. *International Journal of Production Economics, 219*, 405–415. doi:10.1016/j.ijpe.2018.07.007

Bataineh, O., Al-Hawari, T., Alshraideh, H., & Dalalah, D. (2019). A sequential TPM-based scheme for improving production effectiveness presented with a case study. *Journal of Quality in Maintenance Engineering, 25*(1), 144–161. doi:10.1108/JQME-07-2017-0045

Bošnjaković, M. (2010). Multicriteria inventory model for spare parts. *Tehnicki vjesnik-Technical Gazette, 17*(4), 499-504. https://hrcak.srce.hr/62926

Chaabane, K., Schutz, J., Dellagi, S., & Trabelsi, W. (2021). Analytical evaluation of TPM performance based on an economic criterion. *Journal of Quality in Maintenance Engineering, 27*(2), 413–429. doi:10.1108/JQME-08-2019-0085

de Jong, S. J., & Beelaerts van Blokland, W. W. A. (2016). Measuring lean implementation for maintenance service companies. *International Journal of Lean Six Sigma, 7*(1), 35–61. doi:10.1108/IJLSS-12-2014-0039

Duarte, A. L. C. M., & Santiago Scarpin, M. R. S. (2022). Maintenance practices and overall equipment effectiveness: Testing the moderating effect of training. *Journal of Quality in Maintenance Engineering*. Advance online publication. doi:10.1108/JQME-04-2021-0033

Duran, O., Capaldo, A., & Duran Acevedo, P. A. (2017). Lean maintenance applied to improve maintenance efficiency in thermoelectric power plants. *Energies, 10*(10), 1653. doi:10.3390/en10101653

EN 13306:2018 Maintenance - Maintenance terminology

Gelei, A., Losonci, D., & Matyusz, Z. (2015). Lean production and leadership attributes: The case of Hungarian production managers. *Journal of Manufacturing Technology Management*, *26*(4), 477–500. doi:10.1108/JMTM-05-2013-0059

Gopalakrishnan, M., & Skoogh, A. (2018). Machine criticality based maintenance prioritization: Identifying productivity improvement potential. *International Journal of Productivity and Performance Management*, *67*(4), 654–672. doi:10.1108/IJPPM-07-2017-0168

Guizzi, G., Gallo, M., & Zoppoli, P. (2009). Condition based maintenance: Simulation and optimization. *Proceedings of the 8th WSEAS International Conference on System Science and Simulation in Engineering, ICOSSSE'09*, 319-325. https://dl.acm.org/doi/abs/10.5555/1938841.1938902

Gupta, K. (2022). A review on implementation of 5S for workplace management. *Journal of Applied Research on Industrial Engineering*, *9*(3), 323–330. doi:10.22105/jarie.2021.292741.1347

Habidin, N. F., Hashim, S., Fuzi, N. M., & Salleh, M. I. (2018). Total productive maintenance, kaizen event and performance. *International Journal of Quality & Reliability Management*, *35*(9), 1853–1867. doi:10.1108/IJQRM-11-2017-0234

Hassan, M. N., Barakat, A. F., & Sobh, A. S. (2020). Effect of applying lean maintenance in oil and gas fields. *IOP Conference Series. Materials Science and Engineering*, *973*(1), 012045. doi:10.1088/1757-899X/973/1/012045

Hooi, L. W., & Leong, T. Y. (2017). Total productive maintenance and manufacturing performance improvement. *Journal of Quality in Maintenance Engineering*, *23*(1), 2–21. doi:10.1108/JQME-07-2015-0033

Jasiulewicz-Kaczmarek, M. (2015). Practical aspects of the application of RCM to select optimal maintenance policy of the production line. *Safety and Reliability: Methodology and Applications-Proceedings of the European Safety and Reliability Conference, ESREL*, 1187-1195. https://sin.put.poznan.pl/publications/details/n5762

Jasiulewicz-Kaczmarek, M., & Saniuk, A. (2017). How to make maintenance processes more efficient using lean tools? In R. Goossens (Ed.), *Advances in Social & Occupational Ergonomics. AHFE 2017. Advances in Intelligent Systems and Computing*. doi:10.1007/978-3-319-60828-0_2

Khalfallah, M., & Lakhal, L. (2021). The impact of lean manufacturing practices on operational and financial performance: The mediating role of agile manufacturing. *International Journal of Quality & Reliability Management*, *38*(1), 147–168. doi:10.1108/IJQRM-07-2019-0244

Kose, Y., Muftuoglu, S., Cevikcan, E., & Durmusoglu, M. B. (2022). Axiomatic design for lean autonomous maintenance system: An application from textile industry. *International Journal of Lean Six Sigma*. Advance online publication. doi:10.1108/IJLSS-01-2022-0020

Lai, N. Y. G., Wong, K. H., Halim, D., Lu, J., & Kang, H. S. (2019). *Industry 4.0 enhanced lean manufacturing. In 2019 8th international conference on Industrial technology and management (ICITM).* IEEE. https://ieeexplore.ieee.org/stamp/stamp.jsp?arnumber=8710669

Makwana, A. D., & Patange, G. S. (2022). Strategic implementation of 5S and its effect on productivity of plastic machinery manufacturing company. *Australian Journal of Mechanical Engineering*, *20*(1), 111–120. doi:10.1080/14484846.2019.1676112

Márquez, A., Moreu de León, P., Gómez Fernández, J. F., Parra Márquez, C., & López Campos, M. (2009). The maintenance management framework: A practical view to maintenance management. *Journal of Quality in Maintenance Engineering*, *15*(2), 167–178. doi:10.1108/13552510910961110

Marttonen-Arola, S., Baglee, D., Kinnunen, S. K., & Holgado, M. (2020). Introducing Lean into Maintenance Data Management: A Decision Making Approach. In J. Liyanage, J. Amadi-Echendu, & J. Mathew (Eds.), *Engineering Assets and Public Infrastructures in the Age of Digitalization. Lecture Notes in Mechanical Engineering*. Springer. doi:10.1007/978-3-030-48021-9_28

Maware, C., Okwu, M. O., & Adetunji, O. (2022). A systematic literature review of lean manufacturing implementation in manufacturing-based sectors of the developing and developed countries. *International Journal of Lean Six Sigma*, *13*(3), 521–556. doi:10.1108/IJLSS-12-2020-0223

Mkaka, A., & Burduk, A. (2022). Implementation of the integrated lean six sigma philosophy in an Angolan manufacturing company–a case study. *Technologia i Automatyzacja Montażu*, *2*, 58–66. doi:10.7862/tiam.2022.1.6

Mostafa, S., Lee, S. H., Dumrak, J., Chileshe, N., & Soltan, H. (2015). Lean thinking for a maintenance process. *Production & Manufacturing Research*, *3*(1), 236–272. doi:10.1080/21693277.2015.1074124

Nakajima, S. (1988). *Introduction to TPM*. Productivity Press.

Nawaiseh, A. L. K., Alawamleh, H., Al Shibly, M., & Almari, M. (2022). The Relationship Between the Enterprise Resource Planning System and Maintenance Planning System: An Empirical Study. *Information Sciences Letters*, *11*(5), 2. https://digitalcommons.aaru.edu.jo/isl/vol11/iss5/2

Patel, B. S., Sambasivan, M., Panimalar, R., & Hari Krishna, R. (2021). A relational analysis of drivers and barriers of lean manufacturing. *The TQM Journal*. Advance online publication. doi:10.1108/TQM-12-2020-0296

Pinto, G. F. L., Silva, F. J. G., Campilho, R. D. S. G., Casais, R. B., Fernandes, A. J., & Baptista, A. (2019). Continuous improvement in maintenance: A case study in the automotive industry involving Lean tools. *Procedia Manufacturing*, *38*, 1582–1591. doi:10.1016/j.promfg.2020.01.127

Pombal, T., Ferreira, L. P., Sá, J. C., Pereira, M. T., & Silva, F. J. G. (2019). Implementation of lean methodologies in the management of consumable materials in the maintenance workshops of an industrial company. *Procedia Manufacturing*, *38*, 975–982. doi:10.1016/j.promfg.2020.01.181

Randhawa, J. S., & Ahuja, I. S. (2018). Empirical investigation of contributions of 5S practice for realizing improved competitive dimensions. *International Journal of Quality & Reliability Management*, *35*(3), 779–810. doi:10.1108/IJQRM-09-2016-0163

Ribeiro, I., Godina, R., Pimentel, C., Silva, F., & Matias, J. (2019). Implementing TPM supported by 5S to improve the availability of an automotive production line. *Procedia Manufacturing*, *38*, 1574–1581. doi:10.1016/j.promfg.2020.01.128

Schindlerová, V., Šajdlerová, I., Michalčík, V., Nevima, J., & Krejčí, L. (2020). Potential of using TPM to increase the efficiency of production processes. *Tehnicki Vjesnik (Strojarski Fakultet)*, *27*(3), 737–743. doi:10.17559/TV-20190328130749

Shou, W., Wang, J., Wu, P., & Wang, X. (2020). Value adding and non-value adding activities in turnaround maintenance process: Classification, validation, and benefits. *Production Planning and Control*, *31*(1), 60–77. doi:10.1080/09537287.2019.1629038

Singh, J., & Singh, H. (2020). Justification of TPM pillars for enhancing the performance of manufacturing industry of Northern India. *International Journal of Productivity and Performance Management*, *69*(1), 109–133. doi:10.1108/IJPPM-06-2018-0211

Singh, J., Singh, H., & Sharma, V. (2018). Success of TPM concept in a manufacturing unit–a case study. *International Journal of Productivity and Performance Management*, *67*(3), 536–549. doi:10.1108/IJPPM-01-2017-0003

Singha Mahapatra, M., & Shenoy, D. (2022). Lean maintenance index: A measure of leanness in maintenance organizations. *Journal of Quality in Maintenance Engineering*, *28*(4), 791–809. doi:10.1108/JQME-08-2020-0083

Smith, R. (2004). What is Lean maintenance? Elements that need to be in place for success. *Maintenance Technology Magazine*. Available at: www.mt-online.com/article/1004smith

Smith, R., & Hawkins, B. (2004). *Lean maintenance; reduce cost improve quality and increase market share*. Elsevier Butterworth-Heinemann.

Tortorella, G. L., Fogliatto, F. S., Cauchick-Miguel, P. A., Kurnia, S., & Jurburg, D. (2021). Integration of Industry 4.0 technologies into total productive maintenance practices. *International Journal of Production Economics*, *240*, 108224. doi:10.1016/j.ijpe.2021.108224

Vaz, E., De Sá, J. C. V., Santos, G., Correia, F., & Ávila, P. (2021). The value of TPM for Portuguese companies. *Journal of Quality in Maintenance Engineering*. Advance online publication. doi:10.1108/JQME-12-2020-0121

Velmurugan, R. S., & Dhingra, T. (2015). Maintenance Strategy Selection and its Impact in Maintenance Function: A Conceptual Framework. *International Journal of Operations & Production Management*, *35*(12), 1622–1661. doi:10.1108/IJOPM-01-2014-0028

Womack, J., & Jones, D. (2003). *Lean Thinking: banish waste and create wealth in your corporation*. Simon & Schuster Inc.

Xiang, Z. T., & Chin, J. F. (2021). Implementing total productive maintenance in a manufacturing small or medium-sized enterprise. *Journal of Industrial Engineering and Management*, *14*(2), 152–175. doi:10.3926/jiem.3286

Yadav, G., Luthra, S., Huisingh, D., Mangla, S. K., Narkhede, B. E., & Liu, Y. (2020). Development of a lean manufacturing framework to enhance its adoption within manufacturing companies in developing economies. *Journal of Cleaner Production*, *245*, 118726. doi:10.1016/j.jclepro.2019.118726

Compilation of References

Chen, T., & Lin, Y. C. (2017). Feasibility evaluation and optimization of a smart manufacturing system based on 3D printing: A review. *International Journal of Intelligent Systems, 32*(4), 394–413. doi:10.1002/int.21866

Cooney, R. (2002). Is "lean" a universal production system? Batch production in the automotive industry. *International Journal of Operations & Production Management, 22*(10), 1130–1147. doi:10.1108/01443570210446342

Deif, A. M. (2011). A system model for green manufacturing. *Journal of Cleaner Production, 19*(14), 1553–1559. doi:10.1016/j.jclepro.2011.05.022

Durakbasa, N. M., Bauer, J. M., Bas, G., & Kräuter, L. (2016). Novel Trends in the Development of Autonomation and Robotics in Metrology for Production in the Future. *IFAC-PapersOnLine, 49*(29), 6–11. doi:10.1016/j.ifacol.2016.11.057

El Jaouhari, A., Arif, J., Fellaki, S., Amejwal, M., & Azzouz, K. (2022). Lean supply chain management and Industry 4.0 interrelationships: the status quo and future perspectives. *International Journal of Lean Six Sigma*, ahead-of-print.

Fercoq, A., Lamouri, S., Carbone, V., Lelièvre, A., & Lemieux, A. A. (2013). Combining lean and green in manufacturing: a model of waste management. *IFAC Proceedings Volumes, 46*(9), 117-122. 10.3182/20130619-3-RU-3018.00164

Ferro, R., Ordóñez, R. E. C., & Anholon, R. (2017). Analysis of the integration between operations management manufacturing tools with discrete event simulation. *Production Engineering, 11*(4), 467–476. doi:10.100711740-017-0755-2

Groger, C., Kassner, L., Hoos, E., Konigsberger, J., Kiefer, C., Silcher, S., & Mitschang, B. (2016). The data-driven factory. *ICEIS, 2016*, 40.

Hallam, C. R., & Contreras, C. (2016, September). The interrelation of Lean and green manufacturing Practices: A case of push or pull in implementation. In *2016 Portland International Conference on Management of Engineering and Technology (PICMET)* (pp. 1815-1823). IEEE. 10.1109/PICMET.2016.7806669

Helu, M., & Dornfeld, D. (2013). Principles of green manufacturing. In *Green Manufacturing* (pp. 107–115). Springer. doi:10.1007/978-1-4419-6016-0_5

Abualfaraa, W., Salonitis, K., Al-Ashaab, A., & Ala'raj, M. (2020). Lean-green manufacturing practices and their link with sustainability: A critical review. *Sustainability, 12*(3), 981. doi:10.3390u12030981

Kim, S. J., & Kara, S. (2012). Impact of technology on product life cycle design: Functional and environmental perspective. In *Leveraging Technology for a Sustainable World* (pp. 191–196). Springer. doi:10.1007/978-3-642-29069-5_33

Khanchanapong, T., Prajogo, D., Sohal, A. S., Cooper, B. K., Yeung, A. C., & Cheng, T. C. E. (2014). The unique and complementary effects of manufacturing technologies and lean practices on manufacturing operational performance. *International Journal of Production Economics, 153*, 191–203. doi:10.1016/j.ijpe.2014.02.021

Kolla, S., Minufekr, M., & Plapper, P. (2019). Deriving essential components of lean and industry 4.0 assessment model for manufacturing SMEs. *Procedia CIRP, 81*, 753–758. doi:10.1016/j.procir.2019.03.189

Leong, W. D., Lam, H. L., Ng, W. P. Q., Lim, C. H., Tan, C. P., & Ponnambalam, S. G. (2019). Lean and green manufacturing—a review on its applications and impacts. *Process Integration and Optimization for Sustainability, 3*(1), 5-23.

Lucantoni, L., Antomarioni, S., Ciarapica, F. E., & Bevilacqua, M. (2022). Implementation of Industry 4.0 Techniques in Lean Production Technology: A Literature Review. *Management and Production Engineering Review.*

Mrugalska, B., & Wyrwicka, M. K. (2017). Towards lean production in industry 4.0. *Procedia Engineering, 182*, 466–473. doi:10.1016/j.proeng.2017.03.135

Netland, T. H. (2016). Critical success factors for implementing lean production: The effect of contingencies. *International Journal of Production Research, 54*(8), 2433–2448. doi:10.1080/00207543.2015.1096976

Nishal, M., Prasad, K. R., Balaji, T. K., & Kalaivanan, K. (2021). Retrofit of two way holding chuck to improve process efficiency and resource management. *Materials Today: Proceedings, 46*, 9697–9701. doi:10.1016/j.matpr.2020.08.024 PMID:33014714

Anastas, P. T., & Zimmerman, J. B. (2003). *Peer reviewed: Design through the 12 principles of green engineering*. Academic Press.

Ojha, R. (2022). Lean in industry 4.0 is accelerating manufacturing excellence–A DEMATEL analysis. *The TQM Journal.* Advance online publication. doi:10.1108/TQM-11-2021-0318

Rauch, E., Dallasega, P., & Matt, D. T. (2016). Sustainable production in emerging markets through Distributed Manufacturing Systems (DMS). *Journal of Cleaner Production, 135*, 127–138. doi:10.1016/j.jclepro.2016.06.106

Shrouf, F., Ordieres, J., & Miragliotta, G. (2014, December). Smart factories in Industry 4.0: A review of the concept and of energy management approached in production based on the Internet of Things paradigm. In *2014 IEEE international conference on industrial engineering and engineering management* (pp. 697-701). IEEE.

Silvestri, L., Gallo, T., Silvestri, C., & Falcone, D. (2022, March). Integration of Lean Manufacturing in Industry 4.0: An overview of tools and applications. In *2022 2nd International Conference on Innovative Research in Applied Science, Engineering and Technology (IRASET)* (pp. 1-5). IEEE.

Skalli, D., Charkaoui, A., & Cherrafi, A. (2022). The Integration of Industry 4.0 in Operations Management: *Toward Smart Lean Six Sigma. In International Conference on Digital Technologies and Applications* (pp. 3-11). Springer.

Sommer, L. (2015). Industrial revolution-industry 4.0: Are German manufacturing SMEs the first victims of this revolution? *Journal of Industrial Engineering and Management*, *8*(5), 1512–1532. doi:10.3926/jiem.1470

Sony, M. (2018). Industry 4.0 and lean management: A proposed integration model and research propositions. *Production & Manufacturing Research*, *6*(1), 416–432. doi:10.1080/21693277.2018.1540949

Testi, D. (2019). *A statistical research on the impact of lean and industry 4.0 on companies in northern Italy*. Academic Press.

Vogel-Heuser, B., Bauernhansl, T., & Ten Hompel, M. (2017). Handbuch Industrie 4.0 Bd. 4. *Allgemeine Grundlagen, 2*.

Bai, C., Orzes, G., & Sarkis, J. (2022). Exploring the impact of Industry 4.0 technologies on social sustainability through a circular economy approach. *Industrial Marketing Management*, *101*, 176–190. doi:10.1016/j.indmarman.2021.12.004

Wagner, T., Herrmann, C., & Thiede, S. (2017). Industry 4.0 impacts on lean production systems. *Procedia CIRP*, *63*, 125–131. doi:10.1016/j.procir.2017.02.041

Walton, S. V., Handfield, R. B., & Melnyk, S. A. (1998). The green supply chain: integrating suppliers into environmental management processes. *International Journal of Purchasing and Materials Management, 34*(1), 2-11.

Womack, J. P., & Jones, D. T. (1997). Lean thinking—Banish waste and create wealth in your corporation. *The Journal of the Operational Research Society*, *48*(11), 1148–1148. doi:10.1057/palgrave.jors.2600967

Wyrwicka, M., & Mrugalska, B. (2015, September). Barriers to eliminating waste in production system. In *Proceedings of the 6th international conference on engineering, project, and production management* (pp. 354-363). 10.32738/CEPPM.201509.0035

Bauer, H., Brandl, F., Lock, C., & Reinhart, G. (2018). Integration of Industrie 4.0 in lean manufacturing learning factories. *Procedia Manufacturing*, *23*, 147–152. doi:10.1016/j.promfg.2018.04.008

Bauters, K., Cottyn, J., Claeys, D., Slembrouck, M., Veelaert, P., & Van Landeghem, H. (2018). Automated work cycle classification and performance measurement for manual work stations. *Robotics and Computer-integrated Manufacturing*, *51*, 139–157. doi:10.1016/j.rcim.2017.12.001

Bonilla, S. H., Silva, H. R., Terra da Silva, M., Franco Gonçalves, R., & Sacomano, J. B. (2018). Industry 4.0 and sustainability implications: A scenario-based analysis of the impacts and challenges. *Sustainability*, *10*(10), 3740. doi:10.3390u10103740

Bortolini, M., Ferrari, E., Galizia, F. G., & Mora, C. (2016). A reference framework integrating lean and green principles within supply chain management. International Journal of Social, Behavioral, Educational, Economic. *Business and Industrial Engineering*, *10*(3), 859–864.

Cardinali, P. G., & De Giovanni, P. (2022). Responsible digitalization through digital technologies and green practices. *Corporate Social Responsibility and Environmental Management*, *29*(4), 984–995. doi:10.1002/csr.2249

Carvalho, H., & Cruz-Machado, V. (2011). Integrating lean, agile, resilience and green paradigms in supply chain management (LARG_SCM). *Supply Chain Management*, 27–48.

Abideen, A., & Mohamad, F. (2020). Improving the performance of a Malaysian pharmaceutical warehouse supply chain by integrating value stream mapping and discrete event simulation. *Journal of Modelling in Management*. doi:10.1108/JM2-07-2019-0159

Afum, E., Li, Y., Han, P., & Sun, Z. (2022). Interplay between lean management and circular production system: Implications for zero-waste performance, green value competitiveness, and social reputation. *Journal of Manufacturing Technology Management*, *33*(7), 1213–1231. doi:10.1108/JMTM-01-2022-0038

Aggarwal, R.N. (1988, October-December). Indian Automobile Industry: Problems and Prospects. *The Indian Economic Journal*, *36*(2).

Akbulut, U. (2011). *Sanayi Devrimleri Dünya Gidişini Değiştirdi.* www.uralakbulut.com.tr

Akmal, A., Greatbanks, R., & Foote, J. (2020, June 1). Lean thinking in healthcare – Findings from a systematic literature network and bibliometric analysis. *Health Policy (Amsterdam)*, *124*(6), 615–627. doi:10.1016/j.healthpol.2020.04.008 PMID:32456781

Akpulat, F. (2019). *Sürdürülebilirlik kavramına farklı yaklaşımlar: Üniversite öğrencileri üzerine bir araştırma*. İstanbul Üniversitesi Sosyal Bilimler Enstitüsü.

Alahyari, H., Gorschek, T., & Svensson, R. B. (2019). An exploratory study of waste in software development organizations using agile or lean approaches: A multiple case study at 14 organizations. *Information and Software Technology*, *105*, 78–94. doi:10.1016/j.infsof.2018.08.006

Al-Balushi, S., Sohal, A. S., Singh, P. J., Al Hajri, A., Farsi, Y. M. A., & Al Abri, R. (2014). Readiness factors for lean implementation in healthcare settings - a literature review. *Journal of Health Organization and Management*, *28*(2), 135–153. doi:10.1108/JHOM-04-2013-0083 PMID:25065107

Altarazi, S. A., & Ammouri, M. M. (2018). Concurrent manual-order-picking warehouse design: A simulation-based design of experiments approach. *International Journal of Production Research, 56*(23), 7103–7121. doi:10.1080/00207543.2017.1421780

Andjelkovic, A., Radosavljevic, M., & Stošić Panić, D. (2017). Effects of Lean Tools in Achieving Lean Warehousing. *Economic Themes, 54*(4), 517–534. doi:10.1515/ethemes-2016-0026

Antony, J., Palsuk, P., Gupta, S., Mishra, D., & Barach, P. (2018). Six Sigma in healthcare: A systematic review of the literature. *International Journal of Quality & Reliability Management, 35*(5), 1075–1092. doi:10.1108/IJQRM-02-2017-0027

Antony, J., Sunder, M. V., Sreedharan, R., Chakraborty, A., & Gunasekaran, A. (2019, August 30). A systematic review of Lean in healthcare: A global prospective. *International Journal of Quality & Reliability Management, 36*(8), 1370–1391. doi:10.1108/IJQRM-12-2018-0346

Antosz K. & Stadnicka D. (2015). Evaluation measures of machine operation effectiveness in large enterprises: study results. *Eksploatacja i Niezawodność - Maintenance and Reliability, 17*(1), 107-117. doi:10.17531/ein.2015.1.15

Antosz, K., Jasiulewicz-Kaczmarek, M., Paśko, Ł., Zhang, C., & Wang, S. (2021). Application of machine learning and rough set theory in lean maintenance decision support system development. *Eksploatacja i Niezawodnosc – Maintenance and Reliability, 23*(4), 695–708, . doi:10.17531/ein.2021.4.12

Antosz, K., Augustyn, A., & Kaczmarek, M. J. (2021). Application of VSM for Improving the Medical Processes-Case Study. In *IFIP International Conference on Advances in Production Management Systems* (pp. 413-421). Springer. 10.1007/978-3-030-85902-2_44

Antosz, K., Pasko, L., & Gola, A. (2020). The use of artificial intelligence methods to assess the effectiveness of lean maintenance concept implementation in manufacturing enterprises. *Applied Sciences (Basel, Switzerland), 10*(21), 7922. doi:10.3390/app10217922

Antosz, K., & Ratnayake, R. M. C. (2016). Classification of spare parts as the element of a proper realization of the machine maintenance process and logistics - case study. *IFAC-PapersOnLine, 49*(12), 1389–1393. doi:10.1016/j.ifacol.2016.07.760

Ardito, L., Petruzzelli, A. M., Panniello, U., & Garavelli, A. C. (2018). Towards Industry 4.0: Mapping digital technologies for supply chain management-marketing integration. *Business Process Management Journal.*

Arlinghaus, J. C., & Knizkov, S. (2020). Lean Maintenance and Repair Implementation-A Cross-Case Study of Seven Automotive Service Suppliers. *Procedia CIRP, 93*, 955–964. doi:10.1016/j.procir.2020.03.144

AUTOSAR (2017). AUTOSAR Layered Software Architecture. *Autosar*, vol. *4*, 163.

AUTOSAR (2017). Virtual Functional Bus. Autosar.

AUTOSAR (2019). Specification of ECU State Manager. Autosar.

AUTOSAR (2020). Requirements on PWM Driver. Autosar.

AUTOSAR. (2016). *Specification of PWM Driver.*

AUTOSAR. (2017). *General Requirements on Methodology and Templates.* Autosar.

AUTOSAR. (2017). *Requirements on MCU Driver.* Autosar.

AUTOSAR. (2017). *Requirements on Port Driver.* Autosar.

AUTOSAR. (2017). *Specification of ADC Driver.* Autosar.

AUTOSAR. (2017). *Specification of DIO Driver.* Autosar.

AUTOSAR. (2017). Specification of Operating System. *System.*

AUTOSAR. (2018). Requirements of I / O Hardware Abstraction, pp. 1–29. Autosar.

AUTOSAR. (2018). Requirements on Operating System. *System.*

AUTOSAR. (2018). *Specification of Port Driver.* Autosar.

Awad, M. M., Hashem, A., & Naguib, H. M. (2022). The Impact of Lean Management Practices on Economic Sustainability in Services Sector. *Sustainability (Switzerland), 14*(15), 9323. Advance online publication. doi:10.3390u14159323

Azadeh, K., De Koster, R., & Roy, D. (2019). Robotized and Automated Warehouse Systems: Review and Recent Developments. *Transportation Science, 53*(4), 917–945. doi:10.1287/trsc.2018.0873

Azevedo, J., Sá, J.C., Ferreira, L.P., Santos, G., Cruz, F.M., Jimenez, G., & Silva, F.J.G. (2019). Improvement of Production Line in the Automotive Industry Through Lean Philosophy. *Procedia Manufacturing, 41.* doi:. doi:1023-1030

Baby, B. N. P., & Jebadurai, D. (2018). Implementation of Lean Principles to Improve the Operations of a Sales Warehouse in the Manufacturing Industry. *International Journal of Technology, 9*(1), 46. doi:10.14716/ijtech.v9i1.1161

Bahrin, M.A.K., Othman, M.F., Azli, N.H.N., & Talib, M.F. (2016). Industry 4.0: a review on industrial automation and robotic. *Jurnal Teknologi, 78*(6–13), 137–143.

Bahrin, M. A. K., Othman, M. F., Azli, N. H. N., & Talib, M. F. (2016). Industry 4.0: A review on industrial automation and robotic. *Jurnal Teknologi, 78*, 6–13.

Bakri, A., Alkbir, M. F. M., Awang, N., Januddi, F., Ismail, M. A., Ahmad, A. N. A., & Zakaria, I. H. (2021). Addressing the issues of maintenance management in SMEs: Towards sustainable and lean maintenance approach. *Emerging Science Journal, 5*(3), 367–379. doi:10.28991/esj-2021-01283

Bala, A., Muñoz, P., Rieradevall, J., & Ysern, P. (2008). Experiences with greening suppliers. The Universidad Autònoma de Barcelona. *Journal of Cleaner Production, 16*(15), 1610–1619. doi:10.1016/j.jclepro.2008.04.015

Ballou, R. (2006). *Gerenciamento da cadeia de suprimentos/logística empresarial*. Editora Bookman.

Ball, P., & Lunt, P. (2020). Lean eco-efficient innovation in operations through the maintenance organisation. *International Journal of Production Economics*, *219*, 405–415. doi:10.1016/j.ijpe.2018.07.007

Balon, V., Sharma, A. K., & Barua, M. K.Author. (2016). Assessment of Barriers in Green Supply Chain Management Using ISM: A Case Study of the Automobile Industry in India. *Global Business Review*, *17*(1), 116–135. doi:10.1177/0972150915610701

Bandyopadhyay, A., & Bose, S. (Eds.). (2019). *Additive manufacturing*. CRC Press. doi:10.1201/9780429466236

Baril, C., Gascon, V., Miller, J., & Côté, N. (2015). Use of a discrete-event simulation model during a Lean process: A case study in healthcare. *European Journal of Operational Research*, *249*. Advance online publication. doi:10.1016/j.ejor.2015.08.036

Barnett, M. W. (2003). *Modeling & simulation in business process management, 10*.

Bataineh, O., Al-Hawari, T., Alshraideh, H., & Dalalah, D. (2019). A sequential TPM-based scheme for improving production effectiveness presented with a case study. *Journal of Quality in Maintenance Engineering*, *25*(1), 144–161. doi:10.1108/JQME-07-2017-0045

Bayar, M. (2020). *Yalın Yönetim Anlayışının, Çalışanların Görev Performansına Etkilerine Yönelik Bir Araştırma, İşletme Araştırmaları Dergisi*, *12*(2), 1984–2001.

Bechtsis, D., Tsolakis, N., Vlachos, D., & Iakovou, E. (2017). Sustainable supply chain management in the digitalisation era: The impact of Automated Guided Vehicles. *Journal of Cleaner Production*, *142*, 3970–3984. doi:10.1016/j.jclepro.2016.10.057

Belis-Bergouignan, M.C., Bordenave., G., & Lung, Y. (2000). Global Strategies in the Automobile Industry. *Regional Studies*, *34*(1), 41–53. doi:10.1080/00343400050005871

Ben-Daya, M., Hassini, E., & Bahroun, Z. (2019). Internet of things and supply chain management: A literature review. *International Journal of Production Research*, *57*(15–16), 4719–4742. doi:10.1080/00207543.2017.1402140

Bertagnolli, F. (2018). *Lean management*. Springer. doi:10.1007/978-3-658-13124-1

Bertozzi, M., Broggi, A., Coati, A., & Fedriga, R. I. (2013). A 13,000 km Intercontinental Trip with Driverless Vehicles: The VIAC Experiment. *Intelligent Transportation Systems Magazine*, *5*(1), 28–41. doi:10.1109/MITS.2012.2225651

Beynon, H. (1984). *Working for Ford* (2nd ed.). Penguin.

Beynon, H., & Nichols, T. (2006). *The Fordism of Ford and Modern Management*. Edward Elgar Publishing.

Bhattacharyya, A., Ghosh, D., & Majumder, A. (2021). A Threadbare Analysis on the State of Affairs of Indian Automobile Sector in the Aftermath of Present Recessional Trend and Its Remedy, Pal, M.K. (Ed.) Productivity Growth in the Manufacturing Sector, 253-267. Emerald Publishing Limited. doi:10.1108/978-1-80071-094-820211019

Bilgili, M. Y. (2017). Ekonomik, Ekolojik Ve Sosyal Boyutlarıyla Sürdürülebilir Kalkınma. *Uluslararası Sosyal Araştırmalar Dergisi, 10*, 559–569.

Birmingham, F., & Jelinek, J. (2007). *Quick Changeover Simplified: The Manager's Guide to Improving Profits with SMED*. CRC Press.

Blunck, E., & Werthmann, H. (2017, October). Industry 4.0–an opportunity to realize sustainable manufacturing and its potential for a circular economy. *DIEM: Dubrovnik International Economic Meeting, 3*(1), 644-666.

Bokrantz, J., Skoogh, A., Lämkull, D., Hanna, A., & Perera, T. (2017). Data Quality Problems in Discrete Event Simulation of Manufacturing Operations. W *SIMULATION* (T. 94). doi:10.1177/0037549717742954

Bolcato, M., Rodriguez, D., & Aprile, A. (2022). Guiding Principles for Surgical Pathways: A Tool for Improving Outcomes and Patient Safety. *Frontiers in Public Health, 10*, 869607. Advance online publication. doi:10.3389/fpubh.2022.869607 PMID:35462846

Bonabeau, E. (2002). Agent-based modeling: Methods and techniques for simulating human systems. *Proceedings of the National Academy of Sciences of the United States of America, 99*(Supplement 3), 7280–7287. doi:10.1073/pnas.082080899 PMID:12011407

Borges, G. A., Tortorella, G., Rossini, M., & Portioli-Staudacher, A. (2019, May 24). Lean implementation in healthcare supply chain: A scoping review. *Journal of Health Organization and Management, 33*(3), 304–322. doi:10.1108/JHOM-06-2018-0176 PMID:31122116

Bošnjaković, M. (2010). Multicriteria inventory model for spare parts. *Tehnicki vjesnik-Technical Gazette, 17*(4), 499-504. https://hrcak.srce.hr/62926

Bozer, Y., & Aldarondo, F. (2018). A simulation-based comparison of two goods-to-person order picking systems in an online retail setting. *International Journal of Production Research, 56*(11), 1–21. doi:10.1080/00207543.2018.1424364

Brailsford, S., & Hilton, N. (n.d.). *A Comparison of Discrete Event Simulation and System Dynamics for Modelling Healthcare Systems*. Academic Press.

Broggi, A., Buzzoni, M., Debattisti, S., Grisleri, P., Laghi, M. C., Medici, P., & Versari, P. (2013). Extensive Tests of Autonomous Driving Technologies. *IEEE Transactions on Intelligent Transportation Systems, 14*(3), 1403–1415. doi:10.1109/TITS.2013.2262331

Buckman, J. (2009). Ford finds its way. *Quality Progress, 42*(6), 14–15.

BuisnessLine. (2021). 39% of new vehicles sold in India will be electric vehicles by 2030: *The Hindu Business Line*.

Buonamico, N., Muller, L., & Camargo, M. (2017). A new fuzzy logic-based metric to measure lean warehousing performance. *Supply Chain Forum: An International Journal, 18*(2), 96–111. 10.1080/16258312.2017.1293466

Cachadinha, N., & Rueff, N. (2011). Lean construction and sustainability– complementary paradigms? A case study. 19th Annual Conference of the International Group for Lean Construction. Lima, Peru.

Calzavara, M., Glock, C., Grosse, E., & Sgarbossa, F. (2018). An integrated storage assignment method for manual order picking warehouses considering cost, workload and posture. *International Journal of Production Research, 57*(8), 2392–2408. doi:10.1080/00207543.2018.1518609

Campbell, S. Basics of the I2C Communication Protocol. Retrieved from https://www.circuitbasics.com/basics-of-the-i2c-communication-protocol/

Capan, M., Wu, P., Campbell, M., Mascioli, S., & Jackson, E. V. (2015). Using electronic health records and nursing assessment to redesign clinical early recognition systems. *Health Systems (Basingstoke, England), 6*(2), 112–121. doi:10.1057/hs.2015.19

Caron, F., Marchet, G., & Perego, A. (2000). Layout design in manual picking systems: A simulation approach. *Integrated Manufacturing Systems, 11*(2), 94–104. doi:10.1108/09576060010313946

Carrizo Moreira, A., & Campos Silva Pais, G. (2011). Single minute exchange of die: A case study implementation. *Journal of Technology Management & Innovation, 6*(1), 129–146. doi:10.4067/S0718-27242011000100011

Casais, B., & Sousa, B. (2019). Portugal, the best destination: The case of a CSR communication that changed mentalities and increased business performance. *World Review of Entrepreneurship, Management and Sustainable Development, 15*(1/2), 29–41. doi:10.1504/WREMSD.2019.098474

Chaabane, K., Schutz, J., Dellagi, S., & Trabelsi, W. (2021). Analytical evaluation of TPM performance based on an economic criterion. *Journal of Quality in Maintenance Engineering, 27*(2), 413–429. doi:10.1108/JQME-08-2019-0085

Chackelson, C., Errasti, A., Cipres, D., & Lahoz, F. (2013). Evaluating order picking performance trade-offs by configuring main operating strategies in a retail distributor: A Design of Experiments approach. *International Journal of Production Research, 0*(20), 1–13. doi:10.1080/00207543.2013.796421

Chan, R. Y. K., He, H., Chan, H. K., & Wang, W. Y. C.Author. (2012). Environment orientation and corporate performance: The mediation mechanism of green supply chain management and the moderating effect of competitive intensity. *Industrial Marketing Management, 41*(4), 621–630. doi:10.1016/j.indmarman.2012.04.009

Chapin, F. S. III, Torn, M. S., & Tateno, M. (1996). Principles of Ecosystem Sustainability. *American Naturalist, 148*(6), 1016–1037. doi:10.1086/285969

Charan, P., Shankar, R., & Baisya, R. K.Author. (2009). Modelling the barriers of supply chain performance measurement system implementation in the Indian automobile supply chain. *International Journal of Logistics Systems and Management*, *5*(6), 614–630. doi:10.1504/IJLSM.2009.024794

Charron, R., Harrington, H. J., Voeh, F., & Wiggin, H. (2014). The lean management systems handbook. CRC Press.

Chatham, A. (2013). Google's Self Driving Cars: The Technology, Capabilities, Challenges. *Embedded Linux Conference*, Linux..

Chen, Y., Chen, H., Gorkhali, A., Lu, Y., Ma, Y., & Li, L. (2016). Big data analytics and big data science: A survey. *Journal of Management Analytics*, *3*(1), 1–42. doi:10.1080/23270012.2016.1141332

Cho, K., Kim, J., Choi, D. Y., Yoon, Y. H., Oh, J. H., & Lee, S. E. (2021). An FPGA-based ECU for remote reconfiguration in automotive systems. *Micromachines*, *12*(11), 2021. doi:10.3390/mi12111309

Chowdhury, S. G., & Chatterjee, S.Author. (2020). Determinants of Indian Automobile Industry Growth. *Eurasian Journal of Business and Economics*, *13*(26), 65–91. doi:10.17015/ejbe.2020.026.04

Ciano, M. P., Dallasega, P., Orzes, G., & Rossi, T. (2021). One-to-one relationships between Industry 4.0 technologies and Lean Production techniques: A multiple case study. *International Journal of Production Research*, *59*(5), 1386–1410. doi:10.1080/00207543.2020.1821119

Claudio, D., Cosgriff, V., Nino, V., & Valladares, L. (2021). An agile standardized work procedure for cleaning the operating room. *Journal of Industrial Engineering and Management*, *14*(4), 701–717. doi:10.3926/jiem.3440

Correia, D., Silva, F. J. G., Gouveia, R. M., Pereira, M. T., & Ferreira, L. P. (2018). Improving manual assembly lines devoted to complex electronic devices by applying Lean tools. *Procedia Manufacturing*, *17*, 663–671. doi:10.1016/j.promfg.2018.10.115

Costa, C., Ferreira, L. P., Sá, J.C., & Silva, F.J.G. (2018). Implementation of 5S methodology in a metalworking company. *DAAAM International Scientific Book 2018*, 001-012.

Cotteleer, M., & Joyce, J. (2014). 3D opportunity: Additive manufacturing paths to performance, innovation, and growth. *Deloitte Review*, *14*, 5–19.

COVID-19 will batter global auto sales and credit quality, March 23, 2020, S&P Global.

Craigen, D., Diakun-Thibault, N., & Purse, R. (2014). Defining cybersecurity. *Technology Innovation Management Review*, *4*(10), 13–21. doi:10.22215/timreview/835

D'Andreamatteo, A., Ianni, L., Lega, F., & Sargiacomo, M. (2015, September 1). Lean in healthcare: A comprehensive review. *Health Policy (Amsterdam)*, *119*(9), 1197–1209. doi:10.1016/j.healthpol.2015.02.002 PMID:25737260

Da Silva, N. A., Abreu, J. L., Klingenberg, C., Antunes, J. A. V., & Lacerda, D. P. (2022). Industry 4.0 and micro and small enterprises: systematic literature review and analysis. *Production & Manufacturing Research, 10*(1), 696–726. doi:10.1080/21693277.2022.2124466

Daimi, K., Saed, M., Bone, S., & Robb, J. (2016). *Securing Vehicle's Electronic Control Units*, (c), 29–34.

Damayanti, D. D., Novitasari, N., Setyawan, E. B., & Muttaqin, P. S. (2022). Intelligent Warehouse Picking Improvement Model for e-Logistics Warehouse Using Single Picker Routing Problem and Wave Picking. *Undefined.* https://www.semanticscholar.org/paper/Intelligent-Warehouse-Picking-Improvement-Model-for-Damayanti-Novitasari/3ff2de88c48b081689f57638162a70613e50eb10

Dangerfield, B. C. (2016). System Dynamics Applications to European Healthcare Issues. *Operational Research for Emergency Planning in Healthcare*, *2*, 296–315. doi:10.1007/978-1-137-57328-5_13

Dave, P. Y. (2020). The History of Lean Manufacturing by the view of Toyota-Ford. *International Journal of Scientific and Engineering Research, 11*(8), 1598–1602.

de Barros, L. B., Bassi, L. de C., Caldas, L. P., Sarantopoulos, A., Zeferino, E. B. B., Minatogawa, V., & Gasparino, R. C. (2021). Lean Healthcare Tools for Processes Evaluation: An Integrative Review. *International Journal of Environmental Research and Public Health, 18*(14), 7389. doi:10.3390/ijerph18147389

de Jong, S. J., & Beelaerts van Blokland, W. W. A. (2016). Measuring lean implementation for maintenance service companies. *International Journal of Lean Six Sigma*, *7*(1), 35–61. doi:10.1108/IJLSS-12-2014-0039

Dehdari, P. (2014). Measuring the Impact of Lean Techniques on Performance Indicators in Logistics Operations. *Measuring the Impact of Lean Techniques on Performance Indicators in Logistics Operations*, 1–191. doi:10.5445/KSP/1000036424

Dekier, Ł. (2012). The origins and evolution of Lean Management system. *Journal of International Students*, *5*(1), 46–51. doi:10.14254/2071-8330.2012/5-1/6

Demirli, K., Kaf, A., Simsekler, M. C. E., Jayaraman, R., Khan, M., & Tuzcu, E. (2021). Using Lean Techniques and Discrete-Event Simulation for Performance Improvement in an Outpatient Clinic. *International Journal of Lean Six Sigma, ahead-of-print.* doi:10.1108/IJLSS-09-2020-0138

Dias, P., Silva, F. J. G., Campilho, R. D. S. G., Ferreira, L. P., & Santos, T. (2019). Analysis and Improvement of an Assembly Line in the Automotive Industry. *Procedia Manufacturing*, *38*, 1444–1452. doi:10.1016/j.promfg.2020.01.143

Dijk, M., & Yarime, M. (2010). The emergence of hybrid-electric cars: Innovation path creation through co-evolution of supply and demand. *Technological Forecasting and Social Change*, *77*(8), 1371–1390.

Doğruel Anuşlu, M., & Fırat, S. Ü. (2019). Clustering analysis application on Industry 4.0-driven global indexes. *Procedia Computer Science, 158*, 145–152. doi:10.1016/j.procs.2019.09.037

Dombrowski, U., Richter, T., & Krenkel, P. (2017). Interdependencies of industries 4.0 lean production systems: A use cases Analysis. *Procedia Manufacturing, 11*, 1061–1068. doi:10.1016/j.promfg.2017.07.217

Duarte, A. L. C. M., & Santiago Scarpin, M. R. S. (2022). Maintenance practices and overall equipment effectiveness: Testing the moderating effect of training. *Journal of Quality in Maintenance Engineering*. Advance online publication. doi:10.1108/JQME-04-2021-0033

Duas, J. A., Ferreira, L. P., Sá, J. C., Ribeiro, M. T., & Silva, F. J. G. (2019). Improving The Order Fulfilment Process At A Metalwork Company. *Procedia Manufacturing, 41*, 1031–1038. doi:10.1016/j.promfg.2019.10.030

Dural Selcuk, G., & Vasilakis, C. (2021). Evaluating the sustainability of complex health system transformation in the context of population ageing: An empirical system dynamics study. *The Journal of the Operational Research Society*, 1–17. Advance online publication. doi:10.1080/01605682.2021.1992307

Duran, O., Capaldo, A., & Duran Acevedo, P. A. (2017). Lean maintenance applied to improve maintenance efficiency in thermoelectric power plants. *Energies, 10*(10), 1653. doi:10.3390/en10101653

Ejsmont, K., Gladysz, B., Corti, D., Castaño, F., Mohammed, W. M., & Martinez Lastra, J. L. (2020). Towards 'Lean Industry 4.0 '–Current trends and future perspectives. *Cogent Business & Management, 7*(1), 1781995. doi:10.1080/23311975.2020.1781995

Elbert, R., Knigge, J.-K., & Sarnow, T. (2018). *Transferability of order picking performance and training effects achieved in a virtual reality using head mounted devices. 51*, 686–691. doi:10.1016/j.ifacol.2018.08.398

EN 13306:2018 Maintenance - Maintenance terminology

Esty, D. C., & Winston, A. S. (2008). *Yeşilden Altına*. MediaCat.

Ferreira, C., Sá, J. C., Ferreira, L. P., Lopes, M. P., Pereira, T., Ferreira, L. P., & Silva, F. J. G. (2019). iLeanDMAIC – A methodology for implementing the lean tools. *Procedia Manufacturing, 41*, 1095–1102. doi:10.1016/j.promfg.2019.10.038

Ferro, R., Cordeiro, G. A., & Ordoñez, R. E. C. (2018). Dynamic Modeling of Discrete Event Simulation. *Proceedings of the 10th International Conference on Computer Modeling and Simulation - ICCMS 2018*, 248–252. 10.1145/3177457.3177477

Financial Express. (n.d.). *India to be world's 3rd largest car market by 2030*. Financial Express. https://www.financialexpress.com/archive/india-to-be-worlds-3rd-largest-car-market-by-2030-study/158001/

Fisher, A. M., Ding, M. Q., Hochheiser, H., & Douglas, G. P. (2016). Measuring time utilization of pharmacists in the Birmingham Free Clinic dispensary. *BMC Health Services Research*, *16*(1), 1–7. doi:10.118612913-016-1787-6 PMID:27687973

Flood, D., Douglas, K., Goldberg, V., Martinez, B., Garcia, P., Arbour, M., & Rohloff, P. (2017). A quality improvement project using statistical process control methods for type 2 diabetes control in a resource-limited setting. *International Journal for Quality in Health Care*, *29*(4), 593–601. doi:10.1093/intqhc/mzx051 PMID:28486632

Furht, B. (2010). Cloud computing fundamentals. In *Handbook of cloud computing* (pp. 3–19). Springer. doi:10.1007/978-1-4419-6524-0_1

Gajdzik, B., & Grabowska, S. (2018). Leksykon pojęć stosowanych w przemyśle 4.0. *Zeszyty Naukowe. Organizacja i Zarządzanie/Politechnika Śląska*, (132), 221-238.

Gan, L. (2003). Globalization of the Automobile Industry in China: Dynamics and barriers in greening of the road transportation. *Energy Policy*, *31*(C), 537–551.

Garcia-Sabater, P. I. ;, Marin-Garcia, J. J. ;, Vidal-Carreras, P. I., Garcia-Sabater, J. J., & Marin-Garcia, J. A. (2022). Applying Value Stream Mapping to Improve the Delivery of Patient Care in the Oncology Day Hospital. *International Journal of Environmental Research and Public Health, 19*(7), 4265. doi:10.3390/ijerph19074265

Gelei, A., Losonci, D., & Matyusz, Z. (2015). Lean production and leadership attributes: The case of Hungarian production managers. *Journal of Manufacturing Technology Management*, *26*(4), 477–500. doi:10.1108/JMTM-05-2013-0059

Ghadge, B., Metha, G., and Kulkarni, A. (2018). Automated Manual Transmission Using Servo Motors for Sequential. *International Journal of Innovative Research in Science, Engineering and Technology*, 7767–7772. doi:. doi:10.15680/IJIRSET.2018.0707025

Gil-Vilda, F., Yagüe-Fabra, J. A., & Sunyer, A. (2021). From Lean Production to Lean 4.0: A Systematic Literature Review with a Historical Perspective. *Applied Sciences (Basel, Switzerland)*, *11*(21), 10318. doi:10.3390/app112110318

Glas, A. H., & Kleemann, F. C. (2016). The impact of industry 4.0 on procurement and supply management: A conceptual and qualitative analysis. *International Journal of Business and Management Invention*, *5*(6), 55–66.

Golzarpoor, H., & González, V. (2013). *A green-lean simulation model for assessing environmental and production waste in construction.*

Goodland, R. (2002). Sustainability: Human, Social, Economic and Environmental, Ted Munn (Ed.), Encyclopedia of Global Environmental Change, içinde (1-3). John Wiley & Sons Ltd.

Goodland, R., & Daly, H. (1996). Environmental Sustainability: Universal And Non-Negotiable. *Ecological Applications*, *6*(4), 1002–1017. doi:10.2307/2269583

Gopalakrishnan, M., & Skoogh, A. (2018). Machine criticality based maintenance prioritization: Identifying productivity improvement potential. *International Journal of Productivity and Performance Management, 67*(4), 654–672. doi:10.1108/IJPPM-07-2017-0168

Görçün, Ö. F. (2016). Dördüncü Sanayi DevrimiEndüstri 4.0. Beta Basım Yayım Dağıtım. Baskı, İstanbul.

Greasley, A., & Owen, C. D. (2018). Modelling People's Behaviour using Discrete-Event Simulation: A Review. *International Journal of Operations & Production Management, 38*(5), 1228–1244. doi:10.1108/IJOPM-10-2016-0604

Green, K. W., Whitten, D., & Inman, R.A. (2012). Aligning marketing strategies throughout the supply chain to enhance performance. *Industrial Marketing Management*, 1008–1018.

Grosse, E. H., & Glock, C. H. (2015). The effect of worker learning on manual order picking processes. *International Journal of Production Economics, 170*, 882–890. doi:10.1016/j.ijpe.2014.12.018

Grosse, E., Glock, C., Jaber, M., & Neumann, W. (2014). Incorporating human factors in order picking planning models: Framework and research opportunities. *International Journal of Production Research, 53*(3), 695–717. doi:10.1080/00207543.2014.919424

Grosse, E., Glock, C., & Neumann, W. (2016). Human factors in order picking: A content analysis of the literature. *International Journal of Production Research, 55*(5), 1260–1276. Advance online publication. doi:10.1080/00207543.2016.1186296

Guizzi, G., Gallo, M., & Zoppoli, P. (2009). Condition based maintenance: Simulation and optimization. *Proceedings of the 8th WSEAS International Conference on System Science and Simulation in Engineering, ICOSSSE'09*, 319-325. https://dl.acm.org/doi/abs/10.5555/1938841.1938902

Guo, D., Li, M., Lyu, Z., Kang, K., Wu, W., Zhong, R. Y., & Huang, G. Q. (2021). Synchroperation in industry 4.0 manufacturing. *International Journal of Production Economics, 238*, 108171. doi:10.1016/j.ijpe.2021.108171

Gupta, K. (2022). A review on implementation of 5S for workplace management. *Journal of Applied Research on Industrial Engineering, 9*(3), 323–330. doi:10.22105/jarie.2021.292741.1347

Gürsoy, Ö. (2021). *Yalın üretim sisteminde dijitalleşme ve endüstri 4.0 uygulamaları ile süreç iyileştirme analizi: bir imalat işletmesinde uygulama (yayınlanmamış doktora tezi)*. Aydın Adnan Menderes Üniversitesi Sosyal Bilimler Enstitüsü.

Gurumurthy, A., Soni, G., Prakash, S., & Badhotiya, G. K. (2013). Review on Supply Chain Management Research—An Indian Perspective. *IIM Kozhikode Society & Management Review, 2*(1), 1–19. doi:10.1177/2277975213496508

Haak, R. (2006). Implementing process innovation—the case of the Toyota production system. In *Management of Technology and Innovation in Japan* (pp. 185–203). Springer. doi:10.1007/3-540-31248-X_9

Habidin, N. F., Hashim, S., Fuzi, N. M., & Salleh, M. I. (2018). Total productive maintenance, kaizen event and performance. *International Journal of Quality & Reliability Management*, *35*(9), 1853–1867. doi:10.1108/IJQRM-11-2017-0234

Haidar, A. M. A., Benachaiba, C., & Zahir, M. (2013). Software interfacing of servo motor with micro-controller, the *J. Electr. Syst.*, *9*(1), 84–99.

Harris, J. M. (2000). *Basic Principles of Sustainable Development, Global Development and Environment Institute.* (Working Paper 00-04).

Hassan, M. N., Barakat, A. F., & Sobh, A. S. (2020). Effect of applying lean maintenance in oil and gas fields. *IOP Conference Series. Materials Science and Engineering*, *973*(1), 012045. doi:10.1088/1757-899X/973/1/012045

Haugh, D., Mourougane, A., & Chatal, O. (2010), *The Automobile Industry in and Beyond the Crisis, OECD Economics Department* (Working Papers, No. 745). doi:10.1787/5kmmp8wg6cmq-en

Hell, M., & Petrić, L. (2021). System Dynamics Approach to TALC Modeling. *Sustainability*, *13*(9), 4803. doi:10.3390u13094803

Helmold, M. (2020). *Lean management and Kaizen*. Springer International Publishing.

Henrique, D. B., Rentes, A. F., Godinho, M., Kleber, F., Esposto, F., Barberato Henrique, D., . . . Godinho Filho, M. (2015). *A new value stream mapping approach for healthcare environments*. doi:10.1080/09537287.2015.1051159

Hermann, M., Pentek, T., & Otto, B. (2015). *Design principles for Industrie 4.0 scenarios: A literature review.* (Working Paper No. 01).

Hofmann, E., & Rüsch, M. (2017). Industry 4.0 and the current status as well as future prospects on logistics. *Computers in Industry*, *89*, 23–34. doi:10.1016/j.compind.2017.04.002

Hofstatter, T. & M. K. (2020, October). Reimagining the auto industry's future: It's now or never. p. 1. accenture. COVID 19: Mobilizing the automotive industry now accenture.

Holmberg, J., & Sandbrook, R. (1992). Sustainable Development: What Is to Be Done? Making Development Sustainable: Redefining Institutions, Policy, and Economics. In J. Holmberg (ed.) International Institute for Environment and Development, p. 19-38. Island Press.

Hooi, L. W., & Leong, T. Y. (2017). Total productive maintenance and manufacturing performance improvement. *Journal of Quality in Maintenance Engineering*, *23*(1), 2–21. doi:10.1108/JQME-07-2015-0033

Ho, Y.-C., & Lin, J.-W. (2017). Improving order-picking performance by converting a sequential zone-picking line into a zone-picking network. *Computers & Industrial Engineering*, *113*, 241–255. doi:10.1016/j.cie.2017.09.014

Huang, C. (2020). Clinical features of patients infected with 2019 novel coronavirus in Wuhan, China. *Lancet*, *395*(10223), 497–506.

Hüttmeir, A., De Treville, S., Van Ackere, A., Monnier, L., & Prenninger, J. (2009). Trading off between heijunka and just-in-sequence. *International Journal of Production Economics, 118*(2), 501–507. doi:10.1016/j.ijpe.2008.12.014

IEA. (2021). Electric Vehicles. *IEA*. https://www.iea.org/reports/electric-vehicles

India Brand Equity Foundation. (2013). *Auto components industry in India.* IBEF. https://www.ibef.org/pages/33363

Indian Brand Equity Foundation. (2008). *Automotive Market and Opportunities*. IBEF. https://www.ibef.org/download/Automotive_250608.pdf

Inozu, B., Chauncey, D., Kamataris, V., Mount, C., & Novaces, L. L. C. (2011). *Performance improvement for healthcare: Leading change with lean, Six Sigma, and constraints management.* McGraw Hill Professional.

Inter-brand. (2013). Creating and managing brand value. *Third annual best global green brands.* Grounded World.

International Organization of Motor Vehicle Manufacturers. (2022). *Media Reports, Press Releases, Union Budget 2021-22.* Department for Promotion of Industry and Internal Trade (DPIIT), Automotive Component Manufacturers Association of India (ACMA), Society of Indian Automobile Manufacturers (SIAM).

IvyPanda. (2021, July 22). *Research Methodology of the BMW Strategy*. IvyPanda. https://ivypanda.com/essays/research-methodology-of-the-bmw-strategy

Iyer, S. (2022). *Top 6 challenges in the Automobile Industry: The Post-COVID-19 Era.* Global Market Insights.

J.D. Power. (2020*). Post-coronavirus resurgence of car sales in China potentially bodes well for U.S. market*. J.D. Power.

Jackson, T. L. (1996). *Implementing a lean management system*. CRC Press. doi:10.4324/9781482278071

Jaghbeer, Y., Hanson, R., & Johansson, M. (2020). Automated order picking systems and the links between design and performance: A systematic literature review. *International Journal of Production Research, 58*(15), 1–17. doi:10.1080/00207543.2020.1788734

Jaguar. (2019). Future Jaguar Land Rover models could help stop the spread of superbugs. Jaguar Land Rover.

Jahangirian, M., Eldabi, T., Naseer, A., Stergioulas, L. K., & Young, T. (2010). Simulation in manufacturing and business: A review. *European Journal of Operational Research, 203*(1), 1–13. doi:10.1016/j.ejor.2009.06.004

Jasiulewicz-Kaczmarek, M. (2015). Practical aspects of the application of RCM to select optimal maintenance policy of the production line. *Safety and Reliability: Methodology and Applications-Proceedings of the European Safety and Reliability Conference, ESREL,* 1187-1195. https://sin.put.poznan.pl/publications/details/n5762

Jasiulewicz-Kaczmarek, M., & Bartkowiak, T. (2016). Improving the performance of a filling line based on simulation. In IOP Conference Series: Materials Science and Engineering (Vol. 145, No. 4, p. 042024). IOP Publishing. doi:10.1088/1757-899X/145/4/042024

Jasiulewicz-Kaczmarek, M., & Saniuk, A. (2018). How to make maintenance processes more efficient using lean tools. *Advances in Intelligent Systems and Computing* 605, 9 - 20 (AHFE 2017 International Conference on Social and Occupational Ergonomics)

Jasiulewicz-Kaczmarek, M., & Saniuk, A. (2017). How to make maintenance processes more efficient using lean tools? In R. Goossens (Ed.), *Advances in Social & Occupational Ergonomics. AHFE 2017. Advances in Intelligent Systems and Computing*. doi:10.1007/978-3-319-60828-0_2

Jasti, N. V. K., & Kodali, R. (2014). A literaturereview of empirical research methodology in lean manufacturing. *International Journal of Operations & Production Management, 34*(8), 1080–1122. doi:10.1108/IJOPM-04-2012-0169

Javaid, M., Haleem, A., Singh, R. P., Rab, S., Suman, R., & Khan, S. (2022). Exploring relationships between Lean 4.0 and manufacturing industry. *The Industrial Robot, 49*(3), 402–414. doi:10.1108/IR-08-2021-0184

Johansen, A. M. (2010). Monte Carlo Methods. W P. Peterson, E. Baker, & B. McGaw (Eds.), International Encyclopedia of Education (Third Edition) (s. 296–303). Elsevier. doi:10.1016/B978-0-08-044894-7.01543-8

Joosten, T., Bongers, I., & Janssen, R. (2009). Application of lean thinking to health care: Issues and observations. *International Journal for Quality in Health Care, 21*(5), 341–347. doi:10.1093/intqhc/mzp036 PMID:19696048

Junior, M. L., & Godinho Filho, M. (2010). Variations of the kanban system: Literature review and classification. *International Journal of Production Economics, 125*(1), 13–21. doi:10.1016/j.ijpe.2010.01.009

Jurík, L., Horňáková, N., & Domčeková, V. (2020). The application of smed method in the industrial enterprise. *Acta Logistica, 7*(4), 269–281. doi:10.22306/al.v7i4.189

Kammel, S., Ziegler, J., Pitzer, B., Werling, M., Gindele, T., Jagzent, D., Schröder, J., Thuy, M., Goebl, M., von Hundelshausen, F., Pink, O., Frese, C., & Stiller, C. (2008). Team AnnieWAY's autonomous system for the 2007 DARPA Urban Challenge. *Journal of Field Robotics, 25*(9), 615–639. doi:10.1002/rob.20252

Kanajan, S., Pinello, C., Zeng, H., and Sangiovanni-Vincentelli, A. (2008). Between Centralized versus Decentralized Automotive Architectures Using a Virtual Integration Environment. *Proceedings of the Design Automation & Test in Europe Conference*, *1*, 117. . doi:10.1109/DATE.2006.243895

Karnon, J., Stahl, J., Brennan, A., Caro, J. J., Mar, J., & Möller, J. (2012). Modeling using Discrete Event Simulation: A Report of the ISPOR-SMDM Modeling Good Research Practices Task Force-4. *Value in Health*, *15*(6), 821–827. doi:10.1016/j.jval.2012.04.013 PMID:22999131

Kennedy, F. A., & Brewer, P. C. (2006). The lean enterprise and traditional accounting—Is the honeymoon over? *Journal of Corporate Accounting & Finance*, *17*(6), 63–74. doi:10.1002/jcaf.20234

Keshavarz, A., Jaafari, D., Khalaj, M., & Dokouhaki, P. (2021). A Survey of the Literature on Order-Picking Systems by Combining Planning Problems. *Applied Sciences (Basel, Switzerland)*, *11*(22), 10641. doi:10.3390/app112210641

Khalfallah, M., & Lakhal, L. (2021). The impact of lean manufacturing practices on operational and financial performance: The mediating role of agile manufacturing. *International Journal of Quality & Reliability Management*, *38*(1), 147–168. doi:10.1108/IJQRM-07-2019-0244

Knigge, J.-K. (2021). *Theoretical Background: The use of Virtual Reality Head-Mounted Devices for Planning and Training in the Context of Manual Order Picking. W J.-K. Knigge (Red.), Virtual Reality in Manual Order Picking: Using Head-Mounted Devices for Planning and Training.* Springer Fachmedien., doi:10.1007/978-3-658-34704-8

Kolberg, D., & Zühlke, D. (2015). Lean automation enabled by Industry 4.0 technologies. *IFAC-PapersOnLine*, *48*(3), 1870–1875. doi:10.1016/j.ifacol.2015.06.359

Kose, Y., Muftuoglu, S., Cevikcan, E., & Durmusoglu, M. B. (2022). Axiomatic design for lean autonomous maintenance system: An application from textile industry. *International Journal of Lean Six Sigma*. Advance online publication. doi:10.1108/IJLSS-01-2022-0020

KPMG International. (2008). *A rough road-financial crisis and automotive industry*. KPMG.

KPMG International. (2010). *Global Auto Executive Survey 2010 Industry Concerns and Expectations to 2014*. KPMG.

Krishnan, S., Gupta, S., Kaliyan, M., Kumar, V., & Garza-Reyes, J.A. (2021), Assessing the key enablers for Industry 4.0 adoption using MICMAC analysis: a case study, *International Journal of Productivity and Performance Management, 70*(5), 1049-1071. doi:10.1108/IJPPM-02-2020-0053

Kulkarni, P. C., & Lahiri, G. (2014). Improving productivity using SMED. *Journal of Manufacturing Engineering*, *9*(4), 253–258.

Kushwaha, G.S.; Sharma, & Kumar, N. (2015). Green initiatives: A step towards sustainable development and firm's performance in the automobile industry. *Journal of Cleaner Production*.

Lai, C.-C. (2020). Severe acute respiratory syndrome coronavirus 2 (SARS-CoV-2) and corona virus disease-2019 (COVID-19): The epidemic and the challenges. *International Journal of Antimicrobial Agents*, *55*(105924). doi:10.1016/j.ijantimicag.2020.105924

Lai, N. Y. G., Wong, K. H., Halim, D., Lu, J., & Kang, H. S. (2019). *Industry 4.0 enhanced lean manufacturing. In 2019 8th international conference on Industrial technology and management (ICITM).* IEEE. https://ieeexplore.ieee.org/stamp/stamp.jsp?arnumber=8710669

Lawson, T., Weekes, L., & Hill, M. (2018). Ensuring success and sustainability of a quality improvement project. *BJA Education*, *18*(5), 147–152. doi:10.1016/j.bjae.2018.02.002 PMID:33456825

Levinson, W. A. (2002). *Henry Ford's Lean Vision. Enduring Principles from the First Ford Motor Plant*. Productivity Press.

Levy, G. (2008). *Computational finance using C and C*. Academic Press.

Lezzi, M., Lazoi, M., & Corallo, A. (2018). Cybersecurity for Industry 4.0 in the current literature: A reference framework. *Computers in Industry*, *103*, 97–110. doi:10.1016/j.compind.2018.09.004

Liker, J. (2004). *Toyota Way: 14 Management Principles from The World Greatest Manufacturer*. McGraw-Hill.

Liker, J. K. (2004). *The Toyota Way. 14 Management Principles from the World's Greatest Manufacturer*. McGraw Hill.

Liker, J. K., & Convis, G. L. (2012). *Toyota way to lean leadership: Achieving and sustaining excellence through leadership development*. McGraw-Hill Education.

Liker, J. K., & Meier, D. (2006). *Toyota way fieldbook*. McGraw-Hill Education.

Lima, R. M., Dinis-Carvalho, J., Souza, T. A., Vieira, E., & Gonçalves, B. (2021, March 20). Implementation of lean in health care environments: An update of systematic reviews. *International Journal of Lean Six Sigma*, *12*(2), 399–431. doi:10.1108/IJLSS-07-2019-0074

Lin, R.J., Tan, K.H., & Geng, Y. (2013). Market demand, green product innovation, and firm performance: Evidence from Vietnam motorcycle industry. *Journal of Cleaner Production*, *40*(C), 101–107.

Lin, C. J., Chen, F. F., & Chen, Y. M. (2013). Knowledge kanban system for virtual research and development. *Robotics and Computer-integrated Manufacturing*, *29*(3), 119–134. doi:10.1016/j.rcim.2012.04.020

Lippolt, C. R., & Furmans, K. (2008). Sizing of heijunka-controlled production systems with unreliable production processes. In *Lean business systems and beyond* (pp. 11–19). Springer. doi:10.1007/978-0-387-77249-3_2

Lizak M. (2016). Methods of measuring the effectiveness of Lean Management. *Production Engineering Archives*, *13*(4), 31-34.

Loske, D., & Klumpp, M. (2020). Smart and efficient: Learning curves in manual and human-robot order picking systems. *IFAC-PapersOnLine*, *53*(2), 10255–10260. doi:10.1016/j.ifacol.2020.12.2757

Luthra, S., Kumar, V., Kumar, S., & Haleem, A. (2011). Barriers to implementing green supply chain management in automobile industry using interpretative structured modeling techniques: An Indian perspective. *Journal of Industrial Engineering and Management*, *4*(2), 231–257.

Macal, C. M., & North, M. J. (2010). Tutorial on agent-based modelling and simulation. *Journal of Simulation*, *4*(3), 151–162. doi:10.1057/jos.2010.3

Makwana, A. D., & Patange, G. S. (2022). Strategic implementation of 5S and its effect on productivity of plastic machinery manufacturing company. *Australian Journal of Mechanical Engineering*, *20*(1), 111–120. doi:10.1080/14484846.2019.1676112

Malhotra, D. (2004). Trust and reciprocity decisions: The differing perspectives of trustors and trusted parties. *Organizational Behavior and Human Decision Processes*, *94*(2), 61–73. doi:10.1016/j.obhdp.2004.03.001

Manda, Kittu, V., & Beatrice, B. B. (2020).The Indian Automobile Sector Slowdown (January 30, 2020). https://ssrn.com/abstract=3528891 or doi:10.2139/ssrn.3528891

Marin-Garcia, J. A., Vidal-Carreras, P. I., & Garcia-Sabater, J. J. (2021). The Role of Value Stream Mapping in Healthcare Services: A Scoping Review. *International Journal of Environmental Research and Public Health, 18*(3), 951. doi:10.3390/ijerph18030951

Marinho, P., Pimentel, D., Casais, R., Silva, F. J. G., Sá, J. C., & Ferreira, L. P. (2021). Selecting the best tools and framework to evaluate equipment malfunctions and improve the OEE in the cork industry. *International Journal of Industrial Engineering and Management*, *12*(4), 1–13. doi:10.24867/IJIEM-2021-4-295

Márquez, A., Moreu de León, P., Gómez Fernández, J. F., Parra Márquez, C., & López Campos, M. (2009). The maintenance management framework: A practical view to maintenance management. *Journal of Quality in Maintenance Engineering*, *15*(2), 167–178. doi:10.1108/13552510910961110

Martin, R. L. (2002). The Virtue Matrix, Harvard Business Review, 80(3), 68-75

Martins Drei, S., & Sérgio de Arruda Ignácio, P. (2022). Lean healthcare applied systematically in a medium-sized medical clinic hospitalization. *Journal of Health Organization and Management*, *36*(5), 666–689. Advance online publication. doi:10.1108/JHOM-05-2021-0194 PMID:35439404

Martins, R., Pereira, M. T., Ferreira, L. P., Sá, J. C., & Silva, F. J. G. (2020). Warehouse operations logistics improvement in a cork stopper factory. *Procedia Manufacturing*, *51*, 1723–1729. doi:10.1016/j.promfg.2020.10.240

Marttonen-Arola, S., Baglee, D., Kinnunen, S. K., & Holgado, M. (2020). Introducing Lean into Maintenance Data Management: A Decision Making Approach. In J. Liyanage, J. Amadi-Echendu, & J. Mathew (Eds.), *Engineering Assets and Public Infrastructures in the Age of Digitalization. Lecture Notes in Mechanical Engineering*. Springer. doi:10.1007/978-3-030-48021-9_28

Masae, M., Glock, C., & Vichitkunakorn, P. (2021). A Method for Efficiently Routing Order Pickers in the Leaf Warehouse. *International Journal of Production Economics*, *234*, 108069. doi:10.1016/j.ijpe.2021.108069

Matsunaga, F., Zytkowski, V., Valle, P., & Deschamps, F. (2022). Optimization of energy efficiency in smart manufacturing through the application of cyber–physical systems and industry 4.0 technologies. *Journal of Energy Resources Technology, 144*(10). doi:10.1115/1.4053868

Maurya, P., Singh, A., & Salim, M. (2022). The Application of Text Mining in Detecting Financial Fraud: A Literature Review. *Business Intelligence and Human Resource Management: Concept, Cases, and Practical Applications*, *243*(C).

Maware, C., & Adetuntji, O. (2019). Lean Manufacturing Implementation in Zimbabwean Industries: Impact on Operational Performance. *International Journal of Engineering Business Management*, *11*, 1–12. doi:10.1177/1847979019859790

Maware, C., Okwu, M. O., & Adetunji, O. (2022). A systematic literature review of lean manufacturing implementation in manufacturing-based sectors of the developing and developed countries. *International Journal of Lean Six Sigma*, *13*(3), 521–556. doi:10.1108/IJLSS-12-2020-0223

Mayr, A., Weigelt, M., Kühl, A., Grimm, S., Erll, A., Potzel, M., & Franke, J. (2018). Lean 4.0-A conceptual conjunction of lean management and Industry 4.0. *Procedia CIRP*, *72*, 622–628. doi:10.1016/j.procir.2018.03.292

Mazzocato, P., Savage, C., Brommels, M., Aronsson, H., & Thor, J. (2010, October). Lean thinking in healthcare: A realist review of the literature. *Quality & Safety in Health Care*, *19*(5), 376–382. doi:10.1136/qshc.2009.037986 PMID:20724397

McKenzıe, S. (2004). *Social Sustainability: Towards Some Definitions, Hawke Research Institute*. (Working Paper Series No 27).

Mehany, M. S. H. M. (2015). Lean construction principles past and present – a business model consistency. *51st Annual International Conference Proceedings.* ASC.

Melton, T. (2005). The Benefits of Lean Manufacturing: What Lean Thinking has to Offer the Process Industries. *Chemical Engineering Research & Design*, *83*(6), 662–673. doi:10.1205/cherd.04351

Mishra, P. & Sharma, P.(2010). Green marketing in India, emerging opportunities and challenges. *Journal of engineering science and management education, 3*(C), pp.9-14.

Mishra, R., Rai, S., Thakur, G., Singh, A., & Shah, A. K. (2022). Impact of leadership styles on Emotional regulation strategies of followers in leader-follower relationship. *Journal of Positive School Psychology*, 130–141.

Mkaka, A., & Burduk, A. (2022). Implementation of the integrated lean six sigma philosophy in an Angolan manufacturing company–a case study. *Technologia i Automatyzacja Montażu*, *2*, 58–66. doi:10.7862/tiam.2022.1.6

Moldan, B., Janousková, S., & Hak, T. (2012). How To Understand And Measure Environmental Sustainability. *Indicators And Targets, Ecological Indicators, 17*, 4–13. doi:10.1016/j.ecolind.2011.04.033

Monden, Y. (1994). *Adaptable Kanban System Maintains Just-In-Time Production.* Springer. doi:10.1007/978-1-4615-9714-8_2

Monden, Y. (2011). *Toyota production system: an integrated approach to just-in-time*. CRC Press.

Monteiro, C., Ferreira, L. P., Fernandes, N. O., Sá, J. C., Ribeiro, M. T., & Silva, F. J. G. (2019). Improving the Machining Process of the Metalworking Industry Using the Lean Tool SMED. *Procedia Manufacturing, 41*, 555–562. doi:10.1016/j.promfg.2019.09.043

Montgomery, D. C. (2004). Intro to Statistical Quality Control 5th Edition with Minitab Student Release 14 Set. John Wiley & Sons.

Monzcka, R. (2009). Purchasing and Supply Chain Management, 4. Cengage Learning.

Morellı, J. (2011). Environmental Sustainability: A Definition for Environmental Professionals. *Journal of Environmental Sustainability, 1*(1), 1–9. doi:10.14448/jes.01.0002

Morell-Santandreu, O., Santandreu-Mascarell, C., & Garcia-Sabater, J. J. (2021). A Model for the Implementation of Lean Improvements in Healthcare Environments as Applied in a Primary Care Center. *International Journal of Environmental Research and Public Health, 18*(6), 2876. doi:10.3390/ijerph18062876

Morrar, R., Arman, H., & Mousa, S. (2017). The fourth industrial revolution (Industry 4.0):A social innovation perspective. *Technology Innovation Management Review, 7*(11), 12–20. doi:10.22215/timreview/1117

Mortimer, F., Isherwood, J., Wilkinson, A., & Vaux, E. (2018). Sustainability in quality improvement: Redefining value. *Future Healthcare Journal, 5*(2), 88–93. doi:10.7861/futurehosp.5-2-88 PMID:31098540

Mostafa, S., Lee, S. H., Dumrak, J., Chileshe, N., & Soltan, H. (2015). Lean thinking for a maintenance process. *Production & Manufacturing Research, 3*(1), 236–272. doi:10.1080/21693277.2015.1074124

Moura, B. (2006). *Logística Conceitos e Tendências*. Edições Centro Atlântico.

Mourato, J., Ferreira, L. P., Sá, J. C., & Silva, F. J. G. (2021). Improving internal logistics of a bus manufacturing using the lean techniques. *International Journal of Productivity and Performance Management, 70*(7), 1930–1951. doi:10.1108/IJPPM-06-2020-0327

Nakajima, S. (1988). *Introduction to TPM*. Productivity Press.

Narayanan, K. (1998). Technology acquisition, de-regulation and competitiveness: a study of Indian automobile industry. *Research Policy, 27*(2), 215–228. doi:https://doi.org/10.1016/S0048-7333(98)00037-7

Nawaiseh, A. L. K., Alawamleh, H., Al Shibly, M., & Almari, M. (2022). The Relationship Between the Enterprise Resource Planning System and Maintenance Planning System: An Empirical Study. *Information Sciences Letters*, *11*(5), 2. https://digitalcommons.aaru.edu.jo/isl/vol11/iss5/2

Nayak, J., Mishra, M., Naik, B., Swapnarekha, H., Cengiz, K., & Shanmuganathan, V. (2021). An impact study of covid-19 on six different industries: Automobile, energy and power, agriculture, education, travel and tourism and consumer electronics. *Expert Systems*. https://doi.org/10.1111/exsy.12677

Nayak, J., Mishra, M., Naik, B., Swapnarekha, H., Cengiz, K., & Shanmuganathan, V. (2021). An impact study of covid-19 on six different industries: Automobile, energy and power, agriculture, education, travel and tourism and consumer electronics. *Wiley Online Library.*

Neese., W., Foxx., W., Eppler., D. B. & Wright, L.T. (2018). The influence of industry-specific personal characteristics on consumer reactions to domestic vs. foreign comparative advertising in the American automobile market. *Cogent Business & Management, 5*(1).

Nino, V., Claudio, D., Valladares, L., & Harris, S. (2020). An Enhanced Kaizen Event in a Sterile Processing Department of a Rural Hospital: A Case Study. *International Journal of Environmental Research and Public Health, 17*(23), 8748. doi:10.3390/ijerph17238748

Nothdurft, T., Hecker, P., Ohl, S., Saust, F., Maurer, M., Reschka, A., & Böhmer, J. R. (2011). Stadtpilot: First fully autonomous test drives in urban traffic. *International Annual Conference on Intelligent Transportation Systems (ITSC)*, pp. 919-924. IEEE. 10.1109/ITSC.2011.6082883

Ohno, T. (1988). *Toyota Production System. Beyond Large-Scale Production*. Productivity Press.

Ohno, T., & Bodek, N. (2019). *Toyota production system: beyond large-scale production*. Productivity Press. doi:10.4324/9780429273018

Oliveira, J., Sá, J. C., & Fernandes, A. (2017). Continuous Improvement through Lean Tools: An application in a mechanical company. *Procedia Manufacturing*, *13*, 1082–1089. doi:10.1016/j.promfg.2017.09.139

Özçelik, T. Ö., and Cinoğlu, F. (2013). Yalın felsefe ve bir otomotiv yansanayi uygulaması. *İstanbul Ticaret Üniversitesi Fen BilimleriDergisi, 12*(23), 79-101.

Pacana, A., & Czerwińska, K. (2020). Improving the quality level in the automotive industry. *Production Engineering Archives*, *26*(4), 162–166. doi:10.30657/pea.2020.26.29

Paris, I. E. (2019). Scaling up the transition to electric mobility. Global EV Outlook

Patel, B. S., Sambasivan, M., Panimalar, R., & Hari Krishna, R. (2021). A relational analysis of drivers and barriers of lean manufacturing. *The TQM Journal*. Advance online publication. doi:10.1108/TQM-12-2020-0296

Peças, P., Faustino, M., Lopes, J., & Amaral, A. (2022). Lean methods digitization towards lean 4.0: a case study of e-VMB and e-SMED. *International Journal on Interactive Design and Manufacturing (IJIDeM)*, 1-19.

Pegels, C. C. (1984). The Toyota Production System— Lessons for American Management. *International Journal of Operations & Production Management*, *4*(1), 3–11. doi:10.1108/eb054703

Peimbert-García, R. E., Gutiérrez-Mendoza, L. M., & García-Reyes, H. (2021). Applying Lean Healthcare to Improve the Discharge Process in a Mexican Academic Medical Center. *Sustainability, 13*(19), 10911. doi:10.3390/su131910911

Pellegrini, S., Shetty, D., & Manzione, L. (2012). *Study and implementation of single minute exchange of die (SMED) methodology in a setup reduction kaizen* [Doctoral dissertation]. University of Hartford.

Peña, E., & Legaspi, M. G. (2020). UART: A Hardware Communication Protocol Understanding Universal Asynchronous Receiver/Transmitter, Visit Analog., 54(4).

Penna, C.R., & Geels, F.W. (2012). Multidimensional struggles in the greening of the industry: A dialectic issue life cycle model and case study. *Technological Forecasting and Social Change*, *79*(C), 999–1020.

Pereira, A. C., Dinis-Carvalho, J., Alves, A. C., & Arezes, M. P. (2019). How industry 4.0 can enhance lean practices. *FME Transactions*, *47*(4), 810–822. doi:10.5937/fmet1904810P

Pereira, A. M. H., Silva, M. R., Domingues, M. A. G., & Sá, J. C. (2019). Lean Six Sigma Approach to Improve the Production Process in the Mould Industry: A Case Study. *Quality Innovation Prosperity*, *23*(3), 103–121. doi:10.12776/qip.v23i3.1334

Pereira, M. T., Sousa, J. M. C., Ferreira, L. P., Sá, J. C., & Silva, F. J. G. (2019). Localization System for Optimization of Picking in a Manual Warehouse. *Procedia Manufacturing*, *38*, 1220–1227. doi:10.1016/j.promfg.2020.01.213

Petersen, C., & Aase, G. (2004). A comparison of picking, storage, and routing policies in manual order picking. *International Journal of Production Economics*, *92*(1), 11–19. doi:10.1016/j.ijpe.2003.09.006

Pietraszek, J., Radek, N., & Goroshko Andrii, V. (2020). Challenges for the DOE methodology related to the introduction of Industry 4.0. *Production Engineering Archives*, *26*(4), 190–194. doi:10.30657/pea.2020.26.33

Pinto, C. M. A., Mendonça, J., Babo, L., Silva, F. J. G., & Fernandes, J. L. R. (2022). Analyzing the Implementation of Lean Methodologies and Practices in the Portuguese Industry: A Survey. *Sustainability*, *14*(3), 1929. doi:10.3390u14031929

Pinto, G. F. L., Silva, F. J. G., Campilho, R. D. S. G., Casais, R. B., Fernandes, A. J., & Baptista, A. (2019). Continuous improvement in maintenance: A case study in the automotive industry involving Lean tools. *Procedia Manufacturing*, *38*, 1582–1591. doi:10.1016/j.promfg.2020.01.127

Pipatprapa, A. (2019). QR Code on Mobile Platform for Improving Order Picking Process of Lean Factory Warehouse. *International Journal of Innovation, Management and Technology*, *10*(1), 56–60. doi:10.18178/ijimt.2019.10.1.836

Pitt, M., Monks, T., Crowe, S., & Vasilakis, C. (2016). Systems modelling and simulation in health service design, delivery and decision making. *BMJ Quality & Safety*, *25*(1), 38–45. doi:10.1136/bmjqs-2015-004430 PMID:26115667

Pizoń, J., & Gola, A. (2023). The meaning and directions of development of personalized production in the era of industry 4.0 and industry 5.0. In Lecture Notes in Mechanical Engineering, 1–13. Springer International Publishing.

Polonsky, M.J., & Rosenberger, P.J. (2001).Revaluating Green Marketing: A strategic approach, *Business Horizon*, 21-30.

Pombal, T., Ferreira, L. P., Sá, J. C., Pereira, M. T., & Silva, F. J. G. (2019). Implementation of Lean Methodologies in the Management of Consumable Materials in the Maintenance Workshops of an Industrial Company. *Procedia Manufacturing*, *38*, 975–982. doi:10.1016/j.promfg.2020.01.181

Porter, M. E., & Heppelmann, J. E. (2014). How smart, connected products are transforming competition. *Harvard Business Review*, *92*(11), 64–88.

Qiao, D., & Wang, Y. (2021). A review of the application of discrete event simulation in manufacturing. *Journal of Physics: Conference Series*, *1802*(2), 022066. doi:10.1088/1742-6596/1802/2/022066

Raghuram, P., & Arjunan, M. (2021). Design framework for a lean warehouse – a case study-based approach. *International Journal of Productivity and Performance Management, ahead-of-print.* doi:10.1108/IJPPM-12-2020-0668

Ragin-Skorecka, K., & Nowak, F. (2017). Process analysis as a tool for rationalization of the organization. *Studia i Prace WNEiZ*, *48*, 77–88. doi:10.18276ip.2017.48/2-07

Rakshit, B. & Basistha, D. (2020). Can India stay immune enough to combat Covid-19 pandemic? An economic query. *Journal of Public Affairs*, *20*, e2157. https://doi.org/10.1002/pa.2157

Rameshan, P. (2021). Crisis Leadership of Covid-19 Fightback: Exploratory Anecdotal Evidence on Selected World Leaders. *IIM Kozhikode Society & Management Review, 10*(2), 136–159. doi:10.1177/2277975220986274

Randhawa, J. S., & Ahuja, I. S. (2018). Empirical investigation of contributions of 5S practice for realizing improved competitive dimensions. *International Journal of Quality & Reliability Management*, *35*(3), 779–810. doi:10.1108/IJQRM-09-2016-0163

Ratten, V., Jones, P., Braga, V., & Marques, C. S. (2019). Subsistence Entrepreneurship: The Role of Collaborative Innovation, Sustainability and Social Goals. In V. Ratten, P. Jones, V. Braga, & C. S. Marques (Eds.), *Subsistence Entrepreneurship* (pp. 1–6). Springer. doi:10.1007/978-3-030-11542-5_1

Reddy, T., & Thomson, R. (2015). Environmental, Social and Economic Sustainability: Implications for Actuarial Science. ASTIN, AFIR/ERM and IACA Colloquia, 23-27.

Régis, T. K. O., Santos, L. C., & Gohr, C. F. (2019). A case-based methodology for lean implementation in hospital operations. *Journal of Health Organization and Management, 33*(6), 656–676. doi:10.1108/JHOM-09-2018-0267 PMID:31625821

Reschka, A. (2016). *Safety Concept for Autonomous Vehicles.* In M. Maurer (Ed.). Autonomous Driving. doi:10.1007/978-3-662-48847-8_23

Ribeiro, I., Godina, R., Pimentel, C., Silva, F., & Matias, J. (2019). Implementing TPM supported by 5S to improve the availability of an automotive production line. *Procedia Manufacturing, 38*, 1574–1581. doi:10.1016/j.promfg.2020.01.128

Ribeiro, P., Sá, J. C., Ferreira, L. P., Silva, F. J. G., Pereira, M. T., & Santos, G. (2019). The Impact of the Application of Lean Tools for Improvement of Process in a Plastic Company: A case study. *Procedia Manufacturing, 38*, 765–775. doi:10.1016/j.promfg.2020.01.104

Rocha, Í. J. A., & de Vasconcelos, C. R. (2021). Lean healthcare implications in an occupational medicine clinic. *International Journal of Lean Six Sigma, 12*(5), 973–991. doi:10.1108/IJLSS-05-2020-0056

Rodič, B. (2017). Industry 4.0 and the New Simulation Modelling Paradigm. *Organizacija, 50*(3), 193–207. Advance online publication. doi:10.1515/orga-2017-0017

Rodrigues, J., Sá, J.C., Ferreira, L.P., Silva, F.J.G., & Santos, G. (2019). Lean Management "Quick-Wins": Results of Implementation. A Case Study. *Quality Innovation Prosperity, 23*(3), 3-21. doi:10.12776/qip.v23i3.1291

Rodrigues, M.; Sousa, B. & Batista da Costa, J. (2019). The improvement of the supply chain channel based on digital transformation: an exploratory study in the sustainable industry 4.0. *Book of Abstracts*, (pp. 66-77).

Romano, E., Falegnami, A., Cagliano, A. C., & Rafele, C. (2022). Lean ICU Layout Re-Design: A Simulation-Based Approach. *Informatics (MDPI), 9*(2), 35. Advance online publication. doi:10.3390/informatics9020035

Rosa, C., Silva, F. J. G., & Ferreira, L. P. (2017). Improving the Quality and Productivity of SteelWire-Rope Assembly Lines for the Automotive Industry. *Procedia Manufacturing, 11*, 1035–1042. doi:10.1016/j.promfg.2017.07.214

Rosa, C., Silva, F. J. G., Ferreira, L. P., & Campilho, R. D. S. G. (2017). SMED methodology: The reduction of setup times for Steel Wire-Rope assembly lines in the automotive industry. *Procedia Manufacturing, 13*, 1034–1042. doi:10.1016/j.promfg.2017.09.110

Ruan, K. (2019). *Cyber Risk Measurement in the Hyperconnected World. W K. Ruan (Red.), Digital Asset Valuation and Cyber Risk Measurement.* Academic Press., doi:10.1016/B978-0-12-812158-0.00004-1

Ruano, J., Hoyuelos, I., Mateo, M., & Angel, A. (2019). Lean School: A Learning Factory for Training Lean Manufacturing in A Physical Simulation Environment. *Management and Production Engineering Review, 10*(1), 4–13.

Sachs, J., Schmidt-Traub, G., & Kroll, C., La Fortune, G. & Fuller, G. (2018). SDG Index and Dashboards Report 2018. Bertelsmann Stiftung and Sustainable Development Solutions Network

Sanders, A., Elangeswaran, C., & Wulfsberg, J. P. (2016). Industry 4.0 implies lean manufacturing: Research activities in industry 4.0 function as enablers for lean manufacturing. *Journal of Industrial Engineering and Management*, *9*(3), 811–833. doi:10.3926/jiem.1940

Santos, A. C., Reis, A. C., Souza, C. G., Santos, I. L., & Ferreira, L. A. F. (2020). The first evidence about conceptual vs analytical lean healthcare research studies. *Journal of Health Organization and Management*, *34*(7), 789–806. doi:10.1108/JHOM-01-2020-0021 PMID:32945155

Santos, C., Montevechi, J. A. B., Queiroz, J., Miranda, R., & Fabiano, L. (2021). Decision support in productive processes through DES and ABS in the Digital Twin era: A systematic literature review. *International Journal of Production Research*, •••, 1–20. doi:10.1080/00207543.2021.1898691

Santos, V. R., Vitorino, T. F., Dias, Á. L., Martinho, D., & Sousa, B. B. (2022). Developing a Commercial Ethics Framework for Analysing Marketing Campaigns. [IJSSMET]. *International Journal of Service Science, Management, Engineering, and Technology*, *13*(1), 1–16. doi:10.4018/IJSSMET.290336

Sarangi, P. K. (2014). Future Trend in Indian Automobile Industry: A Statistical Approach. *Journal of Management Sciences and Technology*, *2*(1), 28–32.

Sartal, A., Llach, J., & León-Mateos, F. (2022). Do technologies really affect that much? exploring the potential of several industry 4.0 technologies in today's lean manufacturing shop floors. *Operations Research*, *22*(5), 6075–6106. Advance online publication. doi:10.100712351-022-00732-y

Schindlerová, V., Šajdlerová, I., Michalčík, V., Nevima, J., & Krejčí, L. (2020). Potential of using TPM to increase the efficiency of production processes. *Tehnicki Vjesnik (Strojarski Fakultet)*, *27*(3), 737–743. doi:10.17559/TV-20190328130749

Schmidt, R., Möhring, M., Härting, R. C., Reichstein, C., Neumaier, P., & Jozinović, P. (2015). Industry 4.0 - potentials for creating smart products: empirical research results. In W. Abramowicz (Ed.), *Business Information Systems. BIS 2015. Lecture Notes in Business Information Processing* (Vol. 208, pp. 16–27). Springer. doi:10.1007/978-3-319-19027-3_2

Schwab, K. (2017). *A Quarta Revolução Industrial.* Lisboa, Edição: Levoir, Marketing e Conteúdos Multimédia, S.A.

Shahid, M., Gupta, H., & Tamang, J. S. (2016). Digital Speedometer with Password Enabled Speed Limiting Feature. *International Journal of Trend in Research and Development*, *3*(3), 513–517.

Shah, R., & Ward, P. T. (2003). Lean manufacturing: Context, practice bundles, and performance. *Journal of Operations Management*, *21*(2), 129–149. doi:10.1016/S0272-6963(02)00108-0

Sharma, P., Khater, S. & Vashisht, V. (2020). Sales Forecast of Manufacturing Companies using Machine Learning navigating the Pandemic like covid-19, 2021 *2nd International Conference on Computation, Automation and Knowledge Management (ICCAKM),* 1-5, doi:10.1109/ICCAKM50778.2021.9357751

Shen, W., Zhang, Q., Chen, Z., Mao, W., & Li, Y. (2021). Testing and analysis of automotive gearshift performance based on gear shift analysis. *Eng. Reports*, *3*(5), 1–12. doi:10.1002/eng2DOI324

Shinde, G.P., & Dubey, M. (2011). Automobile Industry and Performance of Key Players. *Asian Journal of Technology and Management Research*, *1*(2).

Shingo, S., & Dillon, A. P. (2019). *A revolution in manufacturing: the SMED system*. Routledge. doi:10.4324/9781315136479

Shou, W., Wang, J., & Wu, P. (2021). The application of simulation in lean production research: A critical review and future directions. *Engineering, Construction and Architectural Management, ahead-of-print*. doi:10.1108/ECAM-10-2020-0853

Shou, W., Wang, J., Wu, P., & Wang, X. (2020). Value adding and non-value adding activities in turnaround maintenance process: Classification, validation, and benefits. *Production Planning and Control*, *31*(1), 60–77. doi:10.1080/09537287.2019.1629038

Shrikanth, R., & Raju D.S. N. (2012). Contemporary Green Marketing-Brief Reference to Indian Scenario. *International Journal of Social Science and Interdisciplinary Research*, *1*(1), 26–39.

Sierzchula, W., Bakker, S., Maat, K., & Wee, B.V. (2012). The technological diversity of emerging eco-innovations: A case study of the automobile industry. *Journal of Cleaner Production*, *37*(C), 211–220.

Silva, S., Sá, J. C., Silva, F. J. G., Ferreira, L. P., & Santos, G. (2019). Lean Green—The Importance of Integrating Environment into Lean Philosophy—A Case Study. Proceedings of the 6th European Lean Educator Conference, (*vol. 122*, pp. 211-219). Springer. 10.1007/978-3-030-41429-0_21

Silva, F. J. G., & Gouveia, R. M. (2020). *Cleaner Production—Toward a Better Future; Springer Nature*. Switzertland. doi:10.1007/978-3-030-23165-1

Silva, F. J. G., Kirytopoulos, K., Ferreira, L. P., Sá, J. C., Santos, G., & Nogueira, M. C. C. (2022). The three pillars of sustainability and agile project management: How do they influence each other. *Corporate Social Responsibility and Environmental Management*, *29*(5), 1495–1512. doi:10.1002/csr.2287

Silvestre, B. S. andTircă, D. M. (2019). Innovations for sustainable development: Moving toward a sustainable future. *Journal of Cleaner Production*.

Simões, A., & Tenera, A. (2010). Improving setup time in a Press Line–Application of the SMED methodology. *IFAC Proceedings Volumes*, *43*(17), 297-302.

Singh, A. (2022). From Crisis to Resilience. In Handbook of Research on Challenges for Human Resource Management in the COVID-19 Era, p.89.

Singh, A., & Kumar, A. (2021). Impact of COVID-19 on monitoring human health behavior through digital medium system. *International Journal of Business Information Systems*, *1*(1), 1.

Singh, A., Das, U., & Kumar, S. (2022). Gender, technology and innovation: The role of women in Indian micro, small and medium enterprises. *World Review of Entrepreneurship, Management and Sustainable Development*, *18*(4), 429.

Singh, A., Singh, H., & Singh, A. (2022). People Analytics: Augmenting Horizon from Predictive Analytics to Prescriptive Analytics. In: Jeyanthi P.M., Choudhury T., Hack-Polay D., Singh T.P., & Abujar S. (eds) *Decision Intelligence Analytics and the Implementation of Strategic Business Management.* Springer. doi:10.1007/978-3-030-82763-2_13

Singh, D., Singh, A., & Omar, A., (2022). Business Intelligence and Human Resource Management: Concept, Cases, and Practical Applications (S. B. Goyal, Ed.). CRC Press.

Singh, D., Singh., A. & Karki, S. (2021). Knowledge Management and Web 3.0: Introduction to Future and Challenges. In S. Kautish, D. Singh, Z., Polkowski, A. Mayura., & M. Jeyanthi (Ed.)., *Knowledge Management and Web 3.0: Next Generation Business Models*, 1-14. Boston: De Gruyter. doi:10.1515/9783110722789-001

Singh, H. K., & Singh, A. (n.d.). Governance and Social Responsibility Practices in Indian Life Insurance Industry. *Pacific Institute of Management & Technology.*

Singh, S., Vrontis, D., & Thrassou, A. (2011). Green marketing and consumer behavior: The case of gasoline products. *Journal of Transnational Management*, *16*(2), 84–106.

Singh, V. (2017). Growth of Automobile Industry and its Economic Impact: An Indian Perspective. *International Journal of Commerce and Management Research*, *3*(8), 6–10.

Singh., A., Nagpal, E., & Mundi, H. S. (2020). Brand personification through celebrity ambassador: A study to investigate the impact on consumer attitude and loyalty. *International Journal of Business Excellence*, *1*(1), 1.

Singha Mahapatra, M., & Shenoy, D. (2022). Lean maintenance index: A measure of leanness in maintenance organizations. *Journal of Quality in Maintenance Engineering*, *28*(4), 791–809. doi:10.1108/JQME-08-2020-0083

Singh, J., & Singh, H. (2020). Justification of TPM pillars for enhancing the performance of manufacturing industry of Northern India. *International Journal of Productivity and Performance Management*, *69*(1), 109–133. doi:10.1108/IJPPM-06-2018-0211

Singh, J., Singh, H., & Sharma, V. (2018). Success of TPM concept in a manufacturing unit–a case study. *International Journal of Productivity and Performance Management*, *67*(3), 536–549. doi:10.1108/IJPPM-01-2017-0003

Singh, S. (2008). *Special Issue on the 2007 DARPA Urban Challenge Part I* (Vol. 25). Wiley Subscription Services, Inc.

Singh, S. (2008). *Special Issue on the 2007 DARPA Urban Challenge Part II* (Vol. 25). Wiley Subscription Services, Inc.

Singh, S. (2008). *Special Issue on the 2007 DARPA Urban Challenge Part III* (Vol. 25). Wiley Subscription Services, Inc.

Siriwardena S., Hunt, G., Teisl, M.F., & Noblet, C.L. (2012). Effective environmental marketing of green cars: A nested logit approach. *Transportation Research Part D, Transport and Environment*, 37–242.

Ślusarczyk, B. (2019). Potencjalne rezultaty wprowadzania koncepcji Przemysłu 4.0 w przedsiębiorstwach. *Przegląd Organizacji*, (1), 4–10. doi:10.33141/po.2019.01.01

Smith, A. (1776). *Ulusların Zenginliği. Cilt 1*, Alan yayıncılık, 4. Baskı, İstanbul, 2004. *Sürdürülebilir Kalkınma Amaçları*, https://www.tr.undp.org/content/turkey/tr/home/sustainable-developmentgoals.html

Smith, K.T. (2010). An examination of marketing techniques that influence millennia's perception of whether a product is environment-friendly. *Journal of Strategic Marketing*, *18*(6), 437–450.

Smith, R. (2004). What is Lean maintenance? Elements that need to be in place for success. *Maintenance Technology Magazine*. Available at: www.mt-online.com/article/1004smith

Smith, I. M., & Bayliss, E. (2022). Recovering staff, recovering services: Massive-online support for recovering a paediatric service using Lean and compassionate communication. *BMJ Open Quality*, *11*(2), e001914. Advance online publication. doi:10.1136/bmjoq-2022-001914 PMID:35750350

Smith, R., & Hawkins, B. (2004). *Lean maintenance; reduce cost improve quality and increase market share*. Elsevier Butterworth-Heinemann.

Song, X. (2020). Design and analysis of automatic transmission for Ravigneaux transmission with four-speed. *Journal of Physics: Conference Series*, *1676*(1), 2020. doi:10.1088/1742-6596/1676/1/012184

Spear, S. J. (2004). Learning to lead at Toyota. *Harvard Business Review*, *82*(5), 78–91. PMID:15146738

Srisuk, K., & Tippayawong, K. Y. (2020). Improvement of raw material picking process in sewing machine factory using lean techniques. *Management and Production Engineering Review*, *11*(1). Advance online publication. doi:10.24425/mper.2020.132946

Stadnicka, D. (2015). Setup analysis: Combining SMED with other tools. *Management and Production Engineering Review*, *6*(1), 36–50. doi:10.1515/mper-2015-0006

Stanek, G., Langer, D., Müller-Bessler, B., & Huhnke, B. (2010). Junior 3: A test platform for Advanced Driver Assistance Systems. *Intelligent Vehicles Symposium (IV)*, (pp. 143-149). IEEE. 10.1109/IVS.2010.5547997

Stiller, C., Färber, G., & Kammel, S. (2007). Cooperative Cognitive Automobiles. *2007 IEEE Intelligent Vehicles Symposium (IV)*. Istanbul, Turkey. 10.1109/IVS.2007.4290117

STMicroelectronics. (2017). *Reference manual stm32f407 advanced ARM-based 32-bit MCUs*. ST Microelectronics. https://www.st.com/content/ccc/resource/technical/document/reference_manual/3d/6d/5a/66/b4/99/40/d4/DM00031020.pdf/files/DM00031020.pdf/jcr:content/translations/en.DM00031020.pdf

STMicroelectronics. (2022). *STM32F405xx, STM32F407xx Datasheet, 176*. ST Microelectrons. https://www.st.com/en/microcontrollers-microprocessors/stm32f407vg.html

Strauch., Y., Carter, A., & Homer-Dixon, T. (2020). However, the pandemic unfolds, it's time for oil use to peak—and society to prepare for the fallout. *Bulletin of the Atomic Scientists*, *76*(5), 238–243. doi:10.1080/00963402.2020.1806577

Sutherland, J., & Bennett, B. (2007). The seven deadly wastes of logistics: applying Toyota Production System principles to create logistics value. *White Paper*, *701*, 40-50.

Teixeira, P., Sá, J. C., Silva, F. J. G., Ferreira, L., Santos, G., & Fontoura, P. (2021). Connecting lean and green with sustainability towards a conceptual model. *Journal of Cleaner Production*, *322*, 129047. doi:10.1016/j.jclepro.2021.129047

Tellini, T., Silva, F. J. G., Pereira, T., Morgado, L., Campilho, R. D. S. G., & Pereira, L. P. (2019). Improving In-Plant Logistics Flow by Physical and Digital Pathways. *Procedia Manufacturing*, *38*, 965–974. doi:10.1016/j.promfg.2020.01.180

Thakur, G., Singh, A., Rai, S., & Mishra, R. (2022). An Ounce of Prevention Is Worth a Pound of Cure: A Study on Emotional Regulation, Thwarted Social Needs, Disposable Income and Its Relationship with Psychological Well-Being. International. *Journal of Work Organisation and Emotion*, *13*(4), 1.

Thuy, M., Goebl, M., Rattei, F., Althoff, M., Obermeier, F., Hawe, S., Nagel, R., Kraus, S., Wang, C., Hecker, F., Russ, M., Schweitzer, M., Leon, F.P., Färber, G., Buss, M., Diepold, K., Eberspächer, J., Heißing, B., Wünsche, H.-J. (2008). Kognitive Automobile - Neue Konzepte und Ideen des Sonderforschungsbereichs/TR28. 3. *Tagung Aktive Sicherheit durch Fahrerassistenz. Garching b.* München, Germany.

Tıraş, H. (2012). Sürdürülebilir kalkınma ve çevre: Teorik bir inceleme. *Kahramanmaraş Sütçü İmam Üniversitesi İktisadi ve İdari Bilimler Fakültesi Dergisi*, *2*(2), 57–73.

Tiso, A., Crema, M., & Verbano, C. (2021). A framework to guide the implementation of lean management in emergency department. *Journal of Health Organization and Management*, *35*(9), 315–337. doi:10.1108/JHOM-01-2021-0035 PMID:34558251

Tjahjono, B., Esplugues, C., Ares, E., & Pelaez, G. (2017). What does industry 4.0 mean to supply chain? *Procedia Manufacturing, 13*, 1175–1182. doi:10.1016/j.promfg.2017.09.191

Tlapa, D., Zepeda-Lugo, C. A., Tortorella, G. L., Baez-Lopez, Y. A., Limon-Romero, J., Alvarado-Iniesta, A., & Rodriguez-Borbon, M. I. (2020). Effects of Lean Healthcare on Patient Flow: A Systematic Review. *Value in Health, 23*(2), 260–273. doi:10.1016/j.jval.2019.11.002 PMID:32113632

Tommelein, I. D. (1997). *Discrete-Event Simulation of Lean Construction Processes*. 121–136. https://www.iglc.net/papers/details/25

Tortorella, G. L., Fogliatto, F. S., Cauchick-Miguel, P. A., Kurnia, S., & Jurburg, D. (2021). Integration of Industry 4.0 technologies into total productive maintenance practices. *International Journal of Production Economics, 240*, 108224. doi:10.1016/j.ijpe.2021.108224

Torun, İ. (2003). Endüstri Toplumu‟nun Oluşmasında Etkili Olan İktisadi ve Sina-i Faktörler. *C.Ü. İktisadi ve İdari Bilimler Dergisi,* Cilt 4. *Sayı, 1*, 2003.

Türkan, Ö. U. (2010). Üretimde yalın dönüşümün temel performans kriterleri. *BalıkesirÜniversitesi Fen Bilimleri Enstitüsü Dergisi, 12*(2), 28–41.

U.S. Department of Transportation & Bureau of Transportation Statistics. (2018). Transportation Statistics, Annual Report 2018. [Data set]. USFG.

Ulutas, B. (2011). An application of SMED Methodology. *International Journal of Industrial and Manufacturing Engineering, 5*(7), 1194–1197.

Urmson, C. (2012). Realizing Self-Driving Vehicles. *Intelligent Vehicles Symposium (IV)*. IEEE.

Ustundag, A., & Cevikcan, E. (2018). *Industry 4.0: managing the digital transformation*. Springer. doi:10.1007/978-3-319-57870-5

Vaidya, S., Ambad, P., & Bhosle, S. (2018). Industry 4.0 - a glimpse. *Procedia Manufacturing, 20*, 233–238. doi:10.1016/j.promfg.2018.02.034

Valamede, L. S., & Akkari, A. C. S. (2020). Lean 4.0: A new holistic approach for the integration of lean manufacturing tools and digital technologies. *International Journal of Mathematical, Engineering and Management Sciences, 5*(5), 851–868.

van Gils, T., Ramaekers, K., Braekers, K., Depaire, B., & Caris, A. (2018). Increasing order picking efficiency by integrating storage, batching, zone picking, and routing policy decisions. *International Journal of Production Economics, 197*, 243–261. doi:10.1016/j.ijpe.2017.11.021

van Gils, T., Ramaekers, K., Caris, A., & Cools, M. (2017). The use of time series forecasting in zone order picking systems to predict order pickers' workload. *International Journal of Production Research, 55*(21), 6380–6393. doi:10.1080/00207543.2016.1216659 van Gils, T., Ramaekers, K., Caris, A., & de Koster, R. B. M. (2018). Designing efficient order picking systems by combining planning problems: State-of-the-art classification and review. *European Journal of Operational Research, 267*(1), 1–15. doi:10.1016/j.ejor.2017.09.002

Vaz, E., De Sá, J. C. V., Santos, G., Correia, F., & Ávila, P. (2021). The value of TPM for Portuguese companies. *Journal of Quality in Maintenance Engineering*. Advance online publication. doi:10.1108/JQME-12-2020-0121

Velmurugan, R. S., & Dhingra, T. (2015). Maintenance Strategy Selection and its Impact in Maintenance Function: A Conceptual Framework. *International Journal of Operations & Production Management, 35*(12), 1622–1661. doi:10.1108/IJOPM-01-2014-0028

Vieira, A. M., Silva, F. J. G., Campilho, R. D. S. G., Ferreira, L. P., Sá, J. C., & Pereira, T. (2020). SMED methodology applied to the deep drawing process in the automotive industry. *Procedia Manufacturing, 51*, 1416–1422. doi:10.1016/j.promfg.2020.10.197

Vivien, F. D. (2008). Sustainable Development. *An Overview of Economic Proposals, SAPIENS, 1*(2), 1–8. PMID:17337322

Von Paul, G., &, H.-W. K. (2016, January). *Automobile revolution-perspective towards 2030.*

Wada, K. (2020). *The Evolution of the Toyota Production System.* Springer. doi:10.1007/978-981-15-4928-1

Wang, Z., Sheu, J.-B., Teo, C., & Xue, G. (2021). Robot Scheduling for Mobile-Rack Warehouses: Human-Robot Coordinated Order Picking Systems. *Production and Operations Management*. Advance online publication. doi:10.1111/poms.13406

Weking, J., Stöcker, M., Kowalkiewicz, M., Böhm, M., & Krcmar, H. (2020). Leveraging industry 4.0–A business model pattern framework. *International Journal of Production Economics, 225*, 107588. doi:10.1016/j.ijpe.2019.107588

Wickramasinghe, N., Al-Hakim, L., Gonzalez, C., & Tan, J. (2014). *Healthcare Delivery in the Information Age Lean Thinking for Healthcare.* Retrieved from https://www.springer.com/series/8783

Wille, J. M., Saust, F., & Maurer, M. (2010). Stadtpilot: Driving autonomously on Braunschweig's inner ring road. *Intelligent Vehicles Symposium (IV)*, (pp. 506-511). IEEE. 10.1109/IVS.2010.5548034

Wilson, J. M. (1995). Henry Ford¢s just-in-time system. *International Journal of Operations & Production Management, 15*(12), 59–75. doi:10.1108/01443579510104501

Winkelhaus, S., & Grosse, E. (2020). Logistics 4.0: A systematic review towards a new logistics system. *International Journal of Production Research, 58*(1), 18–43. doi:10.1080/00207543.2019.1612964

Winner, L. E., Reinhardt, E., Benishek, L., & Marsteller, J. A. (2022). Lean Management Systems in Health Care: A Review of the Literature. *Quality Management in Health Care*, *31*(4), 221–230. doi:10.1097/QMH.0000000000000353 PMID:35180733

Wolniak, R. (2014). Relationships between selected lean management tools and innovations. *Zeszyty Naukowe. Organizacja i Zarządzanie/Politechnika Śląska*, (75), 157-166.

Womack, J. P. (2007). Moving beyond the tool age. *Manufacturing Engineer*, *86*(1), 4–5. doi:10.1049/me:20070101

Womack, J. P., & Jones, D. T. (1996). *Lean thinking: Banish waste and create wealth in your corporation*. Simon & Schuster.

Womack, J. P., Jones, D. T., & Roos, D. (1990). *The Machine that Changed the World: The Story of Lean Production*. Harper Collins Publishers.

Womack, J., & Jones, D. (2003). *Lean Thinking: banish waste and create wealth in your corporation*. Simon & Schuster Inc.

World Bank. (2018). *World Development Indicators*. World Bank.

World Health Organization. (2020). *Laboratory testing for coronavirus disease 2019 (Covid-19) in suspected human cases: interim guidance, 2 March 2020. No. WHO/Covid-19/laboratory/2020.4*. World Health Organization.

Xia, Y., & Tang, T.P. (2011). Sustainability in Supply chain management: Suggestions for the auto industry. *Management Decision*, *49*(4), 495–512.

Xiang, Z. T., & Chin, J. F. (2021). Implementing total productive maintenance in a manufacturing small or medium-sized enterprise. *Journal of Industrial Engineering and Management*, *14*(2), 152–175. doi:10.3926/jiem.3286

Yadav, G., Luthra, S., Huisingh, D., Mangla, S. K., Narkhede, B. E., & Liu, Y. (2020). Development of a lean manufacturing framework to enhance its adoption within manufacturing companies in developing economies. *Journal of Cleaner Production*, *245*, 118726. doi:10.1016/j.jclepro.2019.118726

Yang, C. C., & Yang, K. J. (2013). An integrated model of the Toyota production system with total quality management and people factors. *Human Factors and Ergonomics in Manufacturing & Service Industries*, *23*(5), 450–461. doi:10.1002/hfm.20335

Yücel, İ. H. (2006). *Türkiye'de bilim teknoloji politikaları ve iktisadi gelişmenin yönü*. TC Başbakanlık Devlet Planlama Teşkilatı.

Zdęba-Mozoła, A., Rybarczyk-Szwajkowska, A., Czapla, T., Marczak, M., & Kozłowski, R. (2022). Implementation of Lean Management in a Multi-Specialist Hospital in Poland and the Analysis of Waste. *International Journal of Environmental Research and Public Health*, *19*(2), 800. doi:10.3390/ijerph19020800

Zepeda-Lugo, C., Tlapa, D., Baez-Lopez, Y., Limon-Romero, J., Ontiveros, S., Perez-Sanchez, A., & Tortorella, G. (2020). Assessing the Impact of Lean Healthcare on Inpatient Care: A Systematic Review. *International Journal of Environmental Research and Public Health, 17*(15), 5609. doi:10.3390/ijerph17155609

Zhang, X. (2018). Application of discrete event simulation in health care: A systematic review. *BMC Health Services Research, 18*(1), 687. doi:10.118612913-018-3456-4 PMID:30180848

Zhou, K., Liu, T., & Zhou, L. (2016). Industry 4.0: Towards Future Industrial Opportunities and Challenges. In *International Conference on Fuzzy Systems and Knowledge Discovery,* (pp. 2147–2152). IEEE.

Żywicki, K., & Buń, P. (2021). Process of Materials Picking Using Augmented Reality. *IEEE Access: Practical Innovations, Open Solutions, 9*, 102966–102974. doi:10.1109/ACCESS.2021.3096915

About the Contributors

Katarzyna Antosz, Ph.D., Ds.C., Eng., Associate Professor, since 2002 has been working at Rzeszow University of Technology, Faculty of Mechanical Engineering and Aeronautics, Department of Manufacturing and Production Engineering and is a member of the Lean Learning Academy Polska. She is a specialist in the field of improving and increasing the efficiency of production in organizations, using the methods and tools of Lean Manufacturing and Six Sigma, and the reliability and operation of machines and maintenance services in enterprises. Author of many publications in this fields.

José Carlos Sá is MSc in Industrial Engineering and Bachelor Degree in Production Engineering, both by University of Minho, Portugal. In 2015 he awarded the title of Specialist in Quality Management, by Polytechnic Institute of Viana do Castelo, Portugal. He was director of quality and continuous improvement, director of production, and was also a consultant for several companies over 20 years. Currently, he is Adjunct Professor and Lean Six Sigma Post-graduation Coordinator on the School of Engineering, Polytechnic of Porto (Portugal). He taught in Higher Education since 2005. He is a member of the Editorial Advisory Board of Technological Sustainability Journal (Emerald) and member of the Editorial Board of Journal of Applied Research on Industrial Engineering. He is also a member of Review Board of International Journal of Environmental Research and Public Health (MDPI). He has more than 60 papers (WOS+SCOPUS) published.

Małgorzata Jasiulewicz-Kaczmarek, Ph.D. D.Sc. Eng., Associate Professor at the Faculty of Management Engineering at the Poznań University of Technology. Her research interests include the issues of maintenance management of technical systems, sustainable manufacturing, and Industry 4.0. She is a member of the Polish Society for Production Management and the Commission for Digital Modeling of Exploitation of the Polish Scientific and Technical Society for Exploitation.

José Machado concluded Habilitation title in February 2019 at University of Minho, Portugal. He received his PhD degree in Mechanical Engineering – Automation, from University of Minho, Portugal and, in simultaneous, from Ecole Normale Superieure de Cachan, France, in 2006. He is Deputy Director of MEtRICs Research Center and Assistant Professor at Mechanical Engineering department of University of Minho. He has authored, or co-authored, more than 220 refereed journal and conference proceedings papers. He coordinates and has coordinated - and participated as collaborator - in several Research and Technology Transfer Projects on Mechatronics and Automation domains. His main interests are related with Industry 4.0, more specifically, on the design and development of Cyber-Physical Systems; design and analysis of dependable controllers for obtaining dependable mechatronic systems; and mechatronic systems design with special focus on medical or biomedical applications, wellbeing and/or rehabilitation. He is member of IEEE and member of IFAC.

* * *

Burcu Arsan is currently a third-year PhD candidate in Management and Organization at Yeditepe University. Her dissertation title is "The formation of CyberCulture in Learning Organizations," and her research focuses on digital transformation processes in organizations, cyberculture, industry 4.0, and lean thinking in organizations. Her research on those themes has appeared or is forthcoming in journals of management, digitalization, and social sciences and her most recently published paper's title is; "The future of artificial intelligence: how will emotions affect AI?". She holds a Master of Business Administration degree from Yeditepe University and a BA degree in Healthcare Management from Acıbadem University. She working as a Project Assistant in Management Application and Research Center (MARC) at Yeditepe University.

Adina Astilean, PhD, is Professor in the Department of Automation at the Technical University of Cluj Napoca. Her research interests mainly include analysis and development of intelligent control systems, discrete event systems and data communications. She is the author and coauthor of 8 books, 4 book chapters and more than 140 papers, published in various scientific journals and refereed conference proceedings. Adina Astilean was also member in many conference program committees and symposiums and reviewer in the fields of distributed systems, telemedicine, control engineering and data communications. She coordinated and was involved in 20 national and international research projects. She supervised more than 40 master and PhD students.

Roberto Bellas is Ph.D. in Industrial Engineering at the University of Vigo (Spain). Associate Lecturer at the University of Vigo. Senior business consultant and CEO of companies for 10 years.

Vitor Braga, PhD, is an Associate Professor at the School of Technology and Management of Felgueiras, Polytechnic of Porto. He joined the school in 1999 and since then he has been involved in many activities within the school besides teaching. He is the director of the Business Sciences BSc, the head of the business sciences department and the director of the MSc in International Management. In 2008, he received a PhD from Middlesex University Business School (London – UK). He is also a MSc in Industrial and Business Economics (Universidade do Minho, Braga – Portugal) and BSc in Economics (Universidade de Trás-os-Montes e Alto Douro, Vila Real – Portugal). In addition, he received a PgCert in Research Methods for Social Sciences from Middlesex University.

José Baptista da Costa, PhD, completed his PhD in Business Management at the University of Seville. MBA from the French Institute of Management. Engineer from the University of Porto. He was administrator of the Port of Leixões, the largest port infrastructure in Northern Portugal. He was director of Metro do Porto, the largest urbanistic project of the 20th century in Northern Portugal. Smart Cities researcher.

Magdalena Dąbrowska, Ph.D., currently, is the Head of the Department of Production Engineering and Logistics at the Faculty of Technical and Economic Sciences of Collegium Witelona State University. Moreover, she is a member of the Education Team and the Faculty Team for the Quality of Education. She is also the chairwoman of the Logistics and Transport faculty Program Committee and is a co-author of a new field of Logistics and Transport at the Faculty of Technical and Economic Sciences. She is a co-author of the Innovative Education Program for the 5th level and a co-founder and supervisor of the Logistics and Transport Laboratory established at the Faculty of Technical Sciences. Ph.D. Magdalena Dąbrowska is the supervisor of projects implemented in cooperation with external stakeholders (employers) as transfer projects. In 2021, she was awarded the Bronze Medal for Long Service by the President of the Republic of Poland.

José Dinis-Carvalho is Associate Professor at the University of Minho. Degree in Production Engineering in 1989 at the University of Minho. MSc in Computer Integrated Manufacturing in 1992 at Loughborough University. Ph.D. at the University of Nottingham in 1997 on Scheduling and Process Planning Integration. Main research interests are in Lean Approaches to any type of operating environment such as industry, hospitals, construction, offices, design, teaching, etc. Stable and

Sustainable Continuous Improvement systems is one of the main focus at the moment. Other research interests are Teamwork, Scrum and Active Learning approaches in engineering education. Dinis Carvalho has participated in numerous scientific projects with external funding where we highlight the "Continental FOF Project" carried out with Continental Antennas and which is related to the development of an innovative system of production planning and control. He also leads the project "HOMLean - Hospital Operations Management: a Lean Healthcare Framework" and participated in other projects such as the "Easy Ride - Experience is Everything" with the company Bosch. In terms of publications he has a book published in Portuguese by Lidel publisher, dedicated to Continuous Improvement, with the title "Melhoria Continua nas Organizações" and dozens of published scientific articles listed on Scopus.

Gozdem Dural Selçuk has been working as an assistant professor in the Department of Business Administration at Social Sciences University of Ankara (SSUA) since 2022. She received her Ph.D. in Management from Hacettepe University (2015). She has an MBA degree from Bilkent University (2010) and holds a B.Sc. in Industrial Engineering from Middle East Technical University (METU) (2007). Before she joined SSUA, she worked as an assistant professor in the Department of Industrial Engineering at Atılım Unversity (2019-2022). She also worked as a post-doctoral research associate at University of Bath, School of Management in 2016, as a research assistant at Hacettepe University (2015-19) and Middle East Technical University (2011-15). Her recent research interests have been focused on operations research methodologies applied in healthcare services, healthcare policies and evaluation of their sustainability and effectiveness.

Dawid Jagaczyński is a Witelon State University of Applied Sciences in Legnica graduate, Faculty of Technical and Economic Sciences, majoring in Management and Production Engineering, specializing in Logistics and Production Management. For his diploma thesis on "The use of selected Lean Management tools in the production process on the example of a production company X - benefit analysis," he was awarded in the competition for the best diploma thesis organized by the Legnica Special Economic Zone. Engineer Dawid Jagaczyński is interested in organizing and optimizing production processes using innovative solutions and modern management concepts with particular emphasis on the automotive industry.

Vanshika Kakkar is a management student of UPES, Dehradun, India. Her research interest is in Industry 4.0, SMEs, Change Management.

Jacek Krzywy is a graduate of the Poznań University of Technology in the field of Management and Logistics. Currently, a doctoral student at the Doctoral School of the Poznań University of Technology in the scientific discipline: Management and quality science. Experience in implementing business analysis projects for manufacturing and service companies, healthcare, and logistics operators. Practical skills in process modeling using the BPMN 2.0 standard and creating process simulation models. Research interests related to low-code and no-code tools and robotization of processes. He successively deepens his knowledge in the field of using new tools for analysis and simulation of processes, actively participating in international scientific conferences.

Vanda Lima is a PhD in Business Sciences. She is an Assistant Professor at ESTG-P.PORTO. She is an integrated researcher at the Center for Innovation and Research in Business Sciences and Information Systems (CIICESI) and her research falls within the field of management, specifically in the knowledge area of strategic management.

Nishal Murali received the Mechanical Engineering degree from Panimalar Engineering College, and Masters in Manufacturing Systems Engineering from Coventry University. He is currently working as Assistant Professor in Sri Venkateswara college of Engineering. His research interest include, Circular Economy, Supply chain management, Sustainable manufacturing, Re-manufacturing, identifying barriers for sustainable process and identifying areas for designing sustainable framework.

Filip Nowak is the Initiator and Head of the Research Group of Process Excellence at Łukasiewicz Research Network - Poznań Institute of Technology. Graduate of the Poznan University of Technology in the Department of Management Engineering - currently working on his doctoral dissertation on the creation of innovations in business processes. Managed dozens of projects in the area of business process optimization. Academic lecturer in MBA and postgraduate studies and an author of scientific publications in the field of improving the efficiency of activities.

Marlene Rodrigues, MsC, holds a master's degree in organizational management at the School of Management of the Polytechnic Institute of Cávado e do Ave (IPCA), in Portugal. She has several years of experience in management domains and industrial context in northern Portugal. Researcher in the areas of marketing, strategy, management and industry 4.0.

Francisco Silva is Associate Professor with Habilitation. He was Director of the Master's Degree in Mechanical Engineering (2014-2022). He was Deputy Director of the Mechanical Engineering Department from 2014 to 2016. He was Director of the Bachelor in Mechanical Engineering from 2003 to 2006 at ESEIG, Vila do Conde, Portugal. He is author of 7 international books. He has supervised more than 190 MSc. dissertations and co-supervised 2 PhD Thesis already finished, co-supervising mor 5 PhD students at the moment. He is co-author of more than 240 scientific papers iHe is Editorial Board Member of the scientific journal Coatings (MDPI), Solids (MDPI), Materials (MDPI) and Machines (MDPI), among others. He has conducted more than 12 Special Issues in MDPI scientific journals. He founded and was the Editor-in-Chief of the journal of Coating Science Technology (LifeScience Global). He awarded the MDPI Top Reviewer Award in 2018 and the Metals Top Reviewer in 2019. One of his papers was awarded with the Best Paper Award of COATINGS (MDPI, 2019).

Anurag Singh is an Assistant Professor of HR & OB in the School of Business, UPES University, Dehradun India. He has several research publications in top tier journals. His research interest is in emotional regulations, emotional intelligence, personality traits, psychological well-being and workplace bullying.

Bruno Sousa, PhD, is Adjunct Professor of Marketing at Polytechnic Institute of Cavado and Ave (IPCA), Portugal and PhD in Marketing and Strategy in Universidade do Minho, Portugal. Head of Master Program - Tourism Management (IPCA) and Tourism Marketing (IPCA). CiTUR research member and UNIAG research member. He has published in the Journal of Enterprising Communities, Tourism Management Perspectives, Current Issues in Tourism, Journal of Organizational Change Management, World Review of Entrepreneurship, Management and Sust. Development, Annals of Leisure Research, among others. https://orcid.org/0000-0002-8588-2422.aac5d92a-6e64-4f88-8f01-362429bd4dc7

Witold Statkiewicz is a Senior Specialist in the Research Group of Process Excellence at Łukasiewicz Research Network, Poznań Institute of Technology and lecturer at Poznan's School of Logistics. Graduate of the Poznan University of Economics. Currently working on his doctoral dissertation. Participated in dozens of projects in the area of business process optimization. Author of scientific publications in the field of improving the efficiency of activities.

Index

M

P

R

S

T

U

V

W

Z

www.ingramcontent.com/pod-product-compliance
Lightning Source LLC
LaVergne TN
LVHW061546290926
849162LV00004B/919
* 9 7 8 1 6 6 8 4 5 6 0 6 4 *